The Global Journalist
News People Around the World

INTERNATIONAL ASSOCIATION FOR MEDIA AND COMMUNICATION RESEARCH

This series consists of books arising from the intellectual work of IAMCR sections, working groups, and committees. Books address themes relevant to IAMCR interests; make a major contribution to the theory, research, practice and/or policy literature; are international in scope; and represent a diversity of perspectives. Book proposals are submitted through formally constituted IAMCR sections, working groups, and committees.

Series Editors
IAMCR Publication Committee

Coordinators

Naren Chitty
John Downing
Elizabeth Fox
Annabelle Sreberny-Mohammadi

The Global Journalist
News People Around the World

edited by
David H. Weaver
Indiana University

with the assistance of
Wei Wu
National University of Singapore

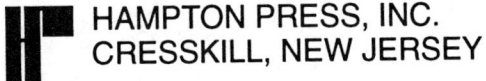
HAMPTON PRESS, INC.
CRESSKILL, NEW JERSEY

Copyright © 1998 by Hampton Press, Inc.

All rights reserved. No part of this publication may be reproduced, stored in a retrieval system, or transmitted in any form or by any means, electronic, mechanical, photocopying, microfilming, recording, or otherwise, without permission of the publisher.

Printed in the United States of America

Library of Congress Cataloging-in-Publication Data

The Global journalist : news people around the world / edited by David H. Weaver ; with the assistance of Wei Wu.
    p. cm. -- (IAMCR book series)
  Includes bibliographical references and index.
  ISBN 1-57273-167-2. -- ISBN 1-57273-168-0 (pbk.)
  1. Journalists--Biography. I. Weaver, David, H. (David Hugh), (1946-   . II. Wu, Wei. III. Series.
PN4820.G56 1998
070.5'092'2--dc21   97-48283
                                                                       CIP

Hampton Press, Inc.
23 Broadway
Cresskill, NJ 07626

To my former students and to those truly professional journalists around the world who have risked, and given, their lives to find and to tell the truth so that all of us might be the wiser

Contents

Series Preface ix
Preface xi

1. Introduction
   David Weaver 1

PART I: FAR EAST/ASIA

2. The Chinese Journalist
   Chongshan Chen, Jian-Hua Zhu, and Wei Wu 9

3. East Meets West: Hong Kong Journalists in Transition
   Joseph Man Chan, Paul S.N. Lee, and Chin-Chuan Lee ... 31

4. Korean Journalists in the 1990s
   Taik Sup Auh, Chang Keun Lee, and Myung Koo Kang ... 55

5. The New Taiwan Journalist: A Sociological Profile
   Ven-hwei Lo 71

PART II: AUSTRALIA/PACIFIC

6. Australian Journalists
   John Henningham 91

7. Journalists in New Zealand
   Geoff Lealand 109

8. Pacific Island Journalists
   Suzanna Layton 125

PART III: EUROPE

9. British Journalists
   John Henningham and Anthony Delano 143

10. The Finnish Journalist: Watchdog with a Conscience
    Ari Heinonen 161

11. The French Journalists
    Aralynn Abare McMane 191

Contents

12. German Journalists in the Early 1990s: East and West
    Klaus Schoenbach, Dieter Stuerzebecher, and Beate Schneider — 213

13. Journalism in Germany
    Siegfried Weischenberg, Martin Löffelholz, and Armin Scholl — 229

14. Hungarian Journalists
    Ildiko Kovats — 257

15. Polish Journalists: Professionals or Not?
    Jerzy Oledzki — 277

16. Journalists in Emerging Democracies: The Case of Spain
    María José Canel and Antoni M. Piqué — 299

PART IV: NORTH AFRICA

17. Algerian Journalists and Their World
    Mohamed Kirat — 323

PART V: NORTH AMERICA

18. Canadian Women Journalists: The "Other Half" of the Equation
    Gertrude J. Robinson and Armande Saint-Jean — 351

19. The Journalists and Journalisms of Canada
    David Pritchard and Florian Sauvageau — 373

20. Journalists in the United States
    David Weaver and G. Cleveland Wilhoit — 395

PART VI: SOUTH AND CENTRAL AMERICA

21. The Brazilian Journalist
    Heloiza G. Herscovitz and Adalberto M. Cardoso — 417

22. Journalists in Chili, Ecuador and Mexico
    Jürgen Wilke — 433

CONCLUSION

23. Journalists Around the World: Commonalities and Differences
    David Weaver — 455

Author Index — 481
Subject Index — 487

Series Preface

In the history of the International Association for Media and Communication Research (IAMCR), the last four years have been very productive. One of the most important contributions of IAMCR has been the series of books launched in 1994 and published by Hampton Press. This series intends to make new and distinct contributions to communication theory and methodology by concentrating on a number of timely topics. The purpose is to make the most recent scholarship widely available and to create a new forum for debate on communication and media issues.

IAMCR is the largest international professional and scientific organization in the field of media and communication research. Established in 1957, the association now has over 2,300 members in some 100 countries. IAMCR has formal consultative relations with UNESCO and is accepted as the international umbrella organization in the field of media and communication research. This status is given to a restricted number of nongovernmental organizations that are broadly international in membership; of proven competence in an important field of education, science, or culture; and with a record of regular major contributions to UNESCO's work. They are invited by the Secretariat to advise UNESCO regularly iin the preparation of its work programs. IAMCR has also been included in the lists of nongovernmental organizations for the United Nations' Economic and Social Council, Council of Europe, the International Labor Organization (ILO), and the Office for Democratic Institutions and Human Rights of the Organization of Security and Cooperation in Europe (OSCE). IAMCR also holds consultative status with the World Intellectual Property Organization (WIPO). Among the associate members of IAMCR are the major regional communication research associations such as AMIC (for Asia), ACCE (for Africa), and ALAIC (for Latin America). Close collaborations also exist with such organizations as the International Institute of Communications, International Federation for Information and Documentation, International Federation of Journalists, Article 19, ComNet, International Peach Research Association, International Political Science Association, Association for Education in Journalism and Mass Communication, International Communication Association, and World Association for Public Opinion Research.

The specific objectives of IAMCR are to provide a forum where researchers, practitioners, and policymakers in the communications field can meet and discuss their work; to stimulate interest in communication research; to disseminate information about research results, methods, and needs; to encourage research and the exchange of information on practices and conditions that impede communication and communications research; and to contribute by means of research and the dissemination of research results to the training of journalists and other media professionals.

Every two years IAMCR holds a General Assembly and Scientific Conference. In addition to the biannual conferences, an off-year conference is also organized. Much of the activity of IAMCR is carried out in its various sections and working groups, which focus on such areas as International Communication, Communication Technology Policy, Documentation and Information Systems, Gender and Communication, History, Law, Local Radio and Television, Media Education Research, Participatory Communication Research, Political Communication Research, Political Economy, Professional Education, Sociology/Social Psychology, and Human Rights.

Thanks to our members' contributions, the diligent work of IAMCR's committee on publications, and the proceedings of the binannual and off-year conferences, we have been able to produce a number of books. The most recent is *The Global Journalist: News People Around the World* edited by David Weaver. The work of journalists in general and issues of journalistic practices and ethics in particular have become more crucial in light of democratic initiatives and the quest of pluralism that has marked the post-cold war era and current changes in international relations. The publication of this volume is timely and relevant as it is one of the first book-length comparative studies of journalists, in 21 countries, focusing on global perspectives of demographics, education, socialization, professionalization, and working conditions. David Weaver, who has been a leading scholar in the field of journalism and media education for many years and whose previous works are know in the professional for their lucidity and originality, has made an outstanding contribution to our knowledge by editing this collection.

The book series, the new affiliated journal, our new format of newsletter and abstracts, and the new IAMCR web page, all contribute to making our publications readily available to all our members as well as the larger community of scholars and policmakers. Indeed, it is extremely rewarding that this volume comes at a time when we are celebrating the 40th anniversary of IAMCR.

Hamid Mowland
President, IAMCR, 1994-1998
Washington, DC

Preface

This book could not have been completed without the encouragement and support of many persons, including friends and colleagues from around the world. Although the idea of pulling together surveys of journalists from many different societies was suggested by former students and colleagues years ago after the 1982-83 study of U.S. journalists by Professor G. Cleveland Wilhoit and me, it was not until the May 1993 conference of the International Communication Association in Washington, DC, that this became a serious proposition in a luncheon talk with Professors Kaarle Nordenstreng of Tampere University in Finland and Jürgen Wilke of the University of Mainz in Germany.

During that talk, I was urged to put together a paper session for the 1994 conference of the International Association for Mass Communication Research (IAMCR) in Seoul, Korea, that would include scholars from various countries who had recently completed surveys of journalists. This session for the Professional Education Section of IAMCR that included studies from Korea, Latin America, Europe, Russia, and the United States became the foundation for this book, along with one that I had organized for the 1993 ICA conference that included studies from Australia, Germany, Hong Kong, and the United States. It was Professor Nordenstreng, longtime president of the Professional Education Section of IAMCR, who really encouraged me to go beyond organizing these paper sessions to a book that could become part of the IAMCR Book Series published by Hampton Press.

This is an especially satisfying book for me to complete because it represents the logical culmination of nearly 20 years of research on journalists, and it includes chapters by many good friends and former students. Among my former doctoral students, of whom I am very proud, are Professor Taik Sup Auh of Korea University; Professor Mohamed Kirat of the United Arab Emirates University and formerly of the Universite d'Alger in Algeria; Dr. Aralynn Abare McMane of the World Association of Newspapers (FIEJ) in Paris, France; Dr. Wei Wu, formerly of Xiamen University in China and now a lecturer at the National University at Singapore; and Professor Jian-Hua Zhu of the University of Connecticut and the City University of Hong Kong. I especially thank Wei Wu, my former research assistant, for all the hours he put into revising and updating the many computer files of the chapters of this book and Nabil Echchaibi, my present assistant, for his careful work on the subject index.

Longtime colleagues and friends include Professor David Pritchard, a fellow faculty member here in the School of Journalism at Indiana University from 1984 to 1993 and now at the University of Wisconsin-Milwaukee; Professor Klaus Schoenbach of the University of Music and Theater of Hannover, Germany, who was a visiting professor here at Indiana University; Professor Siegfried Weischenberg of the Westfalische Wilhelms University in Muenster, Germany, who was also a visiting professor here at Indiana; and of course my mentor and co-author on the U.S. journalist studies, Professor G. Cleveland Wilhoit of the School of Journalism here at Indiana University, with whom I have been working for 30 years as a graduate student and faculty member, and without whose support I would not be where I am today.

In addition to these friends and colleagues, I thank Professors Brenda Dervin of Ohio State University and Robert White of The Gregorian University in Rome for their patience and good will in negotiating the contract with Hampton Press as representatives of the IAMCR Publications Committee. I especially thank Bob White for his speedy and constructive review of the manuscript of this book at a very busy time, and I thank Barbara Bernstein, President of Hampton Press, for her interest and support.

Most of all, I thank the authors of the chapters of this book for their many hours of work, often in a language not their own, and their willingness to meet my demands and to accept my editing of their work. Without their studies and their willingness to contribute, there would be no book.

And, finally, I thank the School of Journalism here at Indiana University, especially Dean Trevor Brown and the Roy W. Howard family, for the support of the Roy W. Howard Chair that makes this and other research projects possible.

I hope that this book will prove useful to those interested in studying and practicing journalism around the world, and that it will help to lead to more professional and ethical journalists and journalism in the next century and millennium.

David Weaver
Bloomington, Indiana

About the Authors

Taik Sup Auh is Professor of Mass Communication at Korea University in Seoul. He received his Ph.D. in mass communication at Indiana University in 1977 and taught at Virginia Commonwealth University in Richmond from 1977 to 1980. Dr. Auh is a former President of the Korean Society for Journalism and Communication Studies and an Advisory Professor of Fudan University in Shanghai, China.

María José Canel is Senior Lecturer in political communication and comparative politics in the Department of Communication at the University of Navarra in Pamplona, Spain. She has published nationally and internationally on the concept of public opinion, electoral communication, media effects, and sociology and newsrooms. She has been "visiting professor" at the London School of Economics and Newhouse School at Syracuse University. She is actively involved in a number of international professional associations including the International Communication Association (ICA), World Association for Public Opinion Research (WAPOR), and the International Association for Mass Communication Research (IAMCR).

Adalberto M. Cardoso is an instructor of Research Methods in Sociology and Sociology of Work at the College of Philosophy and Social Sciences of Universidade Federal do Rio de Janeiro (Federal University of Rio de Janeiro). He is also an associate researcher at Cebrap (Brazilian Center of Analyses and Planning) of Sao Paulo and has worked as a researcher from 1982 to 1996. Cardoso received his Ph.D. in sociology, Universidade de Sao Paulo, Brazil, in 1995 and both bachelor's and master's degrees in sociology, Universidade de Sao Paulo, Brazil, in 1991 and 1982.

Joseph Man Chan is Associate Professor and Chair at the Department of Journalism and Communication, the Chinese University of Hong Kong. He received his Ph.D. in mass communication from the University of Minnesota and the International Communication Association's Kyoon Hur Dissertation Award in 1986. He has published many articles in international journals and book chapters on international communication, political communication, and the impact of information technology, as well as on communication and social change. He has co-authored *Mass Media and Political Transition: The Hong Kong Press in China's Orbit* (Guilford, 1991) and *Hong Kong Journalists in Transition* (Hong Kong Institute of Asia-Pacific Studies, 1996).

Chongshan Chen is Senior Research Fellow at the Journalism Research Institute of the Chinese Academy of Social Sciences, where Wei Bu and Xiaohong Liu are Associate Research Fellows.

Anthony Delano is Senior Research Fellow at the London College of Printing, one of the main centers for journalism training and education in the United Kingdom. Before turning to an academic career he was managing editor of the British national daily newspaper, the *Daily Mirror*, and director of new media for the Mirror Newspapers publishing group. He holds a master's degree in communication and is writing a Ph.D. thesis on the formation of the modern British journalist.

Ari Heinonen is a journalism teacher and researcher at the Department of Journalism and Mass Communication, University of Tampere, Finland. He was formerly a professional journalist and holds a Lic. Soc. Sc. degree.

John Henningham is Foundation Professor of Journalism and Head of the Department of Journalism at the University of Queensland, Brisbane, Australia. He edits the academic journal, *Australian Studies in Journalism*, and is the author of *Looking at Television News* (Longman Cheshire, 1988) as well as editor of *Issues in Australian Journalism* (Longman Cheshire, 1990) and *Institutions in Australian Society* (Oxford University Press, 1995). He has written more than 60 journal articles and chapters on news media topics.

Heloiza Golbspan Herscovitz is currently a Ph.D. candidate at the College of Journalism and Communications, University of Florida. She received her master's degree in mass communications from the University of Montevallo in 1984 and her bachelor's degree in mass communications, with a concentration in journalism, from the Pontifical Catholic University (PUC), Porto Alegre, Brazil, in 1976. She has been an Instructor of Journalism Writing and International Communication at PUC since 1989 and has much experience as a journalist and a media consultant in Brazil.

Myung Koo Kang is Professor of Communication at Seoul National University in Seoul. He received his Ph.D. in mass communication at the University of Iowa in 1985 and taught at Hanyang University in Seoul from 1985 to 1987.

Mohamed Kirat has been Associate Professor at the Universite d'Alger in Algeria and Communication Adviser for the Ministry of Health, United Arab Emirates. He is now Associate Professor in the Department of Mass Communication at the United Arab Emirates University where he teaches international communication, news writing, research methods, and development communication. He received his Ph.D. in mass communication from the School of Journalism at Indiana University in 1987. He has published more than one dozen articles and is the author of the book *The Communicators: A Portrait of Algerian Journalists and Their Work* (Universite d'Algers, 1993).

Ildiko Kovats is a researcher in the Communication Science Research Group of the Hungarian Academy of Sciences. The group is also associated with the Eotvos Lorand Scientific University. She worked for 18 years in the Hungarian Institute for Public Opinion research, where she headed the communication research department. She was the scientific director for the Hungarian Journalism Association's School of Journalism in Budapest.

Suzanna Layton has master's degrees in communication and Pacific Islands studies from the University of Hawaii and a doctorate in journalism from the University of Queensland in Australia. She edited the weekly *Arawa Bulletin* in Bougainville, Papua New Guinea from 1983 to 1986 and has since maintained a strong research interest in Pacific Islands media. Layton has lectured on international and comparative media at the University of Queensland in Australia and is now a Lecturer in print journalism at Griffith University in Nathan, Australia.

Geoff Lealand teaches in the Department of Film and Television Studies at the University of Waikato in New Zealand. His research interests include journalism training, children and media, media education/literacy, and audience research. He has published extensively on these topics, both in New Zealand and abroad, as well as advising New Zealand broadcasters on matters concerning children's television.

Chin-Chuan Lee is Professor of Journalism and Communication at the Chinese University of Hong Kong and the University of Minnesota. Among his English publications are *Media Imperialism Reconsidered: The Homogenizing of Television Culture* (Sage, 1980), *Voices of China: The Interplay of Politics and Journalism* (Guilford, 1990, editor), *Mass Media and Political Transition: The Hong Kong Press in China's Orbit* (Guilford, 1991, co-author), *Sparking a Fire: The Press and the Ferment of Democratic Change in Taiwan* (AEJMC, 1993), and *China's Media, Media's China* (Westview Press, 1994, editor).

Chang Keu Lee is Associate Professor of Mass Communication at Kwang-Woon University in Seoul. Before receiving his Ph.D. in mass communication at the University of Wisconsin in 1988, he had worked as a reporter for Tongyang Broadcasting Company in Seoul from 1978 to 1980.

Paul S.N. Lee is Associate Professor in Journalism and Communication at the Chinese University of Hong Kong. He received his Ph.D. in communication from the University of Michigan. His research interests are telecommunications policy, international communication, development communication, and media issues. He has coauthored two books on international communication and media criticism and co-edited or edited two books on Hong Kong communication research and China telecommunications. His scholarly publications also appear in *Telecommunications Policy, Journal of Communication, Gazette, Asian Journal of Communication,* and *Australian Journal of Chinese Affairs.*

Ven-hwei Lo is professor and chair of the Department of Journalism, National Chengchi University in Taipei, Taiwan. He holds a bachelor's degree in journalism from National Chengchi University, a master's degree in journalism from the University of Oregon, and a Ph.D. in journalism from the University of Missouri-Columbia. Previously, he was a reporter for the *China Times* and the *China Post*. He is the author of three books and numerous articles about news media performance and effects of news media. He thanks Edward Neilan, visiting professor of journalism, National Chengchi University, for his editorial assistance on the chapter on Taiwanese journalists.

Martin Löffelholz is Associate Professor at the Universität Leipzig in Germany (Department for Journalism). Between 1981 and 1988, he studied journalism, mass communication, political science, and sociology. Between 1984 and 1988, he was a reporter for the German Broadcasting Corporation in Cologne. Between 1988 and 1994, he was an Assistant Professor at the Westfälische Wilhelms-Universität Münster (Institute for Communication Science). His most recent publication, with Siegfried Weischenberg and Klaus-Dieter Altmeppen, is *Die Zukunft des Journalismus: Technologische, ökonomische und redaktionelle trends* [The future of journalism: Technological, economics and editorial trends] (Opladen, 1994).

Aralynn Abare McMane is director of educational programs for the World Association of Newspapers (FIEJ) based in Paris, France. She has worked in journalism education, research, and newspapers in both France and the United States. She earned her Ph.D. in mass communication at Indiana University's School of Journalism.

Jerzy Oledzki is Professor of International Communication at the Department of Journalism and Political Science, University of Warsaw, Warsaw, Poland. He is chairperson of the Sociology of Mass Communication Division there, as well as of the Integrated Media

Marketing Laboratory. His first Ph.D. is in political science, with a second Ph.D. in humanistic study, and a master's degree in Polish literature and postgraduate study in journalism. Widely published in Polish periodicals, Oledzki has also coauthored several books on mass media and international understanding. He is author of *Americans about Poland and Poles* (1985), *Democratization of Communication in the Third World* (1987), *International Flow of Information* (1992), *Professionalism in Journalism* (1994), and editor of the annuals *Business Guide to Poland* (since 1993), and *Business & Pleasure* (since 1994).

Antoni M. Piqué is Professor of Newsroom Management at the University of Navarra in Pamplona, Spain, and is currently European Director of the Society of Newspaper Design (SND). He is a former section editor at *La Vanguardia* (Barcelona), one of the leading Spanish papers. As a consultant for Innovación Periodística/University of Navarra, he has been training and helping to reorganize newsrooms, improving coverage and content and giving workshops in several dailies of all sizes in Spain and Latin America. He has also given lectures in a variety of forums: World Newspaper Association, Society of Newspaper Design, Spanish Society of Print Media Marketing, and others. He is a founding member of the Sindicat de Periodistes de Catalunya, the first professional and independent union of journalists in Spain.

David Pritchard, Professor of Mass Communication at the University of Wisconsin-Milwaukee, has a long-standing interest in Canada and Canadian news media. He attended York University in Toronto as an undergraduate and spent the 1991-92 academic year in Quebec City as one of the United States' first Fulbright scholars in Canada. His research on Canadian media systems has attracted funding from the governments of Canada and Quebec, in addition to the Fulbright. Pritchard has served as guest editor for a special issue of *Québec Studies* focusing on the media. During the 1994-95 academic year he was a research fellow of the Center for Twentieth Century at the University of Wisconsin-Milwaukee. His Ph.D. in mass communications is from the University of Wisconsin-Madison, and he was a faculty member of the Indiana University School of Journalism from 1984 to 1993.

Gertrude J. Robinson is Professor and past Director of the Graduate Program in Communications at McGill University in Montreal, Canada. She has written extensively on Canadian media professionals, new technologies, and Canadian regulatory issues. She presently holds a Canadian Social Science and Humanities Research grant to investigate women's progress in media professions from the 1970s to the 1990s.

Armande Saint-Jean was associated with l'UQAM (Université du Québec à Montréal) for 10 years as co-head of the Journalism program, after having worked as a professional journalist and broadcaster for more than 20 years. In 1994, she joined l'Université de Sherbrooke, where she is responsible for the master's program in writing and communication. She holds a Ph.D in communications from McGill University in Montreal. Her research interests are focused on journalistic and media ethics, women's conditions, and feminist theory as well as communication research methodology. She is presently conducting research projects on journalistic ethics both in Canada and in Québec.

Florian Sauvageau, who heads the Centre d'études sur les médias (The center for media studies) in addition to teaching journalism at Université Laval, is one of Canada's best known and most prolific journalism educators and communication policymakers. He has published or co-coauthored seven books and numerous articles and is a former president of the Canadian Communication Association. In addition to his scholarly work, Sauvageau was on the research staff of the Canada's Royal Commission on Newspapers in 1981 and was co-chair of the federal Task Force on Broadcasting Policy in 1985-86. He is a former managing editor of *Le Soleil*, one of Quebec's largest newspapers.

Beate Schneider is Professor of Media Science at the Department of Journalism and Communication Research and Vice President of the University of Music and Theater, Hannover, Germany. She was formerly at the Department of Political Science of the University of the German Armed Forces, Hamburg. Supported by a Fulbright Scholarship, she was a graduate student at the University of Arizona, Tucson, and completed her Ph.D. in international relations at the University of Mainz.

Klaus Schoenbach is Professor of Journalism and Communication Research and Director of the Department of Journalism and Communication Research at the University of Music and Theater, Hannover, Germany. He was formerly with the departments of Mass Communication at the Universities of Muenster and Munich and worked as a visiting professor at Cleveland State University, Indiana University, and San Jose State University. After completing his Ph. D. in mass communication in 1975 at the University of Mainz (advisor: Elisabeth Noelle-Neumann), he became director of the content analysis department of ZUMA, Mannheim. He earned his "habilitation" at the University of Muenster in 1982.

Armin Scholl is Assistant Professor at the Free University of Berlin in Germany (Institute for Communication Science). Between 1989 and 1994, he studied journalism, communication research, and methodology at the Westfälische Wilhelms-Universität Münster (Institute for Communication Science). His most recent publication, with Siegfried Weischenberg, is "Konstruktivismus und Ethik im Journalismus," in

About the Authors

Konstruktivismus und Ethik [Constructivism and Ethics in Journalism] (DELFIN 1995).

Dieter Stuerzebecher is research assistant and previously assistant professor at the Department of Journalism and Communication Research at the University of Music and Theater, Hannover, Germany. He was formerly with the Department of Social Sciences at the University of Marburg (Hesse).

Siegfried Weischenberg is Professor of Communication and Journalism at the Westfälische Wilhelms-Universität Münster (Institute for Communication Science), Germany. From 1979-82, he worked as a Professor of Journalism at the University of Dortmund (Institute for Journalism), Germany. For more than 10 years he was an editor and freelancer for dailies, journals, broadcasting stations, and news agencies. He received his Ph.D. from the Ruhr University in Bochum, Germany, and he has published 12 books on journalism, media technologies, newswriting, journalism education, and sports reporting, as well as many journal articles and book chapters. His most recent book is *Journalistik: Einführung in die Theorie und Praxis vermittelter Kommunikation* [Journalism: Introduction to Theory and Practice of Media Communication] (Opladen, 1992 and 1995).

David H. Weaver is the Roy W. Howard Professor in Journalism and Mass Communication Research at Indiana University's School of Journalism, where he has taught since 1974. He holds a bachelor's degree in journalism and sociology from Indiana University, a master's degree in journalism from Indiana, and a Ph.D. in mass communication research from the University of North Carolina. He has worked as a journalist on four daily newspapers. He has published nine books, including *The American Journalist in the 1990s* (with G. Cleveland Wilhoit in 1996), and numerous book chapters and articles on journalists, the agenda-setting role of the media in election campaigns, foreign news coverage, and newspaper readership.

Wei Wu was a doctoral student in Mass Communications at Indiana University's School of Journalism from 1993-1997, where he completed his PhD. He holds a master's degree in journalism from Stanford University and both a master's and bachelor's degree in English from Xiamen University, China, where he was an Associate Professor and Director of the Communication Research Institute. He is presently a lecturer in the Department of Organisational Behaviour at the National University of Singapore.

G. Cleveland Wilhoit is Professor of Journalism and former Director of the Bureau of Media Research at Indiana University, where he has taught since 1967. He was Associate Director of the Institute for

Advanced Study at Indiana from 1988 to 1993. He holds bachelor's and master's degrees as well as a Ph.D. in mass communication research from the University of North Carolina. He is co-author (with David Weaver) of *Newsroom Guide to Polls and Surveys* and editor of the first two volumes of the *Mass Communication Review Yearbook*. He and Weaver have also written on news media coverage of U.S. senators and foreign news coverage. With Dan Drew, Wilhoit has conducted three national studies of U.S. editorial writers.

Jürgen Wilke is Professor (and currently Director) at the Institut für Publizistik, Johannes Gutenberg Universität, Mainz (Germany). He graduated from this university and taught journalism for some years at the Katholische Universität Eichstätt. In 1993, he was Visiting Scholar at the University of Washington in Seattle. His research interests include history and the structure of mass communication, analysis of news production and news agencies, and international communication. Among others, he edited and partly wrote three volumes on mass media systems in Latin America.

Jian-Hua Zhu is Associate Professor of Communication Sciences at the University of Connecticut and Associate Professor of English at the City University of Hong Kong. He earned his Ph. D. in mass communication at Indiana University's School of Journalism in 1990.

1

Introduction

David Weaver
School of Journalism, Indiana University

The decade from the mid-1980s to the mid-1990s has seen a flowering of systematic surveys of journalists around the world, as journalists have come to play more prominent roles in both newer and older political systems, especially those in transition from authoritarian to more democratic. Many of these studies have been modeled on the three major surveys of U.S. journalists conducted in 1971 (Johnstone, Slawski, and Bowman 1976), 1982-83 (Weaver and Wilhoit 1986), and 1992 (Weaver and Wilhoit 1996), and some have been presented at conferences of the International Association for Media and Communication Research (IAMCR), especially the 1994 meeting in Seoul, South Korea. This book presents the results of such surveys from 21 different countries and territories, including Algeria, Australia, Brazil, Britain, Canada, Chile, China, Ecuador, Finland, France, Germany, Hong Kong, Hungary, Korea, Mexico, New Zealand, the Pacific Islands, Poland, Spain, Taiwan, and the United States.

Many scholars have lamented the fact that these studies are widely scattered in various papers, dissertations, articles, and reports. Several have urged me to pull together these studies into one volume and to try to provide a more general synthesis of their findings across national borders and differing cultures. This book is the result of my efforts to do this, with the generous cooperation and help from many friends and colleagues. Given the number of new studies of journalists conducted in recent years and the increasing interest around the world in the occupation of journalist or communicator as we enter a new information age, I believe the time is right for a book that takes a global perspective on the demographics, education, socialization, professionalization, and working conditions of journalists. I hope the reader will agree.

ORGANIZATION AND PURPOSE

This volume groups the studies of journalists by region of the world, including Asia and the Far East, Australia and the Pacific, Europe, North Africa, North America, and South and Central America. Although not everyone will agree with this classification scheme, it does illustrate that the studies come from most of the major areas, with the exception of sub-Saharan Africa, the Middle East, and Eurasia and Central Asia. Because these studies were not planned in advance, and because representation in this book depended on my knowledge of each study and the willingness of the individual authors to meet deadlines and to make revisions requested by me, some countries where there have been recent surveys of journalists are not represented, such as Belarus, Egypt, Iran, Italy, Russia, Slovakia, South Africa, Sweden, and the Ukraine. I regret that these nations are not included, and I hope that future comparative studies of journalists will remedy this.

In addition to presenting the findings of each survey separately, the final concluding chapter attempts to make rough cross-national comparisons with respect to the basic characteristics, working conditions, and professional values of the more than 20,000 journalists included in these surveys. The aim of these comparisons, which are admittedly post hoc and based on measures that are not always as similar as they could be if preplanned, is to try to identify some similarities and differences that may give us a more accurate picture of where journalists come from, how they think about their work, and whether they are becoming more professional as we prepare to leave the 20th century behind and begin a new century and millennium.

The major assumption is that journalists' backgrounds and ideas have some relationship to what is reported (and how it is covered) in the various news media around the world, in spite of various societal and organizational constraints, and that this news coverage matters in terms of world public opinion and policies.

Obviously this approach is much more inductive than deductive, mainly because this is one of the first cross-national studies of journalists involving more than two countries at a time. Although there are various theories of journalistic socialization and professionalization that have been developed (Ettema, Whitney, and Wackman 1987; Shoemaker and Reese 1996), the primary goal of this book is not to elaborate or test such theories, but rather to discover patterns of similarities and differences that can provide a foundation of empirical data for future theorizing about the influences on journalists and their influences on the news.

EVIDENCE

Table 1.1 illustrates the sample sizes, response rates (where reported), dates, survey methods, and sponsors (where reported) of the surveys that form the basis for the chapters included here. In several countries, more than one survey was conducted (Australia, Germany, and Canada), and in two cases (Canada and Germany) two separate chapters were written to report the results.

The findings reported in this book are based on surveys of 20,280 journalists from 21 countries or territories during the years of 1986 to 1996. The response rates of these surveys vary from a low of 32% in Brazil to a high of 95% among Canadian women journalists. Twelve of the surveys were conducted by mail, five by personal (face-to-face) interviews, and six by telephone. The Algerian survey was conducted by a combination of mail and face-to-face methods, and the French survey also involved personal delivery of some questionnaires as well as mail. In Hungary, it was not clear which interviewing methods were used. The sponsors included several journalists' associations, one national foundation (in Germany), and two private foundations (in the United States and Brazil).

Although most of these surveys were conducted independently in the various societies represented here, the task of comparing the findings was made easier by the fact that many had borrowed questions from our original questionnaire (Weaver and Wilhoit 1986), which was modeled on the first large-scale national study of U.S. journalists done by sociologists at the University of Illinois at Chicago in 1971 (Johnstone et al. 1976). However, some of the surveys employed their own questions or modified somewhat the original wordings. And there is, of course, always the slippage in meaning involved in translating from one language to another.

Nevertheless, the thousands of interviews of journalists from these 21 countries and territories constitute an excellent foundation of data for cross-national comparisons, keeping in mind the admonition of Blumler, McLeod, and Rosengren (1992) that things compared should be comparable.

Table 1.1. Sample Sizes, Dates, Methods and Sponsors of Journalists Surveys.

	Sample Size	Response Rate	Date of Study	Method Used	Sponsor
I. Asia/Far East					
China	5,867	71%	1994	Mail survey	UNESCO
Hong Kong	522	75%	1990	Mail survey	—
Korea	727	72	1993	Mail survey	Korea Press Institute
Taiwan	1,015	78	1994	Face-to-face	
II. Australia/Pacific					
Australia (1)	1,068	90	1992	Phone interview	
(2)	173	85	1993	Phone interview	
New Zealand	1,214	38	1994	Mail survey	N.Z. Journalists Org.
Pacific Islands	164	60	1992	Mail survey	
III. Europe					
Britain (U.K.)	726	81	1995	Phone interview	
Finland	900	58	1993	Mail survey	Journalists Union
France	484	70	1988	Mail survey	
Germany (West)	983	—	1992	Phone interview	
Germany (East)	585	—	1993	Phone interview	
Germany (Total)	1,500	60	1993	Face-to-face	Deutsche Forschungsgemeinschaft
Hungary	400	—	1992	—	Journalists Association
Poland	276	—	1994	Face-to-face	
Spain	600	—	1991	Mail survey	

Table 1.1. Sample Sizes, Dates, Methods and Sponsors of Journalists Surveys (con't).

	Sample Size	Response Rate	Date of Study	Method Used	Sponsor
V. North Africa					
Algeria	75	—	1986	Mail survey + face-to-face	
V. North America					
Canadian Women (1)	186	95	1994	Face-to-face	
(2)	134	92	1995	Mail survey	
Canada	554	75	1996	Mail survey	
United States	1,410	81	1992	Phone interview	Freedom Forum
				Phone interview	
VI. South/Central America					
Brazil	355	32	1994	Mail survey	Ford Foundation
Chile	116	—	1992	Mail survey	
Mexico	100	—	1991	Face-to-face	
Ecuador	146	—	1991	Mail survey	
TOTAL N	**20,280**				

The things about journalists that can be reasonably compared in the concluding chapter of this book include basic characteristics such as age, gender, size of workforce, marital status, minority representation, education levels, and the proportions studying journalism in college. The working conditions compared include perceptions of amount of autonomy or freedom, job satisfaction (including predictors of this in a few societies), and commitment to journalism (intention to remain working as a journalist).

Professional values or orientations that can be compared include perceptions of the importance of different journalistic roles (such as reporting the news quickly, providing analysis and interpretation, investigating claims of government, etc.), proportions belonging to journalistic organizations, opinions about which questionable reporting methods might be justifiable (such as revealing confidential sources, paying for information, etc.), opinions on the importance of different aspects of the job (pay, autonomy, public service, etc.), and journalists' images of their readers, viewers, and listeners.

The patterns of similarities and differences that emerge from these cross-national comparisons are not easily explained by conventional political, economic, and cultural categories or by existing theories of mass communication, but they are striking and intriguing in their variety. I hope that future comparative studies will undertake the exciting task of trying to explain these patterns as we move into a new century and a new millennium.

REFERENCES

Blumler, Jay G., Jack M. McLeod, and Karl Erik Rosengren. 1992. *Comparatively speaking: Communication and culture across space and time.* Newbury Park, CA: Sage.

Ettema, James S., D. Charles Whitney, and Daniel B. Wackman. 1987. Professional mass communicators. In *Handbook of communication science*, edited by Charles R. Berger and Steven H. Chaffee, pp. 747-780. Newbury Park, CA: Sage.

Johnstone, John W.C., Edward J. Slawski, and William W. Bowman. 1976. *The news people.* Urbana: University of Illinois Press.

Shoemaker, Pamela J. and Stephen D. Reese. 1996. *Mediating the message: Theories of influences on mass media content.* 2nd ed. White Plains, NY: Longman.

Weaver, David H. and G. Cleveland Wilhoit. 1986. *The American journalist: A portrait of U.S. news people and their work.* Bloomington: Indiana University Press.

Weaver, David H. and G. Cleveland Wilhoit. 1996. *The American journalist in the 1990s: U.S. news people at the end of an era.* Mahwah, NJ: Erlbaum.

I

ASIA/FAR EAST

2

The Chinese Journalist*

Chongshan Chen, Jian-Hua Zhu, and Wei Wu
with Wei Bu, Xiaohong Liu, Xiuxia Chen, Lidan Chen, Yaokui Xu, Dahong Min, Siyi Li, Xiaowei Song, Guangrong Yuan, Yuzhang Dai, Hailan Liu, Xiaoying Wang, Janice Engsberg, and Huixin Ke

As in almost all other societies, the thoughts and behaviors of Chinese journalists are profoundly shaped by the media system for which they work. Even the reasons why they become journalists and the process of how they join the profession are largely determined by the media system and the society at large. Thus, it is necessary to describe the basic characteristics of the Chinese media system before we take a close look at the media professional employees.

---

*The survey reported in this chapter is supported by a grant from the United Nations Education, Science and Cultural Organization (UNESCO) to the Journalism Research Institute of the Chinese Academy of Social Sciences and the All Chinese Journalists Association. Support for the preparation of this chapter was given to Jian-Hua Zhu by the Committee on Scholarly Exchange with China, with support from the United States Information Agency, and by the City University of Hong Kong Research Office (#9030449). The Roy W. Howard Chair at the School of Journalism, Indiana University, provided travel support for Chongshan Chen and Jian-Hua Zhu to attend a working conference at Indiana University in March 1995 to discuss this study.

All news media in China are state owned. Therefore, all Chinese journalists are state employees. By circulation, Chinese news media can be stratified into four levels: national, provincial, municipal, and county. By function, the press can be classified into three groups: party organ, special interest, and entertainment.

All news media in China are under the control of the propaganda department of the Communist Party and the news and publishing bureau of the government (for the print media) or radio and television bureau (for the broadcast media) of the corresponding level. For example, those media at the national level such as the *People's Daily*, Xinhua News Agency, Chinese Central Television (CCTV), and the Central People's Radio Station (CPRS) are under the direct supervision of the Propaganda Department of the Party's Central Committee, which selects and appoints all senior personnel of these media and sets the tone for their editorial policies. However, their budget and other managerial affairs are handled by the state government, such as the Ministry of Radio, Television and Films (MRTF) and the State Bureau of News and Publishing (SBNP). The same is true for news media at all other levels. Most editors-in-chief of the news media also hold senior positions at the propaganda department to further strengthen the close tie between the department and the medium.

During the Cultural Revolution, party secretaries of the news media were the de facto bosses. Since 1978, editors of the newspapers and directors of the radio and television stations have been given more power in the daily operation of their media.

Despite the ongoing economic reform, which has privatized many public sectors, the Chinese government does not allow the privatization of the news media. Even joint ventures in the news media sector are still prohibited, although there had been several aborted attempts. For example, the *Hong Kong Standard* tried to publish a mainland edition in cooperation with China Daily in 1994, but the Chinese government abruptly stopped the publication despite a three-year contract (Murphy 1995). In 1995, media mogul Rupert Murdoch's News Co. started a joint venture with the *People's Daily,* but its business is only limited to distribution of electronic data information (Karp 1995).

There is no press law in China, although as early as 1983 some representatives at the National People's Congress called for the draft of a Press Law. The mid-1980s saw the peak time for the momentum of drafting the Press Law. The State Council even set up a Press Law Research Group to coordinate the draft. The research group and other research institutions had come up with several versions of the draft, but the whole process was shelved after the Tiananmen events in 1989.

In sum, what has happened to the news media sector since 1978 reflects the Chinese government's policy: pursuing economic reform without yielding the political control on ideology. On the one hand, the government has cut the subsidies to the news media, pushing them into the market and forcing them to become financially self-sufficient. On the other hand, the government still tightly controls the media, especially their editorial policies and senior personnel.

Before the reforms in 1978, all the Chinese news media were subsidized by the state. Under the strict planned economy, the news media's budgets, circulations, and sizes of staff were all decided by the state government. The Post Office had a monopoly on all press circulations. Most subscriptions came from work units and were paid for by the government. Advertising was banned. Government funding became the sole source for the news media, which did not have any concern for profit.

Things have changed since the economic reforms started in 1978, especially since the mid-1980s. Although news media are still treated as state-owned institutions, they are now run as enterprises. In other words, they are supposed to seek profit in order to become financially self-sufficient.[1] The government has been gradually cutting its subsidies to the news media.

On January 28, 1979, the Shanghai-based *Liberation Daily* (*Jiefang Ribao*) ran the first advertisement in more than two decades. Since then, advertising revenue for the news media has been growing at an average rate of more than 50% annually. By 1994, advertising revenue reached RMB¥16 billion (about US$1.88 billion).[2] In addition, the monopoly of the Post Office on circulations was broken. Since the mid-1980s, about 500 newspapers have set up their own circulation networks. By 1994, about one third of the papers were financially self-sufficient (Qiu 1995).

However, a majority of news media, especially the print media, are under growing financial pressure during the reforms. A major threat has come from dwindling circulation. One major reason for the drop has been declining subscriptions by government.[3] Another reason has been the increase in production costs because of the price hikes of newsprint

---

[1] In fact, the current trend is not new. For a few years after the communists took over the power in 1949, newspapers were considered "enterprises" and were supposed to be financially self-sufficient. It was until the Three Reform movement in the mid-1950s that newspapers were considered "institutions" and became totally dependent on government funding.

[2] According to the official exchange rate in 1994, US$1 ≈ RMB¥8.5.

[3] The decline in subscriptions by the government hit party organ newspapers hardest because they were more dependent on government subscriptions and had a very limited number of private subscriptions and street sales. For example, in October 1992, the *People's Daily*, the largest party organ newspaper in the country, sold only about 100 copies everyday on street stands in Beijing, which has a population of 10 million (Chen and Song 1993).

and equipment. In order to attract more subscriptions, newspapers keep expanding by adding more pages, which has further increased production costs. For example, in 1994, the *People's Daily* doubled the number of its pages from 8 to 16. To cover the cost, it had to raise its price from 25 cents to 45 cents. As a result, in 1994, the *People's Daily* circulation dropped by 16% over the previous year, from 2.74 million to 2.3 million copies (Qiu 1995). Almost all other major newspapers have suffered similar sharp drops of circulation in the past decade.[4]

The tough competition for readers and audience among news media has forced them to change their content and programs. Many of them have to publish or broadcast more "soft" or sensational news. Since the late 1980s, most newspapers, even some major party organs, have put out tabloid-type weekend editions or evening newspapers, which are filled with racy crime stories and anecdotes of movie stars and popular singers (Polumbaum 1994).

As advertising has become the major source of revenue, audience ratings have become more important. Television and radio stations of all levels are still obliged to broadcast the primetime news programs of CCTV and CPRS. However, more and more stations are depending on popular imported programs, especially cheap soap operas from Hong Kong and Taiwan, to attract larger audiences.

The financial pressure facing the news media has also led to some practices that are presumed to violate professional ethics, such as selling time slots or space to businesses and carrying stories that are in fact public relations pieces of business and corporations. Many journalists write stories about companies or their products and receive "commissions" for their work. Such "paid journalism" practices have drawn more and more complaints from the readers and audiences and have caused the government's concern. In January 1991, the All China Journalists Association issued a comprehensive Guidance of Professional Ethics Codes for Chinese Journalists. In 1995, the first advertising law was implemented.

A projection at the first national conference on journalism education in 1983 predicted that China might need 90,000 journalists by 1990. This led to a rapid expansion of journalism programs across the country. By early 1990, there were 51 journalism programs accredited by the State Education Commission with more than 5,000 students, compared to 16 programs with 1,400 students in 1982 (*Memo* 1990). However, the 1983 prediction did not take into account that journalism schools were not the only source for new journalists. In fact, in 1983, when the predic-

---

[4]In 1993, all party organ newspapers at the provincial level in mainland China saw a drop in their circulation by an average of 10.2% over the previous year (Min 1993).

tion was made, only 6.1% of Chinese journalists had a journalism degree (Fan et al. 1992). As with most of the government organizations, Chinese mass media were run based on the Soviet model. Because of the news media's importance, political soundness took a higher priority than professional skills in the hiring of journalists. Many media recruit from the huge network of their "freelance correspondents," most of whom are information officers at various governmental agencies or enterprises. These freelance correspondents are not formal employees of those media and are paid by stories (mostly local stories) they contribute. Many of them do not even have any college education, but they are supposed to be politically more dependable than journalism graduates. In addition, as journalism is considered a privileged profession, many people without any journalism training but with strong personal connections have entered the media.

A very recent practice by many media organizations is to openly recruit reporters and editors from the general society, which often attracts thousands of young people to apply for a few positions. An entrance examination is typically involved. Because of the keen competition, successful candidates usually have a college degree, although not necessarily with a major in journalism or communication.

As a result, although the number of graduates from those 51 journalism programs was much smaller than predicted in 1990, many could not find a job in a news media organization. The 1990 seminar of deans and chairmen of journalism schools/departments concluded that "there was a surplus of journalism graduates and there were too many journalism programs" (*Memo* 1990).

In 1983, the Chinese government started granting professional titles to journalists. By 1990, about 100,000 journalists were granted titles ranging from assistant reporter/editor to senior reporter/editor.

METHODS

The data for this study come from a nationwide survey of 5,800 Chinese journalists. Funded by a grant from the United Nations Educational, Scientific and Cultural Organization (UNESCO), the original objective of this survey was to provide a profile of Chinese women journalists. For comparison, men journalists were also included in the sample.

However, unlike other studies of journalists (e.g., Weaver and Wilhoit 1996) that drew inferences about the journalistic population from a probability sample, we do not project to the Chinese journalistic population based on this survey data for two reasons. First, certain demographic parameters about the Chinese journalistic population, such as the total size of journalistic workforce, the ratio between men and women, and the ratio between junior and senior journalists, are readily available from governmental sources. In fact, as is described in detail later, our sample was stratified against these known parameters. Thus, a projection from the sample to the population will merely confirm these parameters.

Second, although many other population parameters such as perceptions and attitudes of Chinese journalists are yet to be known, they should not be inferred from the respondents of this sample who were selected through a quota scheme. Like any other quota samples, ours is subject to certain unknown bias(es). Based on these considerations, we use published and unpublished governmental statistics to present a demographic profile of the Chinese journalistic population, while confining the survey results to the sample itself.

The quota scheme for the survey was developed through a three-stage procedure. In the first stage, we compiled a complete list of Chinese news organizations based on two official publications: the *Chinese Journalism Yearbook* (1992-1994) and the *Chinese Broadcasting Yearbook* (1993-1994). These two publications list 2,001 newspapers that have been registered with the State Bureau of News and Publishing and 987 radio stations and 684 television stations licensed by the Ministry of Radio, Television and Films. The only two news agencies (the Xinhua News Agency and the China News Service) are not listed in the publications but were added to our list because of their vital importance and large staffs.

Excluded from the list are the enterprise press, magazines, and cable television stations. There are thousands of enterprise publications in China, published by large-size companies for internal consumption. They are similar to the trade publications in the United States that were excluded from the 1992 U.S. journalists survey conducted by Weaver and Wilhoit (1996). All magazines are excluded from this survey because most of them are primarily entertainment publications on a monthly or longer basis. Magazines of this kind were also excluded from Weaver and Wilhoit's survey. There are very few news magazines (e.g., *Outlook* and *Biweekly* are subsidiaries of the Xinhua News Agency that is already included in our sampling frame). One exception is the English weekly, *Beijing Review*, which is not included in the sample. Nearly 1,000 cable television stations in China are excluded because most of them do not produce news programs.

The 3,674 media organizations included in our list were stratified along two dimensions: industry and locality. The industry dimension includes two categories: print (newspapers and news agencies) and broadcasting (radio and television stations). The locality dimension consists of four tiers of economic development. There are currently 2,371 administrative localities in China, including 185 provincial- and district-level cities, 294 county-level cities, and 1,892 rural counties. The county-level cities and rural counties have been classified by the State Bureau of Statistics (SBS) Rural Survey Unit into four tiers, with Tier I being the most developed areas and Tier IV the least developed, based on such economic indicators as personal income and gross domestic products (Zhu 1992). We followed SBS's categorization to stratify the 185 provincial- and district-level cities and align them with equivalent county-level cities and counties. Of the total 2,371 cities and counties, 346 (or 15%) fall into Tier I, 1,024 (43%) Tier II, 384 (16%) Tier III, and 617 (26%) Tier IV. By the end of the first stage, the 3,674 news organizations in our list were stratified into a 8-cell (2 industries x 4 tiers of locality) scheme.

In the second stage, we drew 461 media organizations, including 2 news agencies, 266 newspapers, 78 TV stations, and 115 radio stations, from the list. The chosen organizations account for 13% of the news media in China, or 100% of the news agencies, 13% of the newspapers, 12% of the radio stations, and 11% of the television stations. The selection followed a random procedure with an unequal probability that assigns more weight to organizations in the less developed localities to ensure a sufficient representation of these media. The unequal weight was later adjusted during the data analysis.

In the third stage, a local coordinator in each of the 461 chosen media organizations was contacted. In some cases, a regional coordinator was also assigned to work with the local coordinators within the region. Most of our local and regional coordinators were administrative officers in the sampled media organizations. Because the survey was carried out under the sponsorship of the All Chinese Journalists Association (ACJA) and the Journalism Research Institute of the Chinese Academy of Social Sciences (CASS), we received good cooperation from the regional and local coordinators.

Each local coordinator was instructed to draw individual journalists from his or her organization based on a predetermined quota specifying the number, the gender ratio, and the job rank distribution of the respondents. The number of respondents drawn from each organization was proportionate to the staff size of that organization, up to a ceiling (no more than 20 from any newspaper or 30 from any broadcasting station). Because the original focus of the survey was on female journalists, women were purposely oversampled, with a ratio of 2 (for women) to 1 (for men). The distribution of junior-, mid- and senior-level journalists was determined based on information provided by the SBNP. The chosen individuals were asked by our local coordinators to complete a self-administered questionnaire. About half the respondents returned the completed questionnaires by mail using a self-stamped envelope provided by us; the other half handed in their questionnaires through our local contacts. Of the 8,240 questionnaires distributed, 5,867 were returned with a completion rate of 71%. This completion rate compares favorably with the 61% for a mail survey of nationwide journalists in 1988 (Yu and Liu 1992).

Before analyzed, the sample was weighted to adjust for the overrepresentation of women and underrepresentation of largest media organizations (due to the ceiling as described previously), based on the known population parameters. For example, according to the information compiled from the Ministry of Personnel, the MRTF, and the SBNP, we estimated that women account for 33% of the journalistic population in China. However, women respondents accounted for 69% of our sample. In the weighting, we scaled down the proportion of women by a factor of 2.17 to reflect their original share in the journalistic workforce. Because the number of male respondents remained constant, the adjustment led to a reduction in sample size from the original 5,867 to the current 2,723. Although this is a conservative approach, we believe the adjusted sample size is still sufficiently large for statistical purposes.

BASIC CHARACTERISTICS OF CHINESE JOURNALISTS

Workforce Size

According to the information compiled from the SBNP and MRTF, there are 86,646 full-time journalists employed by more than 3,600 news media in China. As shown in columns 2 and 3 of Table 2.1, 42,096 (or 48.6%) of them work for newspapers, 1,320 (1.5%) for news agencies, 19,331 (22.3%) for TV stations, and 23,899 (27.6%) for radio stations. If we combine newspapers and news agencies into the print industry, and radio and television into the broadcasting industry, each industry has an even share of the journalistic workforce.

It should be noted that the governmental statistics reported here understate, probably to a substantial extent, the actual size of the Chinese journalistic population because those working for the media organizations without a formal professional title are not registered in the governmental roster. A professional title, ranging from Assistant Reporter/Editor, Reporter/Editor, and Deputy Senior Reporter/Editor to Senior Reporter/Editor, is granted by the government only to the news editorial staff on permanent payroll. There are at least two types of journalists working full time in the media without a professional title: those young staff members without a college degree,[5] and those who are recruited on a contract basis (as opposed to a permanent basis), a pop-

---

[5]The requirement for a college degree is less stringent for the older journalists with extensive media working experience.

Table 2.1. Full-Time Journalistic Workforce in China.

	Number of Organizations	Number of Journalists	Percentage of Journalistic Population	Percentage Shared by Women Journalists
Newspapers	2,001	42,096	48.6	28.6
News Agencies	2	1,320	1.5	29.2
Print total	2,003	43,416	50.1	28.6
TV Stations	684	19,331	22.3	37.5[a]
Radio Stations	987	23,899	27.6	37.5[a]
Broadcast total	1,671	43,230	49.9	37.5[a]
Total	3,674	86,646	100.0	33.0

Source: Data compiled from the State Bureau of News and Publications, the Ministry of Radio, Television and Film, and the Ministry of Personnel.
[a]estimated values (for a more detailed explanation, see discussion in text).

ular measure under the reform era. Unfortunately, neither the government statistics nor our survey data permit us to estimate the number of these "untitled" journalists.

Geographic Distribution

As divided by the four tiers of locality based on economic development, Chinese journalists are disproportionally concentrated in the most developed areas. On the one hand, as shown in Table 2.2, two thirds (66%) of the newspaper journalists and over half (52%) of the broadcasting journalists live in Tier I (the most developed) areas, which account for only one fifth (21%) of the general population. On the other hand, although 14% of the general population reside in Tier IV (the least developed) areas, only 4% of the print and 6% of the broadcasting professionals work there.

The journalists in four tiers of locality differ mostly in their educational and industrial background. As one can expect, the journalists in Tier I are the best educated, whereas those in Tier IV are the least educated. For example, 8% of the respondents from Tier I did not have any college education as compared to 19% in Tier II, 26% in Tier III, and 27% in Tier IV. The journalists in Tier I are also more likely to have gone through a formal journalism education program than their counterparts elsewhere. Although about one third (32%) of the journalists in the Tier I localities had a degree in journalism, only 21% in Tier II, 18% in Tier III, and 16% in Tier IV did so. The journalists in Tier I are more likely to be

Table 2.2. Geographic Distribution of General and Journalistic Populations.

Locality	General[a] Population (N = 1.13 billion) (%)	Journalists[b] Newspapers (N = 42,096) (%)	Broadcasting (N = 43,230) (%)
I. Most Developed	20.9	65.9	51.8
II. Quite Developed	53.6	23.2	32.5
III. Less Developed	11.3	6.8	9.7
IV. Least Developed	14.2	4.2	6.0
Total	100.0%	100.0%	100.0%

[a]Data compiled from the *1990 Population Census of China,* 1993.
[b]News agency journalists are not included here.

working for print media (55%), as compared to 41%, 40%, and 39% in the remaining localities, respectively. However, the journalists in the three less developed areas are more likely to work for radio (36% for Tier II, 46% for Tier III, and 42% for Tier IV, as compared to 23% in Tier I).

Gender Ratio

As stated earlier, 33% of the Chinese journalistic population is female. This figure was estimated not from the survey, but from various governmental statistics. For example, the Ministry of Personnel provides the proportion of women journalists for newspapers (28.6%) and news agencies (29.2%). However, for the broadcasting media, only the percentage of female anchors (66.6%) is known. Assuming that the same gender ratio of the print media holds for the broadcasting media, we estimate that women account for 37.5% of the total broadcasting journalistic workforce that includes reporters, editors and anchors. The 33% overall female share is the weighted average between the print and broadcasting media.

The 33% share of women in the journalistic workforce is somewhat lower than the female proportion in the general working population (37.3%; *Statistical Yearbook of China* 1994). It is also lower than the female percentage in such professional occupations as education (40.0%), and culture and arts (38.5%). However, the female proportion in the media is comparable to that in science and technology (33.5%) and is much higher than that in governmental and CCP agencies (22.6%).

Age

Age and all other characteristics of Chinese journalists presented here are based on the survey results. The median age of the journalists in the sample is 34.9, with men being 5.4 years older than women (37.1 vs. 31.7). Compared to the median age of the general working population (25.6; *The 1990 Population Census of China*, 1993), journalists are substantially older. However, no comparison can be made to other professional occupations, a more appropriate reference of comparison, because the median age for other professions is unknown.

The age difference between men and women can be accounted for by a number of gender-related factors. For example, the normal retirement age for journalists without a professional title of senior reporter/editor is 55 for women, but 60 for men. Thus, when both men and women aged 56 or older are dropped out of the analysis, in order to remove the influence of the retirement system, the age difference between the sexes is reduced to 4.3 years. A breakdown by job rank further reveals that the gender difference in age is only 1.6 years for regular staff, 0.5 year for mid-level supervisors, but 5.4 years for top-level executives who are disproportionally male.

There is a smaller difference between men and women in terms of their professional age (years in mass media). The median professional age is 9.9 for the male respondents and 8.1 for female, with 9.6 being the median for the entire sample. Compared across media industries, newspaper journalists (median age = 35.8) are older than their counterparts in television (34.2) and radio (34.4). However, radio journalists have had more working experience (median professional age = 10.0) than those in either print (9.2) or television (8.9).

Ethnic Background

There are 56 ethnic minorities in China, accounting for 8% of the general population, 7.5% of the working population, and 7.2% of professional occupations including science, education, culture, and medicine (*The 1990 Population Census of China*, 1993). Of our sample, 11% are from 33 ethnic minorities, with the remaining 89% being the Han majority. Thus, ethnic minorities are well represented in the sample. The largest minority groups surveyed include Mongol (3.2%), Hui (1.8%), Manchu (1.8%), and Tibetan (1.0%).

To find out who these minority journalists are and how they are doing, we compared them with their Han counterparts on various individual and organizational characteristics. No systematic difference was detected between the two groups in terms of age, gender ratio, job rank, and professional title. However, the minority journalists were found to be less likely a CCP member, somewhat less educated, more likely to work in radio but less likely in newspapers or television, and more likely to live in a less developed locality (Table 2.3). For example, 47% of the minority journalists are CCP members, as compared to 51% of the Han journalists. Twenty-three percent of the minority journalists did not have any college education, as compared to 12% of the Han journalists. These differences may suggest that it is relatively easier for the minority journalists without a college degree to enter journalism and receive a professional title. However, 41% of the minority journalists are affiliated with radio stations, compared to only 27% of the Han majority. Although almost two thirds (63%) of the Han majority journalists live in a mostly developed locality (Tier I), only one third (35%) of the minorities reside there. This pattern is nevertheless in line with the geographic distribution of minorities in the general population.

Table 2.3. Significant Differences between the Ethnic Majority and Minority Journalists.

	Han Majorities ($N = 2,387$) (%)	33 Minorities ($N = 336$) (%)
CCP Membership	51.3	47.3
Education		
High School	12.2	23.2
3-year Polytechnic	40.3	31.5
4-year University +	47.5	45.3
Industry		
Print	50.1	43.2
Television	22.4	15.8
Radio	27.4	41.0
Locality		
Most Developed	62.6	34.9
Next Most Developed	27.5	30.8
Less Developed	5.9	22.5
Least Developed	4.0	11.8

Note: All the two-way comparisons between the majority and minority journalists are statistically significant at .05 or beyond.

CCP Membership

More than half (54%) of the sample are members of the Chinese Communist Party (CCP), with another quarter (24%) being affiliated with the Chinese Communist Youth League. Less than 1% of the sample belong to various so-called "democratic parties" that are not an opposition but an advisory body to the ruling CCP.

As one can expect, job rank has the strongest association with CCP membership, based on a multivariate log-linear analysis. For example, although 34% of the ordinary staff are CCP members, 80% of the mid-level directors or 89% of the top-level executives have joined the CCP. However, even after job rank is taken into account, other individual variations still hold. For example, in the rank-and-file staff, more CCP members can be found among men than women (40% vs. 26%), more in the print media than in broadcasting (39% vs. 31%), and more in older generations than in younger cohorts (23% for the 18 to 34-year-olds vs. 50% for the 35 to 49-year-olds vs. 73% for the 50-year-olds and older). Although the age-, gender-, and industry-related differences are much less dramatic for those mid- and high-level journalists, one exceptional group is the young executives (34 years or below). Only 44% of them (or 16 out of 37) are CCP members, a rate lower than not only the older executives (93%), but also the young mid-level directors (62%).

EDUCATION AND TRAINING

The journalists included in our survey appear to be well educated. In the sample 86% have had some college education—39% with a three-year polytechnic degree, 44% with a four-year university degree, and 3% with a graduate degree. However, this may overestimate the educational attainment of Chinese journalists because, as noted before, the sample does not include those full-time news editorial staff without a professional title (who are presumably less educated).

Nearly one third (32%t) of the college-educated, or 27% of the total sample, have majored in journalism. Most of the remaining college graduates studied other social sciences and humanities (including foreign languages, with less than 10% of the college educated from a science, technology, or medical major).

Although the Chinese journalists surveyed were well trained in college, they have received very limited retraining after entering the media profession. When asked, "Totally, how much time have you participated in retraining since becoming a journalist?", nearly half (49%) of the sample answered "none." Another 14% said that they have received less than one month of retraining throughout their journalism career. Among the remaining of the sample, 21% have participated in retraining from one to six months, and 16% over seven months.

To understand why some of the respondents have received on-the-job training, whereas others have never had such opportunities, we performed a logistic regression using various individual and organizational characteristics as explanatory variables. The results (not shown here) suggest that, other things being equal, men, long-term veterans, media executives (as compared to either ordinary staff or mid-level directors), TV journalists (as compared to print or radio personnel), CCP members, and those living in the least developed localities are more likely to be given chances. However, university degree holders (as compared to high school or three-year polytechnic graduates) had less opportunities for retooling, presumably because they are considered to have had enough training in college.

In the survey, the journalists clearly took note of this lack of retooling. We asked the respondents to select, as many as applicable, "the most troubling aspect(s) of your life and work" from a list of 14 items. Surprisingly, 50% of the sample picked "lack of retraining and slow improvement in job-related skills" as a major concern, as compared to 30% naming "low income," 28% "housing," and 15% "lack of promotion." Similarly, 82% of the sample disagreed somewhat or completely with the statement that "You have often received retraining opportunities," as compared to 15% who somewhat or completely agreed.

WORKING CONDITIONS AND JOB SATISFACTION

Job Duties

The journalists included in our sample can be classified into three levels in terms of their job responsibilities: 15% are executives of the organizations (e.g., publishers, chief editors and general managers), 19% departmental directors, and 66% rank-and-file staff.[6] Among the staff, 23% are exclusively involved in news reporting, whereas 32% are only engaged in editing. Another 30% of the staff perform both reporting and editing. Most of the remaining 16% of the staff are either news anchors or program hosts in radio or TV stations. As one moves up along the managerial hierarchy, he or she is less likely to go out to gather news but more

---

[6]Two percent of the sample are both department-level directors and media executives (most often, deputy editor-in-chief or deputy general manager). They are classified into the directorate group in which their primary responsibilities lie.

likely to stay in the newsroom to edit others' work. For example, 18% of the departmental directors and 9% of the executives are primarily involved in news reporting, as compared to 40% of the directors and 46% of the executives who deal exclusively with editing.

Salaries

The median monthly salary for our sample, as of January 1995, is estimated to be RMB¥586. However, because the salary was roughly measured on a 7-point scale, a precise comparison with the general population is not warranted. Comparisons within the sample seem to be more appropriate. Following Weaver and Wilhoit (1996), we focus on the gap between men and women. Overall, calculated by the median income, male journalists make ¥72 (or 13%) more than their female colleagues each month.

When age is taken into account, the gender gap appears to concentrate on the older generation. The largest gap is found in the 45 to 54-year-old cohort, followed by the oldest group, 55-year-olds and above. The difference between men and women is much smaller among those between 25 and 44. Interestingly, for the youngest (under 30), women make more (¥43 or 10%) than men. The overall pattern, except in the youngest cohort, is consistent with what Weaver and Wilhoit (1996) observed in their study of U.S. journalists.

The gender difference virtually disappears when other factors come into play. Based on a multiple regression analysis, the salary difference between the sexes can be adjusted to ¥4, a highly nonsignificant difference ($p > .80$). Five other factors come out significantly in predicting Chinese journalists' income level: locality, industry, professional title, age, and ethnicity, in that order. The first two, locality and industry, can be considered "structural factors," whereas the last three can be termed "individual factors." The distinction is crucial because the structural factors are beyond individual journalists' control. The regression analysis examining both main effects and interactions of these factors reveals that the structural factors have a uniform effect on everyone in the sample, whereas the impact of individual factors is largely confined to certain segments of the sample. For example, the journalists in a more developed locality always earn more, and newspapers always pay better than TV stations, which in turn pay better than radio stations.

However, the impact of professional title on salary does not extend to broadcasting journalists in Tier I localities (the most developed areas), who account for about a quarter of the sample. For these journalists, the deciding factor is age, but age does not play a role in any other localities. Likewise, ethnicity affects only those with a professional title of

Assistant Reporter/Editor in Tier III (next to the least developed) localities, where minority journalists (*n* = 39) reported earning ¥63 less than what the Han majority staff with the same professional title claimed (*n* = 78). No systematic difference was found between the two groups in terms of their age, gender, education, job rank, working experience and other characteristics.

Job Autonomy

In the survey, we asked a set of 20 questions, based on a 4-point scale, regarding job-related experiences. Five of the items dealt with job autonomy in the newsroom. As reported in Table 2.4, although the majority (ranging from 54% to 79%) of the sample responded positively to these items, only 8% firmly believed that they had a great deal of autonomy, and 5% completely agreed that they could put their reform efforts into practice. Thus, the journalists surveyed appear to be somewhat reserved about the latitude they have in their daily work. They seem to

Table 2.4. Perceived Autonomy of Chinese Journalists.

	Agree (%)	Somewhat Agree (%)	Somewhat Disagree (%)	Disagree (%)	Refusal (%)
You enjoy a great deal of autonomy in your job	8	55	30	7	2
You can often materialize your efforts to reform the news	5	49	30	9	7
Your supervisors listen patiently to your opinions and suggestions	11	62	19	5	4
Your supervisors often give you an important assignment	7	55	26	6	6
Your self-initiated stories/programs are often substantially altered	2	11	48	31	7

be a little more certain about attention and support from their supervisors. The most clear-cut case is that only a small number (13%) of the respondents complained that their self-initiated stories/programs have been altered substantially.

As one can expect, the rank-and-file staff reported less autonomy than their supervisors. For example, although 60% of the staff completely or somewhat agreed on their autonomy, 66% of the mid-level directors and 72% of the executives did so. Half the staff said they could put their news reform ideas into practice, whereas 65% of the directors and 79% of the executives said so. The most striking difference is that 28% of the staff claimed to find no instance in which their self-initiated news stories or programs were substantially altered, as compared to 39% of the mid-level directors and 51% of the top-level executives.

Job Satisfaction

When asked on a 5-point scale about their satisfaction with the current job, 10% of the respondents responded "very satisfied" and 62% "satisfied." On the other contrary, 15% were "somewhat dissatisfied" and 3% "dissatisfied." The remaining 11% took a neutral position, and 2% refused to answer. Overall, the Chinese journalists surveyed (72%) appear to be content with their jobs. The degree of their job satisfaction seems comparable to that of their U.S. counterparts: 77% of them were either "very satisfied" or "fairly satisfied" with their jobs (Weaver and Wilhoit 1996).

Also consistent with what Weaver and Wilhoit found, Chinese journalists' job satisfaction has less to do with material rewards such as salary or housing than with their perceptions of job autonomy. For example, 89% of those who said they had a great deal of autonomy were "very satisfied" or "satisfied" with the current job, as compared to 34% of those who felt little autonomy. In fact, in a regression analysis, job autonomy alone explains 20% of the variance in job satisfaction, whereas more than 20 other individual or organizational characteristics together account for only 5% of the variance.

PROFESSIONALISM

Perceived Media Roles

Following Weaver and Wilhoit, we asked the respondents to rate the importance of various roles the news media should play. Of the original 10 items used by Weaver and Wilhoit, we adopted seven that seemed to be acceptable to ask in China, with some rewording (items 1, 2, 3, 4, 6, 8, and 9 in Table 2.5). In addition, we added two items of our own to the list (items 5 and 7). In doing so, we departed somewhat from Weaver and Wilhoit, who were primarily interested in the relationship between the objective and the participatory roles. Our purpose is to explore the extent to which Chinese journalists subscribe to a variety of normative roles of the press as either prescribed by the government (e.g., items 3 and 7) or introduced from the West (e.g., items 4 and 8). Thus, each of the items is treated as a unique role, and our focus here will be placed on the relative importance of these items rather than on the interrelationship among them. Table 2.5 shows the results in the order of ranked importance.

Our respondents chose the dissemination of news quickly and accurately ("information role") as the most important, with 79% of the sample naming it as "very important." The next most important role, endorsed by 72% of the sample, requires the media to provide analysis and interpretation of major social issues, which may be called a "correlation role" according to Lazarsfeld and Merton (1948). The "mouthpiece role" came in third, with 64% considering the dissemination and explanation of governmental regulations and CCP policies to be very important. A slightly smaller number of respondents supported the "watchdog role" by looking over either the government (61%) or the negative sectors of the society (60%).

The least popular role among the Chinese journalists surveyed is entertainment, endorsed by 19% of the sample. The "public forum role," offering a free marketplace of ideas to ordinary citizens, also lacks widespread support, as less than a quarter (24%) viewed it as very important. Contrary to the strong support for the mouthpiece role, only one out of three respondents accepted the "indoctrination role" in promoting Communist role models. The journalists' preference of mouthpiece over indoctrination role is consistent with our previous studies (e.g., Zhu 1990), in which Chinese audiences were found to be responsive to media messages about governmental policies but resistant to campaigns promoting Communist ideology.

Similar to the findings by Wu, Weaver, and Johnson (1996) that little of the variance in Russian and U.S. journalists' perceptions of media roles could be explained, we found few strong predictors of Chinese journalists' professional attitudes. One of the exceptional cases is the impact of job rank on the perceptions of indoctrination and public forum roles. For example, the promotion of Communist role models is viewed as "very important" by 46% of the organization-level executives, but by only 38% of the mid-level directors and 30% of the ordinary staff. However, 17% of the media executives subscribe to the idea that the media should be a public forum, as compared to 24% of the mid-level directors and 26% of the staff.

Table 2.5. Perceived Media Roles.

How important is each of the following roles performed by the news media in our country?	Very Important (%)	Important (%)	Somewhat Important (%)	Unimportant (%)	Refusal (%)
1. Report domestic and foreign news quickly and accurately	79.3	18.5	.8	.3	1.0
2. Provide analysis and interpretation of social issues concerned by the public	71.8	25.6	1.2	.1	1.2
3. Disseminate and explain government regulations and Party policies	63.8	31.6	2.7	.4	1.5
4. Exercise opinion supervision on Party and government institutions and civil servants	60.7	32.0	3.0	2.2	2.1
5. Expose and criticize negative phenoma in the society	60.2	35.1	2.6	.4	1.6
6. Disseminate modern science, technology and cultural knowledge	48.2	45.3	4.5	.3	1.7
7. Promote hero role models	33.2	52.6	10.0	2.4	1.8
8. Provide the public opportunities to publish and express opinions	23.7	57.0	14.6	2.2	2.5
9. Provide cultural relaxation and entertainment	19.4	62.9	14.2	1.5	2.0

Note: Items 1, 2, 3, 4, 6, 8, and 9 are modified versions of Weaver and Wilhoit's 33 A, B, G, D, H and C, respectively. Items 5 and 7 were developed by us.

Commitment to Journalism

In response to the question, "Given a second chance, what will you choose to do?", 57% of the sample said they would stay in journalism. The most popular alternative choice is a career in business (12%), followed by cultural/arts/sports (5%), education (4%), science and technology (4%), and health care (4%). Less popular is to join the CCP or governmental apparatus (3%), law enforcement (3%), or the army (2%). The least desirable is to go into industry (0.5%) or agriculture (0.4%). Finally, a noticeable 6% of the respondents did not answer the question.

We have examined all possible causes for the commitment to journalism and found the decision to stay or leave is largely independent of personal characteristics such as sex, age, education, and ethnic background. Job rank, pay, and housing also appear to have no impact on the respondents' career aspirations. The most important factor is the level of job satisfaction, followed by perceived job autonomy. For example, of those who are "very satisfied" with the current job, 79% said they would stay. In comparison, only 43% of the "very dissatisfied" journalists made such a commitment. Similarly, 27% of those who claim to enjoy a great deal of autonomy said they would like to leave the news profession, whereas 59% of those who feel little job autonomy would opt to depart journalism.

CONCLUDING REMARKS

We have presented a profile of Chinese journalists based on information from two sources: governmental statistics and a survey of more than 5,800 journalists. Following Weaver and Wilhoit, we depict a "typical" Chinese journalist to summarize the major findings reported earlier. The journalist is a 35-year-old male, from the Han ethnic majority, who is a member of the ruling Communist Party, and has worked on a newspaper for 10 years. He attended a four-year university with a major in humanities or social sciences (not in journalism or communication) and was assigned by the state to be a journalist (i.e., rather than his own choice), but has not received on-the-job training for more than one month. He is married, with one child, earning RMB ¥586 per month, and living in one of the most developed localities, where one fifth of the general population reside. His professional title is a Reporter/Editor (i.e., the second lowest rank in a four-tier system), with primary duties in news reporting, mostly on economic affairs. The journalist believes that he has some degree of autonomy in his job, is somewhat satisfied with the job, and plans to stay in the profession given a chance to choose. He believes that the Chinese media should perform chiefly as information provider, interpreter for current affairs, and government mouthpiece, but should not be advocate of ideology, forum for free expression, or entertainer. Of course, there are many cases that deviate from these norms, as our survey results have shown.

Are Chinese journalists "professional" by the international standard described by Weaver and Wilhoit (1996)? The current study provides some positive evidence for the question. For example, the journalists surveyed are well educated, work for social impacts more than material incentives, and plan to stay in the profession. However, the majority of them have not received special training in journalism either in college or on the job. The lack of exposure to journalistic professionalism is reflected in their inconsistent perceptions of media roles. On the balance, we may consider that Chinese journalists are in the midst of professionalization.

This study has raised more questions than answers about the professionalism of Chinese journalists. One crucial issue is the extent to which what the journalists in the survey say is congruent with what they do in daily practice. Inconsistency appears to exist between this survey and other studies of media content. For example, as Polumbaum (1994) observed, the Chinese print and broadcasting media have become increasingly interested in providing "junk-food journalism." However, our respondents expressed a clear-cut preference for the information role over the entertainment role. Future research needs to compare the perceived and the practiced journalistic professionalism by Chinese journalists.

REFERENCES

Chen, Lidan and Xiaowei Song. 1993, May. *On the news consumption in our country*. Paper presented at the seminar on Socialist Market Economy and the Press. Jiangsu, China

Fan, Dongshen and the News Media and Modernization in China Task Force. 1992. *Journalism and modernization in China*. Beijing: Xinhua Press.

Karp, Jonathan. 1995. Buttering up Beijing: News Corp's venture with Chinese newspaper *People's Daily. World Press Review*, 42, 9: 32.

Lazarsfeld, Paul F. and Robert K. Merton. 1948. Mass communication, popular taste and organized social action. In *The communication of ideas*, edited by L. Bryson, pp. 95-118. New York: Cooper Square Publishers.

Memo of the First National Seminar of Deans/Chairmen of Journalism Schools/Departments. June 1990. Xiamen, China.

Min, Anxiang. 1993, May. *Competition of news or competition of media*. Paper presented at the seminar on Socialist Market Economy and the Press. Jiangsu, China.

Murphy, Kevin. 1995, January. China Shuts Newspaper. *International Herald Tribune*, p. 6

The 1990 population census of China. 1993. Beijing: China Statistical Publishing House.

Polumbaum, Judy. 1994, August. *Between propaganda and junk-food journalism: Exploratory terrains in mainland Chinese news coverage*. Paper presented at the annual meeting of the Association for Education in Journalism and Mass Communication. Atlanta.

Qiu, Zhengyi. 1995. Some Issues on the orientation of news media market and press reform. *Fudan Journal*, No. 3: 226-232.

Statistical yearbook of China. 1994. Beijing: China Statistical Publishing House.

Weaver, David H. and G. Cleveland Wilhoit. 1996. *The American journalist in the 1990s: U.S. news people at the end of an era*. Mahwah, NJ: Erlbaum.

Wu, Wei, David Weaver and Owen V. Johnson. 1996. Professional roles of Russian and U.S. journalists: A comparative study. *Journalism and Mass Communication Quarterly*, 73, 3: 534-548.

Yu, Guomin and Xiayang Liu. 1992. *Research on Chinese public opinion*. Beijing: The Chinese People's University Press.

Zhu, Jian-Hua. 1990. *Information availability, source credibility, and audience sophistication: Factors conditioning the effects of communist propaganda in China*. Doctoral dissertation, School of Journalism, Indiana University, Bloomington, Indiana.

Zhu, Qingfang. 1992. *Applications of social indicators*. Beijing: Chinese Statistical Publishing House.

3

East Meets West: Hong Kong Journalists in Transition

Joseph Man Chan, Paul S.N. Lee, and Chin-Chuan Lee
Chinese University of Hong Kong

Hong Kong is a confluence of the East and West. It is a Chinese society that has been under British rule since 1840. Adopting primarily a nonprotectionist cultural policy, Hong Kong opens itself to influences from China, the West, and other parts of the world. Chinese traditions linger on as Western practices and ideas are taking root, resulting in a hybrid culture of the East and West. The journalistic culture of Hong Kong is an integral part of this. It can thus be viewed as illustrative of the interactions between a Chinese press system and Western conceptions of journalism.

Although the prototype of the Chinese press can be traced far back to the Tang dynasty, its modern version did not emerge until the late 19th century when China came into contact with the Western powers. It is no coincidence that the first Chinese-language newspapers were born in the colonies of Hong Kong and Shanghai. Throughout the 20th century, the press was mobilized as an essential instrument of public enlightenment, moral uplifting, reform, and revolutions. The Hong Kong press has from the beginning reflected this instrumentalist orientation and nationalist sentiment (Lin 1937).

As Hong Kong transformed itself from a fishing village off the Southeast coast of China into a metropolis with a population of 6 million and a per capita income of about US$24,000 in 1997 (Staff 1997), its press has also taken on characteristics that are often associated with the commercial systems of the West. The growing affluence in recent decades has given rise to a formidable advertising industry upon which the mass media of Hong Kong thrive.

Although Hong Kong has some stringent press laws, they were seldom enforced, and the press was left to operate primarily within a market structure, resulting in a high degree of press freedom in Hong Kong, second only to Japan in Asia (Shen 1972; Chan and Lee 1991a). Hong Kong is a free port of information that allows the free flow of media in and out. Although only a handful of electronic media are licensed to operate, anyone can apply for a business license and start a publication. The government does set some limits on the publication of pornographic and politically sensitive materials; however, it rarely practices editorial censorship.

Presently, Hong Kong has four television broadcast channels, two of which are saturated with local productions. Radio broadcasting has three operators, one government-owned, two commercial, running a total of 12 channels. Hong Kong is a hotbed of publications. It has more than 20 daily newspapers and hundreds of magazines. It is also a regional center in news transmission, publications, popular songs, movie production, and telecommunications (Chan and Lee 1991b; Lee 1991). Cable television and regional satellite television were introduced after this survey was done.

Prior to the 1990s, politics in this colonial "administrative no-party state" (Harris 1978:11) was sharply divided on the line of the struggle between the Chinese Communist Party (CCP) on the mainland and the Chinese Nationalist Party (KMT) in Taiwan. The press in effect became an extension of the CCP-KMT rift when both parties set up propaganda outposts in Hong Kong decades ago (Chan and Lee 1991a). Not until the early 1970s did "centrist" newspapers, critical of both Beijing and Taipei, begin to prosper. These profit-motivated papers are beneficiaries of Hong Kong's rapidly expanding economy and advertising. Although devoting significant coverage to Chinese politics, they focus more on immediate local concerns.

Hong Kong did not have its own political party until 1990 when the United Democrats formed in anticipation of the maiden Legislative Council election in the following year. From then on, other Hong Kong parties began to crop up, resulting in some rudimentary forms of local party politics. Thus far, the mass media have not made any explicit editorial endorsement of the parties, not to mention financial and organizational linkages.

The electronic media are much less partisan than the press. Neither CCP nor KMT are allowed to own and run television or radio, even though individual owners may have economic or ideological ties with either party. With the exception of Radio and Television Hong Kong (RTHK), which is publicly owned, all other electronic media are commercial operations, which tend to take a "centrist" position ideologically.

Hong Kong has entered a period of political transition since 1984 when Britain agreed to return it to China in 1997. The transition is characterized by the formation of a dual power structure, with China becoming a contender to colonial British rule. Being the political master-to- be and having immense resources at its disposal, China has become very active in coopting the local elites, including the media owners and journalists (Chan and Lee 1991a). The Hong Kong government has become a lame duck that seeks to retain its authority by democratizing the political system of Hong Kong, which has met with strong opposition from China. The impending power transfer has resulted in the mass media's accommodation of China at the institutional and professional levels.

It is against this backdrop that Hong Kong journalists were surveyed. Adapted from Weaver and Wilhoit's (1986) questionnaire in their study of U.S. counterparts, this survey covers Hong Kong journalists' demographics, career paths, working conditions, professional and news values, and ethical standards. We also asked questions about journalists' social outlooks, aspired media roles, and journalistic practices during political transition. What follows is a summary of the findings.

METHOD

The survey was done in the summer of 1990. Journalists surveyed included reporters, editors, and news translators working in television, radio, newspapers, and news magazines. Excluded from this study were correspondents of international media as well as journalists specializing in sports, entertainment, photography, and noneditorial columns. A total of 25 news organizations were involved, covering all the local electronic media and dailies that publish regular news.[1] In other words, virtually every news organization was represented in the sample.

---

[1] Specifically, the sample included these news organizations: (a) television: *Asia Television Limited, Television Broadcasting Limited Radio Television Hong Kong*; (b) radio: *Commercial Radio, Radio Television Hong Kong*; (c) newspapers: *Ching Pao Daily, Express Daily, Hong Kong Commercial Daily, Hong Kong Daily News, Hong Kong Economic Journal, Hong Kong Economic Times, Hong Kong Standard, Hong Kong Times, Ming Pao Daily, New Evening Post, Oriental Daily, Sing Pao Daily, Sing Tao Yat/Wen Pao, South China Morning Post, Ta Kung Pao, Tin Tin Daily, Wah Kiu Yat Po, Wen Wei Po*; and (d) news magazines: *Contemporary, Pai Shing, Yazhou Zhoukan*.

Because quite a few Hong Kong media treated their staff roster with strict confidence because of political sensitivities, we had to create the sampling frame with the aid of informants. They compiled the names of 1,381 journalists working in each news organization by rank and by job nature between mid-June and mid-July 1990. Among them, 95 were expatriates from two English-language newspapers or English news departments of the electronic media. A systematic sample with an interval of 2 was drawn from this population, yielding a sample of 692.

The questionnaire had Chinese and English versions. Questionnaires were distributed and collected with the aid of one or more acquaintances working in each of the sampled institutions. We finished data collection between mid-July and late August 1990. Named questionnaires were delivered to the distributors in bulk, who, in turn, handed them to their colleagues in the office. Respondents returned the questionnaires directly to our informants or mailed them back to us. A response rate of 75% ($N = 522$) was obtained after follow-up phone calls and reminders. This rate is consistent across media (print vs. broadcast), types of journalists (reporters vs. editors), and journalists of differing partisan persuasions.

BASIC CHARACTERISTICS

The total workforce of the whole media industry should be much larger than what the size of our sampling frame (1,381) may suggest because it would also include international media, wire agencies, and non-news publications. An overwhelming majority of Hong Kong journalists work for newspapers (72%), with the rest thinning out into television (13%), radio (8%), and news magazines (2%). The newspapers outnumber other media in employment because of the large number of dailies—about 20—in Hong Kong.

The Typical Journalist

An analysis of the survey data shows that the "typical" Hong Kong journalist is young, mobile, well educated, relatively underpaid, procapitalism, prodemocratization, neutral toward the KMT-CCP strife, and gloomy about the future of press freedom in Hong Kong (Chan, Lee, and Lee 1996). However, this portrait should also be viewed against other journalists of diverse backgrounds and orientations.

Gender and Age

Our survey finds that males (65%) outnumber females (35%) by a ratio of nearly 2:1 in spite of the lopsided proportions in favor of the female in journalism schools. There are at least two reasons that account for this apparent discrepancy. First, a sizeable portion of journalists are spot reporters, who have traditionally been dominated by males, presumably because of their higher capability for dealing with crisis situations such as accidents, disasters, and tragedies. Second, many female reporters find themselves less mobile when they start marriage and childrearing, thereby becoming housewives or leaving journalism for jobs that pay better and have more regular working hours. Consequently, the male journalists have a higher tendency to stay on and take up more senior positions.

Although Hong Kong's journalism can be traced back to the mid-19th century, its present practitioners are young, with a median age of only 30. About half (51%) are below the age of 30, and about 85% are below 41. Only 7% of the journalists are older than 51. This is a result of the rapid turnover of personnel in news industry.

Consistent with the low age of Hong Kong journalists, more than half are single (54%), and married journalists account for only 41%. In contrast, the more mature and stable news industry of the United States registers about three fifths of its journalists as married (Weaver and Wilhoit 1993). The majority of Hong Kong journalists are relatively inexperienced as well. The median of experience in journalism is only 5 years and 9 months, a far cry from the U.S. journalist's median experience of 12 years.

Political Attitudes

Unlike journalists in the United States, where partisan ideology plays a less important role in news media, the political ideology of Hong Kong journalists has been observed to have affected self-selection in newspaper recruitment, resulting in high ideological congruence between journalists and newspapers (Chan and Lee 1988; Chan, Lee, and Lee 1992).

We measured journalists' political ideology by asking them to identify their position on an 11-point Likert scale with regard to (a) their affinity toward Taiwan or Beijing, (b) their preference for socialism or capitalism as a way of life, (c) their preference for slowing down or speeding up Hong Kong's democratization at present, and (d) their priority concerning the interests of the upper social strata or those of the lower strata.

Hong Kong journalists, as a whole, lean quite strongly toward capitalism (median = 8.0, mean = 7.3) and favor a more rapid pace of democratization (median = 8.0, mean = 7.7). Their tendency to identify with class interest is less marked, tilting slightly in favor of the lower class (median = 5.0, mean = 4.3). Although the partisan rift between Taiwan and mainland China has shaped Hong Kong's press structure, the journalists appear to be distancing themselves from this interparty conflict. As many as 65% claimed to opt for the neutral point along the measurement scale (median = 5.0, mean = 4.9).

In light of the impending change of sovereignty in 1997, it is not surprising that Hong Kong journalists have exhibited strong inclinations toward the choice of social systems and the issue of democratization because both are related to the potential threat of China as a disrupter of Hong Kong's *status quo*. Hong Kong, noted for its capitalist success, dreads the idea of becoming part of socialist China in spite of China's promise of "one country, two systems." At the same time, many people tend to think that democratization, independent of its own intrinsic merits, will help fend off undue interference from mainland China. It should be noted that the ideological strife between the KMT and the CCP that shaped the press structure in the past is losing its relevance at the level of journalists who mainly support a neutral stance. This is coterminous with Taiwan's fading influence and China's looming importance in the political life of Hong Kong.

EDUCATION AND TRAINING

Before the 1970s, most Hong Kong journalists had low levels of education. Some reporters covering societal news were retired or sacked policemen hired for their good police connections (personal communication with a veteran journalist). Being unable to express themselves in good Chinese, many had to rely on their colleagues for writing up the stories. More college-educated students began to enter journalism in the 1970s. Their improved proficiency in English and Chinese, coupled with their concern for society, made them more effective reporters than their predecessors.

In general, Hong Kong journalists are quite well educated. About 78% of them have received some level of college education, and the majority of the remainder are matriculators (Table 3.1). Although many college-educated journalists received their undergraduate training in colleges not officially recognized, it is safe to say that an overwhelming majority of Hong Kong journalists have received some level of tertiary education at least close to a bachelor's degree.

Table 3.1. Education.

Education	Level (%)
Junior High School	1
Senior High School	7
Matriculation	11
Tertiary (College) Education	72
Graduate School	6
No Answer	3
Total	100
(N)	(522)

Of all the respondents, about half (48%) majored in journalism or communication in their undergraduate studies. Among degree holders, communication majors make up 62%, in contrast to only 39% for their U.S. counterparts (Weaver and Wilhoit 1993).

Many practicing journalists think that more training courses are needed. However, the managers in most media are not as supportive as they should be. For instance, many journalists have complained that they are not exempted from work even on the few days that they take special training seminars offered by the Journalism Training Board. Very often they have to report to work after spending the entire day in tiring seminars. Only a few enthusiasts will therefore register for these training sessions. The slighting of external training is coupled with the general lack of in-house training.

WORKING CONDITIONS AND JOB SATISFACTION

Type of Work

As expected, journalists in Hong Kong are ranked in a pyramidal fashion with the reporters at the base and the managing and chief editors at the top. Regular reporters (49%) and senior reporters (12%) together constitute the majority of journalists. In some newspapers, the senior reporters also perform a management role that includes job assignment and team coordination for special coverage. Most media depend on the news assignment editors, who make up 6% of the journalistic workforce, for the daily management of reporters. About 14% are editors who review the news stories filed by the reporters. At the top of the news organization are the managing editors (1%), and the deputy and chief editors (4%), who supervise and direct the whole news operation. Hong Kong media organizations rarely station correspondents in foreign territories on a regular basis. Instead, they rely on news translators (4%) who in many cases help select and edit news from the wire services.

Job Satisfaction

Table 3.2 shows that, with three exceptions, all specific items measuring job satisfaction are rated more often as satisfactory than unsatisfactory, although the percentages of those saying "very satisfied" are low. The journalists generally feel satisfied with the opportunity for creativity and initiative, perceived social contribution of their job, opportunity to learn new knowledge, opportunity to influence the public, flexibility in time, autonomy, and access to important people. Only small proportions are dissatisfied with their jobs' perceived social contribution (4%) and influence on the public (11%). Twelve percent are dissatisfied with the creative environment, 12% with access to important people, and 19% with job autonomy.

The three items rated more often as unsatisfactory than satisfactory are pay for a modest living, promotion prospects, and influence on editorial policy. Only 19% of journalists are satisfied with their pay and promotion prospects, and about one fourth (24%) are content with their influence on editorial policy. Nearly half (44%) feel dissatisfied with their pay, and more than one third (38%) are dissatisfied with promotion prospects. These findings suggest that journalists in Hong Kong tend to find the material rewards inadequate.

Predictive Model of Job Satisfaction

Using a total of 17 independent variables identified from the literature, including job attributes, non-job attributes, and political tendencies, a predictive model of job satisfaction was constructed (Lee, Chan, and Lee, 1996).

Table 3.3 lists all the variables involved and the result of regressing job satisfaction on the independent variables. For space consideration, we leave the detailed methodological procedures to another report (Chan et al. 1996). Suffice it for us to mention that only independent variables that correlate significantly with job satisfaction at a level of .05 are included in the regression.

Table 3.2. Level of Job Satisfaction.

Factors	Very Satisfied (%)	Satisfied (%)	Somewhat (%)	Dissatisfied (%)	Not very satisfied (%)	(N)
Present Job	4	36	52	7	2	(509)
Chance for Creativity & Initiatives	8	46	34	9	3	(502)
Chance to Learn	7	41	37	10	6	(499)
Social Contribution	10	47	39	3	1	(477)
Influencing the Public	5	32	52	10	1	(447)
Flexible Time	4		28	37	22	(484)
Autonomy	6	36	39	14	5	(499)
Access to Important People	8	38	42	8	4	(439)
Pay	3	16	37	28	16	(493)
Promotion Prospect	3	16	43	27	11	(437)
Influence on Editorial Policy	4	20	38	26	12	(435)

Note: Percentages may not add up to 100 due to rounding.

Table 3.3. Predicting Job Satisfaction With Stepwise Regression ($N = 263$).

Independent Variables	Standardized B
Chance for creativity & initiative	.24***
Satisfaction with pay	.26***
Chance to learn	.20***
Gender (Male)	.12*

$R^2 = .24$ $F = 22.01, p < .001$

Variables not in the equation	
Age	.01
Marital status	.09
Salary	.05
Rank	-.01
Time worked with present organization	.02
Access to important people	.08
Chance for advancement	.06
Autonomy	.08
Importance of job to society	.05
Influence on editorial decision	.07
Chance to influence the public	.07
Time flexibility	.05
Organization's attitude toward democratization	.06

*$p < .05$, ***$p < .001$

Four predictors stand out in the equation: (a) chance for creativity and initiatives, (b) satisfaction with pay, (c) sex, and (d) chance for learning. Altogether they explain 24% of variance in job satisfaction (adjusted $R^2 = .24$, $F = 22.01$, $p < 0.001$). As Table 3.3 indicates, the strongest negative predictor of Hong Kong journalists' job satisfaction is their satisfaction with the pay (B = .26, $p < .001$). The actual amount of salary, however, is insignificant. The next strongest predictor is the chance for creativity and initiatives in the news organization (B = .24, $p < .001$), followed by the chance for learning new knowledge (B = .20, $p < .001$). The B for this variable is not surprising given that 85% of Hong Kong journalists are below age 41. Young professionals may have a greater need to learn and improve themselves. Sex was also a significant predictor of job satisfaction (B = .12, $p < .05$). Male journalists tend to be more satisfied than females in Hong Kong. The other variables are all insignificant in predicting journalists' satisfaction levels.

MEDIA PROFESSIONALISM AND AFFILIATION

Judging from the membership figures, Hong Kong journalists are quite loosely organized. Only about 13% of the respondents are members of the Hong Kong Journalists Association, and 5% are members of the Hong Kong News Executives Association. In contrast, 36% of the U.S. journalists belong to a professional organization of some sort (Weaver and Wilhoit 1993). One of the major characteristics of a profession is its ability to enforce norms through peer reviews. Without a strong journalism organization, it is difficult for the journalists to carry out such peer reviews at the industrial level. Although it has stopped short of being a well-organized union that fights for the economic benefits of its members, the Hong Kong Journalists Association is emerging as an outspoken pressure group on issues related to journalism issues and a professional organization that provides ethical guidelines and occasional training. The News Executive Association is less outspoken and is more like a socializing venue for journalists at the management level.

Media Roles

Table 3.4 indicates that the Hong Kong journalists share many professional values with their Western counterparts. For instance, a great majority of them consider it important or very important to report objectively (95%) and with balance (78%). Thus objectivity, long hailed as the hallmark of media professionalism in the West, is almost universally accepted by Hong Kong journalists. Although highly regarded, balanced reporting is not as strongly held as objectivity and accuracy. It appears that Hong Kong journalists endorse professional values more readily at the conceptual level than at the operational level of balanced reporting (Lee, Chen, Chan, and Lee 1996).

Johnstone, Slawski, and Bowman (1976) classify U.S. journalists into two professional orientations, "neutral" and "participant," whereas Weaver and Wilhoit (1986) identify three types—"adversarial," "interpretive," and "disseminator." The Hong Kong journalists do not seem to fall neatly into either of these two schemes. The survey shows that Hong Kong journalists are ambivalent in their attitudes toward two professional dimensions. One relates to the tension between the "neutral-informative"

Table 3.4. Importance of Various Professional Values.

	Very Important (%)	Somewhat Important (%)	Somewhat (%)	Somewhat Unimportant (%)	Very Unimportant (%)	(N)
To Report Objectively	71	24	5	0	0	(503)
To Inform Public Promptly	65	30	6	0	0	(513)
To Analyze & Interpret Complex Issue	55	37	7	1	0	(508)
To be Watchdog of Government	58	30	10	1	1	(506)
To Speak for Public	41	39	17	2	1	(502)
To Report in a Balanced Way	48	30	14	3	5	(459)
To Assist in Promoting Government Policy	7	26	46	15	7	(493)
To Educate Public	28	43	23	5	1	(504)
To Raise Cultural Level of Masses	16	45	30	7	2	(497)
To Provide Entertainment	8	31	50	10	2	(501)
To Meet Popular Taste	8	28	41	15	8	(493)

Note: Percentages may not add up to 100 due to rounding.

and the "participant-interpretive" roles, and the other relates to that between media roles as "watchdog of government" and "mouthpiece of government."

"Neutral-informative" vs. "Participant-interpretive." On the one hand, most Hong Kong journalists value a neutral position in reporting. On the other hand, they favor the interpretive and participant role. As mentioned earlier, an overwhelming majority (95%) regard "objective reporting" as important (Table 3.4), and nearly all of them (95%) think that "rapid dissemination of information" is important to news organizations. These findings suggest that Hong Kong journalists choose a "neutral-disseminator" position for themselves.

However, an overwhelming majority (92%) also regard "analyzing and interpreting complex issues" as important. And 8 of 10 journalists consider it important for the news media to "speak for the people." In other words, the journalists also see the "participant-interpretive" role as important for themselves.

"Watchdog of Government " vs. "Mouthpiece of Government." The second dimension that reflects Hong Kong journalists' professional ambivalence is their attitude toward the news media's relationship with the government. Our study shows that 88% of journalists consider it important for the media to serve as a watchdog of government (Table 3.4). A further analysis shows that the perceived importance of the "watchdog" function holds across all news media regardless of their political orientations. The same patterns hold for the function of "speaking for the people."

Nevertheless, the survey shows that about one third (33%) of journalists regard it as important to assist in promoting government policies, and less than one quarter (22%) regard it as unimportant; most (46%) hold an ambivalent attitude (Table 3.4). This finding suggests that the media might transform themselves into a mouthpiece of the government because the "ambivalent" group could switch to the publicity function without denying their original position on government publicity. It is interesting to note that although an overwhelming majority think that the news media should serve as a watchdog of government, many still consider it important to assist in government publicity. Probably the journalists who hold both attitudes do not consider themselves to be self-contradicting because they could criticize the "bad" policies while publicizing the "good" and/or "important" policies. What is clear is that Hong Kong journalists do not assume an "adversarial" position toward government.

Elitist and Anti-commercial Tone. Hong Kong journalists are found to possess an "elitist" and "anti-commercial" orientation. Seven in 10 journalists (71%) consider it important to "educate the public," and 6 in 10 think that it is important to "raise the cultural level of the masses" (61%; Table 3.4)[2] Only a little more than one third (36%) of journalists consider it important for news organizations "to meet the popular taste" and "to provide entertainment" (39%). The journalists tend to be less agreeable to the business and entertaining side of the media. This is probably due to the high educational level of Hong Kong journalists who tend to regard the general mass as somewhat "uneducated" and of "low taste."

Further analysis shows that educational level does make a difference in the perceived importance of meeting popular taste. Significantly, more journalists with tertiary education regard the role of meeting popular taste as less important than journalists with lower education. The duration of working as a journalist also makes a difference in the perceived importance of meeting popular taste. More people who have worked in the profession for a longer time (i.e., four years or more) say that it is important to meet popular taste. In other words, the longer one works in journalism, the greater is the weight attached to meeting popular taste.

Media Partisanship and Professionalism

Partisanship as defined by the media's linkage with the CCP (leftist) and KMT (rightist) has been found to have shaped the press structure and the world views of journalists in Hong Kong (Chan and Lee 1991a; Chan et al. 1992; Lee et al. 1996). Although media partisanship is losing its influence during the political transition, it continues to have an uneven impact on the journalists' endorsement of professional values. In summary:

1. The centrist (commercial)-media and rightist-media journalists are more likely than their leftist-media colleagues to attach greater importance to norms aimed to "provide analysis for complex problems" and to "report news in a balanced way." The differences on these norms all reach statistical significance.
2. The centrist-media journalists are more likely than their partisan counterparts (both rightists and leftists) to assign greater significance to norms aimed to "publicize (the Hong Kong) government policy" and to "raise public cultural appreciation." As expected, the centrists are less likely to value the norm of "providing a clear political stance."

---

[2]Consistent with this observation is that 60% of the journalists agree that news media should mold public opinion.

3. Journalists respond positively to norms ranging from balanced reporting, media as a government watchdog, getting information to the public quickly, to educating the public—in fact, their response is so overwhelmingly positive as to make journalists' partisan affiliation inconsequential. Likewise, their lack of high enthusiasm for the media's functions of providing entertainment or meeting popular taste does not vary with media partisanship.

Ethical Standards

Media professionalization includes the development of codes of practice on the part of journalists. A significant indicator of journalistic ethics is the extent to which various favors from interviewees are accepted without question. Our findings show that Hong Kong journalists respond to different gifts in a wide range of ways.

They generally find meals (48%) and souvenirs (49%) acceptable. Talking over meals appears to be a common form of social exchange that applies to all circles in Hong Kong, including journalism. Standardized and usually inexpensive souvenirs also do not pose great ethical strain on the Hong Kong journalists. Acceptability drops quite drastically when it comes to more expensive junkets or free trips provided by interviewees (16%). For gifts, acceptability declines even further (11%), presumably because they are often personalized and valuable. With monetary favor, there is a virtual consensus—97% find it unacceptable or absolutely unacceptable. With the exception of monetary favor, about one third of the journalists find it difficult to decide on the acceptability of each of the other kind of favors. In general, the more valuable is the advantage, the more unacceptable it is.

Another ethical concern of journalists focuses on the practices of gathering and publishing information. Table 3.5 indicates that Hong Kong journalists generally consider it wrong to breach promised confidentiality (95%), use personal documents without authorization (74%), disguise their identities to get information (56%), copy other media without attribution (57%) and pay others for confidential information (48%). Although the journalists tend to be strict in keeping their honor, they take more casual attitudes toward using government confidential documents (only 21% consider it wrong), using business confidential documents (26%) and badgering the unwilling for information (15%). This is reasonable as the government and corporations are generally more newsworthy than private citizens. Only 17% of Hong Kong journalists disapprove of the practice of "exchanging information with fellow reporters." This finding helps to explain why the news media in Hong Kong seldom break exclusive stories.

Table 3.5. Attitudes Toward Ethical Issues.

Ethical Issues	Absolutely Improper (%)	Improper (%)	Hard to Say (%)	Proper (%)	Absolutely Proper (%)	(N)
Break Promise in Confidentiality	63	32	5	0	1	(502)
Unauthorized Use of Personal Documents	32	42	21	4	1	(497)
Use Confidential Government Documents	6	15	35	35	10	(482)
Use Confidential Business Documents	6	20	38	30	6	(482)
Get Employed in a Firm for Information	22	34	26	16	3	(484)
Claim to be Somebody Else	27	35	26	11	1	(493)
Badger Unwilling Informants	3	12	22	47	15	(487)
Pay Others for Confidential Information	24	24	32	16	3	(491)
Exchange Information with Other Journalists	5	12	27	45	12	(483)
Plagiarism	17	40	25	15	3	(473)

Note: Percentages may not add up to 100 due to rounding.

Newsworthiness

Table 3.6 reflects the weights Hong Kong journalists attach to various influences on news judgments. An overwhelming majority (92%) name "social significance of event" as influential, whereas 73% consider "source of information," 66% "past journalism training," and 59% "supervisors" as having influence on their judgment of what is newsworthy. It is interesting to note that only about one third (35%) regard the political stance of the news organization as an influence on their news judgment. This percentage is lower than one would have expected, especially at a time when Hong Kong has been politicized by the pending exchange of sovereignty.

The lack of influence of the news media's political stance is probably due to the dominance of nonpartisan media in Hong Kong. Nonpartisan media do not stick to a particular political stance, thus making the media's political orientation less important in the journalists' news judgments. Further analysis supports this explanation. The number of journalists working with centrist media almost doubles that of the leftist and rightist media in ruling out the influential role of the media's political stance on news judgment. In contrast, more than half the journalists in both the leftist and rightist media think otherwise.

Colleagues and external media tend to be perceived as less influential on news judgments. About one third of the journalists (32%) consider their colleagues as having influence. Even fewer (30%) consider their acquaintances in other media as influential, although 39% think that major media competitors have influence. Among external media, about one third (32%) say that leading newspapers' news treatment has influence on their news judgment, whereas one quarter point to the impact of television (26%) and radio (24%).

Journalists and Political Transition

When asked to evaluate the importance of certain media roles during the political transition, journalists place the strongest emphasis on their function in maximizing Hong Kong's autonomy. An overwhelming majority (86%) maintain that the Hong Kong news media "should fight to maximize Hong Kong's autonomy beyond 1997." Obviously, whether Hong Kong can have a high level of autonomy when China regains its sovereignty is perceived to be very critical for the future. An overwhelming majority of journalists also think that the mass media should fight for citizens' interest from China and Britain (78%). The proportions of journalists agreeing with these views are even higher than those supporting the media's role in maintaining social stability (53%)—perhaps the most cherished value in Hong Kong.

Table 3.6. Factors Affecting News Judgment.

News Factors	Great Influence (%)	Some Influence (%)	Somewhat (%)	No Influence (%)	None at All (%)	(N)
Social significance of event	47	45	6	2	0	(504)
Source of information	20	53	16	8	2	(502)
Colleagues	3	29	34	27	7	(500)
Acquaintances in other media	3	27	37	26	8	(495)
Supervisors	14	45	24	13	4	(497)
Journalism training	22	44	23	9	3	(436)
Audiences/Readers	9	34	30	21	7	(481)
Major media competitors	4	35	37	21	4	(485)
TV news treatment	2	24	43	24	8	(487)
Radio news treatment	0	24	43	26	8	(487)
Leading newspapers' news treatment	2	30	40	23	5	(489)
One's own political stance	5	33	29	26	8	(473)
Political stance of one's news organization	8	27	27	27	11	(471)

Note: Percentages may not add up to 100 due to rounding.

This observation is further evidenced by journalists' ideas about conflicts between China and Hong Kong. Sino-Hong Kong conflicts have arisen in recent years, and more are expected in the future. When asked which side Hong Kong's news media should take if China and Hong Kong should clash, 46% of the journalists insist that the media should stay "neutral," 31% go with Hong Kong, and less than 1% side with China. The rest either have other qualified attitudes (17%) or no opinion (5%). These findings attest to the journalists' adherence to professional neutrality, on the one hand, and their strong tie with local interest on the other.

Self-Censorship

Self-censorship toward China has been a haunting question for journalists during the political transition. We (Chan et al. 1992) defined self-censorship as the dilution or omission of certain information to avert adverse consequences that may befall journalists or their employing organizations. For fear that the full disclosure of information unfavorable to the power center may invite retaliation, some journalists exercise self-censorship against their better professional judgment. This fear can be induced by the power center, which does not have to exert any real pressure. In other words, self-censorship is a form of information control that is anticipatory and preemptive.

In this study, we measure self-censorship by asking journalists to indicate their agreement or disagreement with the statement that they are "apprehensive when criticizing China." As many as 23% of the journalists admit that they are "apprehensive" when criticizing the Chinese government. However, slightly over half of the respondents (55%) maintain that they are not. The rest (22%) are "uncertain" or have "no opinion." We estimate that the self-censorship figures may be underreported because it is socially undesirable to admit self-censorship. When we ask if "the majority of journalists are apprehensive in criticizing China," the proportion of journalists that agree or strongly agree jumps to 51%. We can safely assume that the actual proportion of journalists that are apprehensive toward criticizing China is over 23%.

SUMMARY AND CONCLUSIONS

Hong Kong journalists can be characterized as young, male, mobile, relatively well educated, and underpaid. The journalists' low age, underpayment, lack of organizational loyalty, and occupational commitment appear to be interrelated. Many young people are known to have joined journalism to earn some experience before looking for more lucrative and stable jobs in other fields, particularly in public relations. A common complaint is that journalism does not pay well, and the prospects are uncertain. If journalism in Hong Kong is to attract and retain talented people, it has to overhaul its salary, promotion, and reward structure.

Four important predictor variables for job satisfaction are identified. They are opportunity to exercise creativity, satisfaction with pay, opportunity to acquire new knowledge, and gender. Male journalists tend to be more satisfied than female journalists. Political factors do not seem to play a role in journalists' satisfaction. Yet after 1997 when the People's Republic of China takes over Hong Kong, the predictors of job satisfaction may take on a more political hue. The predictive model of job satisfaction identified in this study may be applicable only to a politically stable society with a liberal media system.

Ideologically, Hong Kong journalists generally favor capitalism and democratization and see these values as instrumental in defending the existing way of life in Hong Kong against possible interference from mainland China. The interparty struggle between the KMT and the CCP has become less salient in defining the journalists' political outlook as the majority opt for a neutral position. This indicates that the tension between China and Hong Kong has emerged as the most important ideological axis around which political discourse in Hong Kong is and will be organized. The KMT-CCP strife is becoming more a vestige of history, particularly in light of the fact that the KMT has been losing power in the democratizing of Taiwan.

Although Hong Kong journalists share professional values such as neutrality, accuracy, and balanced reporting that originated in Western democracies, they exhibit some ambivalence in professional orientation. While they try to be detached, they embrace a participant role. They consider it important for news media to act not just as a watchdog of government, but also as a channel for publicizing government policies. Most Hong Kong journalists have an elitist orientation with an anti-commercial tone. They think that the media should educate the masses, raise their cultural standards, and pay less attention to meeting popular taste.

Hong Kong journalists' professional orientation is further demonstrated by their ethical judgments. Although their responses to accepting favors from interviewees vary with the kind of favors in question, almost every one agrees that monetary favor is unacceptable. This contrasts sharply with the mainland Chinese journalists and journalists in other developing countries, who often trade news for fees (Chan 1993). The disapproval of monetary favor in Hong Kong is linked to their professional outlook and to the seriousness of the government in enforcing the laws against corruption. While Hong Kong journalists also find favors in the form of gifts and junkets somewhat unacceptable, they think that meals and souvenirs are relatively more acceptable.

Hong Kong journalists also show a range of ethical standards in reporting. In general, they do not endorse breaking a promise of confidentiality, using personal documents without authorization, disguising identity to get information, copying other media without attribution, and paying for confidential information. However, they are less hesitant in using confidential business and government documents and badgering unwilling informants for information.

Uncertain of the feasibility of the political future of Hong Kong, an overwhelming majority of Hong Kong journalists are found to have a very gloomy view of Hong Kong's press freedom when China regains its sovereignty in 1997. Neither are they very optimistic about press freedom in the runup to power exchange. This pessimism is based on the journalists' understanding of China's authoritarian rule. Given CCP's notorious record in suppressing dissenting voices, no wonder few journalists expect China to act otherwise when it gains control over Hong Kong.

As it stands now, China has woven an extensive web of bondage with Hong Kong journalists and publishers through skilled cooptation and united-front campaigns (Chan and Lee 1991a). The effectiveness of such cooptation is linked to China's significant control over business opportunities, advertising, and information resources in Hong Kong as well as on the mainland. China has periodically made implicit and explicit threats toward Hong Kong journalists. Tension culminated when China, in the wake of the Tiananmen crackdown, openly accused Hong Kong media of spreading rumors, agitating demonstrators, and subverting the motherland (Lee and Chan 1990). China is also observed to have a growing influence at the level of media ownership in Hong Kong (Fung and Lee 1994).

This anticipatory fear of China has been translated into self-censorship by about a quarter of Hong Kong journalists, who admit to have exercised self-censorship with regard to Chinese authorities. Even though this figure may seem an understatement, it is wrong to assume that all journalists are about to give up their professional roles to serve as China's propaganda outlets. Coupled with the media market and social pluralism in Hong Kong, journalists' concerns for its autonomy and local interest will likely serve to limit the pace and extent to which the news media bend with the political wind. Indeed, about 9 out of 10 journalists agree that the Hong Kong media should fight to maximize their autonomy after 1997.

If China is truly serious about the "one country, two systems" policy, press freedom must be maintained. To contain the Hong Kong press within tolerable limits, China cannot resort to naked force but must sooner or later return to the mixed tactics of overt threat and subtle incorporation. Amidst the increased political pressure, the press must attend to its own credibility and legitimation in order to survive the intense market competition. The press will have to strike a working (or workable) balance between political demands and market imperatives. As a result, the future news order will likely be uneven, indeterminate, and full of internal contradictions that entail partial compromises, advances and withdrawals.

As stated earlier, most journalists in Hong Kong are vibrant and idealistic. Although some have reportedly imposed self-censorship, many others are guarding with vigilance against any signs of infringement on press freedom. The whole process is likely to be a continual contest between control and anti-control, pressure and counter-pressure. While there are many reasons to believe that press freedom will decline, market competition will ensure that Hong Kong's transparency will remain relatively high—even if the process will be twisted and indirect. In conclusion, media professionalism will probably suffer, but it will not be lost.

This survey will provide a baseline for future comparisons in the runup to 1997 and beyond. Meanwhile, it should provide a basis for both implicit and explicit comparison across nations.[3] This is made possible by virtue of the fact that similar surveys were done, for instance, in the United States (Weaver and Wilhoit 1993), Germany (Schoenbach and Schneider 1993), and Australia (Henningham 1993).

REFERENCES

Chan, Joseph M. 1993. Commercialization without independence: Media development in China. In *China Review 1993*, edited by Joseph Cheng and Maurice Brosseau, pp. 25:1-19. Hong Kong: Chinese University Press.

Chan, Joseph M. and Chin-Chuan Lee. 1988. Press ideology and organizational control in Hong Kong. *Communication Research* 15, 2: 185-197.

Chan, Joseph M. and Chin-Chuan Lee. 1991a. *Mass media and political transition: The Hong Kong press in China's orbit.* New York: Guilford Press

Chan, Joseph M., Chin-Chuan Lee and Paul S.N. Lee. 1992. Fighting against the odds: Hong Kong journalists in transition. *Gazette* 50: 1-20.

Chan, Joseph M., Paul S.N. Lee and Chin-Chuan Lee. 1996. *Hong Kong journalists in transition.* Hong Kong: The Hong Kong Institute of Asia-Pacific Studies, the Chinese University of Hong Kong.

---

[3]For reports of preliminary attempts, see Lee, Chan, and Lee (forthcoming) as well as Chan et al. (1996).

Chan, Joseph M. and Paul S.N. Lee. 1991b. Communication indicators in Hong Kong: Conceptual issues and findings. In *Proceedings of the symposium on social indicators in Chinese societies*, edited by S.K. Lau et al., pp. 175-204. Hong Kong: The Hong Kong Institute of Asia-Pacific Studies, Chinese University of Hong Kong.

Fung, Anthony Y.H. and Chin-Chuan Lee. 1994. Hong Kong's changing media ownership: Uncertainty and dilemma. *Gazette* 53: 127-133.

Harris, Peter. 1978. *Hong Kong: A study in bureaucratic politics*. Hong Kong: Heinenmann Asia.

Henningham, John. 1993, May. The Australian journalists in the 1990s. Paper presented at the International Communication Association Annual Convention, Washington, DC.

Johnstone, John W.C., Edward J. Slawski and William W. Bowman. 1976. *The news people*. Urbana: University of Illinois Press.

Lee, Chin-Chuan and Joseph M. Chan. 1990. The Hong Kong press coverage of the Tiananmen protests. *Gazette* 46: 175-195.

Lee, Chin-Chuan, Joseph M. Chan and Paul S.N. Lee. forthcoming. Professionalism among journalists in comparative perspective. *Journal of Asian Pacific Communication*.

Lee, Paul S.N., Joseph M. Chan and Chin-Chuan Lee. 1996. Determinants of job satisfaction among journalists in Hong Kong. In *Beyond 2000: Future directions in journalism education*, edited by Jim Tully, pp. 134-153. Christchurch, New Zealand: University of Canterbury.

Lee, Chin-Chuan, Chi-hsien Chen, Joseph M. Chan and Paul S.N. Lee. 1996. Professionalism and partisanship: Hong Kong journalists in transition. *Gazette* 57: 1-15.

Lee, Paul S.N. 1991. Media and communications. In *The other Hong Kong report*, edited by Joseph Cheng and Paul Kwong, pp. 383-403. Hong Kong: The Chinese University Press.

Lin, Yutang. 1937. *History of the press and public opinion in China*. Chicago: University of Chicago Press.

Schoenbach, Klaus and Beate Schneider. 1993, May. The German journalist in the 1990s. Paper presented at the International Communication Association Annual Convention, Washington, DC.

Shen, James. 1972. *The law and mass media in Hong Kong*. Hong Kong: The Chinese University of Hong Kong.

Staff. April 25, 1997. *Asiaweek*, p. 71.

Weaver, David and G. Cleveland Wilhoit. 1986. *The American journalist*. Bloomington: Indiana University Press.

Weaver, David and G. Cleveland Wilhoit. 1993, May. The American journalist in the 1990s. Paper presented at the International Communication Association annual convention, Washington, DC.

4

Korean Journalists in the 1990s

Taik Sup Auh
Korea University
Chang Keun Lee
Kwang-Woon University
Myung Koo Kang
Seoul National University

The inauguration of president Kim Young Sam in the spring of 1993 ushered into Korean life a wave of reforms unprecedented in its breadth. Populist in motivation, these changes were to affect virtually every sector of Korean society in which unfair privilege or wealth had been perceived to exist. President Kim's very first decision—made during week one of this administration—was to cut back drastically the military security around the Blue House, the official presidential residence. For the first time in contemporary memory, ordinary citizens of Seoul, out on a Sunday morning hike, could look down at the grounds of the president's home from the surrounding hills.

The symbolism of Kim's action was obvious: Some 40 years of authoritarian (and at times autarchic) military rule were being supplanted by a government that would be open to scrutiny and influence by everyone. More pointedly, Kim was presaging a cluster of revisions to come in the way the military managed its affairs, revisions that would have the overall effect of weakening the political influence of career military personnel. A stop would shortly be put to the bribing endemic to the system by which field grade officers were promoted, legislative and prosecutorial investigation would be conducted into the previous two administrations' military procurement programs, and preferential treatment once the prerogative of members of semi-secret military clubs (*Hana-hoe*) would be crushed.

Change did not end with the military; everyone of any prominence in politics and government would be affected by the institution of the "Real Name System," a replacement of the vast array of phantom bank accounts in which corruptly gained wealth had been for decades secreted, far from inspection by prosecutors and tax auditors. The Real Name System, along with a mandatory property asset disclosure by all prospective executive and judicial appointees as well as all sitting legislators, met with fierce resistance from some politicians both in Kim's party and in the main opposition party. Both measures, however, were instituted on the wave of Kim's popularity with common people, thoroughly disgusted with entrenched political corruption. In addition, corruption in education and business was also to be exposed. In sum, business as usual was about to end.

In this veritable ocean of change, Korean journalists have had to feel their way in unprecedented and unfamiliar roles as their profession itself has been transformed. Although in the past the agenda and content of Korean press coverage was virtually dictated by the government, suddenly this has no longer been the case. Precipitously, Korean journalists have been forced to operate with a degree of liberty for which they are institutionally unprepared. This liberty, moreover, is not only novel, but burdensome: Accompanying it have come the responsibilities of journalistic maturity in a democracy.

In brief, a democratically responsible press operates at the very nucleus of national policy, tabling for consideration a catalogue of important issues and monitoring the public's reactions to them. These reactions are in turn incorporated into governmental policies. At the same time that the press monitors, it anticipates and focuses public opinion. These are the functions the Korean press has suddenly had thrust on it. Needless to say, if performed ethically and professionally, they do not serve the prior interests of politicians or the government. Such a portrayal of the role of the press can only be ideal, as any working journalist must candidly acknowledge.

METHODS

To determine how closely the Korean press—in its own estimation—has approximated this ideal following Kim Young Sam's inauguration, the Korea Press Institute (KPI) in May 1993 commissioned to the present authors a survey of the country's journalists. In general, the survey asked about journalists' perceptions of their responsibilities as well as their standards of ethical performance. Guilt feelings in the case of failure were also assessed. This survey was the third of its kind, following ones in 1989 and 1991 also carried out by the KPI. It employed a mailed questionnaire and involved a total of 727 working journalists. The respondents ranged in rank from editorial writer to young reporter, and the fields of journalistic expertise covered everything from the sciences to the arts.

The sample was drawn from the *Directory of the Korean Journalists* (1993) published by the Korea Press Center. A total of 1,010 people working for the newsroom and editorial departments of newspaper, broadcasting, and wire service companies in Korea were chosen according to the location (central and regional) and type of media (general and specialized). Questionnaires were mailed or hand delivered in bulk to each of the 40 selected media companies and distributed among the intended target respondents within the media organizations. Of the 1,010 questionnaires distributed, 727 completed questionnaires were returned for a response rate of 72%.

BASIC CHARACTERISTICS OF JOURNALISTS

Size of Journalistic Workforce

As of 1995, a total of 40,897 men and women were working in journalism in Korea—22,087 were employed by newspaper companies, 18,088 by broadcast media, and 722 by wire service news agencies. The number of journalists has steadily increased over the last 15 years. Of the 8,861 people working for Seoul metropolitan dailies, a plurality worked in the newsroom (2,576), followed by 909 people engaged in newspaper production and 867 people working in general affairs. It is noteworthy that 10% of those working for Seoul's dailies were engaged in editing and producing various publications and periodicals other than daily newspapers.

Age and Gender

Korean journalism is a predominantly male market, in which only 14.1% of the workforce is female.[1] The dominance of male journalists was most pronounced in the case of wire service news agencies (92%). In newspapers, females constituted 19% of the workforce—the largest percentage of females of all the various media. It is clear from Table 4.1 that journalism in Korea, as in many other countries, is a young person's occupation, with those in their 30s most numerous and an average age of 36.7.

Ethnic and Religious Origins

There is no linguistic, ethnic, or cultural variance among the working journalists because Korea is a homogeneous country. The majority of Korean journalists were found to have no religious affiliation (58%). Of the survey respondents, 19% were Christians, 11% were Catholics, 11% were Buddhists, and 2% were from other religious beliefs.

Political Attitudes

The ideological spectrum of Korean journalists shows a symmetrical, unimodal distribution resembling a normal curve. Of the 698 respondents, about two thirds said they were politically neutral (64%). On one extreme side, 16% reported being "somewhat progressive," and 4% reported being "very progressive." On the other end of the continuum, 11% thought they were "somewhat conservative," whereas 6% thought of themselves as "very conservative." In comparison with their own ideological orientation, the respondents felt that the media organizations they worked for were leaning further to the right (32% were "somewhat conservative" and 32.4% "very conservative"). It may very well be because of the perceived difference of political leanings of their news organizations from the journalists' own that disputes often arise over "unfair" journalistic practices within the media companies.

---

[1]This percentage is based on the population total. The sample studied here included 8.2% women journalists.

Table 4.1. Age Distribution of Korean Journalists.

Age	Frequency	(%)
20	117	(16.4)
30	391	(54.3)
40	135	(18.7)
50	78	(10.6)
Total	721	(100.0)[a]

[a] The total in the table does not equal the total number of respondents because six did not give their age.

EDUCATION AND TRAINING OF JOURNALISTS

Years of Schooling

By any standard, Korean journalists enjoy impressive academic backgrounds, with an overwhelming majority (94%) being university graduates or better. Those with junior college or lower educational backgrounds were primarily working for provincial media. It is worth noting that 1.6% of the metropolitan daily newspaper employees were holding doctoral degrees in various fields of specialization.

Fields of Study

Korean journalists represent a wide variety of academic backgrounds. Thirty-five percent majored in humanities, including Korean literature, English literature, history, philosophy, and psychology. The field of social sciences was yet another important discipline. Thirty-four percent studied political science, law, public administration, and sociology. Leading the pack of social science majors were—quite expectedly—journalism majors, at 13.5%. The rest of the workforce was divided into economics and business majors (9.8%) and engineering and natural science majors (6.6%). The remainder came from other disciplines.

Continuing Education

With the recent development in communication technologies and the accompanying changes in audience needs for information and entertainment, it appears that media management is stepping up its efforts to reeducate media professionals by means of a wide variety of educational training programs available through internal and external agencies. Educational programs include language training, computer education, and specialized reporting courses. Increasingly, overseas training is becoming available for a large number of Korean journalists. A recent survey conducted by the KPI showed that approximately 30% of the Korean working journalists had participated in continuing education or training provided by their own organizations or the Korean Press Institute.

WORKING CONDITIONS

By far the largest workforces within the news organizations are affiliated with the newsrooms (37%), in which the day-to-day activities of the reporters and editors are constantly monitored and critically assessed, often producing friction with their peers and superiors.

Perceived Autonomy

About two thirds of the working journalists in Korea felt that they enjoyed reasonable autonomy and freedom to select and present stories as they saw fit. About one in every five people felt that he or she enjoyed absolute freedom (22%) whereas about 1 in every 10 people felt that he or she had little or no freedom as a journalist (13%). Perceived journalistic autonomy or freedom was more strongly held by nonunion members (30%) than union members (20%).

Reporters' autonomy to select and cover stories was perceived to be compromised most frequently by heads of departments (66%), followed by newsroom managers, including editors and managing editors (16%); newspaper management, including the publisher (9%); senior reporters (3%); the news source (3%); and sometimes by advertisers (2%).

On a 100-point scale, the respondents were asked to rate the degree of freedom that they thought they were enjoying under the present and the two previous governments, with a 0 grade being "absolutely controlled" and a 100 "absolutely free." They gave a passing grade of 70.3 to the present Kim Young Sam government, 50.5 to Roh Tae Woo's Sixth Republic, and 24.6 to Chun Doo Whan's Fifth Republic. The older the respondent, the higher was the grade for the present government, but there was no appreciable difference in the respondents' ratings among journalists of various staff positions.

Communication with Others

More often than not, Korean journalists are subject to criticism and even protests for what they report about. The internal and external sources who offer such criticism "often and regularly" are, in the order of frequency, higher ups in the newsroom (66.2%), colleagues in the same news organization (53.3%), news sources (44.3%), and audience members (43.9%). Criticism comes less frequently from colleagues in other media companies.

Images of Audiences

The majority of Korean reporters felt that their audiences were more interested in straight news coverage of various events than in-depth analyses of issues (64.5% agreed, and 10.7% absolutely agreed). They believed that their readers and viewers were gullible and apt to fall prey to deceptive information (62.4% agreed and 11.9% absolutely agreed). What does that suggest? Does it mean that Korean journalists look down on their audiences? Not necessarily, but these findings do reflect the Korean journalists' concern regarding the susceptible, gullible nature of their audiences.

Job Satisfaction

About three fourths of Korean journalists were satisfied with their jobs "somewhat" (59%) and "very much" (17%), whereas 21% were "somewhat dissatisfied," and 3% were "very much dissatisfied."

Reasons for dissatisfaction with their jobs were many. In order of importance, they were dissatisfied with the way they were being treated by their superiors, their "lower" salary (Korean journalists are in fact paid much more than U.S. journalists), their lack of job security, their lack of ability to serve social justice, the editorial policy of their own news organization, the lack of autonomy and freedom in their journalism performance, and, finally, the lack of promotional opportunities.

Quality of News

Accuracy, balance, relevance, and neutrality are the most representative values to be found in news reporting. Asked to evaluate on a 5-point scale—superior (1), excellent (2), fair (3), average (4), and poor (5)—the respondents by far gave the highest mark to reporters for their ability to write news stories that were "relevant" to society. Relevance had an average rating of 2.4, followed by accuracy with a rating of 2.5, neutrality with a rating of 3.1, and last of all balance with a rating of 3.1.

PROFESSIONALISM

Readership of Professional Journals

Korean journalists, for the most part, do not show an interest in the many publications specializing in journalism and communication. Eight of 10 journalists did not read such publications.

Journalistic Practices

The respondents were given the following list of undesirable and unprofessional journalistic practices: unfair reporting, accepting of *chonji* (financial gratuities offered in exchange for special consideration, including playing up or down a news story), infringement on privacy rights, voluntary compliance with political elites, withholding or playing down certain stories under lobbying or other outside pressure, and, finally, heavy reliance on government news releases for story material. The respondents were asked to indicate whether these activities had been aggravated, improved, or left unaffected following Kim Young Sam's inauguration. Table 4.2 shows that the first three improved more than the last three, in the opinion of the surveyed journalists, especially the accepting of *chonji*.

Among the important attributes of a free and responsible press are fairness and impartiality. Included in the many factors impairing these, as Table 4.3 shows, the survey respondents cited "lack of effort" on the part of the media (31%); "lack of professional ethics" (26%); "intervention and control from management" (15%), and "government control, both overt and covert" (15%). This last figure is particularly interesting because in earlier surveys government control was one of the most important factors (25% in 1989 and 28% in 1991). In short, in the 1993 survey, Korean journalists seemed to be blaming themselves for the unfairness and partiality of coverage they find rather than their managers or the government.

Journalistic Functions

Responding to a comprehensive set of 11 items designed to encompass the full range of journalistic functions, the journalists assessed Korean

Table 4.2. Undesirable Journalistic Practices and Their Present Condition Compared with the Past (in percentages).

Journalistic Practice	Aggravated Much	Aggravated Somewhat	About the Same	Improved Somewhat	Improved Much
Unfair reporting	0.0	1.4	34.2	60.4	4.0
Accepting chonji	0.1	0.7	15.5	54.7	29.0
Invasion of privacy	0.3	4.3	46.9	42.9	5.7
Voluntary compliance with political elites	2.4	8.1	51.1	33.7	4.7
Withholding stories under lobbying or pressure	0.4	4.3	55.1	33.3	6.8
Heavy reliance on government news releases	0.1	2.2	79.4	15.8	2.4

Table 4.3. Factors Impairing a Free and Responsible Press (in percentages).

Factor	1989	1991	1993
Management control	13.2	14.2	15.3
Lack of media effort	30.2	18.7	31.1
Lack of professional ethics	22.9	33.0	26.3
Government control	25.4	27.6	15.1
Advertiser control	3.4	2.3	9.2
Control from various social institutions	4.2	4.0	2.6
Labor union control	0.7	0.2	0.4
Total	100.0	100.0	100.0

press performance as a whole. A 5-point rating scale was employed for each item on the survey, with 5 being "excellent" and 1 "unacceptable." By far the highest category of press performance, in the opinion of the respondents, was "rapid news delivery," with an average score of 3.9. The second highest mark elicited was for "human interest features and programs" (3.8). Tied for third place, with an average score of 3.3, were the press's "entertainment fare" and the job done by the press as "watchdog of government officials." These were the only four items meriting better than the average mark of 3.0.

The remaining seven categories from the bottom up included: "reportorial investigation of the accuracy of government releases" (2.4), "critical scrutiny of business activities" (2.5), "critical discussion of formative government policies" (2.5), "the withholding of unconfirmed information" (2.5), "the espousal of well-formulated opinions about major contemporary issues" (2.7), "stimulation of readers' intellectual curiosity" (2.8), and "the provision of in-depth analysis and interpretation of complex issues" (2.9).

There was no major difference between the print and broadcast media in terms of the journalistic activities evaluated except on speedy delivery of news and information, withholding of unconfirmed news, and elevating intellectual and cultural interest. On these three items, the broadcast media were perceived to do a better job than newspapers.

To sum up, Korean journalists by no means hold their own activities in high esteem. Those five items in which they gave themselves the lowest ratings are all related to the so-called "watchdog" function expected of a responsible press in a free democracy, whereas the three items in which they scored highly are considered the hallmark of "commercial" journalism.

Ethics

A popular and persistent charge against Korean journalists concerns the widespread tradition of *chonji* (literally, "small will")—financial gratuities (usually in small white envelopes) offered in exchange for special consideration. More than three of four Korean journalists attested to the survival of this tradition. At the same time, more than half denied accepting *chonji* themselves. In most cases, the survey indicates, *chonji* is given directly to reporters by persons or organizations outside the media (81%). At other times, *chonji* is transmitted through the press corps covering government agencies (15%). Surprisingly, *chonji* is said to be passed for the most part simply because of custom (57%), rather than in exchange for favorable coverage (29%) or to play down or suppress embarrassing facts (10%).

The survey also contained several forced-choice questions in which the respondents had to divide between two incompatible, but at least superficially reasonable, claims dealing with journalistic ethics. A majority of our respondents opposed participation by journalists in the new *Moon-min* government because of its inherent danger of marriage between press and government (60% opposed; 40% were in favor). A strong majority objected to the idea of major business enterprises owning and operating media outlets (85%t opposed; 15% were in favor). Almost three fourths of the reporters surveyed claimed optimistically that the doctrine of objectivity in reporting could be satisfied by Korean journalists if they made this their goal and worked diligently toward its fulfillment (72% were optimistic; 27% pessimistic). When asked whether the greatest need facing Korean journalists today was greater freedom or greater responsibility, slightly more than 6 in 10 chose greater responsibility.

Korean journalists seemed on the whole to have a low opinion of their own performance in the political processes of the nation. For example, only 14% of our respondents said that the press had taken an aggressive role in the political democratization of Korea during the dark period of military dictatorship from 1980 to the initiation of civilian government in 1993. Even more deplorable, a resounding majority (86%) said that the Korean press was prone to jump on whatever bandwagon happened to predominate at any given time.

Inaccuracy in reporting perennially ranks among the most difficult problems in journalism, and in all three surveys it was considered. In the two earlier surveys, reporter carelessness was found to be the single most

Table 4.4. Reasons for Inaccurate Reporting (in percentages).

Reason	1989	1991	1993
Reporter carelessness	41.5	43.5	22.7
Faking news stories	1.3	0.5	0.3
News source error (unintentional)	4.2	2.0	2.5
News source error (intentional)	12.6	10.9	10.6
Deadline pressure	4.6	4.6	6.9
Competition among the media	20.3	20.8	39.5
Lack of journalists' professionalism	15.2	17.5	16.5
Other	0.3	0.2	1.0
Total	100.0	100.0	100.0

important cause of inaccuracy, as Table 4.4 shows. By 1993, instead of carelessness, competition within the media was cited as the major culprit. These data suggest that because of the recent influx of additional media outlets, the media market has become a breeding ground of sensationalism, which in turn has degraded reporter accuracy.

At least as serious are libel and the violation of privacy by journalists; these, again, were ascribed primarily to uncontrolled competition within the news media. It is important to note that the percentage of journalists who find a lack of professionalism in their ranks rose sharply from 13.5% in 1989 and 12% in 1991 to 29% in 1993. Simultaneously, there was a perceived decrease in feelings of condescension by journalists toward the general public (22% in 1989, 16% in 1991, and 9% in 1993). In this connection, it is worth mentioning that print and broadcast journalists write an average of only two corrections per year for inaccurate or offensive news items. Additionally, our respondents freely admitted that the right to reply by complainants is frequently ignored by the news organizations in which they work, with 22% saying that their organizations permit no replies at all, and 55% saying that replies are seldom allowed.

Like working journalists anywhere, the men and women working for the Korean press are under heavy pressure to reveal their news sources when they write controversial stories and articles potentially damaging to politicians. In the absence of a shield law, Korean journalists are vulnerable to possible pressure to reveal their sources. As many as 42% of the subjects of the 1989 survey confided that they had experienced such pressure to disclose news sources, but this dropped to 38% in 1991 and 24% in 1993.

Reporting Methods

It is widely believed by the general public that journalists leave no stone unturned when investigating news stories. In this connection, the respondents were given a list of questionable reporting methods and were asked to indicate their opinions on the justifiability of these activities (Table 4.5). They identified as not justifiable breaking promises of confidentiality (82% of the respondents); harassing news sources (73%); using personal letters, pictures, and documents without permission (61%); paying for secret information (60%); and faking company employment to gain access to inside information (51%). The respondents indicated as justifiable such practices as concealing their identities or making false claims of professional employment (59%) and printing or airing government or company documents without permission (50%).

Influence on Public Opinion

The survey asked the respondents three interrelated questions dealing with the influence of public versus published opinion on politics as a whole. In response to the question, "To what extent do you think press opinion should influence major government decisions?" about 39% of the respondents said "a great deal," 21% said "somewhat," and 40% said "not a lot." In a follow-up question asking the journalists to what extent press opinion *does* influence major government decisions, strikingly more (63%) said "quite a lot," 20% said "somewhat," and 16% said "not a lot." In answer to the third question, "To what extent does public opinion influence major government decisions?", the majority of journalists (58%) said "not much," 14% said "somewhat," and only 22% said "a lot."

These results suggest that journalists believe they exert more influence on the political administrative process and government affairs than they should, certainly far more than the collective population. It is interesting to note that the longer his or her career in journalism, the stronger is the journalist's opinion regarding the extent of his or her impact on government decisions.

Provided with a list of professions, the respondents were also asked to check the one they believed exerted the greatest political influence, the one that needed the most self-discipline and reform, the one that in comparison to its past has gained the most power and influence, and the one that in comparison to its past has lost the most power and influence.

Politicians were singled out as constituting the most influential profession and the group that needs the most self-discipline and reform. Journalists, themselves, picked their own profession as having gained

Table 4.5. Justifiability of Journalistic Practices Employed in Investigative Reporting (in percentages).

Journalistic Practice	Justifiable	Unjustifiable	Not sure
Paying for secret information	27.3	60.1	12.5
Using company/government documents without permission	49.8	36.2	14.0
Faking one's identity	58.7	32.8	8.5
Breaking promises of confidentiality	9.2	82.2	8.6
Harassing news sources	17.0	72.7	10.2
Using personal letters, pictures and documents without permission	26.8	60.8	12.4
Faked employment to gain inside information	36.8	50.6	12.6

the most political power and as the one needing the least self-discipline and reform. Quite expectedly, the military was viewed as having lost the most power. Using the Multi-Dimensional Scaling (MDS) method, it is clear that journalists view themselves as being unique and quite different from bureaucrats, businessmen, professors, religious personalities, lawyers, soldiers, and politicians.

CONCLUSIONS

There are some inconsistencies in opinion among the journalists who responded to the survey. Although the majority of the respondents said they enjoyed a reasonable amount of autonomy and freedom on the job, they also admitted to performing poorly in all areas relating to the journalist's role as a check on the workings of government—the very role that distinguishes the journalist as the "fourth estate" or public "watchdog," a responsibility that not only establishes the autonomy of the journalist from other areas of government, but also helps establish the autonomy of an entire public within a democratic society.

Yet the results of the survey also suggest that Korean journalists are tentative about the role of the journalist as a check on government. Although a majority of the respondents said the media do in fact influence government decisions, a plurality of the respondents said they believed the media should not, in an ideal situation, exert its influence on the formation of government policy. In other words, the journalists' perceived *actual* influence on government policy exceeds the perceived *ideal* influence. Such a discrepancy suggests that Korean journalists are unclear about the role of a journalist, especially as it pertains to their "watchdog" responsibility. It is perhaps this very confusion that is most accountable for their poor performance—as perceived by themselves—in the way of independent, critical reporting.

The recent reform campaign, started by president Kim Young-Sam, unquestionably commands overwhelming public support, and, notwithstanding its many faults, the press must be credited with having done an adequate job of rallying public support behind Kim's reformative aims. Because of the gravity of the problems at hand, the very strength of public opinion has with equal strength necessitated enlightened criticism and the airing of alternative views on the issues. It has been the press's destiny—a destiny that it has never long shirked historically—to play the role of devil's advocate, to present unpopular views and opinions. If forthcoming, constructive criticism by the press will, in the long run, enrich the quality of the current social reform movement.

REFERENCES

Kang, Myung Koo. 1993. *A sociology of the journalism profession in Korea*. Seoul: Nanam Publishing Co.

Korea Press Center. 1993. *Directory of the Korean journalists*. Seoul, Korea.

Korea Press Institute. 1989. *The responsibility and ethics of the journalists: The first national survey of professional attitudes of the Korean journalists*. Seoul, Korea.

Korea Press Institute. 1991. *The responsibility and ethics of the journalists: The second national survey of professional attitudes of the Korean journalists*. Seoul, Korea.

5

The New Taiwan Journalist: A Sociological Profile

Ven-hwei Lo
National Chengchi University

The New Taiwan Journalist is a "new" sociological phenomenon because of the drastic and dramatic changes in the press structure, political diversity and pluralism, evolution of the democratic election process at every level, economic growth, and rise in personal income that have characterized Taiwan since the lifting of martial law in 1987. Taiwan, an island nation of 21 million people situated about 100 miles off the southeast coast of mainland China, is governed by the Republic of China, or the Nationalist government, which retreated to Taiwan in 1949 after being defeated by the Communists on the mainland.

Although the Chinese began to settle Taiwan as early as the 7th century A.D., large-scale immigration from southern China did not begin until the 17th century. The latest and very significant influx started in the late 1940s and continued in the early 1950s when the Communists took control of the mainland, and the Nationalist government, accompanied by some two million people from every mainland province, moved to Taiwan.

Many of these mainlanders were highly educated and well-experienced government officials, scholars, business owners, and journalists.

Consequently, they dominated Taiwan's political power. They also had a commanding position in the government, military, education, and news media.

By contrast, the Taiwanese, who are the descendants of early immigrants who came from China's Fukien and Guangdong provinces during the past centuries, were deprived of their full political rights. Inevitably, tension and conflict developed between the two groups of Chinese. This mainlander-Taiwanese division, as Lee (1993) suggests, has been a major source of political friction in Taiwan since the late 1940s. Although the distinctions between these two groups are no longer definitive in most recent decades due to intermarriages and common use of Mandarin, the official language, most people in Taiwan still identify unequivocally with one group or the other (Harrell and Huang 1994).

In the early 1950s, Taiwanese outnumbered mainlanders four to one. Now the Taiwanese constitute 84% of the population, whereas mainlanders and their descendants make up only 14%. The remainder (2%) are mostly Malay-Polynesian aborigines who reached Taiwan thousands of years ago.

In recent years, Taiwan has been marked by its rapid economic growth and political reform. In the early 1950s, Taiwan was a poor, rural society with a per capita GNP less than US$100 (Sun 1994). In 1994, Taiwan outstripped most other developing countries with a per capita GNP of US$11,597 (CNA 1996).

Before the lifting of martial law in 1987, Taiwan was a one-party state. The Nationalist Party, or the Kuomintang (KMT), was Taiwan's only legal, active political party, and no opposition party was allowed to form, although non-KMT members had contested seats in elections at various levels.

As a result of the lifting of martial law, many political parties were established. In 1994, there were 75 registered parties in Taiwan (CNA 1996), but only the two largest opposition parties , the Democratic Progressive Party (DPP) and the New Party, were able to challenge the KMT in both local and national elections.

In the 1995 legislative election, for example, the KMT took more than 46% of the popular votes compared to 33% of the votes received by the DPP and 13% by the New Party. In addition, the DPP's candidate Shui-bian Chen won the 1994 Taipei Mayoral election by garnering 43.7% of the vote, trailed by the New Party's Jaw Shau-kong and the KMT's Ta-chou Huang, with 30.2% and 25.9% of the votes respectively.

Prior to 1987, all news media in Taiwan were under direct or indirect control of the government. All three television stations and most of the radio stations were controlled by the triple alliance of the ruling KMT, the government, and the military (Lo, Cheng, and Lee 1994).

In addition, all newspapers must be registered with the government, which imposed a registration ban in 1951 on the number of newspapers and number of pages (Tien 1989). Before the removal of the registration ban on the number of newspapers and pages in 1988, there were only 31 daily newspapers in Taiwan.

Through the registration ban, the government had effectively restricted freedom of the press by facilitating government ownership of newspapers and by preventing newspapers from falling into the hands of the opposition leaders (Lee 1993). Consequently, 14 of the total 31 daily newspapers were owned by the government and the KMT, and, over the years, most newspapers favored the KMT (Cheng 1988).

After lifting the ban, the number of newspapers increased drastically. By June 1994, there were 288 registered newspapers, although only 40 were widely read (Government Information Office 1995). The largest and most prestigious newspapers are the privately owned *China Times* and the *United Daily News* (Lo 1993), each with a circulation of around one million (Lee 1993). These two privately owned newspapers account for more than two thirds of the total daily newspaper circulation in Taiwan (Lee 1993).

In recent years, Taiwan's news media have enjoyed broader freedom in news coverage (Lo 1994). In 1993, the government lifted a 22-year ban on the establishment of new television stations and enacted a law to legalize the island's booming cable industry (Peng 1994). The stringent control of radio stations also has been greatly eased. As a result, many privately owned cable television and radio stations have entered this lucrative market. Taiwan's broadcast industry has entered a new phase marked by unprecedented competition and broader freedom in news coverage.

On March 23, 1996, voters in Taiwan went to the polls in the first presidential election. President Lee Teng-hui, the KMT candidate, was the resounding winner, receiving 54% of the total votes. Peng Ming-min, the DPP candidate, received only 21% of the votes. Candidate Lin Yang-kang, who was supported by the New Party, earned 14.9% of the votes.

As the first democratically elected President in 5,000 years of Chinese history, President Lee's challenge is now to contemplate the future of Taiwan-China relations. Without a coherent policy for maintaining peace with China, the future of Taiwan will be trembling in the balance.

Methods

This study is based on a national survey of 1,015 working journalists in Taiwan in 1994. The purpose of the survey was to examine journalists' basic characteristics, their education and training, working conditions, and professional values and ethics. It is the first national survey that attempts to provide a comprehensive portrait of the Taiwan journalist.

In this survey we followed the definition of *journalist* used by Weaver and Wilhoit (1986). We also used many of the same questions, although a number were altered to make them more suitable to Chinese respondents. Following Weaver and Wilhoit (1986: 168), we defined *journalists* as those "who have editorial responsibility for the preparation or transmission of news stories or other information." Unlike Weaver and Wilhoit, however, our definition of journalist includes researchers, photographers, and camera operators. In other words, the population of our survey is the full-time editorial personnel including all reporters, editors, wire editors and translators, correspondents, columnists, researchers, news announcers, photographers, and camera operators employed by the Chinese-language radio and television stations and daily newspapers in Taiwan.

This study used a multistage sampling plan. In the first stage we compiled a list of Chinese-language daily newspapers, radio, and television stations in Taiwan. In December 1993, there were three TV stations, 33 radio stations, and 276 newspapers registered with the Government Information Office (GIO). Through the GIO media source book, we were able to obtain a list of Chinese-language news media including three television stations, 32 radio stations, and 43 daily newspapers.

The second stage was to estimate the number of journalists employed by each of these daily newspapers, radio, and television stations. We called the directors of personnel departments of all these news organizations, explaining our survey and asking them to tell us the total number of journalists working in their organizations. By so doing we were able to estimate the total full-time journalists in Chinese-language daily newspapers, radio, and television stations in Taiwan in 1994 to be around 5,500, with 90% of them employed by daily newspapers.

The third stage was to draw a random sample of individual newspapers. First, the 43 daily newspapers were divided into five strata based on the number of editorial personnel: those with more than 500, those with 200 to 499, those with 100 to 199, those with 20 to 99, and those with less than 20. The largest newspapers in the first stratum, the *China Times* and the *United Daily News*, were arbitrarily included. Then four newspapers were randomly selected from each of the four remaining strata. In total, 18 newspapers were selected in our sample.

The fourth stage was to obtain lists of all journalists working for these three television stations, 32 radio stations, and 18 daily newspapers. We called the managing editors and the directors of personnel departments of all these news organizations and requested them to provide names and positions of all editorial personnel working for their organizations. Only one radio station refused to cooperate. In all, we were able to obtain lists of all journalists working for all these three television stations, 31 radio stations, and 18 daily newspapers.

The final stage was to draw a random sample of individual journalists. This was done in two steps. The first step was to draw a random sample of daily newspaper journalists. From the names of journalists provided by each of these 18 daily newspapers, we selected a random sample of 1,001 daily newspaper journalists.

The second step was to draw a systematic sample of broadcast journalists. From the names of broadcast journalists provided, we estimated the total full-time journalists working for these radio and television stations to be around 600. A sample of 299 broadcast journalists was drawn systematically, including 158 television and 141 radio journalists. We deliberately oversampled radio and television journalists because we wanted to ensure adequate numbers for comparison with each other and with daily newspapers.

Before formal interviews were conducted, we sent a letter to each of these 1,300 journalists in our sample telling them the purposes of the study and asking for their cooperation. In addition, the questionnaire was pretested twice, and minor changes were made in the wording of some of the questions. Personal interviews were conducted during a four-week period in May 1994. Of the total 1,300 journalists, 1,015 (78%) completed the questionnaires for analysis. Of those responding to the questions, 138 (13.6%) were radio journalists, 108 (10.7%) were television journalists, and 769 (75.7%) were daily newspaper journalists. A total of 60 interviewers were employed and trained for this study. All of them were students at the National Chengchi University.

GENERAL CHARACTERISTICS OF JOURNALISTS

Age and Gender

From information obtained from our 1994 national survey of 1,015 journalists in newspapers, radio, and television stations, the average age of Taiwan journalists is 35.8 years old. Table 5.1 reveals that Taiwan journalists tend to be under 45 years of age, with most (83%) falling between the ages of 25 to 44. The largest age group (48%) is 25 to 34 years old, and another third (35%) are between 35 and 44.

There are very few journalists under the age of 25 or over the age of 55. Compared to the total Taiwan labor force, Taiwan journalists are disproportionally overrepresented in the 25-to-44 age group and are

Table 5.1. Age and Sex of Taiwan Journalists (in percentages).

	Radio N = 138	Television N = 108	Newspaper N = 769	Total N = 1,015
Age				
Under 24	4.3	0.0	2.3	2.4
25-34	55.1	65.7	44.2	48.0
35-44	29.7	24.1	37.5	35.0
45-54	8.7	7.4	10.8	10.2
55-64	0.0	.9	2.9	2.3
65 and older	2.2	1.9	2.2	2.2
Total	100.0	100.0	99.9	100.1
	N = 138	N = 108	N = 764	N = 1,010
Sex				
Male	45.6	64.8	64.9	62.3
Female	54.4	35.2	35.1	37.7
Total	100.0	100.0	100.0	100.0

underrepresented both in the under 25 and over 55 age groups. These findings suggest that journalism in Taiwan tends to be a younger person's occupation, and people tend to enter it relatively late and leave it relatively early. This also suggests that Taiwan's news media may experience a considerable exodus of their most experienced journalists.

Analysis of the age distribution shows that newspaper journalists are slightly older than their broadcast counterparts. The average age for newspaper journalists is 36.5 compared to 33.7 in radio and 33.5 in television. In addition, male journalists are significantly older than are female. The average age for male journalists is 38.1 years, whereas the female average is 32.1. Table 5.1 also reveals that Taiwan journalists are predominately male—62% are men and 38% are women. These are very close to the 1990 census figures for the percentage of men (61.8) and women (38.2) in the full-time Taiwan labor force (Ministry of the Interior 1995). However, there is considerable variation in the extent to which the three news media are dominated by male journalists. About 54% of those working in radio are women compared to 35% for daily newspapers and television.

Significantly more women journalists are employed by radio stations than by the other media, probably because women perform better in announcing the news. More significantly, the proportion of female journalists between the ages of 25 and 34 is extremely high (64%), and 52% of all journalists under the age of 34 are female, suggesting there has been a rapid increase in the percentage of women employed in the news media in recent years. This also suggests that if the news media are able to retain these young female employees, the proportion of women journalists will significantly increase in the future.

Provincial Origins and Political Attitudes

Taiwan journalists are substantially overrepresented by those of mainland origins. In our sample, 48% of the journalists identified themselves as mainlanders compared with 14% of the total population reporting mainland origins. Compared with the total population, Taiwanese and aboriginal journalists are all underrepresented. About 51% of the journalists identify themselves as Taiwanese compared with 84% of the total population. The most striking imbalance is for aborigines—only .4% of journalists identify themselves as aborigines compared with 2% of the total population.

Of course, the percentage of journalists from mainland origins varies tremendously by medium, from 43% in daily newspapers to 60% in radio and 66% in television. Radio and television stations hire considerably more journalists from mainland origins than from other origins, probably because those of mainland origin speak better Mandarin, which is considered by the broadcast media as one of the most important criteria in recruiting their new editorial staffs.

It is clear that Taiwan's news media should recruit more Taiwanese and aborigines in order to increase their representation. As to general political leanings, most Taiwan journalists (49%) claim they do not support any political party; 27% say they support the KMT, 16% New Party, 8.5% DPP, and .2% other parties.

It is widely known in Taiwan that provincial origins affect people's political attitudes. In our sample, Taiwanese (58%) are more likely to claim they do not support any political party than those from mainland origins (40%). Journalists from mainland origins are more likely than others to support the KMT and New Party, whereas native Taiwanese are more likely to support the DPP.

Respondents were also asked to indicate the political leanings of their organizations. The results show that 63% claim their organizations support the KMT, 9.4% the DPP, and 5.7% the New Party. Only 22% feel that their organizations do not support any political party.

There are significant differences when television, radio and daily newspapers are compared on this question. In our sample, 92% of the television journalists claim their organizations support the KMT, compared to 81% of the radio journalists and only 55% of the newspaper journalists. These differences probably reflect the fact that the three television stations and most of the radio stations are controlled by the government, whereas most of the leading newspapers are privately owned. There are no significant differences among journalists of various origins in terms of perceptions of their organizations' political leanings.

Education and Training

In general, the educational levels of the Taiwan journalists are high. Table 5.2 reveals that 93.5% of contemporary Taiwan journalists have received some level of college education, 30% hold (three-year) college degrees, 60% hold bachelor's degrees, 15% have pursued some graduate studies, 11% hold graduate degrees, and .3% hold doctoral degrees.

Among college degree holders, more than half (57%) majored in journalism or communications, compared to 19% in humanities, 10% in social sciences, 5% in natural sciences, 4% in business, and 1.5% in law. Among graduate degree holders, 53% majored in journalism or communications compared to 23% in social sciences, 12% in humanities, 4% in natural sciences, and 3% in business. No significant differences were found when television, radio, and daily newspapers were compared on this question.

These patterns illustrate that although journalism and communications are the most popular major fields for Taiwan journalists, the news media do contain a large number of persons whose college preparation is in other fields.

Working Conditions

The most important indicator of working conditions is salary. Our survey indicates that the median income of Taiwan journalists is US$1,700 per month. Only 1% of the respondents report monthly incomes less than US$750, and 14% more than US$2,700. The most common monthly income is in the US$1,100 to US$1,900 range (44%), and 28% of the incomes fall between US$1,901 and US$2,700. However, Taiwan journalists usually receive one or two months' bonus salary by the end of each year. Therefore, the average annual income of a typical Taiwan journalist is about US$23,000.

Table 5.2. Education and Training of Taiwan Journalists (in percentages).

	Radio N = 136	Television N = 108	Newspaper N = 759	Total N = 1,003
Highest Education				
Graduated from high school	11.8	3.7	5.9	6.5
Graduated from 3-year college	37.5	28.7	28.9	30.0
Some university	3.7	2.8	3.8	3.7
Graduated from university	30.9	40.7	48.0	44.9
Some graduate training	4.4	4.6	3.3	3.6
Master degree	11.0	19.4	9.9	11.1
Doctoral degree	.7	0.0	.3	.3
Total	100.0	99.9	100.1	100.1
	N = 115	N = 97	N = 715	N = 927
Major Field in College				
Journalism	26.1	30.9	33.6	32.4
Communications	38.3	28.9	22.5	25.1
Social Sciences	11.3	12.4	9.8	10.3
Business	1.7	2.1	4.5	3.9
Sciences	4.3	4.1	5.6	5.3
Humanities	17.4	18.6	19.2	18.9
Law	0.0	1.0	1.8	1.5
Others	.9	2.1	3.1	2.7
Total	100.0	100.1	100.1	100.1
	N = 24	N = 34	N = 122	N = 180
Major Field in Graduate School				
Journalism	29.2	44.1	29.5	32.2
Communications	16.7	20.6	22.1	21.1
Social Sciences	29.2	20.6	22.9	23.3
Business	0.0	0.0	4.9	3.3
Sciences	8.3	2.9	3.3	3.9
Humanities	16.7	11.8	11.5	12.2
Law	0.0	0.0	.8	.6
Others	0.0	0.0	4.9	3.3
Total	100.1	100.0	99.9	99.9

Journalists' salaries varied significantly by medium. Journalists at television stations earned the most (US$2,000 per month), followed by those at daily newspapers (US$1,700). Those at radio stations earned the least (US$1,350).

There was also a significant salary discrepancy by gender. Male journalists had a median monthly income of US$1,830, compared to US$1,500 for women. Most of the disparity can be explained by differential experience. Male journalists have longer years of experience in journalism than female—an average of 10.7 years for men compared to 7.4 years for women.

Perceived Autonomy

Another indicator of working conditions is perceived autonomy. Table 5.3 indicates that 6% of the journalists claim they have almost complete freedom in making news decisions affecting their works, 41% claim they have considerable freedom, 44% claim they have some freedom, and only 5% claim they have almost no freedom at all. There is a slight tendency for male journalists to be more likely to say they have complete or considerable autonomy than females.

Considerable differences in perceived autonomy are also found in the various news media. In our sample, 50% of the daily newspaper, 44% of the radio, and 25% of the television journalists claim that they have complete or considerable freedom in their own work. Journalists at daily newspapers appear to have the highest perceived autonomy, whereas television journalists tend to have the least.

Table 5.3. Perceived Autonomy of Taiwan Journalists (in percentages).

	Radio N = 136	Television N = 107	Newspaper N = 762	Total N = 1,005
Perceived Autonomy				
Almost Complete Freedom	5.9	2.8	6.6	6.1
Considerable Freedom	38.2	22.4	43.8	40.8
Some Freedom	41.9	58.9	42.8	44.4
Almost no Freedom	6.6	11.2	3.9	5.1
No Opinion	7.4	4.7	2.9	3.7
Total	100.0	100.0	100.0	100.1

Job Satisfaction

Our survey also asks the respondents to indicate their levels of job satisfaction in a single question: "All things considered, how satisfied are you with your present job—would you say very satisfied, satisfied, dissatisfied, or very dissatisfied?"

Table 5.4 reveals that although few Taiwan journalists say they are very satisfied with their present jobs, the majority appear to be satisfied. All things considered, nearly 69% of the respondents say they are very satisfied or satisfied with their jobs, and 23% are dissatisfied or very dissatisfied (see Table 5.4).

Regression analysis shows that several factors appear to be significant predictors of job satisfaction. The most important predictor is perceived autonomy. Journalists who claim a higher level of autonomy in their jobs tend to have greater job satisfaction. The second most important predictor of job satisfaction is journalists' ratings of their news organization. Journalists who rate their organization more highly in news reporting tend to express higher levels of job satisfaction.

Not surprisingly, salary level is also a significant predictor of job satisfaction. Those who earn a higher salary are more likely to express greater job satisfaction. Type of news medium is also related to job satisfaction. In our sample, 70.5% of journalists at daily newspapers are satisfied with their jobs compared to about 66.7% at radio and 59.4% at television. Age and gender are not significant predictors of job satisfaction, however. Men and women journalists do not differ much with respect to job satisfaction, nor do younger and older journalists.

Table 5.4. Job Satisfaction of Taiwan Journalists (in percentages).

	Radio N = 135	Television N = 106	Newspaper N = 760	Total N = 1,001
Job Satisfaction				
Very Satisfied	1.5	4.7	6.2	5.4
Satisfied	65.2	54.7	64.3	63.4
Dissatisfied	20.2	31.1	20.3	21.4
Very Dissatisfied	2.2	2.8	1.6	1.8
No Opinion	10.9	6.6	7.6	8.0
Total	100.0	99.9	100.0	100.0

Journalists' Rating of Their Organization

The perception of how well one's organization is doing in informing the public can be considered an indicator, as well as a predictor, of job satisfaction. Our survey asks the respondents to rate their organizations' performance in news reporting. Although few (6.8%) Taiwan journalists think their organizations are doing an outstanding job, most of them think of their organizations as very good (31.4%) or good (33%) in news reporting. Only 6% think their organizations are doing a poor job, and 3% have no opinion.

Among those who rate their organizations as outstanding or very good in news reporting, 42% work for daily newspapers compared to 26% for radio and 26% for television. It is clear that newspaper journalists are more likely to rate their organizations more highly than their broadcast colleagues.

Employment Aspirations

Another indicator of job satisfaction is the future plans of working journalists. Although a majority (56%) of Taiwan journalists want to work for the same organization five years from now, 15% desire work in a different news organization, 12% plan to leave the field of journalism in five years, and another 17% are undecided. The relatively high proportion of those who plan to leave the field during the next five years is a disturbing development because it may predict an exodus of highly experienced journalists.

Considerable media differences emerge with regard to journalists' future employment aspirations. Newspaper journalists (59%) are more likely to say they plan to work for the same organization five years from now than are broadcast journalists, and radio journalists (42%) are least likely to say this. In addition, radio journalists (33%) are far more likely to say they plan to move to a different medium than are those in television (10%) or newspapers (13%). Television journalists are slightly more likely to want to work outside the news media (15%) than are those in radio (12%) or newspapers (11%).

Discriminant analysis reveals several factors that are important for distinguishing those who want to work for the same organization five years from now and those who plan on working different jobs or are undecided. The results of the analysis show that job satisfaction is the most important factor in distinguishing these two groups. Journalists who claim higher levels of job satisfaction are more likely to say they want to work for the same organization five years from now.

The second most important factor in distinguishing these two groups is years of experience in journalism. The longer a journalist has been in journalism, the more likely he or she will want to remain in the same organization.

Salary appears to be another influential factor in determining employment aspirations. Those who earn a higher salary are more likely to say they plan to work for the same organization. The other influential factors are journalists' ratings of their organization, perceived autonomy, journalism education, and gender. Those who rate their organizations more highly, perceive higher autonomy, major in journalism or communications, and are male are more likely to say they plan to work for the same organization during the next five years.

PROFESSIONALISM

Membership in journalism organizations is one indicator of professionalism of journalists. Respondents were asked whether they belong to any journalistic organizations or associations. The results show that 65% of Taiwan journalists belong to one or more professional organizations. About 40% say they belong to one or more nonunion professional associations. Another 36% say they are members of trade unions. There is a slight tendency for male journalists to be more likely to join trade unions or professional associations than female journalists. Broadcast journalists are more likely to join professional organizations than are those working on newspapers.

Although a substantial majority of Taiwan journalists claim membership in journalism associations or trade unions, there is no single organization that embraces even a small minority of the journalists. Moreover, only 40% of all Taiwan journalists belong to any nonunion professional associations, which indicates a fairly low involvement of journalists in a professional community and a weaker organizational identity than in other major professional occupations.

Perception of Journalistic Roles

Another aspect of professionalism is perceptions of journalistic roles. Following Weaver and Wilhoit (1986), the journalists in our sample were asked to rate the importance of 11 possible roles of the news media, ranging from "extremely important" to "not really important."

Table 5.5 shows that three journalistic roles are seen as extremely important by a majority of Taiwan journalists: reporting the news accurately, getting information to the public quickly (58%), and

Table 5.5. Perception of Various News Media Roles.

News Media Roles	Percentages Saying Extremely Important $N = 998$
Report News Accurately	75.8
Get Information to Public Quickly	57.6
Avoid Stories with Unverified Content	53.1
Develop Intellectual/Cultural Interests	42.4
Provide Analysis of Complex Problems	39.8
Discuss National Policy	30.8
Investigate Government Claims	27.3
Concentrate on Widest Audience	27.0
Provide Entertainment	16.3
Serve as Adversary of Government	2.2
Serve as Adversary of Business	1.8

avoiding stories with unverified content. There are no significant differences among journalists from the different media types on the perceptions of importance of these journalistic roles.

It appears that Taiwan journalists tend to view "information dissemination" as the most important role of the news media, but they also view the interpretative and investigative role as important. In our sample, 42% view "developing the public's intellectual and cultural interest" as extremely important, 40% so regard "provide analysis of complex problems," 31% "discuss national policy," and 27% consider "investigate government claims" as extremely important.

There is a tendency for newspaper journalists to be more likely to view the interpretative and investigative role as more important than their broadcast colleagues. Although a majority of Taiwan journalists appear to embrace both the information dissemination and interpretative and investigative roles, only a very small minority accept the adversary role. In fact, only 2.2% of the respondents view "adversary of government" as extremely important, and slightly less than 2% consider "adversary of business" as extremely important. No significant differences are found when radio, television, and newspaper journalists are compared on their perceptions of the adversary role of the news media.

Compared to research conducted by Weaver and Wilhoit (1993), Taiwan journalists are more likely to view the information dissemination role as the most important, where U.S. journalists tend to consider the interpretative and investigative role as the most important.

Ethical Perceptions

Another indicator of professionalism of journalists is their views on the ethics of various reporting practices. Our survey asked the respondents to indicate their agreement with eight statements adapted from previous research (Weaver and Wilhoit 1986) concerning various reporting practices.

Table 5.6 shows that Taiwan journalists tend to disagree with all these models. Greatest disagreement is indicated with two: "divulging confidential sources" and "using personal documents without permission." A majority of Taiwan journalists also disagree with "using confidential documents," "using hidden microphones," "paying for confidential information," and "badgering sources."

Highest agreement is with the two practices that involve the use of false identification in reporting: "posing as someone else" and "getting employed to obtain inside information."

No significant difference is found between male and female journalists. Radio journalists, however, are significantly more likely than others to disagree with almost all reporting practices, except the practice of badgering sources. The reason for the difference is probably because radio journalists experience less pressure in daily news reporting, whereas newspaper and television journalists face heavy competition in covering the news.

Table 5.6. Ethical Perceptions of Various Reporting Practices (in percentages).

	($N = 998$)		
Reporting Practices	Agree or Strongly Agree	Disagree or Strongly Disagree	No Opinion
Using False Identification	43.7	47.7	8.7
Employment Under False Pretenses	40.3	50.9	8.8
Badgering Sources	37.7	55.0	7.3
Using Hidden Microphones	29.5	62.3	8.2
Paying for Confidential Information	27.8	60.7	11.5
Using Confidential Documents	26.5	67.3	6.2
Using Personal Documents Without Permission	12.7	82.4	4.9
Divulging Confidential Sources	9.6	88.6	1.8

CONCLUSIONS

The purpose of this study was to examine Taiwan journalists' basic characteristics, education and training, working conditions, and professional values and ethics. The results of the study show a sharply different profile from 10 or 20 years ago, reflecting the economic and sociological changes in Taiwan itself. The average or typical "new" Taiwan journalist of today is a married male who has a bachelor's degree, is 36 years old, and earns about US$1,700 per month, has worked in journalism more than nine years, does not support any particular political party, works for a daily newspaper, likes his job, and plans to stay with the same news organization another five years.

Compared to U.S. journalists (Weaver and Wilhoit 1993), Taiwan journalists are nearly as well educated, are more likely to major in journalism and communication, are about the same age, have less experience in journalism, and earn lower salaries. More significantly, Taiwan journalists are less likely than their U.S. colleagues to say they are very satisfied with their jobs. They are also much less likely to claim they have almost complete freedom in making news decisions affecting their work than are U.S. journalists.

Perhaps the most striking finding of this study is that although most Taiwan journalists do not support any particular political party, a substantial majority claim their organizations support the KMT, suggesting that government and the ruling KMT still have a great influence on the news media.

During the past decades, the government and the KMT had been very effective in controlling the news media in Taiwan by adopting a press policy of "incorporation" marked by a combination of high inducement and high constraint (Lee 1993). It was not only coercive force but also vast political and economic interests that made the news media more compliant.

When the political system became more free and democratic, the newly acquired political freedom and market forces have encouraged the news media, especially the privately owned newspapers, to be more liberal and critical of the government and the KMT (Lo 1994). Furthermore, the emergence of cable television and the impressive expansion of radio stations, in which the government has no control, have made the government's control of the press more difficult.

Consequently, Taiwan journalists are looking for greater autonomy in their work. Even those who work for the state-controlled media are eager to see a reduction in political supervision. In the early 1990s, the topic of internal media democracy won wide attention in Taiwan, principally through the vigorous activities of the journalists of the *Independent*

Evening Post and the newly established Association of Taiwan Journalists (Tu 1996).

It is apparent that the expanding market economy and the free and open political atmosphere will lead the Taiwan press and journalists toward greater freedom and a more independent journalistic approach in news coverage and commentary. Another significant finding of this study of Taiwan journalists is that although journalists are predominately male, females are a growing force in the newsroom. They make up 38% of the total news workforce and 52% of all journalists under the age of 34.

However, this study also reveals that women have lower commitment to their present jobs. They are more likely than men to want to work for a different news organization or to leave the field of journalism in five years. It appears that males will continue to dominate the newsroom if the news media cannot retain those highly experienced female journalists.

In fact, the challenge of retaining the best and brightest journalists, both men and women, will be the most difficult problem faced by the news media in Taiwan. This study clearly indicates that many of the most highly experienced journalists plan to leave the field relatively early because of low job satisfaction and autonomy and lack of money and esteem for the job their organization is doing.

These findings leave little doubt that the news media have to significantly improve the working conditions of their editorial staff by increasing their salaries, improving their job satisfaction, providing them with more autonomy, and helping them advance in order to become seasoned journalists.

This said, there are some significant implications for the future to be drawn from this study of the new Taiwan journalist. First, if the recent (March 23, 1996) presidential election marked a turning point in political development and democratization for Taiwan and as an example for Asia, the same may be said of the media and journalists.

Covering the presidential election shoulder to shoulder with some 690 foreign correspondents, the combined media experience was one of the freest and most sophisticated ever in Asia, according to many observers (Neilan, Sun, and Lo 1996).

Just as the Taiwan model of political development is likely to be followed in Mainland China's eventual evolution toward democracy, so too is media development in the world's most populous nation likely to follow the Taiwan model of progression toward a free and professional press. The new Taiwan journalist stands at center stage of this important and mind-boggling prospect for the future.

REFERENCES

CNA. 1996. *The Chinese world almanac.* Taipei: The Central News Agency.

Cheng, Jei-cheng. 1988. *Examining mass media.* Taipei: CommonWealth.

Harrell, Steven and Huang Chun-chieh. 1994. *Cultural change in postwar Taiwan.* Taipei: SMC Publishing.

Lee, Chin-Chuan. 1993, April. Sparking a fire: The press and the ferment of democratic change in Taiwan. *Journalism Monographs.* No. 138.

Lo, Ven-hwei. 1993. *News media credibility.* Taipei: National Science Council Research Report.

Lo, Ven-hwei. 1994, July. *Press coverage of the 1992 National Assembly Election in Taiwan.* Paper presented to the International Association for Mass Communication Research. Seoul, Korea.

Lo, Ven-hwei. 1995. *Professional values of the journalists.* Taipei: National Science Council Research Report.

Lo, Ven-hwei, Jei-cheng Cheng, and Chin-Chuan Lee. 1994. Television news is government news in Taiwan. *Asian Journal of Communication* 4, 1: 99-110.

Ministry of the Interior. 1995. *1994 Taiwan-Fukien demographic fact book Republic of China.* Taipei: Ministry of Interior.

Neilan, Edward, Mine-ping Sun, and Ven-hwei Lo. 1996. *Dateline Taipei: Foreign journalists' coverage of Taiwan's first-ever presidential election.* Unpublished manuscript.

Peng, Bonnie. 1994. The regulation of new media in Taiwan. *Asian Journal of Communication* 4, 2: 97-110.

Sun, Chen. 1994. Investment in education and human resource development in postwar Taiwan. In *Cultural change in postwar Taiwan,* edited by Steven Harrell and Huang Chun-chieh, pp. 91-110. Taipei: SMC Publishing.

Tien, Hung-mao. 1989. *The great transition: Political and social change in the Republic of China.* Taipei: SMC Publishing.

Tu, Chien-Feng. 1996. The editorial statute movements in Taiwan. *Mass Communication Research* 52: 35-48.

Weaver, David H. and G. Cleveland Wilhoit. 1986. *The American journalist: A portrait of U.S. news people and their work.* Bloomington: Indiana University Press.

Weaver, David H. and G. Cleveland Wilhoit. 1993, August. *The American journalist in the 1990s: Traits, education, work, and professional attitudes.* Paper presented at the annual meeting of the Association for Education in Journalism and Mass Communication, Kansas City.

II

AUSTRALIA/PACIFIC

6

Australian Journalists

John Henningham
University of Queensland

Journalists in Australia work within a relatively free media environment. Although freedom of the press lacks specific constitutional protection, significant High Court judgments in 1992 and 1994 have pointed to an implied right of free political speech in the Australian constitution.

As a country comprising what were until 1901 a group of British colonies, Australia has a media culture that has traditionally been modeled on that of Britain, although since the introduction of television in the 1950s, the United States has become a dominant influence. The influence, however, is not only one-way. One of Australia's sons, Rupert Murdoch, is among the world's most powerful media proprietors, and many journalists from Australia have risen to prominence in news media in the northern hemisphere.

About 4,500 journalists are employed by mainstream news media organizations, although as many work in non-news media, entertainment or specialist magazines, public broadcasting, or as freelancers. Members of the Australian Journalists Association (now a section of the Media, Entertainment & Arts Alliance) number about 12,000, although this figure includes photographers, book editors, and public relations practitioners.

Comparison with the United States shows a considerably smaller proportion of journalists to population in Australia: For every million people in the United States there are 450 journalists, compared with 250 journalists for every million people in Australia. The number of print journalists per 1,000 circulation in Australia is 0.7, compared with a figure of 0.9 in the United States (Henningham 1995a).

There is no consensus on what proportion of journalists is desirable to serve the needs of a democracy, but the lower Australian figure may result from the economies of scale flowing from oligopolization in the local media market. One company, Rupert Murdoch's News Limited, controls the circulation of two thirds of the metropolitan daily newspapers, whereas a second company, the Fairfax Group, controls most of the remainder.

Australia has a population of only 18 million, occupying a continent similar in size to the United States (less Alaska). The greater part of the population is clustered in five major coastal cities plus several smaller regional areas. Only 10 metropolitan daily newspapers have survived ownership concentration and mergers in the 1980s, although there are two viable national newspapers (the *Australian* and the *Australian Financial Review*).

In addition there are 38 regional daily newspapers, just over 100 nondailies and more than 200 magazines and special interest newspapers. Two public and three commercial television networks, plus a range of commercial and public radio broadcasting services, have been joined only as recently as 1995 by cable television services.

Most news media are within a fairly narrow, quality-popular spectrum, leaning more toward the popular. But with only two cities (Sydney and Melbourne) supporting two competing metropolitan dailies each, newspapers are striving to appeal to mixed markets. As elsewhere in the world, circulation figures have been in decline since the 1950s, and young people have largely rejected newspapers.

Several newspapers, including the two nationals and Sydney's *Herald* as well as Melbourne's *Age*, are newspapers of quality (with the latter two included in John Merrill's, 1991, list of the world's top 20 elite newspapers).

METHODS

The profile of journalists reported in this chapter is based on data from a national telephone survey of 1,068 news media people conducted in 1992 and a smaller survey in 1994. The major survey covered journalists in all media and all regions and represented a response rate of 90%.

Questions replicated major surveys of journalists in the United States conducted by Johnstone, Slawski, and Bowman (1976) and Weaver and Wilhoit (1991), as well as exploring local issues. Journalists drawn at random from all 50 provincial, metropolitan, and national daily newspapers were interviewed, as well as samples of journalists from all 44 commercial television stations, Australian Broadcasting Corporation stations, the national wire service, and news magazines. Respondents were also drawn from a random sample of about one third of the nation's 104 paid weekly newspapers and the 160 commercial radio stations. The follow-up survey of 173 journalists, also by telephone, achieved a response rate of 85%. A summary of journalists' characteristics is shown in Table 6.1.

Table 6.1. Occupational Backgrounds of Australian Journalists (in percentages).

Age	Median	32		
Sex	Male	67%	Female	33%
Socioeconomic background (based on father's occupation)	Professional & managerial	44		
	Clerical and sales	17		
	Skilled trade	17		
	Semi-skilled, unskilled	12		
	Agriculture	10		
Type of secondary schooling	State school	56		
	Catholic school	23		
	Private non-Catholic school	20		
Highest education level	Secondary only	45		
	Some tertiary	16		
	Diploma	4		
	University degree	31		
	Some postgraduate study	2		
	Postgraduate degree	2		
Major at university (of those who had attended university)	Journalism	33		
	Communication	8		
	Other humanities/ social sciences	41		
	Economics, business	6		
	Science	3		
	Other	10		
Religious denomination (in which brought up)	Roman Catholic	32		
	Anglican	31		
	Other protestant	22		
	Orthodox	1		

Table 6.1. Occupational Backgrounds of Australian Journalists (in percentages) (con't).

Age	Median	32		
Sex	Male	67%	Female	33%

	Jewish	1
	Other	1
	No religion	12
Is religion practiced now?	Yes	26
	No	74
Political leaning	Pretty much to the left	4
	Little to the left	35
	Middle of the road	41
	Little to the right	14
	Pretty much to the right	2
Voting intention	Labor Party	37
	Liberal Party	29
	National Party	2
	Aust Democrats	3.5
	Other	11
	Don't know	13
	Refused	4
Mean number of years in journalism	13 (median 10)	

BASIC CHARACTERISTICS

Age

A generation ago there were signs that journalism had become a "young man's profession": The press, and in particular the ranks of reporters, were dominated by males who were predominantly in their 20s or early 30s. Hart (1970) described this as a "drop out at 30" phenomenon, which he saw as indicating a degree of alienation from journalism as a career, as well as a result of the financial attractions of careers in advertising or public relations.

By the 1980s, greater vocational commitment had emerged in television news, in which the introduction of attractive salary packages and the promotion of television journalists as stars resulted in an upward shift in the median age (Henningham 1988). By the 1990s, a greater proportion of journalists in print media as well as television were remaining in the occupation into middle age. The median age of Australian journalists is now 32, similar to the median for the workforce in general, but lower than the U.S. journalists' median of 36. Australian journalists have been in their occupation for 10 years (median), compared with U.S. journalists' 12 years (Weaver and Wilhoit 1992, 1996).

Gender

The proportion of women in mainstream journalism in Australia is almost identical to that in the United States—one third—and is also the same as the proportion of women in the paid full-time workforce. There has been a threefold increase in the proportion of women journalists since the early 1970s, when only 10% of journalists were women. As a result of the relatively recent recruitment of women to media positions, women journalists are significantly younger than men (median age 27, compared with men's 37) and have had on average fewer years in journalism (eight years compared with men's 16). As a consequence, women are far less likely to occupy executive or managerial positions. Almost two thirds of women journalists (64%) work as reporters, compared with 44% of men. Only 3% of women occupy the position of newspaper editor or deputy editor, or broadcast news director, compared with 12% of men. Women's median salary is $35,000, compared with men's $45,000.

Culture and Religion

Journalists are overwhelmingly Caucasian. A total of 85% indicated that their ancestors were from the British Isles, compared with 13% from continental Europe and 1% from Asia. Of journalists, 81% are Australian-born, compared with 75% of the population. Of journalists born overseas, two thirds are from the British Isles or New Zealand, compared with less than 30% of the population. Those whose native language is not English are in a small minority in Australian newsrooms.

Most journalists had been brought up in mainline Christian denominations, with the proportions closely reflecting those of the general population: Catholic 32%, Anglican 31%, Uniting (an amalgamation of Methodist, Presbyterian, and Congregationalist churches) 18%, other protestant denominations 4%, and Orthodox 0.6%. Only 1% were Jewish, and 1% had been brought up in other faiths. Most journalists do not practice a religion: only 26%, compared with 37% of the population (Henningham 1995b).

Politics

Politically, journalists lean a little more to the left than to the right. Although 4% describe themselves as "pretty far to the left," 35% are "a little to the left," 41% "middle of the road," 14% "a little to the right," and 2% "pretty far to the right" (other, refused, and don't know total 4%; Henningham 1995c). They resemble U.S. journalists in this respect, although U.S. journalists are a bit less likely to choose the middle ground: 47% of U.S. journalists were left of center compared with 41% of Australians, whereas 22% of U.S. journalists were right of center compared with 17% of Australians (middle of the road total 30% U.S. and 43% Australia; Weaver and Wilhoit 1996).

Australian journalists were more inclined to vote for the Labor Party or for a minor "liberal" party (the Australian Democrats) than for the conservative Liberal and National Parties (Labor 52%; Democrats 5%; Liberals 41%; Nationals 3%; don't know, other, and refused were excluded). A scale of ideological values (Henningham 1996b, 1996c) found that journalists were significantly more liberal than the general population in social, moral, and economic values.

EDUCATION AND TRAINING

For much of this century journalism has been taught on the job in Australia, through a formal cadetship system (Lloyd 1985). That system, originally involving four years' part-time training for recruits with a secondary school education, has largely given way to one-year cadetships for graduates, supplemented by in-service courses in later years.

Education is one of the areas of major change in Australian journalists' characteristics. In 1963, only 5% of newspaper journalists had a university degree (Hudson 1963). In the 1990s, 39% had a tertiary qualification, whereas a further 16% had undertaken some tertiary study. The proportion with degrees (35%) is, however, somewhat short of the British figure (49%; Delano and Henningham 1995) and considerably less than the U.S. figure of 82% (Weaver and Wilhoit 1996). Although only 4% of U.S. journalists have no formal education beyond secondary school, 45% of Australian journalists lack any tertiary education (Henningham 1993).

As would be expected given the change over time toward formal education, younger journalists tend to be better educated than older ones. Of those aged over 40, about 60% have no education beyond secondary school, double the proportion of those in their late 20s.

Of graduates, the greatest proportion (40.5%) had studied humanities and/or social science subjects as part of an Arts degree. Just under a third (32.5%) had studied journalism, whereas 8% had studied communications. Commerce, economics, or business degrees were taken by 6% of graduates, whereas just under 3% had studied science. Other disciplines, including law, accounted for 10%.

Attitudes to the value of tertiary education are mixed. Just over half (53%) believe it is desirable that future recruits to journalism have a university degree; however, only 27% believe recruits should have a degree in journalism (Henningham 1993).

WORKING CONDITIONS

Most Australian journalists work as reporters or writers. A total of 51% describe themselves as reporters, whereas 8% are feature writers, leader writers, or columnists. Production roles account for a large proportion of journalists—the classification of "subeditor" (equivalent to the term more commonly used in the U.S. of copy editor) applies to 18% of journalists, whereas 5% are television or radio news producers. Middle-management roles such as chief of staff, news editor, or chief subeditor are held by just under 5% of Australian journalists. The senior editorial position of editor or deputy editor in newspapers, or news director or executive producer in broadcast news, is held by 9%.

Just over half the journalists (51.5%) indicate they have no content-based area of specialty. Of those who do have a specialized round (or beat), by far the largest number are sports reporters—22%—with politics the next largest round, at 16%. Ten percent specialize in finance, business, or economics, and 6% work on police rounds.

Job Satisfaction

Australian journalists are generally happy with their work, with most indicating they are at least fairly satisfied. A total of 29% said they were very satisfied with their jobs, 51% fairly satisfied, 16% somewhat dissatisfied, and 4% very dissatisfied. There was little difference between print and broadcast journalists, and the highest levels of satisfaction were recorded by elite groups within each medium—news magazines and Australian Broadcasting Corporation (ABC) current affairs programs.

However, journalists generally believe their colleagues are cynical: Some 69% believe that the level of cynicism of Australian journalists is high or very high. A slightly lower proportion ascribed a high level of cynicism to themselves (50%).

Two thirds of journalists described the level of stress they experienced in their work as high or very high, and 68% believed stress levels were increasing.

Men were slightly more satisfied with their jobs than women. This may be related to the fact that most women journalists believe that a gender bias exists in Australian newsrooms. In answer to the question, "Do you think it is more difficult for capable women journalists to get ahead in their careers (in comparison with capable men journalists)?", 72% of women said "yes." Male perceptions are quite different, with only 39% of men answering yes to the question. Asked whether they had personal experience or knowledge of women being the victims of prejudice in the newsroom, 66% of women said yes, compared with 35% of men.

Similarly, ethnic background affected perceptions of difficulties faced by minorities. Just 50% of journalists of British Isles ethnic background agreed that it was more difficult for journalists of ethnic or racial minorities to get ahead in their careers, compared with 57% of those of continental European background and 72% of those of other ethnic groups (including those of Asian, Middle-Eastern, or Aboriginal background). As to whether they had experienced or knew of newsroom prejudice against minority journalists, 16% of British Isles background journalists said yes, compared with 26% of those of European background and 45% of those of other ethnic or racial backgrounds.

Technology

Technological developments have had a significant impact on Australian print and broadcast newsrooms in the past decade, as they have internationally. Australian journalists have generally positive views of the introduction of new technologies in newsrooms, with more than 80% believing that time savings and quality improvements had resulted (Henningham 1995d). Print journalists have become accustomed to the first generation of computer typesetting technology introduced into newspapers, but they are only beginning to make use of full-screen pagination and the Internet.

The journalists most receptive to technological developments are those in the Australian Broadcasting Corporation's radio news service, where digital audio editing has been pioneered. Across other media, older journalists are predictably less happy with new technologies than are the younger generation. Less predictable, given studies suggesting they are less comfortable with technology than men, is the fact that women as a group seem more happy than men with newsroom technologies. This follows from the fact that women in journalism are on average a decade younger: when controlling for age there is no statistically significant gender difference.

Media Performance

Journalists have a fairly rosy view of the performance of the news media: A total of 60% consider that the news media are overall doing a good or very good job in informing the public. Approval of their own organization is even higher, at 72%.

Most journalists (53%) see the level of press freedom in Australia as high, although a very high proportion (44%) believe press freedom is decreasing. Many are concerned with the concentration of ownership, with 82% believing the federal government should prevent increased ownership concentration. The majority (53%) also believe that the dominant News Ltd., headed by Rupert Murdoch, should be required to divest some newspapers.

Concerns are also high over foreign ownership of the media, with a maximum foreign ownership level of 25% of print and broadcast media recommended by journalists. Currently, 90% of the circulation of metropolitan and national daily newspapers is under the control of companies headed by businessmen who are not Australian citizens.

Despite such concerns, many journalists are happy with standards of journalism in Australia. Asked to compare current standards with those of 20 years ago, 44% believe standards have improved, 32% say they have worsened, whereas 12% say they have stayed the same.

Public Opinion

Annual surveys on the public's view of the ethics of a range of occupations have never been kind to journalists. Newspaper journalists are judged as high or very high in terms of honesty and ethical standards by only 7% of the public, a decline from double-digit ratings a decade ago. Television journalists fare somewhat better, with a rating of 12%, which is still well below the traditional professions (Bulletin 1996).

Journalists have a rather better opinion of themselves. Asked how they would rate Australian journalism in terms of the overall honesty and ethical standards of its practitioners, 11% said "very high" and 47.5% said "high."

The public's collective attitude to journalists is interesting in the context of media influence. Journalists believe the media are very influential in the formation of public opinion, although they have reservations about their level of influence. Asked to rate the media's influence on a 10-point scale (with 10 indicating very great influence), journalists gave a median rating of 8. Asked how strong the media's influence should be, the median rating was 6.

PROFESSIONALISM

The perennial question of whether journalism is a profession has occupied academic rather than journalistic minds in Australia. Australia has a quasi-professional association—the Australian Journalists' Association (AJA)—formed early this century as a trade union to alleviate poor working conditions and low pay (Lloyd 1985). Membership of the AJA is very high, with the 1992 survey indicating that 86% of journalists were members. The AJA is limited in acting as a full professional association as it normally excludes senior journalists employed in news media executive positions (such as editors, editors-in-chief, news editors, and executive producers). It has, however, played a leading role in professional issues, including development of an ethics code and lobbying for such legislation as freedom of information and shield laws. In 1992, the association was absorbed into a larger grouping of unions named the Media, Entertainment and Arts Alliance.

About two thirds of Australian journalists prefer the term *profession* to describe their occupation; others are more comfortable with such terms as *craft* (23%) or *trade* (6%). The concept of journalism as a profession appears to be age-related. Younger journalists are more likely to describe journalism as a profession, but most of those over 50 reject the term. Level of education is not in itself related to professional consciousness, but journalism graduates are considerably more likely to see themselves as members of a profession than are arts or communication graduates, suggesting a process of professional socialization in journalism schools. Professional identification is also stronger among those from middle-class backgrounds.

The desire to be a journalist does not seem to be a vocation in the traditional sense. Only a small proportion of journalists (4%) are attracted to the occupation by public service ideals. For many, the reasons for entering journalism are related either to being "good at writing" at school (27%) or because of the perceived excitement or interest in journalism (19%). Others cite an intrinsic interest in news or current affairs (16%).

Job Aspects

In the 1992 survey, journalists' levels of professional orientation were tapped by use of items devised by Johnstone et al. (1976) and used subsequently in the later U.S. studies of Weaver and Wilhoit (1991, 1996). The surveys asked journalists to indicate the level of importance of various aspects of their jobs. Responses, comparing Australian and U.S. journalists, are shown in Table 6.2.

Table 6.2. Professional Orientations (Percentages saying "very important").

	Australian Journalists (1992) (N = 1,068)	United States Journalists (1992) (N = 1,156)
Job security	58	61
Editorial policies of organization	55	69*
Chance to get ahead in organization	51	39*
Amount of autonomy you have	51	51
Chance to help people	44	61*
Chance to develop specialty	40	40
Freedom from supervision	39	—
Pay	23	21
Fringe benefits	7	35*

*Statistically significant difference (based on t-tests of mean responses).

Five of the items (editorial policies, autonomy, helping people, developing a specialty, and freedom from supervision) have been designed to test a specifically professional orientation. The remaining questions are concerned with security aspects of the job.

Of the professional items, the majority of Australian journalists support only two as "very important"—editorial policies and autonomy. The nonprofessional item—job security—attracted the highest support, perhaps indicating an uncertain employment environment in Australia in the 1990s, with unemployment running at 10%, and several newspapers and radio news services having closed or amalgamated. However, Australian journalists do not attach a very high importance to pay or to fringe benefits.

As seen in Table 6.2, Australian and U.S. journalists are similar in their responses to many of the items. However, U.S. journalists place relatively more emphasis on editorial policies, helping people, and fringe benefits. In both countries, however, journalists tend to give more support to professional factors than to nonprofessional factors (with the exception of job security).

Women and those with higher levels of education were more professionally oriented (as measured on a scale of the five professionally oriented job aspects) than were men or those with less education. Age was unrelated to the scale.

Roles

The professional values of the journalists were also indicated by their perceptions of the functions or roles of the news media. The Australians were asked a set of questions devised by Johnstone et al. (1976) and augmented by Weaver and Wilhoit (1991, 1996). It was found that investigation of government claims was the most valued news media role, judged as extremely important by more than 8 out of 10 journalists. Getting information to the public quickly was the second most important, valued by three quarters of the journalists, just ahead of analysis and interpretation. The only other role supported by more than half the journalists is the discussion of national policy while it is still being developed.

The individual items in the scale elicited stronger support from Australian journalists than from U.S. journalists, although the rankings were similar, as Table 6.3 shows.

These results indicate a commitment both to the information-processing and the investigative roles of the news media. Entertainment, by contrast, received little support. The adversarial role of media proved to be the preference of a minority. Factor analysis of the items indicated a threefold pattern of values—information seeking, investigation, and advocacy—identical to the pattern found among U.S. journalists by Weaver and Wilhoit (1991).

Commitment to an information-seeking role is relatively stronger among journalists with less formal education and with right-of-center political leanings, as well as among those who had been in journalism longer. An orientation toward analysis is more related to those with higher levels of education and with left-of-center views. An adversarial stance is also associated with higher education.

Ethics

Adoption of ethical codes is generally seen as basic to the development of an occupation as a profession (Henningham 1990). Australian journalists' positions on ethical issues were examined by using a set of questions used by Weaver and Wilhoit (1991, 1996) and an earlier European study (Table 6.4). The questions in an extended form were applied to U.S. journalists in Weaver and Wilhoit's 1992 study and were also used in the American Society of Newspaper Editors' study (1989), as well as in a variety of studies internationally.

Two areas in which Australian and U.S. journalists were in total agreement were protection of confidential sources and use of confidential government or business material. Only 4% of the Australian journalists (and 5% of U.S. journalists) considered that it "may be justified" to

Table 6.3. Australian and U.S. Journalists' Attitudes to Media Functions (Percentages saying "extremely important").

	Australian Journalists (1992) (N = 1,068)	United States Journalists (1992) (N = 1,156)
Investigate claims & statements made by the government	81	67*
Get information to the public quickly	74	69*
Provide analysis & interpretation of complex problems	71	48*
Discuss national policy while it is still being developed	56	39*
Stay away from stories where factual content cannot be verified	45	49
Concentrate on news which is of interest to the widest possible public	38	20*
Develop intellectual and cultural interests of the public	37	18*
Be an adversary of public officials by being constantly skeptical of their actions	30	21*
Provide entertainment & relaxation	28	14*
Be an adversary of businesses by being constantly skeptical of their actions	27	14*

*Statistically significant difference (based on t-tests of mean responses)

break an agreement to protect confidentiality. (Their commitment to this value is further confirmed by several cases of Australian journalists going to jail since the 1980s for refusing to reveal sources to courts.) At the other end of the scale, 79% of Australians (81% of U.S. journalists) believed it could be justified to use confidential business or government documents without permission.

Australian journalists were a little more inclined than U.S. journalists (55% to 49%) to "badger unwilling informants" in the quest of a story, but the difference is slight. One area of significant difference is that of "checkbook journalism"—almost a third of Australian journalists (compared with only one fifth of U.S. journalists) felt it could be justified to pay for confidential information.

Table 6.4. Views on Ethical Issues: Australian and U.S. Journalists (Percentages who say "may be justified").

	Australian Journalists (1992) (N = 1068)	U.S. Journalists (1992) (N = 1156)
Using confidential business or government documents without permission	79	81
Badgering unwilling informants to get a story	55	49*
Getting employed in a firm or organization to gain inside information	46	63*
Making use of personal documents such as letters and photographs without permission	39	47*
Paying people for confidential information	31	20*
Claiming to be somebody else	13	22*
Agreeing to protect confidentiality and not doing so	4	5

Question: "Journalists have to use various methods to get information. Given an important story, which of the following methods do you think may be justified on occasion and which would you not approve under any circumstances?"

*Statistically significant difference (based on t-tests of mean responses).

However, Australian journalists were less inclined to use subterfuge as a means of gathering news than were U.S. journalists. Thus, only 13% of Australians, compared with 22% of U.S. journalists, approved of "claiming to be somebody else." Just under half the Australian journalists (46%) approved of "getting employed in a firm or organization to gain inside information," compared with 63% of U.S. journalists. Australian journalists were also less likely to approve of the use of personal documents without permission (Australian journalists 39%; and U.S. journalists 47%).

When evaluating responses to these questions, the wording has to be kept in mind: "Journalists have to use various methods to get information. Given an important story, which of the following methods do you think may be justified on occasion and which would you not approve under any circumstances?" Thus, the importance of a story may justify shedding any of the ethical constraints in the quest for truth.

As argued elsewhere (Henningham 1996a), the ethics questions may be to some extent testing caution versus risk taking in news-gathering practices, rather than ethical values. Construction of a scale composed of the ethics items found that those more inclined to support use of the controversial behaviors were younger, better educated, and less politically conservative.

CONCLUSIONS

Journalists in Australia resemble their colleagues in other Western democracies by being a young, fairly well-educated, middle-class group with liberal social values and somewhat left-of-center political views. There has been important change in some aspects of the workforce in the last generation. Journalists are on average somewhat older than they were in the 1970s, indicating a greater commitment to careers in journalism. Education levels have increased, especially among younger journalists, and there is a greater tendency to have studied journalism or communication academically. Women remain a minority in journalism, but the numbers of women in the occupation has increased considerably.

Australian journalists show mixed professional values. Job security is more important for many of them than are the various purely professional values. However, few are in the occupation for the money or the fringe benefits. Most value autonomy and the importance of editorial policies.

They are strongly committed to the primary functions of news media as information dissemination and critical analysis. A minority support an adversarial approach. In ethical areas, most reject controversial news-gathering practices, except for using leaked government information or putting pressure on sources in the case of an important story. They are more likely to disapprove of the use of deceit than are U.S. journalists. They very strongly support protection of confidential sources.

Journalists in Australia value freedom of the press and are reasonably happy with current levels of media freedom in Australia. They are, however, concerned about ownership concentration, particularly in the press, as well as foreign ownership.

Australian journalists currently face the challenges posed by concentration of media ownership and introduction of new technologies. The extent of their professional and ethical commitment, related to their capacity to convince a somewhat skeptical public of the importance of their work, will determine their success in maintaining a free and vibrant media culture into the 21st century.

REFERENCES

American Society of Newspaper Editors. 1989. *The changing face of the newsroom*. Washington, DC: Author.
Bulletin. 1996. Nurses rate highest for ethics and honesty. *The Bulletin* April 30: 38.
Delano, Anthony and John Henningham. 1995. *The news breed: British journalists in the 1990s*. London: London Institute.
Hart, Brian. 1970. *The Brisbane journalist*. BA Honors thesis, University of Queensland, Brisbane, Australia.
Henningham, John. 1990. Is journalism a profession. In *Issues in Australian journalism*, edited by John Henningham, Melbourne: Longman Cheshire.
Henningham, John. 1993. Australian journalists' attitudes to education. *Australian Journalism Review* 15, 2: 77-90.
Henningham, John. 1995a. Journalism in the USA and Australia: Some comparisons. *Australian Journal of Communication* 22, 1: 77-91.
Henningham, John. 1995b. Australian journalists' religious views. *Australian Religious Studies Review* 8, 2: 63-77.
Henningham, John. 1995c. Political journalists' political and professional values. *Australian Journal of Political Science* 30, 2: 321-334.
Henningham, John. 1995d. Australian journalists' reactions to new technology. *Prometheus* 13, 2: 225-238.
Henningham, John. 1988. *Looking at television news*. Melbourne: Longman Cheshire.
Henningham, John. 1996a. Australian journalists' professional and ethical values. *Journalism Quarterly* 73: 206-218.
Henningham, John. 1996b. How political correctness shapes the media. *Independent Monthly*, February: 16-20.
Henningham, John. 1996c. A 12-item scale of social conservatism. *Personality and Individual Differences* 20, 4: 517-519.
Hudson, W.J. 1963. *Metropolitan daily journalism in Australia*. MA thesis, University of Melbourne (School of Political Science).
Johnstone, John W.C., E.J. Slawski, and W.W. Bowman. 1976. *The news people*. Urbana: University of Illinois Press.
Lloyd, Clem. 1985. *Profession: Journalist*. Sydney: Hale and Iremonger.
Merrill, John. 1991. The world's top 20 newspapers. *Sydney Morning Herald* October 1: 11 [reprinted from *Gannett Centre Journal*, Fall 1990].
Weaver, David and G.C. Wilhoit. 1991. *The American journalist: A portrait of U.S. News people and their work*, 2nd ed. Bloomington: Indiana University Press.

Weaver, David and G.C. Wilhoit. 1992. *The American journalist in the 1990s: A preliminary report of key findings from a 1992 national survey of U.S. journalists.* Arlington, VA: The Freedom Forum.

Weaver, David H. and G. Cleveland Wilhoit. 1996. *The American journalist in the 1990s: U.S. news people at the end of an era.* Mahwah, NJ: Erlbaum.

7

Journalists in New Zealand

Geoff Lealand
University of Waikato

A small, bicultural, and democratic nation of 3.6 million people (or "Kiwis") set in the South Pacific, New Zealand has been described as one of the most media-saturated nations of the late 20th century. Most of its political and social traditions continue to take their reference points from Britain, but the media (television, radio, newspapers, and magazines) have always been wide open to the fluxes and flows of international culture.

New Zealand has also led the world in the deregulation of its broadcasting structures, passing legislation in 1990 that permitted full foreign ownership of television and radio networks. As yet, the most profitable systems have not been sold off, but the Canadian conglomerate CanWest Global Systems now holds a controlling interest in the private television channels TV3 and TV4. TVNZ Television, the other main television broadcaster, continues to operate as a highly profitable State-Owned Enterprise (SOE), returning a very healthy profit to its "shareholders" (the New Zealand Government) while serving commercial imperatives.

Free market doctrines have driven recent changes in broadcasting, which include a five-channel pay-television network (Sky Networks, providing broadcast subscription television with primarily off-shore feeds for 265,000 subscribers); commercial, regional, and music video television; several localized cable systems; and extraordinary growth in local and networked radio stations (in excess of 400 AM or FM frequencies). In April 1996, cross-media trends intensified with the sale of the 41-station Radio New Zealand commercial network to a consortium of Wilson and Horton (publishers of New Zealand's largest daily, *New Zealand Herald*, Australian Provincial Newspaper Holdings, and the U.S. radio giant Clear Channel Communications.

Despite the size of its population, New Zealand continues to support a high number of metropolitan and provincial daily newspapers (28 in 1994), together with steady growth in suburban give-aways and in local magazine publishing (600 titles). However, ownership of the print media tends to be concentrated in two major companies: Independent Newspapers Limited (of which international media magnate Rupert Murdoch owns 40 percent) and Wilson and Horton Limited, 45 percent of which is owned by the Ireland-based Independent Press holdings. Most of the major magazine titles are owned by Kerry Packer's Australian Consolidated Press. The high level of media outlets and institutions offers both entry and exclusion for budding journalists in New Zealand. Although some sectors of journalism expand (suburban newspapers, public relations), other sectors contract (the displacement of radio journalists by computer technology, the disappearance of some evening metropolitan newspapers), providing a climate of both opportunity and uncertainty for New Zealand journalists.

SURVEYING NEW ZEALAND JOURNALISTS

There have been two surveys of New Zealand journalists that provide substantial and up-to-date information on the profession. In 1987, the New Zealand Journalists Training Board commissioned a population survey of New Zealand journalists, with nearly 3,000 questionnaires distributed throughout the country and 1,249 (42%) returned. Numerical comparisons were made with the 2,682 New Zealanders who identified themselves as "Journalist or Reporter/Editor or Sub-Editor" in the 1986 New Zealand Census of Population and Dwellings. Information from this 1987 Survey was published as the "National Survey of New Zealand Journalists 1987," authored by Geoff Lealand.

Another population survey in 1994, commissioned by the renamed New Zealand Journalists Training Organization (NZJTO), and also authored by Geoff Lealand, used the same research method of self-completed questionnaires widely distributed to journalists. In order to replicate the process of 1987 and obtain a high return, 3,200 questionnaires were distributed and 1,214 returned, a return rate of 38%. Although direct case-by-case comparisons were not possible (all responses were anonymous), the similar number of returns in the 1987 and 1994 surveys enabled comparisons and the identification of significant trends.

In both cases, even though the survey instruments did not reach all journalists working in New Zealand, the views and experiences contained in the 1987 and 1994 surveys represent a substantial body of data. In some specific areas of journalism there was a high level of representation, with more than half of New Zealand television journalists included in 1994 survey.

Such incomplete responses to surveys of journalists appear to be the norm. For instance, in his 1991-92 survey of Australian journalists, Henningham (1993) used a sample base of 1,068 journalists, or about one in four of the estimated 4,200 journalists working in the mainstream news media.

CHARACTERISTICS OF NEW ZEALAND JOURNALISTS

Size of the Workforce

In addition to the census figures presented earlier, the levy figures of the NZJTO provide an estimate of journalists currently employed in New Zealand. According to these figures, in the period 1994-95, 1,738 journalists were working for city, provincial, or community newspapers and state-owned or private radio or television stations. However, this figure excludes freelancers, public relations people, and probably many journalists working on individual contracts.

Age and Gender

Of the 1,214 journalists who participated in the 1994 survey, 70% were 39 years or younger. A similar number were in this age group in 1987, but there were considerably fewer very young journalists in 1994, suggesting that the cadet journalist is becoming an increasingly endangered species. Nearly three quarters of these young journalists occupied less senior positions in news organizations, with most directors and editors being both male and older.

In addition, a greater proportion of these young journalists were female (67% were aged 35 years or less, compared with 40% of males in the same age group). There were 658 males and 546 females in the 1994 survey. The phenomenon of an "increasing feminization" of New Zealand journalism observed in the 1987 survey seemed to have reached a plateau by 1994.

Gender was also the primary factor in determining who held the most senior positions in news organizations, Even though substantial numbers (84) of women held editor or sub-editor positions, most of these were with smaller news organizations such as magazines or community newspapers, with only a handful of women occupying senior positions of authority on major metropolitan newspapers.

Ethnicity

Giving a voice to all elements of the New Zealand population is particularly important in New Zealand, given the partnership clauses of the 1846 Treaty of Waitangi agreement between the Pakeha (white) settlers represented by the British Crown and the Maori population (*tangata whenua*) in contemporary New Zealand life—a partnership that officially sanctions the sharing of resources and the use of Maori as the second official language of New Zealand. In addition, the large Pacific Island groupings in New Zealand (Auckland, New Zealand's largest city, also has the largest Pacific Island population of any place in the world) now seek better coverage of their languages and interests.

However, this variety of languages and interests is not reflected in the composition of the New Zealand journalistic workforce, despite recent efforts to increase numbers and opportunities. There have been only two training courses dedicated to training Maori and Pacific Island journalists—a course for Maori journalists at Waiariki Polytechnic (Rotorua) and a course for Pacific Island journalists at Manukau Polytechnic.

Such courses have not yet made much numerical difference in the ethnic composition of the New Zealand journalistic workforce. In the 1994 survey, there were just over 4% of Maori journalists and less than 1% were from a Pacific Islands background. The experiences of 50 Maori journalists were represented in the 1994 survey, compared with McGregor's 1991 survey, which reported responses from 92 Maori journalists, or a response rate of 73% from a targeted survey.

Few Maori journalists in the 1994 survey occupied senior positions in a profession largely dominated by Pakeha journalists (94%) and, many would argue, Pakeha interests and news values.

Political Attitudes

No direct questions were asked regarding political affiliation, attitudes, or aspirations in both the 1987 and 1994 surveys. Most probably the majority of New Zealand journalists would pride themselves on the lack of formal political links, even though the general motivation for their career choice and motivation is more likely to be in the liberal, mainstream traditions. In her unpublished 1994 doctoral thesis, Pahmi Winter wrote of New Zealand television journalists:

> The journalists' professional responsibilities are constructed in terms of contributing to a citizen being informed so s/he can develop an opinion about particular issues and participate in the democratic process. Implicit in some journalists' formulation of "professional duty" is the notion of advocacy journalism, the journalist as an agent of justice. (Winter 1994:155)

In the case of television journalists, this role is shaped and constrained by institutionally determined factors, most particularly "impartiality," a "populist ethos" regarding the audience for television news, "rules of relevance," "logistical burdens," and technology (Winter 1994).

EDUCATION AND TRAINING OF JOURNALISTS

Schooling and Professional Training

New Zealand journalists are highly educated, with nearly two thirds of those participating in the 1994 survey having participated in tertiary (college)-level education. More than one third (37%) had completed an undergraduate degree in the humanities or social sciences. These figures represent a rise from the numbers reported in the 1987 survey, supporting the claim that the general education level of the profession is on the rise. In the 1994 survey, 7% had also completed postgraduate studies, and considerable numbers had participated in a wide variety of educational opportunities ranging from dance and drama to teacher training and management studies.

In the majority of cases, the contribution of such studies to their subsequent work as journalists was regarded as either essential or helpful. Of the journalists in the 1994 survey, 519 or 43%, indicated they had participated in pre-entry journalism training courses, a considerable increase from 35% in the 1987 survey.

In 1994, there were eight journalism training courses available in New Zealand, all based at polytechnic institutes except for a postgraduate one-year course at the University of Canterbury. With the exception of the Auckland Institute of Technology shorter course, all courses ranged across a full academic year. In 1994, a distance-taught National Diploma of Journalism, designed for midcareer journalists, was added to training opportunities.

Of the journalists in the 1994 survey, nearly two thirds (62%) had done their pre-entry training in the previous 10 years, indicating again the relative youth of journalists in New Zealand.

On-the-Job and Off-the-Job Training

In both the 1987 and 1994 surveys, journalists were asked to describe their experiences with professional training that took place in their workplace or as scheduled short-term training courses outside the workplace. Just over one third had experienced such training in the period 1987-1993, with most training opportunities being offered by the NZJTO or by large employers such as Independent News Limited.

In most cases, such training was judged to be beneficial in terms of improving skills or increasing a sense of professionalism, but on-the-job training was largely unstructured and infrequent. There was a general desire for better and coherent structure for training in the workplace, with training scheduled more frequently and regularly.

WORKING CONDITIONS

Job Satisfaction

As a large proportion of journalists in the 1994 survey were relatively new to the profession, with slightly more than half having worked nine or fewer years in journalism, their opinions regarding the quality of their working conditions were probably tempered by their relatively junior status in news organizations. In addition, there was a high level of mobility across news organizations, with over one third of the journalists having worked for more than four.

A very large proportion of journalists (86%) in the 1994 survey expressed their satisfaction with journalism as a career choice, with only a minority offering criticisms, which ranged from complaints over pay rates to more general worries about the commercial thrust of their news organizations. There was also a significant drop in the number of journalists seriously considering leaving the profession, down from nearly half in the 1987 survey to a minority (18%) in the 1994 survey.

Discrimination in the Workplace

Nevertheless, a large number (252 journalists) reported they had encountered serious barriers in their career path, with 108 reporting they had encountered overt or covert sexual discrimination. The majority were female, but there were also cases of discrimination against gay journalists. Another important area of discrimination was being regarded as too old or too young for positions of responsibility in news organizations. In more than 100 cases, such instances of sexual or age discrimination had occurred within the previous three to four years.

Feedback in the Workplace

In the 1987 survey, encouragement from those in more senior positions was regarded as the most positive influence on the professional development of journalists. In the 1994 survey, however, the importance of this factor had declined, down from 91% in 1987 to 72% in 1994. Other factors such as encouragement from colleagues, the perceived importance of pre-entry and university training, and ongoing training were regarded as more important in 1987 than in 1994. One possible explanation for a decline in the perceived value of such influences could be to the greater number of senior journalists in the 1994 survey, many of whom would have had the primary experience of learning on the job without benefit of formal training. Henningham's (1993) research on Australian journalists supports the contention that the perceived value of university training for journalists, for example, is inversely related to age and seniority.

In addition, the importance of encouragement from senior colleagues may reflect the actual amount of encouragement received. Little more than one quarter of journalists in the 1994 survey had their work performance assessed in a regular or formal manner, even though there was a strong desire for this to happen.

Images of the Audience

Nevertheless, encouragement and helpful criticism from immediate colleagues remains the primary source from which New Zealand journalists seek approval and legitimization of their craft, even though the proportion of journalists turning to this source is declining. One possible reason for this is a more openly competitive environment in some sectors of the media, such as financial weekly newspapers, women's magazines, and prime-time television news. This was reflected in the considerable attention paid to "customer response" in the 1994 survey. However, less attention appears to be paid to formal measurements of media consumption such as ratings or circulation figures, even though such figures feature prominently in the language and rationales of senior executives, programmers, and media owners.

Generally, it would seem, journalists in New Zealand have rather narrow and self-referential notions of their audiences. In the majority of cases, their professional peers and/or immediate circles of friends and family provide the primary sites for judgment on performance, be it positive or negative.

Professional Development

The division between lower ranked journalists and more senior journalists was also reflected in responses to a question about which groups or sectors in the workplace were in the greatest need of further skills and development. As might be expected, most nominated a group or sector that was not their own; more junior journalists pointed to a need for supervisors and managers to improve skills in interpersonal and people management, whereas supervisors and managers pointed to a perceived need for journalists under their supervision to improve writing and grammar skills.

When asked what specific areas of training or professional development would be of direct personal benefit, journalists in the 1994 survey nominated a range of specific areas, headed by training in defamation/media law and ethics, specialization in layout and design, editing and subbing, computer and new technology skills, general writing skills, and acquisition of Maori language and/or cultural perspectives.

New Zealand Journalism as a Profession

Because both the 1987 and 1994 surveys were primarily designed to provide base data for a training needs analysis, they did not venture far into questions about the more qualitative or social aspects of the lives of New Zealand journalists such as political affiliations or more philosophical musings on the roles and purposes of news gathering and dissemination. As a consequence, information or speculation on the more elusive and underinterrogated aspects of the profession have to be sought in other sources that are often fragmentary, unsubstantiated, or display a particular critical agenda, such as academic or political criticisms of news agendas or news performance.

ISSUES IN NEW ZEALAND JOURNALISM

Monoculturalism and Biculturalism

As already described, fair and culturally sensitive reporting of Maori and other ethnic interests continues to be a major issue in the New Zealand media and increasingly a site of polarization of opinion. In 1995, for example, a number of land occupations by Maori (*iwi*) groups seeking redress through direct action for 19th-century land confiscations led to prolonged and headline news exposure, much of it sensational or confrontational. Such recent examples have been cited as further proof of inaccurate or unacceptable reporting by non-Maori of Maori issues, demonstrating a lack of knowledge that continues to keep the mainstream media offside with Maori. Maori broadcaster Tawini Rangihau points to a situation in which an estimated 90% of journalists come through an educational system that gives them little knowledge of things Maori (Knight 1995).

Even though the renaissance of Maori culture, language, and media of the past decade has produced increased outlets, most particularly in community or regional radio stations and glossy magazines such as *Mana*, these tend to speak primarily to particular audiences and not the wider New Zealand public.

As demonstrated in both the 1987 and 1994 surveys, journalists identifying with their Maori or other ethnic backgrounds are grievously underrepresented in the mainstream media, with their particular views of events often muted or misreported. As Michael King (1994) points out, however, Maori opinion leaders also expect to see more Maori faces in journalism. They expect a stronger commitment to the coverage of Maori issues and a greater expertise in dealing with them than has been apparent from non-Maori journalists in the past.

The opportunities for these faces to be seen will most probably increase, with a Maori national television channel planned for 1997. Yet given the current number of Maori journalists, and the disappearance of dedicated training courses for Maori journalists, there may be real difficulties in filling the spaces. Likewise, media outlets for Samoan, Tongan, and other Pacific Island voices will experience the same problems in finding trained professionals.

The News Media and Commercial Pressures

With few exceptions, the media in New Zealand are fully commercial, that is, they operate to specific commercial imperatives, most specifically the discourses of competition and economic rationalization. In the late 1980s, for example, politicians and the New Zealand Treasury maintained that it was no longer appropriate to treat broadcasting as a public good, arguing instead for deregulation and submission to "market forces." Competition, it was claimed, would guarantee that audience interests were adequately met through media choice (proliferation of media outlets) and measurements of performance such as ratings.

Such objectives, according to the advocates of the free market, are being achieved, or will be fully achieved once the remaining state involvement (Television New Zealand, Radio New Zealand) is passed over to private interests. For others—a mixture of academics, former broadcasters, members of the viewing public—the consequences of market solutions are negative, with news sources such as the top rated "One Network News" (Television New Zealand) putting profits, ratings, and entertainment ahead of accuracy, fairness, soberness, and impartiality.

Criticisms have been leveled at the marginalization or depoliticization of the public arena in television news (Cocker 1990, Atkinson 1992), the influence of U.S. modes of news construction and formatting that encourage the use of "sound bites" and "news morselisation" (Atkinson 1992), especially the blurring of entertainment values and conventional news content in late night programs such as TVNZ's "Newsnight" and early evening personality-led shows such as "Holmes" and the primacy of certain narrow constructions of television news audiences. In response, television news executives have called on ratings to argue for viewer satisfaction for current professional practice, adding to what one British academic has characterized as a "dialogue of the deaf" (Collins 1992).

Commercial pressures are also a factor in other areas of the New Zealand media. There is fierce competition among weekly and monthly magazine titles, reflected in the battles for readers and advertising. Daily newspapers are facing declining evening readership and more competition from community or free newspapers, and there is increasing computerization and networking of news and music output from radio stations. As a result, some employment sectors are shrinking (newspaper journalism, specialist television journalism), whereas some employment sectors are expanding (public relations, community-based or local news reporters).

The Journalist as Salesperson

According to a 1994 newspaper feature, "Inducing a former journalist to become an advertising tool is becoming common practice" (Calder 1994:3). Certainly familiar faces and voices from television news and radio can now be seen and heard extolling the virtues of all kinds of goods and services, including fronting campaigns for government reforms. Many of these journalists regard such activities as a two-way street, crossing back to straight journalism after plugging some product or service on radio or television, most usually for generous financial rewards. There are, however, critics such as journalism lecturer Jim Tully, who disagree with this rationale, arguing, "journalists who cross the tracks have forever tainted their credibility as reliably free from affiliations or alignments and should not be able to work as journalists again. . . . It's not a two-way street" (Calder 1994:3).

Yet it happens all the time. What is less clear is the effect it has had on the public's perceptions of the credibility of those journalists who indulge in such practices. Journalists themselves argue that it is their right to "cross the tracks," particularly when they regard the credibility they have built up in journalism as intellectual property.

Certainly the rewards of product or service endorsement will continue to offer serious temptations to New Zealand journalists, particularly when they compare their salaries to those of their colleagues in public relations and as numerous journalists refer to such extracurricular activities as providing for their retirement.

Public relations continues to recruit mainstream journalists in large numbers, offering more generous salaries and possibly more prestige. The New Zealand public relations industry earns NZ$100 million a year and employs about 500 people, equally divided between independent consultancies and salaried positions in public and private sector organizations, hiring more women than men.

Another major employer of former journalists is the political system. Political parties, whether in power or not, have shifted away from public service appointments to positions as press secretaries or advisors to Ministers of the Crown as more open political appointments. Previously press secretaries were expected to be neutral public servants; now they are expected to promote their ministers' political interests actively—in other words, to be propagandists. "They are a new breed of political minders" (Munro 1993).

The demands of this role are very much eased by the money such "minders" earn, with most in the highest salary brackets for New Zealand. Many former journalists earn even more fronting as publicists or public relations advocates for large corporations, further accentuating what some critics already see as a pro-business bias in the media.

The Threat of Defamation and Punishment

A successful defamation case against the Auckland city magazine *Metro* in 1994—awarding twice as much as the largest amount in any previous court case—heralded a new era in legal action against New Zealand journalism. Previously, the complexity and low rewards of court proceedings deterred most of the recipients of real or imagined defamation from taking action. The winning barrister in the 1994 case argued: "Defamation proceedings are lengthy, complicated and very costly and publishers can burn off a plaintiff very easily. The fact is that the level of court costs awarded is so low that a plaintiff needs a substantial sum of compensation before they can even break even" (MacLennan 1994:7).

The *Metro* case, and other recent defamation cases, have led some commentators to fear for the future of free speech and unbridled commentary in the media, in the face of possible litigation and increased caution by news media owners. Their fears may be exaggerated, but there is now an onus on journalists and media writers to establish "truth" as an absolute defense, with opinions standing in defense only if they are "genuine" and can be proven to be based on substantially true facts.

Another formal avenue for complaints and their redress is through the Broadcasting Standards Authority (BSA). This government-funded body was set up in the wake of the deregulation of television and radio in 1988. Full economic deregulation was encouraged, but the National Government hesitated in allowing full editorial freedom, setting up the BSA to police standards in the areas of "balance, fairness and accuracy" on all New Zealand radio and television. Although the Authority is primarily a reactive body (reacting to complaints rather than establishing policy) and is not held in high regard by broadcasters, it does have the powers to fine them or demand they close down broadcasts for stipulated periods. For some lobby groups and individuals, the BSA is regarded as an ally in a battle with perceived excesses in the New Zealand media.

SOME CONCLUDING COMMENTS

Journalism educator Jim Tully, in the erratically published *New Zealand Journalism Review* wrote of "overstretched journalists, under-reported news":

> The number of journalists employed by news organizations in New Zealand continues to fall as advertising revenues decline. Staff cuts

may be inevitable in these tough economic times but the implications are serious for the quality and range of news presented to readers, listeners and viewers . . . the most obvious pointers to an understaffed daily newspaper are an increasing reliance on New Zealand Press Association stories, freelance contributions and stories syndicated from other newspapers in the same group. (1991:1)

Some four or more years later, the situation is both the same and different. Tully addressed his remarks mainly at newspapers, and there have been further newspaper closings, falling circulations for tabloid newspapers, and job redundancies in this sector. Yet most New Zealand cities and towns continue to publish a daily newspaper, and the community/free newspaper sector is burgeoning. New niche markets have emerged in the magazine or specialist publishing area.

The radio news market is simultaneously contracting (through computer automation and networking) and expanding (through the spread of community-based radio, the development of news-talk radio, the development of specialist news feeds such as Mana Maori Media), but it still remains the cheapest form of mass communication available to New Zealanders. The daily National Public Radio Morning Report continues to attract audiences considerably larger than any other radio news source.

Television advertising revenue continues to increase, with record profits being reported by Television New Zealand for the past three years. Television now takes the largest slice of the advertising dollar, and much of the success of the dominant broadcaster Television New Zealand is attributed to its 6 p.m. flagship news service "ONE Network News." Television news continues to be the most prestigious place for journalists to work, and despite the persistent complaints from academics, critics, and some dissatisfied viewers about the emphases and style of top rated television news programs such as "ONE Network News" and "Newsnight," the reality is that, year after year, such local programs top the ratings. In 1995, for example, the second highest rated program for all viewers was "ONE Network News," with the New Zealand version of "60 Minutes" at number 10.

Even though employment prospects in some sectors of the media do not look promising, and the overall job market remains unstable, training opportunities for budding journalists or further training for current journalists continue. However, these need to be structured within the new environment of industry-accountable training, with national assessment standards established by the New Zealand Qualifications Authority, and new or existing courses being accredited and moderated by the New Zealand Journalists Training Organization. This dual requirement of national standards and industry moderation is proving to be a problem for university-based journalism training because it is perceived as a challenge to academic freedom.

Even though there are more opportunities for journalist training generally, the areas of greatest need are not being provided for. The Manukau Polytechnic Pacific Islanders course closed, and the Waiariki Polytechnic Maori course narrowly escaped closure, in 1995. This is in direct contradiction to an obvious underrepresentation of Maori and Pacific Island journalists in the New Zealand workforce. Stop-gap methods such as a "buddy" or mentoring system have been proposed, but they will not replace the hole left by the disappearance of one or possibly two dedicated training courses.

There are other areas of structural discrimination. Female journalists combining a career and motherhood are disadvantaged by a lack of child-care provision in the workplace. In fact, Television New Zealand is the only media employer providing workplace child-care facilities. Female journalists comprise nearly half (45% in the 1994 survey) of the profession in New Zealand, but equity in terms of positions of responsibility and salary is not yet a reality.

To generalize about New Zealand journalists, however, it is possible to say that they are well educated, well trained, and, in many cases, possess considerable power and influence in shaping public debates about New Zealand political and social life. As in other countries, the New Zealand public respond to the use of such power and influence with a great deal of ambivalence; the journalist is permitted his or her role as the "public watchdog," but there is also disquiet about real or imagined excesses of journalistic investigation, invasion of privacy, and misreporting.

New Zealand does have a long tradition of freedom of the press, but there is also a counter-tradition of generalized blaming of the media for social unrest, favoring entrenched interests, political instability, and all kinds of social ills. Public opinion polls reflect the ambivalence many New Zealanders feel toward journalists; a nationwide random survey of 750 people in 1992 placed journalists in tenth place out of 21 occupations being judged for the public respect they hold, slightly below public servants ("NBR opinion poll" 1992). A more recent poll rated journalists 5.37 on a scale of 1 (no respect) to 10 (enormous respect), below lawyers but above stockbrokers and politicians (NBR-Consultus poll 1997).

Of course, the New Zealand public's mixed feeling about the role and performance of journalists is matched by journalists' often narrow or underarticulated vision of their public and, most particularly, their frequent inability to accept or consider criticism—as others have noted, being very good at "dishing it out" but not at receiving it. To some extent, this tendency to reject criticism or fall back on the explanation of professional practice is encouraged by the lack of public forums for debating issues about journalism. There is, for example, no regular professional publication available to New Zealand journalists such as *Journalism Quarterly* or the *Australian Journalism Review*.

Journalism in New Zealand will continue to change and be shaped and reshaped by market forces and the evolving demographics of the workforce, but it will also be affected in the near future by changes in the workplace, as new technology redefines what is news, how news is gathered, and how news is disseminated. Given that it is a predominantly young and professionally committed occupation, there will continue to be a central place for journalism in New Zealand's social fabric.

REFERENCES

Atkinson, Joe. 1992. *The state, the media and thin democracy*. Auckland, New Zealand: University of Auckland Winter Lecture Series.

Calder, Peter. 1994, February 5. Credibility for sale. *New Zealand Herald*, p. 3.

Cocker, Alan. 1990, May 2. Time to save our screens. *New Zealand Herald*, p. 17.

Collins, Richard. 1992. Public service broadcasting and freedom. *Media Information Australia* 66: 3-15.

Henningham, John. 1993, July-December. Australian journalists' attitudes to education. *Australian Journalism Review*, pp. 77-90.

King, Michael. 1994. *Kawe Korero: A guide to reporting Maori activities*. 2nd ed. Wellington: New Zealand Journalists Training Organization.

Knight, Richard. 1995, July 19. Message for the media. *Waikato Times*, p. 9.

Lealand, Geoff. 1988. *A national survey of New Zealand journalists 1987*. Wellington: New Zealand Journalists Training Board.

Lealand, Geoff. 1994. *A national survey of New Zealand journalists 1994*. Wellington: New Zealand Journalists Training Organization.

MacLennan, Catriona. 1994, May 5. Satire takes a long hard look at itself. *The Dominion*, p. 7.

Munro, Mike. 1993, May 20. The minders. *The Dominion*, p. 7.

NBR-Consultus poll. 1997, February 7. *National Business Review*, p. 14.

NBR opinion poll rates police highest and politicians at the bottom. 1992, March 20. *National Business Review*, p. 25.

Tully, Jim. 1991. Over-stretched journalists, under-reported news. *New Zealand Journalism Review*, Winter 4:1.

Winter, Pahmi. 1994. *The masters of truth and justice? TVNZ news culture 1989-1992*. Doctoral thesis, University of Waikato, New Zealand.

8

Pacific Island Journalists

Suzanna Layton
University of Queensland

Pacific Island nations and territories are among the smallest and most isolated in the world. In the northern and eastern Pacific, the isolation is that of tiny atolls and crumb-like volcanic archipelagos dotting literally thousands of square miles of ocean. Among the continental islands of the southwestern Pacific, isolation is imposed by rugged, impenetrable mountain ranges often dropping straight into the sea. Some of the hardest fought battles of the Second World War took place in the Southwest Pacific.

Pacific populations are also small and scattered. Pitcairn Island, the last remaining British territory in the Pacific, boasts 65 residents descended from the HMS Bounty mutineers and their Tahitian wives. The atoll populations of Tokelau (1,577), Niue (2,532), Tuvalu (9,045), and Nauru (9,919) are equivalent in size to the student body of a metropolitan U.S. high school. The single exception is Papua New Guinea (PNG), whose 3.9 million people share half the continental island of New Guinea with the Indonesian province of Irian Jaya (Douglas and Douglas 1994).

The area is divided into three macroculture regions: Micronesia (small islands), Polynesia (many islands), and Melanesia (black islands).

Polynesia, and to a certain extent Micronesia, is traditionally characterized chiefly by systems of political and social power. Melanesian political systems are based on the successful accumulation and distribution of wealth and resources. Although all independent and self-governing countries save one entered the postcolonial era as presidential or parliamentary democracies (Tonga is a monarchy), traditional sensibilities remain influential in the political process. Of these sensibilities, the issue of land ownership is perhaps the most important because land remains overwhelmingly in indigenous hands.

The regional economy is based on primarily subsistence agriculture, with extractive resource industries (mining, forestry, and fishing), cash cropping, migrant remittances, and aid forming the balance of national budgets. Few people starve thanks to the tenacity of traditional kinship systems based on indigenous land and fishing rights, but the accelerating drift of unskilled villagers into regional capitals has resulted in a crisis of social services there.

The rising urbanization of the 1980s paralleled a period of rapid development for media in the Pacific Islands (Layton 1992). Titles (156) and circulation (683,000) doubled since the early 1970s, and daily circulation rose by more than half—indicating larger urban markets, better distribution methods, and healthier profits. Desktop publishing technology saturated the region after 1985, transforming the look and frequency of many of these titles. A different technology, that of the facsimile machine, and the regionalization of the profession—through regular meetings of the Pacific Islands News Association (PINA), the formation of the Pacific Islands Broadcasting Association (PIBA), and the launch of the regional news exchange Pacnews—saw more regional and international news filling the pages of the region's national newspapers. The 1980s were also the years broadcast television finally came to the South Pacific.

Newspaper organizations themselves went from mainly one- and two-person operations in the 1970s to three-tier structures akin to those of small-town and country papers, comprising an editor, a chief of staff, and the staff itself. Indigenous editors began to outnumber their expatriate colleagues, and indigenous ownership increased as well, from 6 titles in the 1970s to 14 in 1989.

The rapid institutionalization of an independent and indigenous regional media system was accompanied in the latter part of the decade by increased stress on media-government relations. The 1987 coups in Fiji, the 1987 draft Media Tribunal Bill in PNG, the 1988 onset of hostilities on Bougainville, and the 1990 talk of newspaper licensing in Fiji all created headaches for Pacific journalists trying to do their jobs. An attempt to understand these changes led to doctoral study in the early 1990s on media freedom in the Pacific, which included in part a quantitative study of journalists' attitudes in the region (Layton 1993).

METHODOLOGY

Quantitative media research has rarely generated huge response rates in the region. Phinney (1985) was perhaps most successful, with his survey of 42 PNG print and radio journalists, prior to the advent of broadcast television in that country. Seventy-four percent of radio journalists responded, as did 52% of newspaper journalists. Phinney (1985) acknowledged that the high rate for radio journalists was most likely due to the personal contact he had developed in his capacity as a radio trainer.

Masterton (1989) drew a more typical response in his survey of news sources and journalists in the area covered by the University of the South Pacific (USP).[1] His opportunity-sample questionnaire, mailed to USP Centre directors and selected journalists, was distributed to, in addition to working journalists, "citizens who are often reported by . . . journalists and to as many others whom the distributor considered intelligent and interested members of the community" (p. 46). He received a response rate 24.6% overall, but noted that the study did not "purport to be . . . comprehensive or statistically satisfactory: both are difficult to achieve in this region" (p. 46).

My 1992 survey sought to overcome some of these difficulties while reaching as many journalists as possible. With a total of 24 media-producing nations and territories in the Pacific, however, some sampling was required. The independent press is less than 20 years old in much of the Pacific, and in most cases is limited to one title per country, if any (Layton 1992). The existence of competing independent papers therefore signifies a comparatively complex media system in regional terms. For the purposes of the study it was assumed that a more complex media system would feature a greater population of journalists, encouraging efficiencies in data collection and analysis. It was also assumed that practical experience with press freedom issues would be more evident, in comparison with less diversified, government-dominated media systems. On this basis, eight countries with English as a national language were identified (the ninth was French Polynesia and omitted from the study due to translation concerns): American Samoa, the Commonwealth of the Northern Mariana Islands (CNMI), Fiji, Guam, PNG, Solomon Islands, Tonga, and Western Samoa (now Samoa).

The survey instrument comprised 25 questions, many taken from previous studies of journalists (McLeod and Hawley 1964; McLeod and Rush 1969a, 1969b; Nayman, Atkin, and O'Keefe 1973; Phinney 1985; Weaver and Wilhoit 1986; Henningham 1988; Shamir 1988), and was pretested at the Pacific Islands News Association annual meeting in Auckland, New Zealand, in October 1991.

---

[1] Cook Islands, Fiji, Kiribati, Nauru, Niue, Solomon Islands, Tonga, Tuvalu, Vanuatu, and Western Samoa.

Media organizations were identified from research conducted in 1989 and updated in 1992 (Layton 1992). The survey itself tried to balance the importance of face-to-face contact in Pacific society with the constraints of time, infrastructure, and isolation. News manager participation was encouraged through background material faxed, and then mailed, ahead of my arrival in the country. In addition, meetings with news managers were held soon after arrival. Questionnaires were then left with management for distribution in their newsrooms. In this way, 300 questionnaires were distributed to 47 organizations. A total of 164 completed questionnaires were subsequently returned, for a response rate of 60%.

BASIC CHARACTERISTICS OF JOURNALISTS

One of the most distinguishing characteristics of Pacific journalists is their youth. Nearly half of those surveyed were between 20 and 29 years old. Pacific populations are youthful, however, with two thirds of people in Fiji, for example, less than 30 years old (EIU 1990). Yet some senior journalists do remain in the profession. Although Phinney (1985) found no journalists aged over 40 in PNG, 8% make up the 1992 PNG sample.

Women in journalism are younger than men, with 69% under 30 compared with 40% of men. Phinney (1985) found eight years previously that 90% of his female journalists were under 30, compared with 66% of males. Today the ratio of women journalists under and over 30 in PNG is approaching that of men nearly a decade ago.

Fiji has the largest group of 20-year-olds in the journalism workforce (65%), followed by PNG with 61% and Guam with 46%. Yet only 15% of Fiji journalists are in their 30s, virtually half the number for PNG (32%) and Guam (30%). This dip may be one result of the exodus of journalists from Fiji after the 1987 coups. The idea that those who emigrated were primarily midcareer journalists is supported by the relatively large proportion of senior Fiji journalists still in the workforce, whose experience would have allowed them to weather post-coup pressures. Nearly one in five (19%) Fiji journalists is at least 40 years old. Guam has an even higher proportion of senior journalists—24% or nearly one in four—and may reflect the stronger career paths of the primarily expatriate U.S. journalist community there (see later). Melanesian journalists are the youngest group overall, with only 8% of journalists over 40.

As Henningham (1988) found with the government-funded Australian Broadcasting Corporation, government media organizations in the Pacific are more likely to employ older journalists, who represent 22% of newsroom staff, than the foreign-owned private media, with 8%.

The security and benefits of public service employment in the Pacific, coupled with the competitiveness of the commercial media, are likely factors of influence here.

Nearly two thirds (64%) of journalists surveyed were male and 36% female. Fifty-fifty representation of men and women exists among journalists in their 20s. A drop in female participation begins in the 30s, with three in four (76%) journalists of that age being male. Of those 40 or over, 19% are female. This figure, however, is high for total paid female employment in the non-American Pacific.[2] In the American Pacific, the totals are even higher: American Samoa 43% (Untalan-Munoz 1987), CNMI 40% (Douglas and Douglas 1989), and Guam 37% (U.S. Bureau of the Census 1992). As an aggregate, women made up 41% of the media professionals surveyed in those areas.

Melanesia is the most male-dominated media system, with 75% of journalists male and 25% female. The ratio was much closer in Polynesia (55% male and 45% female) and Micronesia (56% male and 44% female). Foreign-owned media workforces were 59% male and 41% female. In comparison, more than two thirds (67%) of journalists working for government media were male.

The three largest ethnic groups represented in the survey were Melanesian (47%), Caucasian (20%), and Polynesian (11%), followed by Mixed and Filipino both at 7%. In Melanesia, 99% of journalists are indigenous Melanesians. In Polynesia, 66% of journalists are indigenous (including both Melanesians and Polynesians).[3] In Micronesia, only 6% of journalists identify themselves as indigenous, although indigenous people form 42% of the population on Guam (Douglas and Douglas 1989).

Caucasian journalists are well in the majority of Micronesia journalists at 57%, followed by Filipinos at 23%. The high presence of Filipino journalists reflects labor recruitment practices in a wide range of employment sectors on Guam and in the CNMI and can be attributed to colonial links with the United States. Only 17% of Guam/CNMI journalists were born in Micronesia and, with the exceptions of the media proprietors themselves, few stay in the islands longer than a couple of years.

The dominance and transience of expatriate journalism in Micronesia differentiates that media system from multi-ethnic Fiji. Most of Fiji's 12% Indo-Fijian, 7% Caucasian, and 5% Chinese journalists were born in and grew up in that country.

---

[2] Women average 17% of the total workforce in PNG, 16% in Western Samoa, and less than 14% in Tonga (Banks 1988).

[3] Fiji was grouped with Polynesia because of the strongly hierarchical social and political structure. Anthropologist R.R. Nayacakalou "once joked that the bodies of Fijians were Melanesian but their cultures [were] Polynesian" (Crocombe 1983: 15).

Fourteen percent of journalists surveyed had fathers in the medical, legal, and accountancy professions, 12% in education, and 12% in the public service. However, few (4%) are second-generation journalists, a similar result to that found in Australia (Henningham 1988). With the 4% of journalists who have politicians for fathers, journalists with middle-class backgrounds number 46%.

In 1985, Phinney presumed that "the parents of the majority of Papua New Guinean journalists are small scale farmers" (p. 42). In 1992, that did indeed hold true (51% of journalists had farmer parents), but it was interesting to note that even in poorly developed PNG, 38% of journalists came from professional backgrounds. This is higher than the regional total of 31%.

The picture that emerges of journalists' backgrounds shows a large cluster of modern middle-class backgrounds on the bottom and a smaller cluster of more traditional agrarian backgrounds on the top. In the middle is the very small number of journalists who come from business or blue-collar homes, highlighting the relative lack of commercial markets and industry in the islands.

EDUCATION AND TRAINING

Pacific journalists are very well educated in comparison to the general population. Forty-eight percent had completed a diploma or undergraduate degree in some subject, and a further 19% had done one to three years of study at tertiary level.

In Guam, 72% had completed a tertiary course, and in PNG 68% (slightly down from 76% in 1984; Phinney 1985). Fiji has, by comparison, few journalists with tertiary degrees (16%), a surprising finding considering the presence of the University of the South Pacific (USP) in Suva.

Thirty-seven percent of university-educated journalists had studied journalism or communication as a major or minor subject, compared with 40% in Australia (Henningham 1996). The next most common, either alone or in conjunction with other subjects, was English (12%), followed by history (8%) and politics (7%). Only 2% of journalists in the U.S.-affiliated areas had not gone on to university, compared with 17% in the former Australian colony of PNG, and 42% in former British colonies.

Fifty-one different institutions were named; 10 in the Pacific. PNG ranked as the leader in tertiary education, with 36% of university-educated journalists having studied in one of the three institutions there. Next is the United States, with 20% of journalists educated in a wide range of colleges, the most popular being the University of Hawaii. Fiji is third with 15%, and Australia a distant fourth with 9%. New Zealand-educated journalists number 5% of the total, and nearly half of those attended the special journalism course for Pacific Islanders at Manakau Polytechnic. Philippines' university alumni total 5% and the UK 4%.

A tertiary education is seen as increasingly important for journalists, as well as more accessible (Petelo, personal communication, October 10, 1991; Fusimalohi, personal interview, July 7, 1992). Only 15% of journalists over 40 were university educated, compared with 36% of journalists in their 30s and 47% in their 20s.

The figures presented here do not register the variety of "short courses" or workshops available to Pacific journalists sponsored by aid agencies and international media organizations. The more prominent journalism trainers are UNESCO, Friedrich Ebert Stiftung, the Asia Foundation, the East-West Center, the Commonwealth Federation of Journalists, the former Australian Journalists' Association (now MEAA), and the Thomson Foundation.

Short courses have been criticized, however, for their overly ambitious curricula, the selection of participants with widely varying levels of professional experience, and the use of consultants with inadequate knowledge of regional society and culture (Fusimalohi 1986). Feedback is also a problem with uncoordinated workshops in that trainers "just turn up, run their courses and go. . . . We never hear from them again" (Petaia 1993: 251). On-the-job training has perceived disadvantages relating to the small staffs and heavy workloads characteristic of most island media (Fusimalohi 1986; Herman 1990; Maka'a 1993) as well as the cultural insensitivity of expatriate tutors (Lawrence 1986). Yet at least one editor believes that one-to-one, on-the-job training is the best solution for small organizations because the journalist remains productive during the training period (Petaia 1993). Masterton (1989) found that journalists and government officials preferred overseas training, whereas media employers and educators believed in-country training to be more useful.

WORKING CONDITIONS

Fifty-five percent of study respondents worked in print media, just under a third (31%) worked in radio, 13% were television journalists, and 2% worked in two or more media. Eighty-six percent of respondents were directly involved in newsgathering or processing as the primary aspect of their job. Fifty-one percent were reporters, 24% were editors, 9% were trainees/cadets, and 2% were bureau chiefs/correspondents.

In rating the importance of nine characteristics of a job in journalism, autonomy ranked near the top of the list, as Table 8.1 indicates. Fifty-four percent of journalists thought it "very important," followed by public service (62%), editorial policy (61%), and job security (57%). The percentage rises to 57 among university-educated journalists and journalists in their 30s and 58% among women. The latter is perhaps indicative of the individualism of women in the profession relative to the societies they come from.

Radio journalists, drawn primarily from government broadcasters, were also more concerned with autonomy and editorial policy than their colleagues in print and television. This is most likely due to the higher level of interference they experience in their work (Honimae, personal interview, May 21, 1992; Usher, personal interview, June 24, 1992; Angiki 1995; Layton 1995a). Governments in the region commonly believe their "public" broadcaster's role is to disseminate government policy and often require government responses be run alongside items critical of the government (Herman 1990). Another type of request censors dissenting political views:

> I was reporting the sugar cane harvest boycott last year [1991] which put the government in a tight situation. As a responsible journalist . . . I reported both sides of the story. As the strike went on the minister called me and told me to omit any comments made by the trade union leader. (Yavala, quoted in Matau and Ritova 1995: 11)

Table 8.1. Importance of Job Characteristics (in percentages; N = 164).

Job Characteristics	Very Important	Fairly Important	Not too Important
The chance to help people	62	32	6
The editorial policies of the organization	61	31	9
Job security	57	31	12
The amount of autonomy	54	43	3
The chance to develop a specialty	51	36	14
The chance to get ahead in the organization	48	39	13
The pay	39	51	11
Freedom from supervision	39	44	17
Fringe benefits	26	50	24
Mean =	49	40	12

Fifty-three percent of journalists strongly felt a journalist should resign if she or he disagreed with editorial policy, and government journalists were more than twice as likely as foreign-employed journalists to do so. Indeed, many senior journalists working today began their careers in the government-owned broadcast media, but left to take up positions in the private media when editorial constraints became too great. This demonstration of professional commitment should be emphasized, given the security, higher wages, and benefits associated with government employment in the region. It can be argued that the effect of such action on the professional community would be great in underscoring the need to maintain professional ideals.

Mala Jagmohan (personal interview, June 26, 1992), editor of *Pacific Islands Monthly*, said private-sector journalists in Fiji sometimes complained that their stories were not being run, but credits this to the lack of sufficient substantiation. Working under *Fiji Times* editor Vijendra Kumar during the coup period, she said Kumar ran all her stories "and my stories are pretty controversial stuff," but Kumar had to be certain that everything had been "checked and cross-checked" for accuracy.

PROFESSIONALISM

As noted in the introduction, the development of professional organizations in the region is a phenomenon less than a decade old. Yet the journalists surveyed indicated a strong belief in the value of professional collectivism—95% agreed that professional organizations should be developed to uphold standards. This increasingly entails a diverse range of organizational emphases.

PINA, a nongovernmental organization primarily made up of the region's independent media (both print and broadcast), has three stated functions: protecting media freedom, organizing professional development seminars, and fostering professional fellowship and cooperation. PIBA, a consortium of the region's public (government) broadcasters, was established in 1988 specifically to oversee multilateral aid projects such as the Pacbroad training project and the Pacnews broadcast news exchange (Fusimalohi 1992).

Many rank-and-file journalists view these two organizations as representing management interests (Australian 1989). There may be some truth in this; 15 years ago newsroom staffs were small or nonexistent. Now, however, staff numbers have increased to that of a sizable professional class, with its own objectives. The Pacific Journalists Association (PJA) was founded in 1989 to improve working conditions through trade union development and to "safeguard media freedoms" that neither "governments, with their political interests, nor media proprietors with their commercial interests" can be trusted to preserve ("Australian" 1989).

National media organizations have in most cases followed the establishment of the regional bodies and are more or less modeled on PINA. Although they receive little outside funding, they emphasize training and fellowship and are quick to react to instances of government pressure on the media.

Press councils are also being discussed in the region, although with some delicacy due to their popularity with regional governments. The PNG Press Council, founded in 1975, was the only such body in the South Pacific at the time of this study.

PROFESSIONAL ROLES

Pacific Islands journalists were found to be remarkably supportive of the critical role of the press; fewer respondents rejected it than in a comparable study of U.S. journalists (Weaver and Wilhoit 1986), although to a lesser extent than Australian journalists (Henningham 1996). One in four Melanesian journalists thought the adversarial role extremely important, although only 13% of Polynesians, who come from more hierarchical and conservative societies, concurred. More than two thirds of the overall sample thought it "extremely important" to investigate government claims, as Table 8.2 indicates.

Government-employed journalists, however, were much less likely than their colleagues from the foreign-owned press to rate adversarial, analytical, and investigative functions as extremely important. They were also more likely to emphasize wide public appeal. Journalists in the foreign-owned press were more likely to highlight entertainment in the news.

Objectivity is a key professional norm in the Pacific, and 54% agreed all information should be disclosed by the media, no matter how sensitive or controversial an issue: "The best thing about Papua New Guinean journalists is [their] readiness to tackle issues that are probably seen as very sensitive" (Dorney, quoted in Littlemore 1992). The manner in which this information is presented, however, demands special consideration. Nearly three of four journalists believe media have a responsibility to promote harmony between differing racial groups, indicating the sensitivity of racial relations in the region. Yet although many journalists would be cautious with reports endangering national unity (64%), a threat derived from ethnic tensions, more than half (53%) disagreed that national image should be a concern when reporting on domestic prob-

Table 8.2. Importance of Media Roles (in percentages; N = 164).

Media Roles	Extremely Important	Quite Important	Somewhat Important	Not Really Important
Get information to the public quickly	86	13	1	1
Investigate claims and statements made by the government	67	24	7	2
Provide analysis and interpretation of complex problems	67	27	5	1
Concentrate on news of interest to the widest possible public	56	29	11	4
Discuss national policy while it is still being developed	40	43	13	4
Develop intellectual and cultural interests of the public	40	37	19	4
Stay away from stories where factual content cannot be verified	37	21	28	14
Provide entertainment and relaxation	22	38	29	12
Be adversary of public officials by being skeptical of their actions	20	30	29	21
Be adversary of business leaders by being skeptical of their actions	18	30	31	21

lems, as Table 8.3 shows. Also strongly rejected was the notion that "criticism of government foreign affairs and security initiatives should be limited" (68%).

Less than a third of the sample agreed positive news should be stressed. The highest agreement (47%) was found, as might be expected, among government-employed journalists. Government-employed journalists also agreed that caution should be exercised in reports threatening national unity, national image, and foreign affairs to a greater degree than those employed by foreign-owned media.

At the same time, both survey and interview data indicate there is a higher commitment on the part of Pacific journalists to a "nationalist" agenda than found with Western journalists, born in part out of recognition that Pacific media are limited in diversity when compared with the West.

> I don't think it's an absolute priority for the nation to learn about how [a particular minister] is conducting his domestic affairs. Perhaps when we have as many newspapers as England, some can be dedicated to carrying junk and others to report good things. . . . If, for nationalistic reasons, there were more important stories to think about than a particular story, then that's news judgement. And very responsible news judgement at that. (Senge Kolma, senior journalist, Papual New Guinea Post-Courier, personal interview, May 27, 1992)

Finally, as Table 8.4 indicates, Pacific journalists show a distinct lack of enthusiasm for the more questionable practices employed by certain sectors of the Western media. The only item to gain significant support (although at the low rate of 43%) of the seven controversial practices provided concerned the use of government or business documents without authorization. This does, however, add support to the finding that Pacific journalists see the watchdog role of the press as intrinsic to their jobs.

DISCUSSION

Debate over the professional status of Pacific journalism has, like that of responsibility in the media, intensified in the last few years. Much of the rhetoric is couched in language reminiscent of the UNESCO "free-flow" debates of the 1970s: "It appears that our learned young men and women in the journalism profession have become deliberately irresponsible and sensational. . . . I condemn this new trend in journalism in this country and call for greater reforms and responsible news reporting" ("Somare will help" 1989: 2).

Table 8.3. Responsibilities by Rank (in Percentages; N = 164).

Responsibilities	Agree	Disagree
When government officials or the police deny access to official information, journalists should seek other sources in order to report accurately on events or issues	93	1
The media should be totally independent in their decision about what to publish and what not to publish	91	7
The media have a responsibility to promote racial harmony	70	18
Locally owned media are more likely to reflect the concerns of their community	69	24
The media must be careful with reports that could damage national unity	64	25
The media must present all information to the public, no matter how sensitive or controversial an issue	54	34
Cultural sensitivities reduce freedom of the press in the Pacific	53	29
Self-censorship is an important part of what governments mean by responsibility in Pacific journalism	51	24
National image should be considered when reporting on domestic problems	37	53
News should stress the positive aspects of the society and state	31	58
It is a fact of life that journalists must show special deference to leaders in the Pacific	28	54
Criticism of government foreign affairs and security initiatives should be limited	16	68

Table 8.4. Justifiable Ethical Practices (in percentages; N = 164).

Ethical Practices	Approve	Disapprove	Unsure
Using confidential business or government documents without authorization	43	38	19
Getting employment in a firm or organization to gain inside information	29	53	18
Paying people for confidential information	20	65	15
Claiming to be someone else	14	70	15
Badgering unwilling informants	14	65	21
Using personal documents such as letters and photographs without permission	12	69	19
Agreeing to protect confidentiality and not doing so	3	91	7

Pacific journalists, however, argue the governments have never taken their profession seriously: "[The] journalism profession in Papua New Guinea [has] no professionally recognised status. Hence there is no pride, respect, dignity . . . there is no distinction between a journalist and a government clerk" (Nash 1990: 28).

They see the threatened imposition of government-formulated codes of conduct as a continuation of this disregard for the quality of professional practice. In addition, although journalists and government officials do agree that the level of training in the profession should be improved, this has yet to be backed up with a strong show of government financial support for such regionally based journalism programs as those of the University of Papua New Guinea and the University of the South Pacific.

Sociologically, the media are a Western institution imported into cultures in which public consensus and respect for leaders are core social norms. As journalists are perceived to reject these in their work, concern for social order demands they be held accountable by some other yardstick—logically the highest standards of professional practice. Professionalism per se is also highly valued in the region, due in part to the long period in which entry into the professions was effectively denied to indigenous people. These two forces converge in the often politically expedient calls by government leaders for more professionalism on the part of journalists. The danger is that criticism about the state of the industry will be followed by government-imposed regulatory agencies should media organizations appear complacent, or worse, recalcitrant, about developing their own. An increasingly professionalized workforce is therefore important for the maintenance of media freedom in the region. Evidence shows that Pacific journalists overall are strongly committed to this goal.

REFERENCES

Angiki, Dykes. 1995. Media freedom: Broadcasting in Solomon Islands. *Pacific Islands Communication Journal* 16(2): 33-38.
Australian, New Zealand backing for unions, PINA called 'bosses' association. 1989, September-October. *PINA Nius*, p. 4.
Banks, A.S., ed. 1988. *Political handbook of the world*. Binghamton, NY: CSA Publications.
Crocombe, Ron. 1983. *The new South Pacific*. Auckland, New Zealand: Longman Paul.
Douglas, Norman and Ngaire Douglas. 1989. *Pacific Islands yearbook*. 16th ed. Sydney: Angus and Robertson.
Douglas, Norman and Ngaire Douglas. 1994. *Pacific Islands yearbook*. 17th ed. Sydney: Angus and Robertson.
Economist Intelligence Unit (EIU). 1990. *Pacific Islands country profile 1990-1991*. London: Economist Intelligence Unit Ltd.
Fusimalohi, Tavake. 1986. Training in broadcast journalism in Tonga. In *Pacific news media: Today and tomorrow*, ed. Sir Leonard Usher, pp. 63-66. Suva: Pacific Island News Association.
Henningham, John. 1988. *Looking at television news*. Melbourne: Longman Cheshire.
Henningham, John. 1996. Australian journalists' professional and ethical values. *Journalism Quarterly* 73(1).
Herman, Francis. 1990. The media in Fiji. In *Pacific eyes: Media in the South Pacific*, pp. 16-21. Brussels: International Federation of Journalists.
Lawrence, John. 1986. News training for the Pacific. In *Pacific news media: Today and tomorrow*, ed. Sir Leonard Usher, pp. 68-70. Suva: Pacific Island News Association.
Layton, Suzanna. 1992. *The contemporary Pacific Islands press*. Brisbane, Australia: University of Queensland Department of Journalism.
Layton, Suzanna. 1993. *Media freedom in the Pacific Island: A comparative analysis of eight nations and territories*. Unpublished Ph.D. dissertation, University of Queensland, Department of Journalism, Australia.
Layton, Suzanna, (ed). 1995a. *Pacific Islands Communication Journal* 16(2): i-101.

Layton, Suzanna. 1995b. Introduction. *Pacific Islands Communication Journal* 16(2): 1-5.

Layton, Suzanna. 1995c. Media legal issues in the South Pacific. *Pacific Islands Communication Journal* 16(2): 61-67.

Littlemore, Stuart. 1992, October 12. *Media watch*. Sydney, NSW, Australia: Australian Broadcasting Corporation.

Maka'a, Julian. 1993. The current situation of the media in the Solomon Islands. In *New views on news*, ed. Frank Morgan, pp. 254-256. Newcastle, New South Wales: Department of Communication and Media Arts, University of New South Wales.

Masterton, Murray. 1989. "Mass" media in the South Pacific. *Media Information Australia* 52: 46-49.

Matau, Robert and Stan Ritova. 1995. Fiji. *Pacific Islands Communication Journal* 16(2): 7-14.

McLeod, J.M. and R.R. Rush. 1969a. Professionalization of Latin American and US journalists. *Journalism Quarterly* 46(3): 583-590.

McLeod, J.M. and R.R. Rush. 1969b. Professionalization of Latin American and US journalists: Part II. *Journalism Quarterly* 46(4): 784-789.

McLeod, J.M. and S.E. Hawley Jr. 1964. Professionalization among newsmen. *Journalism Quarterly* 41(3): 529-538, 577.

Nash, Sorariba. 1990. The status of journalism in Papua New Guinea. In *Pacific eyes: Media in the South Pacific*, pp. 28-29. Brussels: International Federation of Journalists.

Nayman, O.B., C.K. Atkin, and G.J. O'Keefe. 1973. Journalism as a profession in a developing society: Metropolitan Turkish newsmen. *Journalism Quarterly* 50(1): 68-76.

Petaia, Uelese Leota. 1993. The PINA view. In *New views on news*, ed. Frank Morgan, pp. 251-252. Newcastle, New South Wales: Department of Communication and Media Arts, University of New South Wales.

Phinney, R. 1985. A profile of journalists in Papua New Guinea. *Australian Journalism Review* 7: 41-48.

Shamir, Jacob. 1988. Israeli elite journalists: Views on freedom and responsibility. *Journalism Quarterly* 65(3): 589-594, 647.

Somare will help change media. 1989, July 25. *Niugini Nius*, p. 2.

Untalan-Munoz, Faye. 1987. *Pacific Island women's conference on employment and labor market development*. Honolulu: East-West Center Pacific Islands Development Program.

U.S. Bureau of the Census. 1992. *Guam 1990 census*. Washington, DC: U.S. Government Printing Office.

Weaver, D.H. and G.C. Wilhoit. 1986. *The American journalist: A portrait of U.S. news people and their work*. Bloomington: Indiana University Press.

III

EUROPE

9

British Journalists

John Henningham
University of Queensland
Anthony Delano
London College of Printing

As the source of the world's robust and multifaceted English-language press, Britain is of particular significance in a globally comparative study of journalism. More than five centuries after Caxton set up his press in Westminster, British publishing of books, newspapers, and magazines continues to have a profound international influence. Similarly, the British structure of public service broadcasting has been a model for systems developed around the world.

Yet changes have been considerable in the last decades of the 20th century. Use of the term *Fleet Street* as shorthand for the British national press has become historical, in the wake of international proprietor Rupert Murdoch's successful breakaway movement to harness new production technologies and to dispense with printing staff. In addition, the reputation for more than a century that the British press had enjoyed for journalism of quality and integrity—both in its intellectual broadsheet forms and in its tabloid popular newspapers—has been undermined by the sensationalist excesses of a small number of commercially successful national tabloids.

Britain has a considerable diversity of news outlets, including some of the world's most respected media. The *Times*, the *Daily Telegraph*, the *Guardian*, and the more recent *Independent* are newspapers with readership and influence well beyond the British Isles, whereas the British Broadcasting Corporation (BBC) is recognized worldwide as the pre-eminent public broadcasting organization and, until the development of CNN, the most valued international broadcaster.

Britain currently has 13 national daily newspapers and 9 national Sunday editions, ranging in style from quality broadsheets to popular tabloids. In addition, there are 91 regional dailies and 10 regional Sunday editions, plus more than 1,100 weekly newspapers.

Television news is broadcast at national and regional levels by the BBC and by the commercial ITV network, whereas radio news is supplied by the BBC and Independent Radio News, supplemented by local services. A pay-TV news service is provided by Sky Television. Major providers of news are the wire services Reuter (international) and the Press Association (domestic), whereas a large number of small news agencies supply stories and photos regionally and to tabloid dailies.

METHODS

The data for this chapter are derived from a national survey of British journalists conducted by the authors in 1995. The study encompassed the United Kingdom of Great Britain: England, Scotland, Wales, Northern Ireland, the Channel Islands, and the Isle of Man.

In parallel with the national studies of U.S. and Australian journalists by Johnstone, Slawski, and Bowman (1976), Weaver and Wilhoit (1996), and Henningham (1996a) on which this research was modeled, the study focused on those employed full time as journalists by the daily or weekly news media. This included national and regional daily and weekly newspapers, television and radio news services, and wire services. Many who contribute to the media in Britain were thereby excluded from the survey—including the growing number of freelance journalists, plus those employed by popular or special interest magazines or engaged in non-news information programs for broadcasting organizations.

Estimates of the total journalistic workforce were based on staff lists obtained from national newspapers and broadcasters, regional organizations, and professional and industry associations. The estimated number of journalists employed full time by mainstream news organizations at the time of the study was 15,175.

A total of 726 journalists were interviewed, representing a response rate of 81% of available journalists approached. Interviews were conducted by On-Line Telephone Surveys, a subsidiary of the national market research firm MORI. The survey instrument, based on the research of Johnstone et al. (1976), Weaver and Wilhoit (1991), and Henningham (1996a), covered standard demographic questions and included attitude scales and other questions concerning various professional areas. Further details on method are included in Delano and Henningham (1995).

Of the sample, one third were employed by national newspapers—30% by national dailies and 4% by national Sundays. The largest single employers were regional dailies (34%), whereas 10% of journalists were with regional weeklies. One in six were with broadcasting—BBC television 6%, BBC radio 1%, independent television 8%, and independent radio 1%. Three percent worked for wire services (Reuter, Press Association, etc.) and 4% for agencies. The final sample somewhat overrepresented national newspaper journalists and underestimated those in regional dailies, but differences were not great. About one third of the journalists were engaged in part-time or freelance work in addition to their main job, most of these in the print media.

BACKGROUNDS AND WORK

Career Patterns

The study emphasized the importance of the provincial press as a recruiting ground for journalists: 44% began their careers with a regional weekly newspaper and 21% with a regional daily. Only 6% started journalism with a national daily. The BBC was first employer of only 6% of journalists (one third of these in television), whereas independent broadcasting accounted for only 4%.

Although for some journalism is a late vocation, most journalists made their career decision in their teens: 23% had decided on journalism when aged 14 or less and 43% when aged between 15 and 19. Only 6% were in their late 20s and only 2% over 30 when deciding to become a journalist. The median age at which journalists in the sample began their first regular paid job in journalism was 21.

In being drawn to journalism as a career, British journalists showed much the same kind of pattern as found in the case of Australian journalists (Henningham 1996a). The largest proportion (29%) became journalists because of their writing skills, whereas almost one in four were attracted by the perceived excitement and interest of the occupation. Only 14% indicated an intrinsic interest in news or current affairs as their prime motivator, whereas a mere 2% named factors related to service to the public ("righting wrongs," "exposing corruption," etc.; see Table 9.1).

Job Satisfaction

Once involved in journalism, most seem happy with their lot. Thirty-three percent said that, "all things considered," they were very satisfied with their present job, and 49% were fairly satisfied. Only 4% were very dissatisfied. More than 4 out of 10 intended to be working for the same organization in five years' time, and only 2% planned to be out of the media altogether (apart from retirees).

In addition, as many as 75% said they would advise their son or daughter or another young person in favor of a career in journalism, and only 15% said they would advise against it.

However, most journalists indicated they felt stressed in their work: 24% said stress levels were very high, whereas 51% said they were high. The great majority, 87%, considered that stress levels were increasing.

Perhaps their insulation from workplace pressures takes the form of cynicism: 36% believed that journalists have a very high level of cynicism and 48% a high level. When considering their own outlook, 16% felt their cynicism level was very high, whereas 45% felt their level was high.

Table 9.1. British and Australian Journalists: Main Reason for Entering Journalism.

	Percentage indicating this reason	
	British journalists (N = 726)	Australian journalists (N = 1,068)
Good at writing	29	27
Exciting, interesting	23	19
Interest in news, current affairs	14	16
Circumstantial, accidental	10	15
Suited ability	7	5
Family influence/relative in journalism	5	7
Service to public	2	4
Family influence	5	3
Other	6	7

Age

U.K. journalists are on average much the same age as their North American colleagues. The median age of a journalist in Britain is 38 (up slightly from the 34.5 for print journalists reported by the Royal Commission on the Press 1977), compared with 36 in the United States. However, the median disguises a great variety within and between media types. Newspaper journalists, especially those with nationals, tend to be older than broadcast journalists. The most youthful group are those working in independent radio, of whom more than 60 percent are aged under 30. Regional weeklies are also heavily populated by under 30-year-olds (42%). The biggest single group working for national Sunday editions are "30-something" (47%).

Social Lives

The vast majority, 71%, are married or live with a partner of the opposite sex. One percent live with a partner of the same sex. Twenty-four percent live alone or with friends. Mixing with other journalists is common, but not dominant in journalists' lives. On average, about 40% of social contacts are with people connected with journalism or other media, and between 10% and 20% work for the same organization. The spouses or partners of those who are married or partnered are, in 29% of cases, also journalists.

Gender

British journalists are predominantly male: Only 25% of full-time journalists are women. The proportion of women has, however, increased in comparison with earlier studies. For example, the Royal Commission on the Press (1977) found that 17% of print journalists responding to its survey were women, most of whom were freelancers or worked in magazines. (Of editors in the Royal Commission's study, only 7% were women.)

However, women are less well represented in U.K. journalism than in the United States and Australia, where they account for 33% of the total in each country. The journalists' figures do not, however, seem to indicate any systemic bias against employment of women in journalism. Of the full-time employed British workforce aged between 20 and 65, 28% are women (Central Statistical Office 1993), compared with 25% in journalism.

Women journalists are significantly younger on average than their male colleagues; indeed, 67% are aged under 35, compared with 36% of males. The median age for female journalists is 33, five years younger for males. Fewer than one in five female journalists are aged over 40, compared with 46% of male journalists (see Table 9.2).

Marriage statistics show a gender-based difference, presumably related to male-female age differences. Although 31% of male journalists are single, similar to the overall male population's figure of 29%, the proportion of women journalists who are single, 53%, is almost three times higher than the female population's figure of 21%. Population figures are based on those aged between 20 and 65 (Central Statistical Office 1993). Women were particularly underrepresented in national daily newspapers (especially tabloids). The highest proportions of women work in independent television and radio and in Sunday newspapers (broadsheet and tabloid).

Perceptions of newsroom sexism are very much a function of respondents' gender, with almost twice as many women (66%) as men (36%) believing it is more difficult for capable women journalists to get ahead in their careers. Moreover, 60% of women said they had personal experience or knowledge of women being the victims of prejudice in the newsroom (of men, 31% had observed such prejudice).

Ethnicity and Religion

Journalism in Britain is literally the domain of White Anglo-Saxon Protestants. Journalists are overwhelmingly British-born (93%), with 90% describing themselves ethnically as "European." Only 1% are Indian or Pakistani (the main source of Asian immigration to Britain), and only 1%

Table 9.2. British Journalists: Percentage in Each Age Group by Sex.

	Men (N = 537)	Women (N =182)
Under 30	19.6	40.6
30-39	33.7	40.7
40-49	27.5	12.0
50 and over	19.2	6.6
Total (N = 726)	74.7	25.3

Black African or Caribbean. The majority of journalists (55%) conceded that it was more difficult "for capable journalists of ethnic or racial minorities to get ahead in their careers" (29% said no), although only 19% indicated personal knowledge or experience of newsroom prejudice.

Just under half (46%) were brought up in England's and Wales' established church, the Church of England, whereas 16% were brought up as Roman Catholics, and 10% in one of the non-Anglican Protestant denominations. Only 1% of the sample were Jewish, whereas other non-Christian religions (including Islam, Buddhism, Hinduism, and Sikhism) accounted for only 1% of the sample between them. Seventeen percent said they had been brought up in no religion. In terms of current religious practice, most journalists are not now religious in any sense. Even with a broad definition of religious practice (including such expressions as attendance at religious services or praying), 72% of journalists said they did not now practice a religion.

Education

Levels of formal education among British journalists are rising. In the late 1960s, only 30% of specialist journalists had degrees (Tunstall 1971), whereas in the mid-1970s, only 17% of print editors were graduates (Royal Commission on the Press 1977).

Given the emphasis since 1965 by both employers and the National Union of Journalists (NUJ) on the essentially practical standards for trainees established by the National Council for the Training of Journalists (NCTJ), the discovery that only 40% of all journalists held NCTJ certificates must have disappointed advocates of this credential. Only 31% wished they had received more formal off-the-job training in journalism.

Although the fast-rising educational levels of journalists need to be put in the context of the increase in the national university population from 50,000 in 1938 to 750,000 in 1992 (CIHI 1995), they must be seen as one of the most significant changed elements in the profile of the British journalist. By the mid-1990s, almost half the journalists in Britain (49%) have a degree, whereas a further 20% have or are attending a tertiary institution. Thus, only about 30% of U.K. journalists have had no exposure to tertiary education, a reversal of the situation a generation before.

The greatest proportion of degrees were in the arts (48%), followed by economics (11%), science (5%), and commerce/business (3%). Only 2% of graduates had undertaken undergraduate studies in journalism. However, 17% of graduates had a postgraduate qualification in journalism. Only 2% had a bachelor's degree in media studies and 1%

a postgraduate diploma in media. Of the graduates, 15% had attended Oxford or Cambridge, whereas the largest proportion (47%) had attended the middle-ranking "redbrick" universities.

Despite the rise in university education, the possession of a degree is not rated particularly highly by journalists. Only 22% of the sample answered "yes" to the question: "Do you think it desirable that future recruits to journalism have a university degree?" (Of graduates, 28% said yes; of non-graduates, 17% said yes.)

Possession of academic qualifications was negatively correlated with age: Although more than 70% of those aged between 25 and 30 were graduates, the proportion was less than one in four for those aged over 45. This generational difference underlines the recency of the significant shift toward tertiary education in journalism.

Until the 1960s a pragmatic grasp of the requirements was often all that was required to become a journalist. Then, while the NUJ was able to enforce it, a loose form of apprenticeship, or at least of structured entry, came into being. In both these eras it seems that people from a wide range of social and educational backgrounds and differing experience found their niche within the journalistic structure. But despite there again being no formal barriers to entry or career progress, the preponderance of graduates suggests that higher education qualifications may have become a de facto prerequisite.

Contemporary journalists may not appear to regard any educational or vocational credentials as essential, but even apart from the striking level of graduate trainees there was evidence to indicate that within the span of a single working generation journalism has come to offer fewer opportunities to anyone with a limited or unconventional education.

Class

Interestingly, and perhaps reflecting the continuation of class structures in Britain, the move toward tertiary qualifications has drawn criticism that journalism has become an elite activity, with limited opportunity for working-class reporters. A spokesman for the Guild of Editors, Mr Sean Dooley, commented: "If we are not careful we are going to have staffs dominated by classes of entrants who have little common experience with the people who they are writing about. It is not a plea for working class journalists, it's a plea for balanced newsrooms" (quoted in Slattery 1995: 1).

However, the British media are already dominated by journalists who come from middle-class homes, as indexed by parental occupation. Forty-five percent of journalists' fathers (or mothers if the main household breadwinners) worked in professional or managerial positions. A further 6% were in journalism. White-collar occupations accounted for a further 12% in clerical or sales work. Only 15% were employed in manual unskilled or semi-skilled work, and 16% in skilled trades occupations. In addition, 6 out of 10 journalists received their secondary education at a private school.

Reporting Area

Most journalists have no particular specialty. The largest single specialty is sports, in which 13% of journalists are involved. Finance (including business and economics) accounts for 6% of journalists and politics and local government 5%. Arts and culture are the specialities of 4% of journalists, and remaining areas are occupied by only 1% or 2% of journalists.

Politics

In their politics, journalists are Labour rather than Conservative by a factor of almost 10 to 1. Asked how they planned to vote at the next general election, 57% said Labour, whereas only 6% said Conservative. Almost as many again, 5%, named the Liberal-Democrats. On a scale of liberalism-conservatism (Wilson 1985; Henningham 1996b), the journalists generally took liberal positions on a range of social, economic, and moral issues.

Mixed results were indicated when journalists were asked their views on issues of freedom and media standards. Threats to press freedom have been a significant issue in Britain in the 1980s and 1990s. A serious concern is the likelihood of a privacy law being introduced on top of the many legislative strictures that already prevent information from being unearthed or published. Most journalists consider that the level of media freedom is high (42%) or very high (10%). However, one in two journalists (49%) believe the level of freedom is decreasing, and only 13% believe freedom is increasing.

Public Services

Only 18% believe that standards of journalism have improved since they started work (and 49% think they have gotten worse). Yet three-quarters of the journalists believe the news media do a good job of informing the public, and 89% hold this view of their own organizations. In addition, 57% declare that they are optimistic about the future of journalism in Britain.

Some misgivings about the media's ethical standards are indicated by the fact that only 7% consider that British journalism can be rated "very high" in terms of the overall honesty and ethical standards of its practitioners. A further 38% indicate a "high" rating, whereas 42% plump for "medium."

At the same time, British journalists believe their influence on the formation of public opinion is considerable. Using an "influence" scale of 0 to 10, with 10 equating maximum influence (Donsbach 1983; Weaver and Wilhoit 1991), journalists determined on average that their influence rated an 8. By contrast, they considered that their influence ought to be at the level of 5. Journalists in Germany, the United States, and Australia all agree that their influence is greater than it should be, but the British gap is higher than that found elsewhere.

There is strong concern about oligopolization of media ownership, with 77% supporting government intervention to prevent further print concentration, and 80% supporting prevention of further broadcast media concentration.

PROFESSIONALISM

Roles

As found in U.S. and Australian studies, British journalists tend to support both the investigative and information-transmitting roles of the news media (see Table 9.3). Application of a scale devised by Johnstone et al. (1976) and developed by Weaver and Wilhoit (1996) found that investigating government claims and getting the news out quickly were seen by British journalists as the two most important media functions (both judged as very important by 88%), followed by analysis and interpretation (83%) and discussion of national policy (64%). Entertainment was seen as more important (47%) than developing intellectual and cultural interests (30%). Moreover, British journalists were considerably more inclined to support entertainment as a legitimate news media role than were U.S. and Australian journalists.

However, British journalists were much more likely than U.S. or Australian journalists to support an adversarial role. Thus, 51% believed that the news media should be an "adversary of public officials by being constantly skeptical of their actions," whereas 45% believed they should be an adversary, in the same sense, of business. By contrast, only 21% of U.S. and 30% of Australian journalists supported adversary of public officials (and 14% and 27%, respectively, were for adversary of business).

Table 9.3. British, Australian, and U.S. Journalists: Importance of News Media Functions.

	Percentage saying "extremely/very important"		
	British journalists (N = 726)	Australian journalists (N = 1068)	U.S. journalists (N = 1,156)
Get information to the public quickly	88	74	69
Provide analysis & interpretation of complex problems	83	71	48
Provide entertainment & relaxation	47	28	14
Investigate claims & statements made by the government	88	81	67
Stay away from stories where factual content cannot be verified	30	45	49
Concentrate on news which is of interest to the widest possible public	45	38	20
Discuss national policy while it is still being developed	64	56	39
Develop intellectual and cultural interests of the public	30	37	18
Be an adversary of public officials by being constantly skeptical of their actions	51	30	21
Be an adversary of businesses by being constantly skeptical of their actions	45	27	14
Set the political agenda	13	—	5
Give ordinary people a chance to express their view on public affairs	56	—	—

Source of U.S. data: From Weaver and Wilhoit (1996: 136) and personal communication.

One would have hypothesized that U.S. journalists would be more adversarial than British journalists, particularly given the strong tradition of crusading journalism in the United States. Again, the difference may indicate British frustration with constraints on media freedom in a country lacking a First Amendment culture.

Professional Status

British journalists have mixed feelings about professional identification. Just half (51%) chose the word *profession* to describe their occupation from a list also including *vocation* (21%), *craft* (16%), and *trade* (10%). Moreover, 67% do not believe journalism can be organized as a profession. Only 5% believed their occupation could be organized into a "closed profession" like law or medicine, whereas 25% considered it could be organized into a "semi-profession" like architecture or accountancy. However, the majority seek a social status for journalism equivalent to that of such occupations as accounting, teaching, and law.

Membership of purely professional associations in British journalism is minute. Historically such associations have been involved in industrial conflict in an occupation that has had in the past a strong union commitment. Thus, joining a professional association has been seen to a large extent as "anti-union," involving a conscious rejection of union-based methods of improving working conditions in favor of attempts to emulate nonunion occupations.

In the period of Conservative Party government that began in 1979 and ended in 1997, legislation effectively abolished the collective bargaining power of trade unions, including the National Union of Journalists (NUJ). In an earlier era of Labour government, the NUJ had established a virtual "closed shop" that compelled journalists to join it irrespective of whether they considered a trade union the type of organization best suited to represent them.

By the 1990s, the NUJ had been widely "derecognized" by employers, who then offered individual contracts to journalists. The union, largely bypassed in wage negotiations and stripped of the power to decide who could work as a journalist, lost nearly half its membership and barely managed to retain a presence in many newsrooms. Yet by 1995, its numbers had begun to rise again. Of those sampled in the present survey, 62% said they were members of the NUJ.

The routing of the NUJ brought no comfort or encouragement to those journalists who argued (as a faction had done for nearly 100 years) that journalists should be recognized as a profession, regulated by a near autonomous body akin to the "chartered" organizations empowered to grant accreditation to engineers or architects. As a vestigial indication of earlier aspirations to professional status, the Institute of Journalists, a chartered body, has lingered on but its membership remains minute. A third organization, the British Association of Journalists, has not flourished. Of the sampled journalists, only 1% belonged to each of these professional organizations. The development of professional protections in British journalism may be seen as necessary by the fact that 44% said they had personally experienced "improper managerial interference with a story."

Use of Johnstone et al.'s professional values scale (as developed by Weaver and Wilhoit) indicated less commitment than was found among U.S. journalists to the importance of the organization's editorial policies, the chance to develop a speciality, and the chance to help people (see Table 9.4). About the same proportion, one in two, put a high value on autonomy. Job security was valued highly, whereas fringe benefits were generally disdained. Overall, comparative application of the scale suggested a less professional orientation on the part of British journalists, which may be related to the limited tradition of professional education in journalism.

Ethics

Similarly, British journalists appeared to be less ethical in their attitudes. The ethical stances of journalists were explored by using an expanded version of a scale first devised in 1980 for comparative research on

Table 9.4. British, Australian, and U.S. Journalists: Importance of Job Aspects of Journalism.

	Percentage saying "very important"		
	British journalists (N = 726)	Australian journalists (N = 1,068)	U.S. journalists (N = 1,156)
Pay	62	23	21
Job security	56	58	61
Editorial policies of organization	56	55	69
Amount of autonomy you have	47	51	51
Chance to get ahead in organization	45	51	39
A sense of identity	44	—	—
Freedom from supervision	33	39	—
Chance to develop speciality	28	40	40
Chance to help people	26	44	61
Fringe benefits	10	7	35

Note: It is important to note the different wording of U.K. questions compared with the U.S. and Australian questions, which may explain some of the differences (especially on pay):

U.S./Australia: "Could I now ask how important a number of things are to you in judging jobs in journalism—not just your job but any job. For example, how much difference does the pay make in how you rate a job in journalism—is pay very important, fairly important, or not too important?"

U.K.: "If you were offered another job within journalism, please could you say how important each of the factors I read out would be to you in assessing that offer. For each item that I read out could you say whether you think it would be very important, fairly important, or not too important."

German and British journalists (Donsbach 1983) and replicated and developed by Weaver and Wilhoit (1991). As in the earlier study, it was found that for the most part British journalists were less concerned with ethical niceties than were U.S. and Australian journalists (Henningham 1996a; Weaver and Wilhoit 1996; see Table 9.5).

On all but one issue, British journalists were more likely than U.S. journalists to respond that the controversial reporting practices

Table 9.5. British, Australian, and U.S. Journalists: Views on Ethical Issues.

	Percentage saying "may be justified."		
	British journalists (N = 726)	Australian journalists (N = 1,068)	U.S. journalists (N = 1,156)
Using confidential business or government documents without permission	86	79	82
Getting employed in a firm or organization to gain inside information	80	46	63
Badgering unwilling informants to get a story	59	55	49
Making use of personal documents such as letters and photographs without permission	49	39	48
Claiming to be somebody else	47	13	22
Paying people for confidential information	65	31	20
Agreeing to protect confidentiality and not doing so	9	4	5
Using hidden microphones or cameras	73	—	60
Disclosing the names of rape victims	11	—	43
Using re-creations or dramatizations of news by actors	78	—	28

Question: "Journalists have to use various methods to get information. Given an important story, which of the following methods do you think may be justified on occasion and which would you not approve under any circumstances?"

Source of U.S. data: From Weaver and Wilhoit (1996: 157).

"may be justified." In some cases, the differences were considerable. Thus, the sample of British journalists was three times more likely (65%) to approve of paying sources for information and twice as likely (47%) to approve of subterfuge (claiming another identity). They were also more likely to approve of use of hidden cameras or microphones and generally unconcerned about dramatizations in news programs. They were also twice as likely (9%) as Australian and U.S. journalists to approve of the breaking of agreements to protect confidentiality.

The only area in which British journalists took a "more ethical" stance than U.S. journalists was in being unwilling to disclose the names of rape victims (11% approved compared with 43% of U.S. journalists).

One can only speculate as to the reasons for these differences. The strongly competitive newsgathering environment in the U.K., particularly in London, may result in a culture in which ethical constraints are somewhat blurred. The relative recency of professional education in journalism may be another factor, together with the lack of a tradition of associations of journalists organized on purely professional (as opposed to union) lines.

However, British journalists may be more inclined to take risks and to contextualize their responses to the question with more attention to the preamble of "if it was an important story, which of the methods . . . may be justified on occasion" (as discussed in Henningham 1996a). Again, this could be a function of competitive pressures.

Consideration of journalists' responses to the ethics questions in terms of type of medium reveals a uniformity in some areas and differences in others. Use of confidential documents was rather universally supported, and there was much the same level of support for the practice of badgering sources. However, broadcast journalists were more relaxed about assuming a false identity than were print journalists, and they were also far happier with the use of hidden cameras/mikes and re-creations of news on television. Interestingly, for most of the items journalists with the internationally respected BBC were more inclined than other journalists to justify the controversial methods (see Table 9.6).

The lower professional and ethical standards of the British news media reflect a recent appraisal by media scholar Jeremy Tunstall:

> By the 1990s the press is both more commercially aggressive and more politically partisan; the occupational consensus has been shattered by sharp antagonism between triumphant managers and a defeated National Union of Journalists. "Standards" by common consent have declined; the Press Council has disappeared. There is less consensus as to the virtues of upmarket newspapers or of public service broadcasting." (Tunstall 1996: 56)

Table 9.6. Views on Ethical Issues, by Type of Media.

Percentage saying "may be justified"

	National paper (N = 243)	Regional paper (N = 315)	Independent radio/TV (N = 63)	Wire/ agency (N = 56)	BBC (N = 4 9)
Paying for information	68	61	73	66	74
Using confidential documents	87	83	86	86	98
Claiming to be someone else	8	41	62	43	63
Not protecting confidentiality	8	10	10	7	14
Badgering	63	57	59	50	63
Using personal documents	51	48	43	46	57
Employed to get inside information	81	76	92	80	88
Hidden cameras	71	68	89	75	96
Disclosing names of rape victims	11	12	6	11	8
Re-creations of news	73	77	95	73	96

Technology

There has been widespread acceptance of technological change in the newsroom. The survey found that 72% of journalists believed the new technology had improved the quality of their work and 68% believed it saved time. This finding is of particular interest given the huge industrial changes sparked in the late 1980s by *Times* and *Sun* publisher Rupert Murdoch's challenge to the Fleet Street print unions. By setting up new printing plants in Wapping, Murdoch led the physical shift of newspapers from Fleet Street as part of their embrace of computer-based typesetting technology that the unions had resisted.

For desk workers, contact with other journalists outside the workplace, once a regularly pursued means of occupational networking, has become much less frequent. The advent of direct copy input, electronic page makeup, automated video editing, and satellite transmitters has meant that journalists must increasingly double as technicians. This, as well as limiting their mobility, has bound their operations ever more tightly to inflexible "windows" of activity.

Perhaps the most alarming consequence of the technology that has transformed newsgathering is the comprehensive surveillance that has virtually stripped individual journalists of the freedom to stray from routine in order to inquire, investigate, socialize with contacts, and follow leads. Shackled to assignment editors and news desks by mobile telephones, satellite links, networked computer screens, all of which can be accessed at ascending levels of supervision, present-day journalists function under constant scrutiny as though within an electronic panopticon.

CONCLUSIONS

The lack of comprehensive national studies of British journalists in the past results in the need for caution in drawing conclusions about trends. Some developments are clear, however, as are some international differences.

British journalists are now far more likely to be university-educated than in the past, with almost one in two of the workforce possessing degrees, and almost all journalists aged under 30 having had a tertiary education. University education is not particularly valued, however, which raises questions about journalists' perceptions of the applied value of current courses and of the profession's (and thereby the media's) perceptions of contemporary universities.

Another trend is the increasing proportion of women in journalism. Although no greater than the proportion of women in the workforce in general, the greater numbers of women in the younger age groups may indicate a steady feminization of the occupation. At present, most women perceive problems of equity in the newsroom.

Other comparisons are more suitably drawn at international levels. On various measures of professional orientation such as membership in associations and job perceptions, British journalists are as a group "less professional" than their U.S. colleagues (and even than the perhaps implicitly disdained Australian journalists!).

As further evidence of this difference, they are far more "gung-ho" in ethical areas. Perhaps their attitude could be characterized as being more disposed toward "getting the story and worrying about the consequences afterwards" than their U.S. and Australian counterparts. This is an intriguing difference, as popular perceptions may suggest that U.S. journalists as a group are far more assertive and aggressive than the diffident British. Why are journalists in the two cultures different from their national stereotypes?

Another interesting difference is that British journalists showed a stronger commitment to an adversarial function for the news media than did their U.S. counterparts. With its First Amendment freedoms, and its development of "-gate" journalism, many may have considered the U.S. media as the home of adversarial journalism. However, the lack of such constitutional protection in Britain may result in a culture in which an adversarial mindset has developed.

These and other questions raised by this study support the need for further research on British journalists as well as those in other countries.

REFERENCES

Central Statistical Office. 1993. *Annual abstract of statistics*, No. 129. London: HMSO.

Council for Industry and Higher Education (CIHI). 1995. *Post-18 education*. London: Author.

Delano, Anthony and John Henningham. 1995. *The news breed: British journalists in the 1990s*. London: London Institute.

Donsbach, Wolfgang. 1983. Journalists' conceptions of their role. *Gazette* 32(1): 19-37.

Henningham, John. 1996a. Australian journalists' professional and ethical values. *Journalism and Mass Communication Quarterly* 73: 206-218.

Henningham, J.P. 1996b. A 12-item scale of social conservatism. *Personality and Individual Differences* 20(4): 517-519.

Johnstone, John W.C., E.J. Slawski, and W.W. Bowman. 1976. *The news people*. Urbana: University of Illinois Press.

Royal Commission on the Press. 1977. *Attitudes to the press: A report by social and community planning research*. London: HMSO (Cmnd 6810-3).

Slattery, Jon. March 6. 1995. Middle class spread. *U.K. Press Gazette*, p. 1.

Tunstall, Jeremy. 1971. *Journalists at work*. London: Constable.

Tunstall, Jeremy. 1996. From gentlemen to "journos." *British Journalism Review* 6(3): 54-59.

Weaver, David and G. Cleveland Wilhoit. 1991. *The American journalist: A portrait of U.S. news people and their work*, 2nd ed. Bloomington: Indiana University Press.

Weaver, David H. and G. Cleveland Wilhoit. 1996. *The American journalist in the 1990s: U.S. news people at the end of an era*. Mahwah, NJ: Erlbaum.

Wilson, Glenn D. 1985. The "catchphrase" approach to attitude measurement. *Personality and Individual Differences* 6(1): 31-37.

10

The Finnish Journalist: Watchdog with a Conscience

Ari Heinonen
University of Tampere

Finnish journalists carry on their profession within a typically Western European mass communication system: Freedom of speech is guaranteed by the constitution with only slight statutory regulation, and the mass media are for the most part privately owned. The media audience in Finland is comparatively well educated, and the level of media consumption ranks among the highest in the world.

Freedom of the press in Finland is based on the Constitution (from 1919), which guarantees freedom of speech and publishing by forbidding prior censorship. In addition to this, there is the Freedom of Printing Act (1919), which confirms freedom of publication but requires that for each publication there is a responsible editor who shall be answerable for any criminal offenses. There is also separate legislation on broadcasting (1927) and on cable television (1987), both of which require a government license. Otherwise there is very little legislation on mass communication in Finland. Criminal legislation contains restrictions on the dissemination of pornographic material, and there are also laws on the right of reply and source protection.

Ownership of the print media in Finland is in the hands of a wide range of private publishers. The biggest publisher is Sanoma Oy, a family-owned business involved in newspapers, magazines, and cable television. Its Helsinki-based but nationally read *Helsingin Sanomat* is by far the biggest newspaper in the country with a daily circulation of about 500,000. The leading regional dailies reach circulations of no more than around 100,000. Local papers appear in large numbers across the country. In earlier years many newspapers were party-affiliated, but today the overwhelming majority declare independence.

In 1993, Finland had a total of some 90 dailies (appearing at least three times a week), some 10 less than in the late 1980s before the onset of the recession. With a population of some five million, Finland's newspaper circulation per capita was the third highest in the world in the early 1990s. The total circulation of newspapers increased steadily up until 1990, peaking at over 4 million copies. Since then, the figures have dropped by some 100,000. One newspaper copy has an average of 2.6 readers. Most Finnish newspapers are delivered direct to the subscriber's door; single copies account for no more than 12% of total circulation, with the country's two evening papers accounting for most of that (Jyrkiäinen and Savisaari 1994; Tommila 1994).

The newspaper business is not very heavily concentrated in Finland. The biggest company Sanoma Oy (see earlier) has a market share of around 20%, whereas the four biggest companies together account for about half of total newspaper circulation. However, most regions of the country have no more than one newspaper (Nordenstreng 1994).

In the magazine sector there are no less than some 2,500 titles in Finland (including business and customer magazines) with a total circulation of some 13 million. General-interest magazines represent 37% of that figure. An outstanding trend of recent years has been the growth of special-interest magazines (such as computer magazines) and the entry of foreign publishers into the Finnish marketplace (Kivikuru and Sassi 1994).

Broadcasting in Finland is based on a mixture of public service broadcasting and private operators. The Finnish Broadcasting Company (YLE), publicly owned and under indirect parliamentary control, operates two national television channels and five radio channels, partly regional. The private operator MTV Oy has one national television channel. In the mid-1990s there were plans to launch a fourth national television channel by private operators. In addition, there are a few very small local television stations, but these are still more or less experimental projects. Since the entry into force in the 1980s of new, more liberal radio legislation, scores of private local radio stations have been set up across the country that concentrate mostly on light music. Commercial cable television is available in larger towns.

In 1992-1993, the average radio listening time in Finland was 3 hours 45 minutes, the figure for television viewing was 2 hours 13 minutes, for magazine reading 42 minutes, and newspaper reading 41 minutes (Erämetsä 1994). In national economy terms, however, the print media represents the most significant sector in the mass media business. In 1992, the turnover of the print media in Finland totaled US$2.5 billion (based on the June 1995 exchange rate), whereas the figure for the electronic media was US$0.7 billion. The total turnover of the media industry (including print and electronic media, advertising, film, book publishing) in 1992 amounted to US$3.4 billion, almost US$0.5 billion less than in 1990. The media industry accounted for 3.1% of Finland's gross national product (GNP) in 1990 (Sauri 1994).

FIRST STUDIES OF FINNISH JOURNALISTS

Despite the rich tradition of media and journalism research in Finland, studies on working journalists have been surprisingly scarce. It was not until 1987 that the first comprehensive survey ("portrait study") of the Finnish journalist was carried out, and that survey was commissioned by the journalists' union who wanted information on its members and their opinions (Kehälinna and Melin 1988). A study on the attitudes of Finnish journalists toward self-regulation in journalism (Heinonen 1994, 1995) added new substance to the portrait. This study was based on a survey among Finnish journalists and shed light on the professional and ethical orientation of Finnish journalists. Basic data were also provided on working conditions.[1] Almost simultaneously the journalists' union repeated its organizational survey (Melin and Nikula 1993). Again, this study, although primarily motivated by trade unionist interests, provided valuable information on journalists' working conditions and professionalism.

This chapter on Finnish journalists, their professionalism, working conditions, and attitudes is largely based on the two latter studies. Both of them covered basically the same population and used the same sampling techniques and interview methods. In both studies the interviews were carried out at the same time—in May and June 1993. In both studies the population was the membership of the Union of Journalists in Finland (UJF). This is not only an easy solution (the union has a computerized membership file) but also fully justified in that there are hardly any professional journalists in the country who are not members of this all-media union. Furthermore, both studies used the method of random sampling, and through collaboration the researchers were able to avoid

---

[1]The study was modeled on the design of a Swedish project (see Weibull 1991).

overlapping in sampling. The data were collected with postal questionnaires that consisted mainly of structured items. The response rate in the UJF study (Melin and Nikula 1993) was 58%, and in the other survey (Heinonen 1994, 1995) 52%. These were considered satisfactory because the sample in both studies was representative.

BASIC CHARACTERISTICS: MIDDLE AGED, MIDDLE CLASS, URBAN

At the end of 1994, the Union of Journalists in Finland had 9,000 members. Bearing in mind that, on the one hand, this figure includes pensioners and, on the other, that there are only few full-time journalists in the country who are not members, the active journalistic workforce in Finland can be estimated at about 8,000. Not surprisingly, large numbers live and work in the south: Helsinki and surroundings alone are the base for 46% of all journalists in Finland (Heinonen 1994). YLE, MTV, and Helsingin Sanomat are, of course, all based in Helsinki, and most national magazines also have their offices in the capital.

The proportion of women journalists is growing. Currently accounting for 49% of the whole profession, women clearly outnumber men (56% vs. 44%) in the age group under 30 (Heinonen 1994). For several years now the majority of students beginning their studies in journalist training institutions in Finland have been female. The average age of Finnish journalists is 40 years, showing some tendency to rise in recent years at least in part because of the recession and the lack of new vacancies since the beginning of the 1990s. Two thirds (64%) of Finnish journalists have been in the trade for at least 10 years (Heinonen 1994).

Newspapers are still the biggest employer of journalists, but numbers employed by the electronic media have been growing (see Figure 10.1). In 1993, some 40% of Finnish journalists worked in the press, compared to 47% in 1987. Radio and television (national and local, public and commercial) employ 26% of the journalistic workforce and magazines 13%. Fewer than 10% of Finnish journalists are freelancers, but it is expected that the use of freelancers and short-term contracts will increase in all the media (Melin and Nikula 1993).

In 1993, Finnish journalists had an average monthly salary of US$2,790, whereas the figure for all wage earners was US$2519 (based on the June 1995 exchange rate). Women journalists earned markedly less than men: Women's salaries amounted to 89% of those paid to their male colleagues. However, the wage gap in journalism is narrower than in most other occupations. Taking all wage earners together, women's earnings were 78% of those paid to men. Half of the journalists were content with their pay, and 22% were not. Not surprisingly, men were less dissatisfied than women (Melin and Nikula 1993).

The Finnish Journalist 165

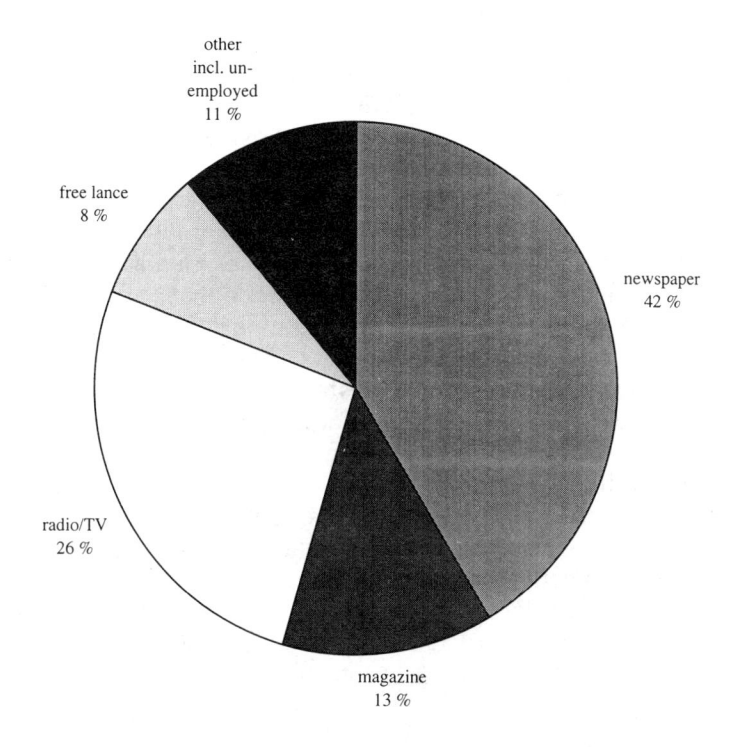

- newspaper 42 %
- magazine 13 %
- radio/TV 26 %
- free lance 8 %
- other incl. unemployed 11 %

Figure 10.1. Journalists in Finland, 1993. Source: Melin and Nikula (1993).

There are two official languages in Finland—Finnish and Swedish. In the whole population, 6% speak Swedish as their first language. Among journalists the figure is higher at 9% (Kehälinna and Melin 1988).

Party political opinions of Finnish journalists have not been studied. This is not by chance; the topic is rather sensitive. An illustrating fact is that the board of the journalists' union considered this to be too delicate a matter to be included in the questionnaire of the organizational surveys. The journalists themselves seemed to agree. In the first organization survey, the respondents said that the credibility of journalism might suffer in the eyes of the public if journalists' political attitudes were publicly known. In general, Finnish journalists participate in different civic organizations more than Finns on average, but these are mostly nonpolitical by nature.

However, in the mid-1980s, 17% of Finnish journalists were members of a political party, which is a higher proportion than in the whole population. Almost half of the respondents said that no political party pursues goals that they personally consider important (Kehälinna and Melin 1988). It is indeed justified to argue that the trend among journalists has been toward nonaffiliation, and this has been an essential feature of the professionalization process of Finnish journalists. Detachment from party politics has taken place hand in hand with the declining importance of the party political press.

More than half of Finnish journalists identify themselves with the middle class (with the other preset options being the working class and the upper class). One third said they did not identify with any social class—another indication of the trend toward nonaffiliation. This was the case most particularly among younger journalists (Kehälinna and Melin 1988).

However, Finnish journalists in the late 1980s experienced social conflicts more acutely and in a different way than Finnish people on average. Journalists tended to attach more importance to the conflict between the requirements of industrial efficiency and environmental protection, whereas in the population at large the accent was more clearly on traditional social conflicts. Banks and major corporations, as far as journalists were concerned, had far too much power in society, whereas universities and parliament had too little. Most other people agreed with journalists on this, but added that political parties have too much and local councils too little power (Kehälinna and Melin 1988).

EDUCATION AND TRAINING

Finland was the first country in Scandinavia to provide regular journalism training at the tertiary level. Training started in 1925 at the Civic College in Helsinki, at which time the program led to an undergraduate degree. In 1947, the College (then called the School of Social Sciences) was granted its first professorship in journalism, and journalism studies were extended to the graduate level. In 1960, the School was moved to Tampere and became the University of Tampere, continuing to offer BA- and MA-level journalism programs.[2]

Programs in journalism are also offered in Helsinki (up to the BA level, but only in the Swedish language) and in Jyväskylä (MA level). The annual intake of students in Tampere is 80 (of whom 40 have journalism and mass communication as their major subject and 40 as a minor subject), and in both Helsinki and Jyväskylä it is 20. The true number of journalism students in the country is markedly higher because in each university large numbers take journalism as a minor subject. Journalism is a

---

[2]For details on journalism studies at the University of Tampere, see the home page of the Department of Journalism and Mass Communication on the World-Wide Web at http://www.uta.fi/laitokset/tiedotus.

very popular subject—only some 5% to 20% of all applicants can be enrolled. The undergraduate degree (BA) requires three to four years of full-time studies, and the MA level a further two to three years.

Although journalism is an open profession in Finland with no formal entry qualifications, more and more new recruits in the media are university educated. In 1993, 40% of the workforce had a university degree in some field, either at the BA or MA level (Heinonen 1994), whereas the figure for 1987 was only 33% (Kehälinna and Melin 1988). In addition to those with a university degree, a further 25% studied at a university but did not complete their degree (Heinonen 1994). During the 1970s and 1980s, premature recruitment of university students into media was indeed quite common in Finland.

However, the majority of journalists in Finland have had no formal professional training. Less than 25% of the workforce have studied journalism as a major or minor subject at a university. Most of them have studied at the University of Tampere (Heinonen 1994). Measured in terms of university degrees and professional training, women journalists tend to be better educated than their male colleagues. Every other female journalist has a university degree, and around 30% have studied journalism. The profession is now witnessing an influx of well-trained, educated young women (Heinonen 1994).

Further education for journalists is rather well organized in Finland. Various universities offer further training courses in different fields for journalists. Based on an agreement between the journalists' union and the publishers' organization, journalists are entitled to a certain amount of further training with full pay, at the employer's expense. In addition, the Ministry of Education and journalists' own foundations have scholarships for further training purposes. More than 50% of the journalists have taken part in further training courses (Melin and Nikula 1993). Recently, university courses have been launched for journalists who want to complete their degree studies.

WORKING CONDITIONS

Before looking at how the journalistic workforce in Finland is divided into different professional categories, it should be noted that reporters in a typical Finnish newsroom enjoy quite a high degree of independence. In smaller newsrooms in particular, copies often go to print without hardly any editing at all. This represents a different journalistic culture than in the Anglo-American countries and means that editing staffs in Finnish newsrooms are relatively small. In fact, more than half (56%) of Finnish journalists are reporters. The rest of the workforce is divided quite evenly—9% work as managing editors or in other managerial positions; 11%

are subeditors, producers, or similar editing staff; and 10% are photographers or artists. The remaining 14% include editorial assistants, fact checkers, and so on (Melin and Nikula 1993). The majority of Finnish journalists describe themselves as general reporters, whereas 46% say that they have some special beat (without necessarily being special correspondents as such). The most common areas of specialism are politics and economy, culture, foreign affairs and sports (Heinonen 1994). More than half of Finland's journalists in managerial positions are men, whereas more than half of the editing staff is female. Women and men are equally represented as reporters, but among photographers the majority are men (Melin and Nikula 1993).

Free But Self-Censored

Finnish journalists said they have a relatively free job, even though two thirds have to work scheduled hours. More than half said they could take a day off at will without losing pay or other benefits. In the journalistic profession the content of work may be regarded as more important than working hours, and in this respect, too, Finnish journalists feel they enjoy considerable freedom. Almost 70% said they could independently choose their assignments (Melin and Nikula 1993).

The notion of a free profession is strengthened by the finding that about 80% of Finnish journalists said they could freely choose the topic on which they want to write. There is very little, if any, pressure—two thirds said they could present their stories as they pleased. Indeed, the majority of journalists maintained that they had not experienced any pressure either on the part of their employers or from the outside (Melin and Nikula 1993).

However, one can presume that external pressures are perhaps of a more indirect nature. According to 90% of the journalists, the factor that most restricted their journalistic freedom was self-censorship. Other restrictive factors identified by Finnish journalists included the publisher's policy (70%) and immediate supervisor, requirements of marketing, and legislation (60%). The majority felt that neither colleagues nor public officials limited their freedom (Melin and Nikula 1993).[3]

---

[3]Traditionally Finnish journalists negotiate with their employers at the collective level. Agreements based on collective bargaining specify terms of employment (salaries, vacations, etc.) but also other aspects. For instance, the agreement on the print media (1995-1996) says that journalists are obliged to follow the editorial policy defined by the publisher, while on the other hand, they are entitled to refuse any assignment that contradicts their conviction (Collective bargaining agreement between the Union of Journalists in Finland and the Federation of the Printing Industry in Finland for 1995-1996, 19§).

An earlier study of journalists' perceptions of their journalistic freedom arrived at the same conclusion that Finnish journalists do not consider lack of freedom a serious problem in their job (Hemánus 1983). Whether this subjective feeling is due to their never having really tested the limits of freedom is an altogether different matter.

Satisfied But Worried

All in all Finnish journalists seemed to be quite content with their lives and their jobs. Over three quarters said they were satisfied with their lives. Men felt living to be a bit harder than women—11% of men were not satisfied with their lives, whereas only 6% of women were (Melin and Nikula 1993). Three quarters also said they were pleased with their job. Only 10% were not satisfied with what they do, both among men and women. Even so, the idea of changing jobs or even one's profession is not unfamiliar to Finnish journalists—more than half (53%) had contemplated changing jobs, and a little less than half (47%) had thought about changing their profession during the previous year.

About half of Finland's journalists (49%) said the most important thing about their present job was that the work was interesting and variable (see Figure 10.2). Second in order of importance was the stability and security of the job (25%). Like typical middle-class professionals, journalists did not mention salary as a very important factor—only 14% said that salary is most important in their job (Melin and Nikula 1993).

However, journalistic work does have its problems. In fact, fully 75% of Finnish journalists admitted to having suffered from burn-out symptoms. This has been most common among freelancers, but there were no differences between men and women. The worst thing about the journalist's job (not only as a cause of burn-out, but in general) is its hectic pace and stressful nature (see Figure 10.3). There is hardly any relief in sight—77% complained that their workload had increased. Ranking second among the worst sides of the job were problems related to organizational culture at the workplace. Hierarchic structures at the workplace were also mentioned quite often as the most negative aspects of the job (Melin and Nikula 1993).

In the early 1990s, Finnish journalists had to come to grips with a problem that, up until then, they had never really encountered before: large-scale unemployment. From 1990 to 1993, the number of unemployed journalists soared from 250 to 1,300.[4] This was caused by the closing down of newspapers, including the leading conservative paper

---

[4] At the time Finland's national economy was in the depths of its worst recession ever, with unemployment at a record high 20% of the workforce.

170 Heinonen

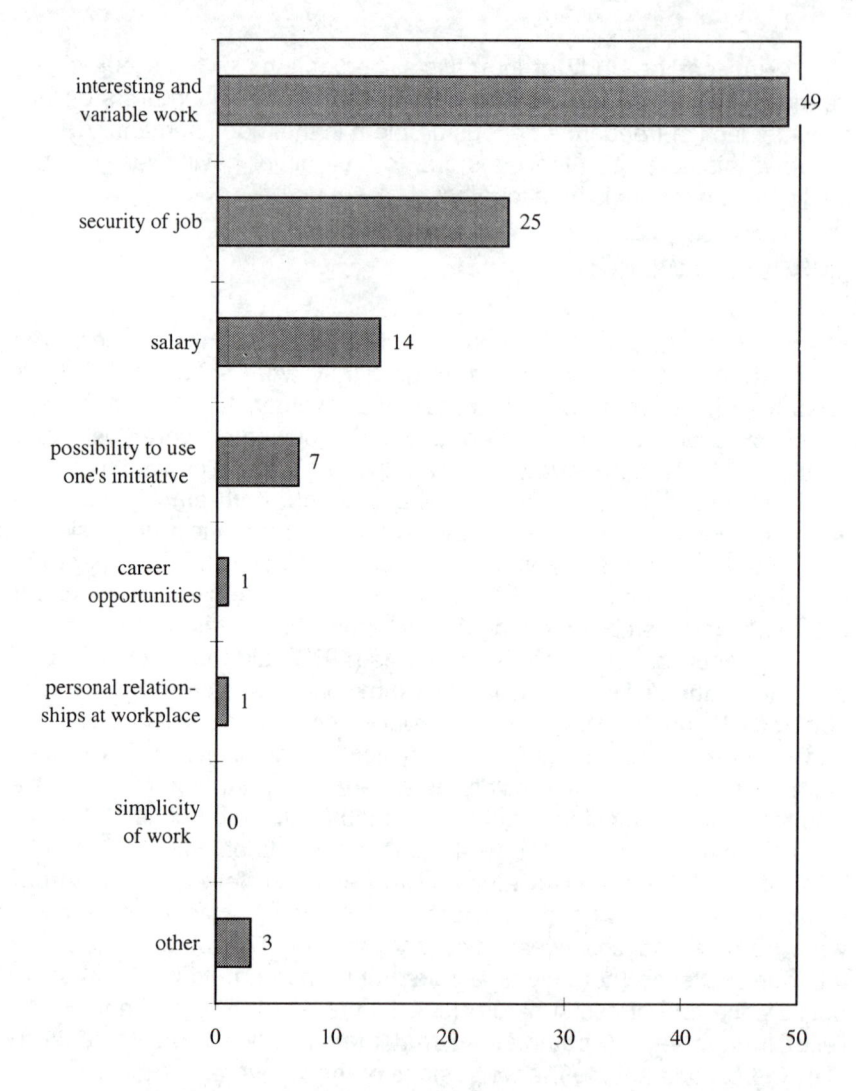

Aspect	%
interesting and variable work	49
security of job	25
salary	14
possibility to use one's initiative	7
career opportunities	1
personal relationships at workplace	1
simplicity of work	0
other	3

Figure 10.2. Most important aspects of job (percentage mentioning). Source: Melin and Nikula (1993).

Uusi Suomi, which had been published for 100 years. In all sectors of the media business expenses were cut back, which meant that staff numbers had to be reduced. Many journalists who were laid off in this wave of economic austerity have since tried to survive as freelancers, and, if the predictions are right, they will probably have to continue to do so because permanent jobs will probably be scarcer even if the unemployment situation changes.

The Finnish Journalist 171

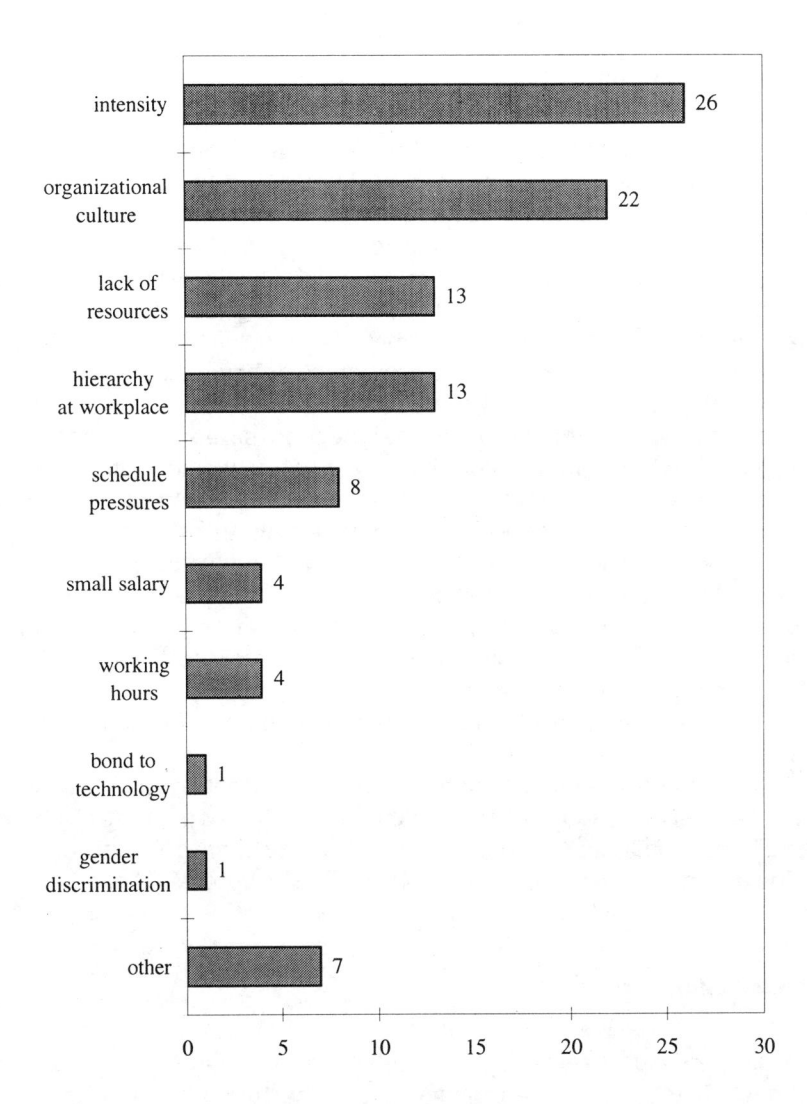

Category	Value
intensity	26
organizational culture	22
lack of resources	13
hierarchy at workplace	13
schedule pressures	8
small salary	4
working hours	4
bond to technology	1
gender discrimination	1
other	7

Figure 10.3. Most negative aspects of job (percentage mentioning). Source: Melin and Nikula (1993).

This was clearly reflected in the opinions of Finnish journalists. Four out of five believed in the growth of part-time jobs in the future, and roughly the same proportion expected to see more freelancers and more journalistic work done by subcontractors. Almost all journalists believed that the number of permanent jobs in the profession would decrease (Melin and Nikula 1993).

Welcome Technology

Finnish journalists may complain about some aspects of their work, but new technology is certainly not one of them. In Finland the invasion of microchips into the newsrooms has been rapid but smooth. PCs are now a standard tool in journalist's work: four out of five Finnish journalists said they used personal computers on a daily basis (Melin and Nikula 1993). Practically all newsrooms in Finland are digitized. Computers are used not only for copy production, but also more and more for layout purposes. Middle-sized newspapers in particular have adopted computer layout methods. By the mid-1990s, more than 60% of the pages in the Finnish newspaper press were designed on screen (Kuusisto and Siivonen 1995). Around 25% of Finnish journalists worked with electronic layout and 20% with digital photo processing (Melin and Nikula 1993).

Information networks are the latest new arrival in newsrooms. As yet there are only a few media companies that provide access to the Internet, but the situation is rapidly changing. For instance, the Finnish Broadcasting Company YLE opened an Internet connection for staff members in 1995. Journalists have apparently realized the potential of information networks; further training courses on the subject have been overcrowded. New media technology is also incorporated into journalism training programs offered at universities.

The overwhelming majority of Finnish journalists take a positive view on the new editorial technology. In 1987, two thirds, or 68% described its influence in positive terms. Since then a great deal has happened in the field, but the proportion of positive evaluations in 1993 remained at a high 72%.

Gender Influence?

The gender issue seems to have cut its way into Finnish newsrooms, although it may not be as incisive as at certain other workplaces. According to a survey conducted in the 1980s (Kuusava, Mäkinen, and Nummijoki 1993),[5] women felt less independent on the job than men. Women also felt they had less influence on editorial policy issues than men. Another gender difference was that women tended to show more so than men a certain diffidence in their professional skills and competence. It seems clear that female and male journalists have experienced their profession, at least to some extent, in different ways. There is also some hard evidence to back up this impression—the higher we go in the

---

[5]The response rate in this survey was only 31%; the findings must be treated accordingly.

newsroom hierarchy, the less we find women. Women have also earned less than men in journalism (see earlier discussion).

However, most journalists, both men and women, said that their gender has not been an important career factor. Three quarters (74%) said that gender has had neither a positive nor a negative influence in general. However, looking into this question in closer detail we found that gender did in fact come into play—41% of the women said that their sex has had a negative impact on their salary, and 34% claimed that it has adversely affected their career opportunities.

PROFESSIONALISM

Membership in the Union—Not Just Financial

Founded in 1921, the Union of Journalists in Finland (UJF) is the only union of professional journalists. In addition to the UJF there are small journalists' associations that are based on ideological grounds (such as the Social Democratic Journalists' Association and the Center Journalists) and several journalists' clubs organized on a professional basis (such as the Sports Reporters' Association and the Association of Investigative Reporting). Members of these organizations are usually members of the UJF as well. The UJF is a member of the International Federation of Journalists (IFJ). Membership numbers have been steadily increasing over the past few years from 8,767 in 1991 to 9,035 at the end of 1994.

Practically all journalists of the print as well as electronic media in Finland are members of the UJF, although membership is voluntary. (Journalists are no exception in that in Finland levels of labor organization are very high throughout. This is partly due to the collective bargaining system.) The UJF is basically a trade union with a traditional role of promoting its members' interests, and the collective agreements set the minimum standards for the field. Another important area in which the union works to defend the interests of its members is in further training—the union has cooperation with employer organizations and various training institutions. The union has regional branches in Finland and a basic organization in most newsrooms.

With the growth of unemployment among professional journalists during the past few years, the reasons for joining the union have changed to some extent. Whereas in 1987 UJF members said they belonged to the union because "organization can help to promote journalists' contractual interests," in 1993 they said "being a member gives

174 Heinonen

you better unemployment benefits" (see Figure 10.4).[6] So although the immediate concern now is more with plain survival, UJF members still tend to consider their organization primarily as a traditional trade union (Melin and Nikula 1993).

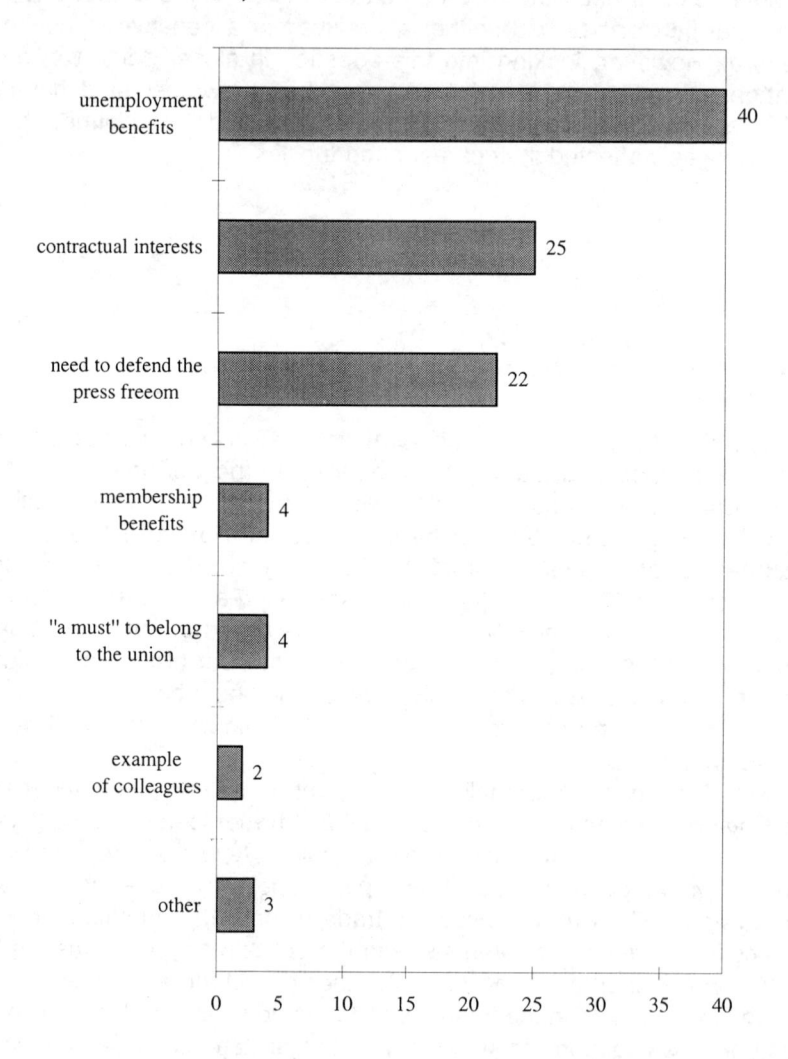

Reason	Percentage
unemployment benefits	40
contractual interests	25
need to defend the press freeom	22
membership benefits	4
"a must" to belong to the union	4
example of colleagues	2
other	3

Figure 10.4. Reasons for belonging to the journalists' union (percentage mentioning). Source: Melin and Nikula (1993).

---

[6]Trade unions have unemployment funds that are financed by membership fees, employers' payments, and subsidies from the state budget. Unemployed members get better benefits than nonmembers who rely entirely on state monies.

Journalists in Finland also regard their organization as an actor in the field of media policy. One fifth (22% in both 1987 and 1993) of the members of the UJF said the reason they joined is that the profession needs an organization that defends freedom of speech and journalists' rights and that works to influence communication policy. Various governmental acts concerning the media field have been submitted to the UJF for review. One of the recent topics was the debate on publicity regulations when Finland entered the European Community in 1995.

The journalists' union has it own newspaper, *Journalisti* ("The Journalist"), which is issued twice a month. It comes free to all members, but it is also read in other circles such as journalism researchers. *Journalisti* is the only journal in Finland that qualifies as a more or less professional publication, although most of its stories deal with trade union questions. The journals published by the Society of Communication Research and the Newspapers' Association are more clearly targeted to academic circles and the management of publishing houses, respectively. *Journalisti,* however, covers all the media and regularly publishes articles by media researchers. Media policy, journalism ethics, and problems with freedom of the press are rather well represented on the pages of *Journalisti.*

Judging by a readership survey conducted by *Journalisti* itself, UJF members consider their paper quite important: 52% said they read most or even all the articles it carried, whereas 44% said they read "the interesting articles." Only 3% said they read the paper only occasionally (*Journalisti* 1993).

The paper's most interesting items, according to the survey, are the debates, advertisements for vacancies, and the resolutions of the press council. Topics that readers think should be given more attention are the ethics of journalism and photojournalism. An interesting finding was that the majority of the journalists (66% of the member readers) said Journalisti should carry more criticism of journalism, even if that meant criticizing the work of other union members. Journalisti does in fact often carry pieces on criticism by professional journalists and scholars.

Professional Roles: Ideal vs. Reality

Finnish journalists' professional role definitions tend to vary depending on the level from which they describe their professional characteristics. On the one hand, Finnish journalists attach to their profession expectations and definitions with strong social dimensions. On the other hand, they admit to having entered the profession in order to fulfill their more individualistic aspirations. There seems to prevail a certain discrepancy between the ideal of the professional role as a journalist and the mundane, everyday journalist.

176 Heinonen

Views on what may be regarded as the ideal journalist were quite consistent (see Figure 10.5). Finnish journalists agreed that the journalist should take an active stance on social issues by criticizing social injustices and keeping a close watch on those who have power in society. At the same time, the ideal journalist should act as an intellectu-

A journalist should...

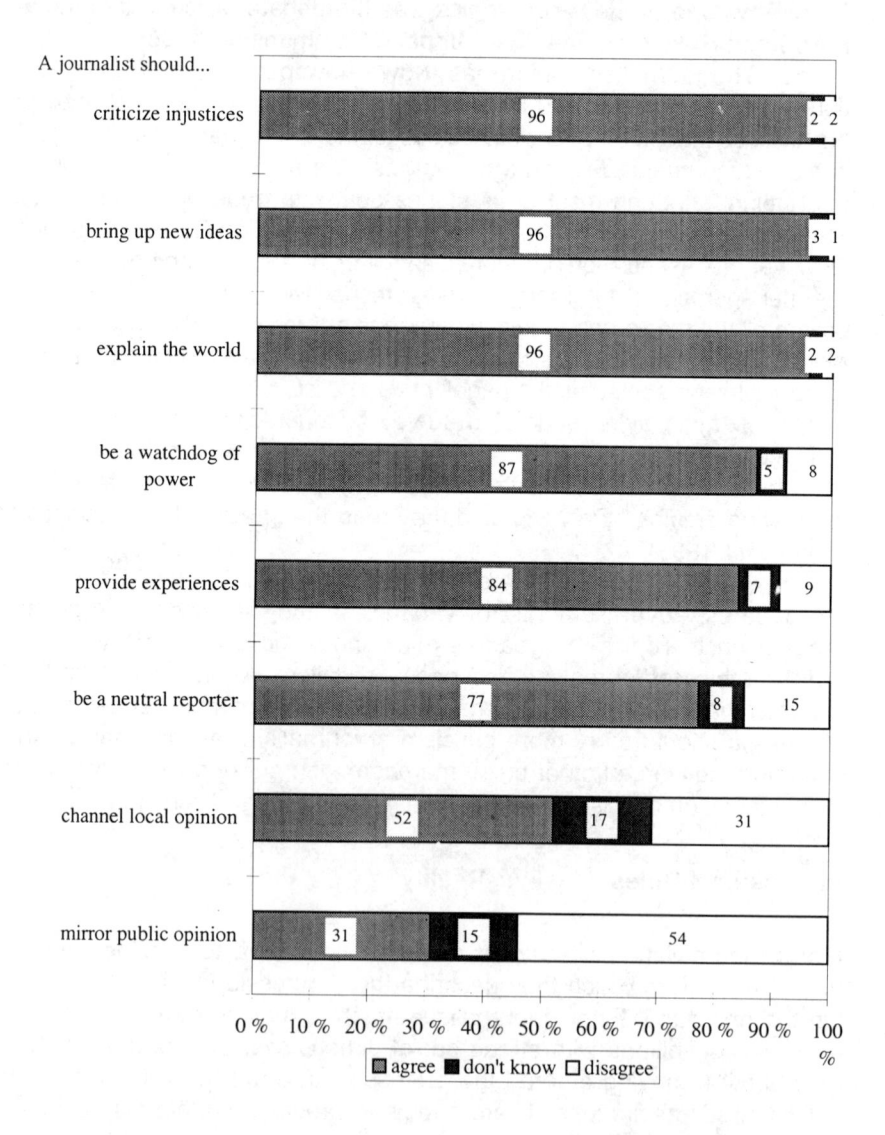

Role	agree	don't know	disagree
criticize injustices	96	2	2
bring up new ideas	96	3	1
explain the world	96	2	2
be a watchdog of power	87	5	8
provide experiences	84	7	9
be a neutral reporter	77	8	15
channel local opinion	52	17	31
mirror public opinion	31	15	54

**Figure 10.5. Ideal professional roles of journalists.
Source: Heinonen (1995).**

al catalyst and educator for civil society by bringing forward new ideas and explaining the complex world to the public. These definitions for the journalist's ideal professional role are endorsed by 87% to 96% of Finnish journalists (Heinonen 1995).

Furthermore, the clear majority (84%) of Finnish journalists agreed that the ideal journalist should aim to provide his or her audience with true experiences. This seems to indicate that journalists themselves consider their profession to involve an emotional dimension as well as an informative one (Heinonen 1995). It is perhaps worth noting that the traditional demand of neutrality does not enjoy as much support among Finnish journalists as does the notion of a socially active role. As expected, the clear majority of journalists (78%) agreed that "a journalist should be a neutral reporter," but 15% disagreed (Heinonen 1995).

The relationship between the public and journalists is more controversial than other dimensions of the professional role. The majority (54%) of Finnish journalists said that a journalist should not mirror public opinion. Opinions were sharply divided here as nearly one third (31%) accepted the statement. However, at a more concrete level, a closer relationship with the public was endorsed—more than half (53%) agreed that a journalist should be a channel for local opinion. Again, opinions were divided: 31% disagreed with this statement. One can assume then that Finnish journalists tend to identify more closely with local community aspirations than with general, often vaguely defined trends. However, both these role definitions were clearly less popular than the others (Heinonen 1995).

What about the journalist of everyday reality? We can draw some conclusions about this side of the journalist's professional role by looking at the motives that brought Finnish journalists into the profession. There is more variation in these than in definitions of the journalist's ideal role (see Figure 10.6). This is quite understandable in view of the fact that we are now dealing with personal questions, whereas definitions of the ideal journalist are more likely to be based on a collective professional mind. The second finding may be more interesting—it seems that individual motives provide a better explanation for career choices than social motives, even though the ideal journalist works first and foremost for the common good.

Indeed, 81% of Finnish journalists said they came into journalism because of the desire to express themselves and the freedom at work. A further 72% said they appreciated journalistic work because it is not one of those 9 to 5 jobs (Heinonen 1995). Linking these rather explicitly individual motives to more social ones is "the possibility to work with news," which was accepted by 72% of the journalists. Hints of individualism can be detected here as well because the emphasis is on personal working conditions rather than on journalism's public service function (Heinonen 1995).

178 Heinonen

The more socially oriented motives carry less weight. Explaining their choice of profession, 56% referred to the possibility of exposing social remedies. About the same proportion accepted the motive of influencing other people. Although these motives of career choice may be individualistic, Finnish journalists are hardly selfish in a material sense.

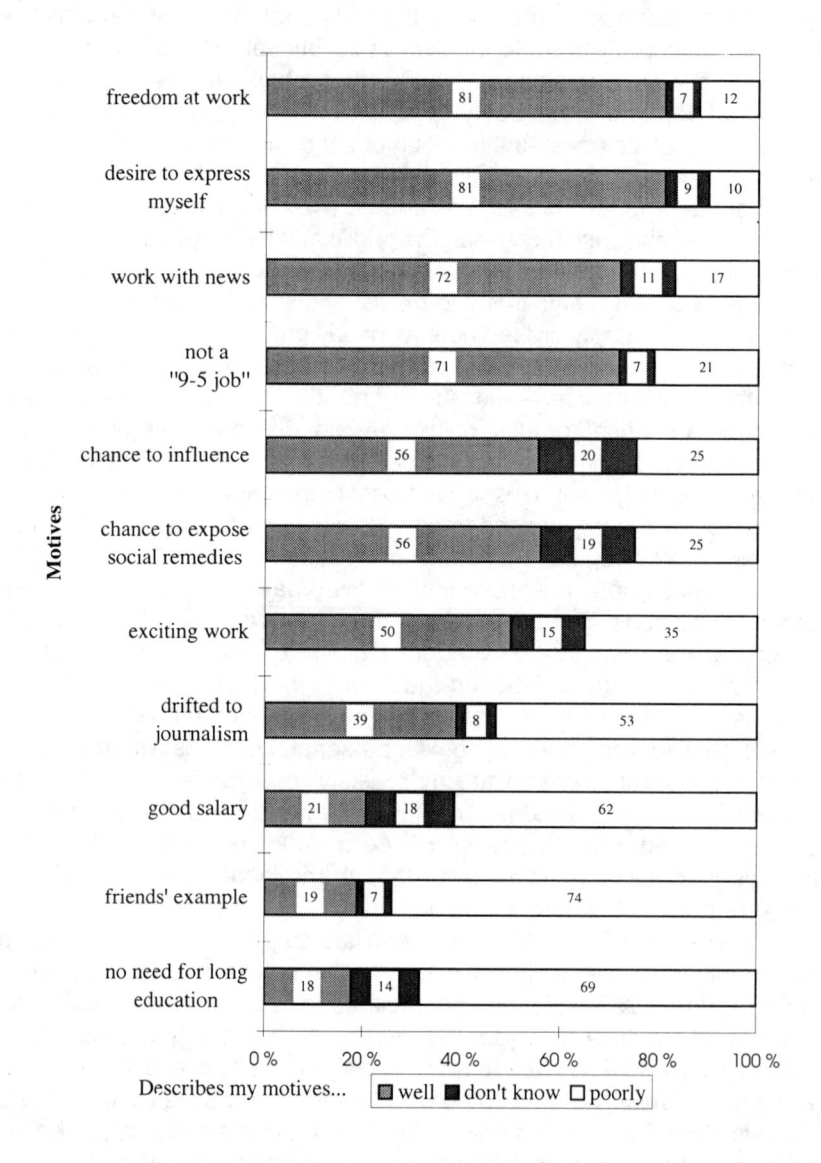

Motives	well	don't know	poorly
freedom at work	81	7	12
desire to express myself	81	9	10
work with news	72	11	17
not a "9-5 job"	71	7	21
chance to influence	56	20	25
chance to expose social remedies	56	19	25
exciting work	50	15	35
drifted to journalism	39	8	53
good salary	21	18	62
friends' example	19	7	74
no need for long education	18	14	69

Describes my motives... ■ well ■ don't know □ poorly

Figure 10.6. Personal motives for career choice. Source: Heinonen (1995).

The majority (62%) deny having entered the profession because journalists are paid well. Moreover, 69% said they were not tempted into journalism by the fact that there is no need for formal education (Heinonen 1995).

Firm on Ethics

Before discussing the ethical attitudes of Finnish journalists, it is useful to introduce the system of self-regulation that prevails in Finnish journalism. Journalistic self-regulation in Finland is based on two institutions: the code of ethics and the press council. The code of ethics—called "The Guidelines for Good Journalistic Practice"—is formally adopted by the Union of Journalists in Finland (UJF). The first code was adopted in 1958, and the latest (fifth) version of the code has been in effect since the beginning of 1992. In practice the code of the UJF has been and still is a national code for all sectors of the media. This has been accomplished by an open and wide drafting of the code. Before the latest version of the code was formally adopted by the UJF national council, the draft(s) of the code were widely circulated for comments among publishers, media experts, journalism scholars, and the press council. The status of the UJF code is strengthened by the fact that there are only a few house codes (most noteworthy is the one of the national broadcasting corporation), no regional codes, and practically no codes of various professional groups.

The Guidelines for Good Journalistic Practice covers the print as well as the electronic media. It is a rather typical code of Western democracies (see White 1989; and for a recent comparison of European codes, see Laitila 1995). The UJF code, first, includes clauses referring to general ethical principles such as commitment to truth and respect for the natural environment. The code also defines the relationship between journalists and society by saying that journalism is founded on the citizens' right to receive correct information on the basis of which they can create a truthful picture of the world and society. Second, the code deals with matters related to human rights such as freedom of opinion and human dignity. Third, there are clauses that define acceptable professional practices such as checking information and using open and honest methods to gather information. Finally, the UJF code includes obligations not only for journalists but also for publishers such as the journalist's right to refuse assignments that conflict with his or her convictions and a detailed formulation of the right of reply and correction.

The press council in Finland, known as the "Council for Mass Media," is another institution recognized by all parties in journalism. Founded in 1968, the council consists of 15 members, of whom 5 are nominated by the journalists' union and 5 by the publishers' organizations.

These "professional" members cover all sectors of the print and the electronic media. The remaining five members and the chairman represent the general public and must have no strings to the mass media. They are nominated by the full council. The council is jointly funded by the respective organizations and the state. State funding in this case does not endanger the council's independence for it is merely part of regular aid for nongovernmental organizations. The council does not have a code of conduct of its own but applies the UJF code, which serves as a frame of reference. The only sanction available to the council is publicity—if a complaint against a medium is upheld, the medium in question is required to publish the resolution. So far this has happened almost without exception. Presently the council issues some 100 resolutions annually.

Respected but distant code. The importance of any professional code of conduct depends largely on the support, or at least acceptance, it enjoys within the professional community concerned. In this respect the status of the code of conduct of Finnish journalists seems to be high. It is well respected by the profession. However, its link with everyday work is weaker. The clauses most actively present in the journalist's day-to-day job are those that concern the social credibility of the profession, whereas clauses defining the rights of the public are of a more passive nature.

The clear majority (88%) of Finnish journalists did not subscribe to the statement that the code is "unnecessary and more likely to be detrimental to journalists' work." Opinions were more divided on its relevance to everyday work: 51% thought the code was important but "not useful in practice." There were, however, large numbers (42%) who felt that the code "often helps in the job." It is fair to conclude, then, that Finnish journalists hardly looked on their code of conduct with indifference, let alone with hostility (Heinonen 1995). Asked to rank the clauses of their professional code in order of importance, the journalists were more or less agreed that the top clause is that which requires journalists to strive for truthful and essential communication. That was followed by the clauses saying that a journalist must repel attempts to influence journalism and that a journalist must respect human rights and democracy (Heinonen 1995).

At the bottom of this ranking were those clauses that state that a journalist should recognize his or her responsibility for the natural environment, and that methods of information gathering should be open and honest. It is somewhat surprising that these clauses were ranked lowest in importance because environmental issues have been widely debated in Finland as well as among the journalists themselves. It is also interesting to see that the clause of openness and honesty in information was ranked so low because, as discussed later, Finnish journalists do not accept questionable methods of information gathering (Heinonen 1995).

To check a new angle on attitudes toward the professional code of conduct, the journalists were asked to identify the clauses that they felt were problematic in their own job and those that were not (for this method, see Löfgren 1991). The list of most problematic clauses was topped by the one that says that a journalist is responsible first and foremost to the public. This was followed by the clauses that deal with textual advertising and with the truthfulness of journalism. The clauses mentioned as least problematic in the everyday job were those dealing with the rights of the public in relation to journalism—the demand not to breach privacy (unless well justified by public interest), the right of reply, and the demand to inform interviewees about the context in which their statements will be used (Heinonen 1995).

When these two lists are combined, we can locate those clauses that are at once important and problematic (i.e., active clauses that may be presumed to have a closer presence in everyday journalistic work than the rest of the clauses), and those clauses that are considered less important and not problematic (i.e., passive clauses—Heinonen 1995; see also Löfgren 1991).

On the basis of this distinction, we find that the active part of the code of conduct is that which deals with the general credibility of journalism—the truthfulness of journalism, journalism's responsibility toward the public, and the rejection of outside pressures on journalism. The passive clauses, however, are those that deal with the rights of the objects of journalism, individual members of the public as sources of information. These included such clauses as the one that defines the right of reply and correction, the clause that says that an interviewee must know in which context his or her statement will be used, and the one that says that privacy should not be breached without good reasons (Heinonen 1995).

Interesting and important press council. Professional journalists take a serious interest in the work and decisions of the press council. The council's resolutions are regularly published in the union's paper *Journalisti*, and 96% of Finnish journalists said they read these resolutions "carefully" or at least "occasionally"; 40% read them carefully (Heinonen 1995).

Finnish journalists also regarded the press council as an important institution of journalism (see Figure 10.7). Three quarters of Finnish journalists described it as important because it provides a channel for the public to voice its discontent with journalism. More than half agreed that the press council protects journalism from statutory regulation. However, 65% disagreed with the statement that the press council deals with unimportant issues, whereas 60% disagreed with the statement that abolishing the council would not adversely affect the quality of journal-

182 Heinonen

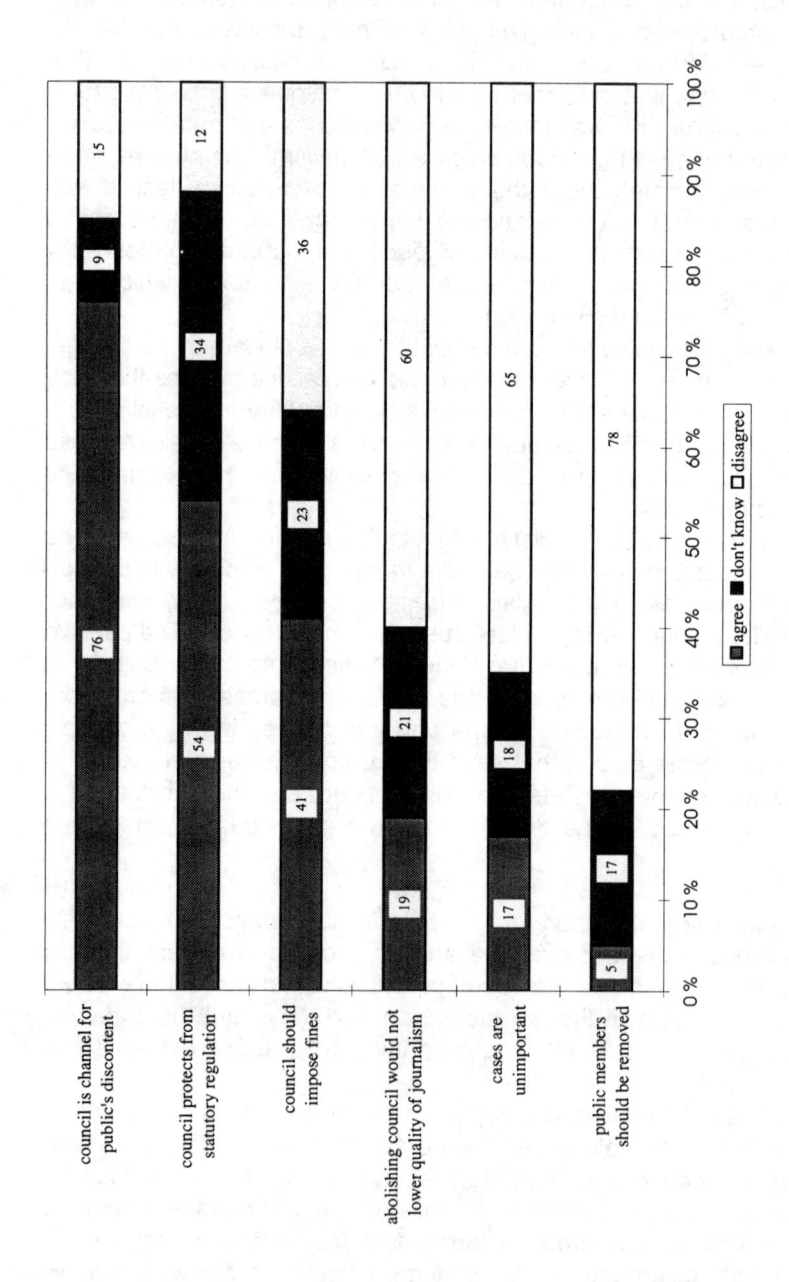

Statement	agree	don't know	disagree
council is channel for public's discontent	76	9	15
council protects from statutory regulation	54	34	12
council should impose fines	41	23	36
abolishing council would not lower quality of journalism	19	21	60
cases are unimportant	17	18	65
public members should be removed	5	17	78

Figure 10.7. Journalists' opinions on the press council. Source: Heinonen (1995).

ism. It was also a strongly held view that the public plays an important role in the council: 78% of the journalists disagreed with having the representatives of the public removed from the council (Heinonen 1995). Finnish journalists were quite firmly in favor of strengthening the press council by granting it harder sanctions—41% agreed that in addition to its current publicity sanction the council should also be entitled to impose fines, whereas 36% were against this proposal (Heinonen 1995).

Looking at the press council from a professional point of view, Finnish journalists again made it clear that they respected the council's work—84% thought that the council's resolutions were usually well founded and accurate, whereas only 2% disagreed. An institution like the press council could be easily criticized for its failure to pay sufficient attention to the practical demands of the profession, but in this case only 11% of the journalists in the country did so. The press council seems to serve as some kind of guide for practical journalism, for 55% of Finnish journalists said that the council's resolutions provide useful advice for everyday work. However, it is interesting that only 30% thought that an upheld complaint was an indication of poor professional competence (Heinonen 1995).

Indiscreet methods rejected. An interesting addition to the picture of Finnish journalists' ethical attitudes is obtained by looking at their views on the use of so-called unusual (or questionable) methods of information gathering. These are methods that at least in theory would be at variance with one or more clauses of the code of conduct. Asked to state their opinion on eight such methods (see Figure 10.8), Finnish journalists appeared to be very discreet. Only a small minority said they could use the proposed methods without hesitation. One quarter would copy a secret document, and one fifth would take a job under a false identity to get inside information. However, for each method at least 25% said they were firmly against this action. Four of the methods listed met with particularly heavy resistance—half or nearly half of the journalists were against unauthorized use of private material, publishing confidential information, threatening sources, and posing as someone else.

However, the concept of good journalistic practice may be changing. Almost half of Finland's journalists said they expected to see the observance of professional codes of ethics become more lenient, whereas only 15% expected to see stricter ethics (Heinonen 1995). One possible explanation lies in the recent tendency of economic austerity, which in many publishing houses has implied an entry of marketing considerations into the realm of journalism. Indeed, many local branches of the journalists' union have filed complaints with the press council about advertisements designed in the form of journalistic products.

Journalists on Journalism

It is a common, if not universal, criticism that journalists have too much power and too little responsibility in society. This has also been heard in Finland. For instance, politicians complain every now and then that the profession has transgressed the limits of responsible journalism by scan-

reporting method	by all means	sometimes	never
publishing confidential material	5	34	61
unauthorized use of private material	5	34	61
threatening sources	9	34	57
posing as someone else	11	42	47
paying for information	16	46	37
paying for interviewee	16	44	39
getting a job with false identity	21	47	30
copying secret documents	24	48	27

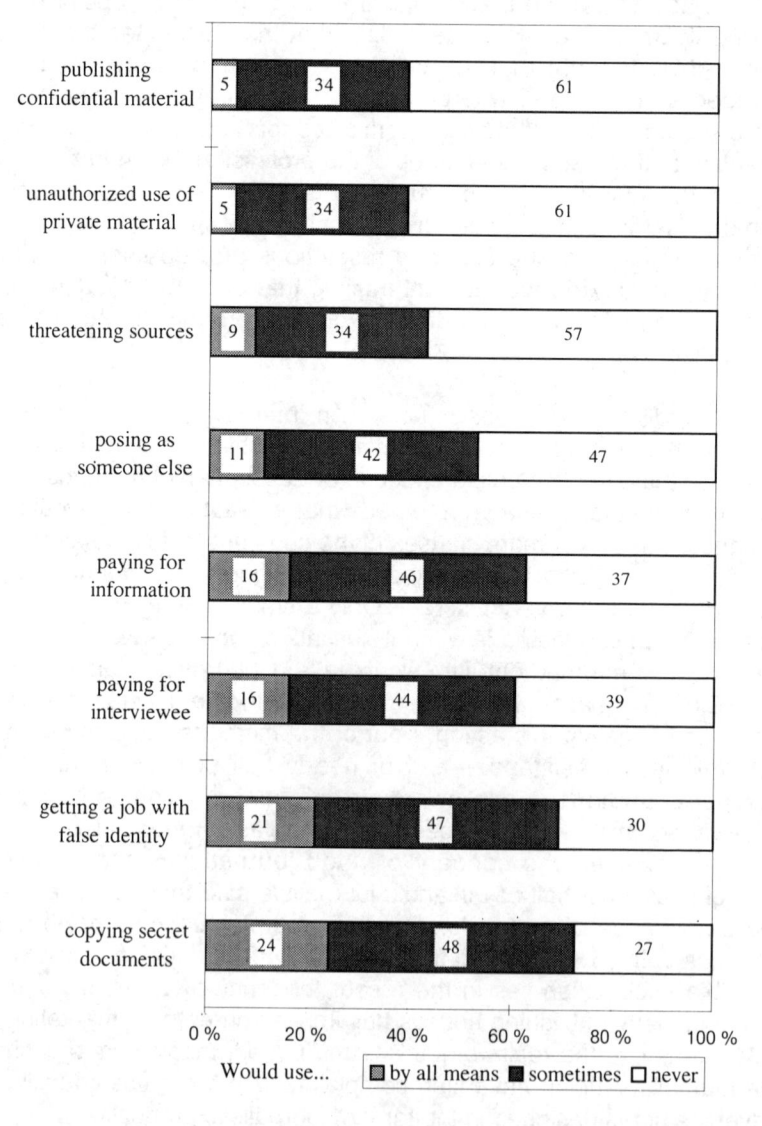

Would use... ▨ by all means ■ sometimes ☐ never

Figure 10.8. Opinions on reporting methods. Source: Heinonen (1995).

dalized and inaccurate reporting. The slogan coined to describe this tendency was *infocracy*, intended to highlight the power of journalists in Finnish society. However, the criticism has not only come from the outside, but journalists themselves have also been sharply critical of the performance of journalism.

Journalists did not share the view that the media have too much power in Finnish society—only 10% agreed, 77% did not. At the same time, however, journalists admitted that certain media institutions do exert some social power. This applies most notably to the biggest newspaper, *Helsingin Sanomat*—59% of the journalists thought that it had too much influence as a social institution. Only 23% to 30% of the journalists in Finland were of the opinion that radio and television, the party political press, and regional leading newspapers had too much power. On the other hand, 70% believed that the media were good in promoting and fostering things that are important to people, whereas 6% said the same about major corporations and 25% about the political parties (Kehälinna and Melin 1988).

When presented with eight statements concerning Finnish news journalism, however, the majority of Finnish journalists agreed with only two positive features—that journalism in Finland is professional (in terms of skill and competence) and that it is responsible. On the contrary, a majority of journalists (52%) agreed that journalism is easily manipulated. Furthermore, 73% disagreed that journalism is courageous, 62% disagreed that journalism has ideals, and 56% disagreed that journalism is critical (see Figure 10.9; Heinonen 1995).

So why were Finnish journalists so sharply critical of their own profession? Something can be inferred from the journalists' own comments when they were asked to give examples of what they thought represented unethical journalism. (The following typology of six clusters and the quotes are from Heinonen 1995: 106-109). The first type of criticism by Finnish journalists of Finnish journalism concerned certain types of journalism that were thought to be dubious. One such line of journalism is so-called celebrity journalism. As one of the journalists in the survey put it: "totally stupid and artificial stories about celebrities. Who divorced whom and who married whom. . . . Totally needless . . . undermines the respect for journalists." Another comparable line was crime journalism. Finnish journalists despised "wallowing in murders" and "feasting with the details of crimes."

The second type of criticism was targeted against certain media. One of these was represented by the evening papers (there are two in Finland). These were accused especially of selling their issues with screaming headlines without any real solid foundation for them. Another type was the magazine that specializes in bloody scandals and gossip. Third, journalists were critical of colleagues who tended to identify too

186 Heinonen

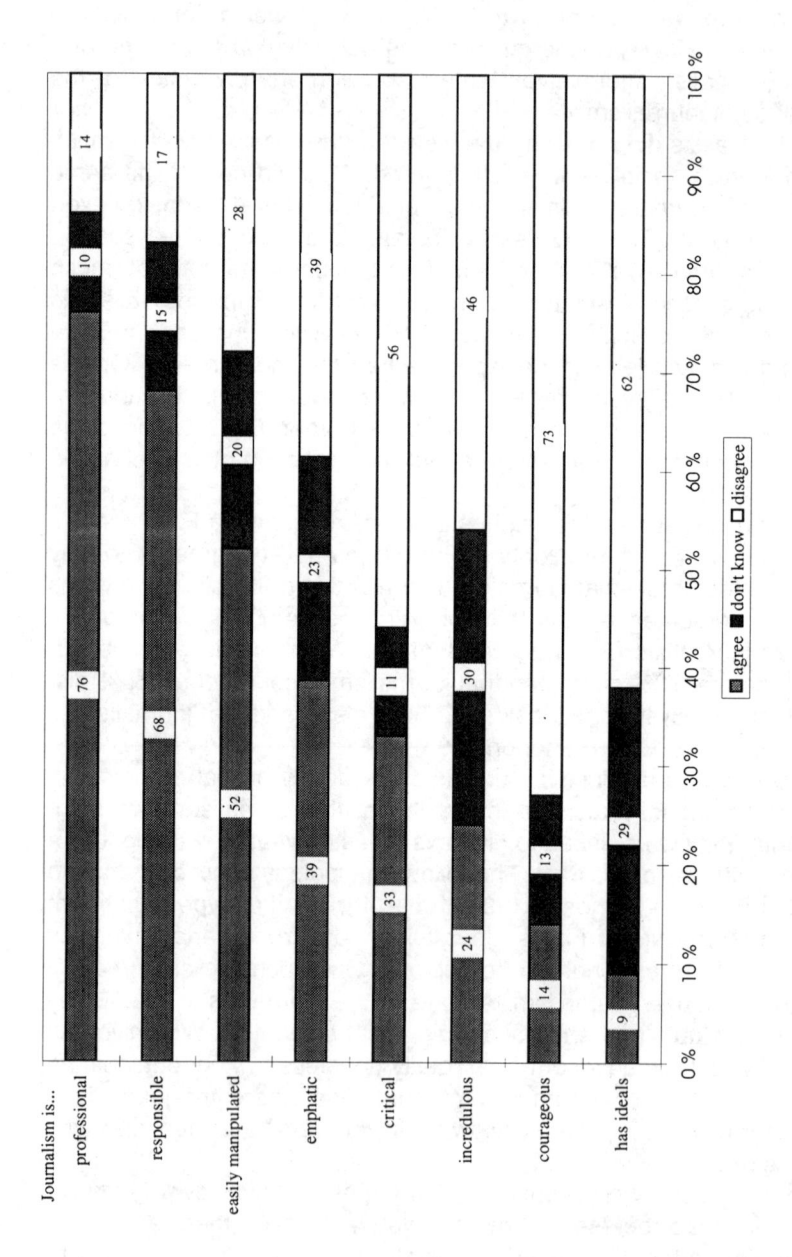

Journalism is...	agree	don't know	disagree
professional	76	10	14
responsible	68	15	17
easily manipulated	52	20	28
emphatic	39	23	39
critical	33	11	56
incredulous	24	30	46
courageous	14	13	73
has ideals	9	29	62

Figure 10.9. Opinions on Finnish journalism. Source: Heinonen (1995).

much with their sources. This problem was related specifically to journalists who cover politics and economic affairs. To some extent the problem stems from the sources' higher level of professionalism (see Luostarinen 1994), but it is exacerbated by the journalists' willingness to be part of the establishment. As one journalist said, "Journalists have become part of the establishment, with the task of offering bread and circus-games to the people." As a consequence, journalists tend to raise themselves above their audience.

The fourth type of problem identified by professional journalists in Finnish journalism has to do with neglecting the rights of the objects of journalism. The criticism here concerned the methods applied by journalists in their job. Typical examples of disliked methods were writing a story without hearing the subject, prying into private affairs, and telling the story of only one side in personal disputes.

General professional sluggishness is perhaps the best description of the fifth type of criticism by Finnish journalists. This does not mean being unprofessional or showing malice, but simply a lack of professional pride, not doing one's very best. In practice this means, for instance, that journalists are content with mechanically repeating the message from their source, without evaluating or checking the information. This is seen to contradict the very mission of journalism: "if important social news are presented to the audience without a proper background, that will leave them with no chance to put things into perspective." Another journalist complained about general "laziness—you cannot justify incompetence by haste."

Finally, Finnish journalists were concerned about the very concept of journalism, that it is being blurred. As we saw earlier, the intense competition in the media field was seen as a threat to the integrity of journalistic values; it was feared that the borderline between journalism and advertising and public relations is fading away. This is not to say that Finnish journalists rejected the commercial face of the media as a whole, but many thought there should be a clear distinction between commercial and journalistic principles.

CONCLUSIONS

Summarizing some of the most important characteristics of the Finnish journalist of the late 1980s and early 1990s, it appears that Finnish journalists were rather typical middle-class urban professionals with a relatively high level of education and income. The profession as a whole is likely to become more heavily dominated by women, but it remains to be seen whether they will succeed in making their way to the upper echelons of the professional hierarchy.

The second conclusion that emerges from our analysis is that perceptions of professional identity were quite strong among Finnish journalists. One part of this professionalism was their close attachment to the journalists' union, which was seen as having an important role to play not only in terms of safeguarding benefits but also in terms of promoting freedom of the press. Finnish journalists also showed a high level of commitment to, and satisfaction with, their jobs. At the same time, however, there was also some discontent with the general performance of journalism, reflecting perhaps a growing concern for the social status of the profession. This concern, and the commitment to maintaining high professional standards, was further evidenced by the fact that the system of self-regulation in journalism is well established among Finnish journalists. However, although the code of conduct and the press council were considered important instruments for the profession, their links to everyday journalistic practice are rather loose. Finally, one may observe that the professional role of the journalist seemed to have two sides in the minds of Finnish journalists—there was the ideal professional journalist of the classic watchdog type with an element of educator, but there was also the mundane working journalist who entered the profession for more individualistic motives.

It may be justified to conclude that journalistic professionalism is not a one-dimensional concept, but rather a cluster of variables that may even contradict one another. Furthermore, the nature and even the meaning of professionalism is subject to change, depending on internal and external factors affecting journalism. For instance, the increase in the number of women journalists may affect prevailing perceptions of how to go about the journalistic profession, and higher education may change the values that underlie journalistic decisions. As part of professional identity, the ethical standards of journalism may also be affected, for instance, heightened media competition may result in slacker journalistic ethics, and as yet it is impossible to know what kinds of effects new information technology will have on the methods of journalism. These changes will in turn have inevitable consequences on the performance of journalism and hence on journalism as a social institution. All this underlines the importance of further research on the development of professionalism in journalism.

REFERENCES

Erämetsä, Harri. 1994. Joukkoviestimien käyttö [Consumption of the mass communication]. In *Joukkoviestintä Suomessa* [Mass communication in Finland], edited by Kaarle Nordenstreng and Osmo A. Wiio, pp. 20-33. Porvoo, Finland: WSOY.

Heinonen, Ari. 1994. *Vahtikoiran omatunto. Journalismin itsesääntely ja toimittajat* [Conscience of a watchdog. Journalists and self-regulation of journalism]. Licentiate's thesis, University of Tampere, Finland.

Heinonen, Ari. 1995. *Vahtikoiran omatunto. Journalismin itsesääntely ja toimittajat* [Conscience of a watchdog. Journalists and self-regulation of journalism]. Tampere, Finland: University of Tampere, Department of Journalism and Mass Communication, Publications, Series A 84/1995.

Hemánus, Pertti. 1983. *Journalistinen vapaus* [Journalistic freedom]. Jyväskylä, Finland: Gaudeamus.

Journalisti. 1993. *Journalisti-lehden lukijatutkimus* [Readership survey of "Journalisti"]. Unpublished report. Suomen Journalistiliitto/Taloustutkimus Oy.

Jyrkiäinen, Jyrki and Eero Savisaari. 1994. Sanomalehdistön nykytila [The newspaper press today]. In *Joukkoviestintä Suomessa* [Mass communication in Finland], edited by Kaarle Nordenstreng and Osmo A. Wiio, pp. 53-59. Porvoo, Finland: WSOY.

Kehälinna, Heikki and Harri Melin. 1988. *Tuntemattomat toimittajat* [Unknown journalists]. Porvoo, Finland: Suomen Sanomalehtimiesten Liitto.

Kivikuru, Ullamaija and Sinikka Sassi. 1994. Aikakauslehdistö [The magazine press]. In *Joukkoviestintä Suomessa* [Mass communication in Finland], edited by Kaarle Nordenstreng and Osmo A. Wiio, pp. 76-91. Porvoo, Finland: WSOY.

Kuusava, Sirkku, Anneli Mäkinen, and Seija Nummijoki. 1993. *Journalismi tasa-arvon tyyssijako?* [Journalism—nest of equality?]. Naistoimittajat ry.

Kuusisto, Olli and Timo Siivonen. 1995. Sanomalehtien tekninen tilasto 1994: Näyttöpäätetaitto ohittamassa perinteisen [Technical statistics 1994 of the Newspapers' Association: On-screen designing superseding traditional methods]. *Suomen Lehdistö* 1: 34-37.

Laitila, Tiina. 1995, June 1. *The journalistic codes of ethics in Europe.* Paper presented at the European Conference of the World Association of Press Councils. Helsinki, Finland.

Löfgren, Monica. 1991. Synen på de yrkesetiska reglerna [Views on professional codes of ethics]. In *Svenska journalister. Ett grupporträtt* [The Swedish journalists. A group portrait], ed. by Lennart Weibull. Stockholm: Tidens Förlag.

Luostarinen, Heikki. 1994. *Mielen kersantit. Julkisuuden hallinta ja journalistiset vastastrategiat* [Sergeants of the mind. Publicity management and journalistic counter-strategies]. Juva, Finland: Hanki ja jää.

Melin, Harri and Jouko Nikula. 1993. *Journalistit epävarmuuden ajassa. Journalistiliiton jäsentutkimus* [Journalists in a time of uncertainty. Organizational survey of the Union of Journalists]. Forssa, Finland: Suomen Journalistiliitto.

Nordenstreng, Kaarle. 1994. The press: A lot but alike. *Intermedia* 3:17-19.

Sauri, Tuomo. 1994. Joukkoviestinnän talous [The economy of the mass communication]. In *Joukkoviestintä Suomessa* [Mass communication in Finland], edited by Kaarle Nordenstreng and Osmo A. Wiio, pp. 190-203. Porvoo, Finland: WSOY.

Tommila, Päiviö. 1994. Suomen sanomalehdistö 1700-luvulta nykypäivään [The Finnish newspaper press from the 16th century to the present day]. In *Joukkoviestintä Suomessa* [Mass communication in Finland], edited by Kaarle Nordenstreng and Osmo A. Wiio, pp.35-52. Porvoo, Finland: WSOY.

Weibull, Lennart. 1991. *Svenska journalister. Ett grupporträtt* [The Swedish journliast. A group portrait]. Stockholm: Tidens Förlag.

White, Robert A. 1989. Social and political factors in the development of communication ethics. In *Communication ethics and global change*, ed. by Thomas W. Cooper with Clifford Christians, Frances Forde Plude, and Robert A. White, pp. 40-65. New York: Longman.

11

The French Journalist

Aralynn Abare McMane
World Association of Newspapers, FIEJ

French journalists of the late 20th century work in an environment of both advantage and limitation that has emerged from a long, rich history (Albert and Terrou 1985). Legally, journalists are protected by a century-old defamation law that puts most of the liability for misdeeds on the director of the news organization. However, other parts of the law continue to leave French journalists unable to legally reveal information that has been routinely reported in many other Western countries, such as background about a person from more than a decade beforehand.

They remain protected ethically by a 1935 "clause of conscience" in the national work code that allows them to leave, with substantial severance pay, a news organization that greatly changes its politics. However, some ethical stances continue to clash with legal realities. For example, an admonition from the national journalist union's 1918 ethical code to maintain the confidentiality of a news source has remained unprotected by law. Economically, French journalists have enjoyed a substantial income tax exemption offered to just a few other categories of workers and have minimum wages, even for freelancers, set under national and regional agreements. However, as elsewhere in Western

Europe, the overall economy of news work has shifted with newspapers, by far the largest employer of journalists, declining in number and losing an increasingly large share of advertising revenues to television.

Television is but one factor that has put French journalists into a setting that mixes tradition with accelerating change. As early as the 18th century, France developed a literary press of opinion in Paris, along with a less interpretive, more information-giving press that thrived later in its regions. The two traditions did cross paths, notably when the Paris press produced mass-circulation newspapers in the late 19th century, but the distinction remained largely intact even as late as the early 1970s when the very opinionated new paper *Liberation* emerged from the student protest movement to become a notable part of Paris newspapers. Soon thereafter, the Paris press lost its circulation dominance, and a regional daily in Rennes, *Ouest France*, took the lead starting in 1976. By the mid-1990s, the role of opinion in the Paris press had become less clear. The next new Paris daily that lasted more than a few months, *Infomatin*, made it a point to tout itself as providing "information and only information" and then increased its commentary and then died. Even the elite and highly interpretive paper *Le Monde* promised potential readers in a 1995 marketing brochure that its own redesign would include a separation and labeling of opinions, although the reality presented far more of a mix of the two.

Television news sectors also saw considerable change in the early 1980s as the privatization movement brought new opportunities and competition. News directors of the state's monopoly broadcast system had routinely held or lost their jobs depending on the desires of the government in power. With the sale of one of the state-run television channels, TF1, in 1987, a new era began of market dependence and debates about newscasters as highly paid, ratings-getting stars. By the 1990s, France had become the home for two all-news stations: the joint European venture Euronews and LCI, and the cable offshoot of the private TF1 channel.

Debates about the proper training and role of the journalist also have a long history in France. For example, one 17th-century observer not only objected to the fact that it was a doctor who was running the country's first successful paper but also found his journalistic values wanting. "I admit that your newspapers make you resemble a newspaperman," the critic wrote, "that is, a writer of stories as likely to be false as true" (Bellanger, Godechot, Guiral, and Terrou 1976:95). Arguments about the possibility that news work might be a profession date at least from the late 1800s, when anti-semitism and other excesses in the coverage of the treason court martial of Alfred Dreyfus prompted some Paris journalists to found the country's first journalism school. Eventually, the commission that awarded journalists cards (described later) "recognized" five, then seven, journalism schools, whose reputations were based on producing a highly controlled number of graduates—about 300 nationally per year by the 1980s—who had been "professionally" trained.

Continuing education became a fixture when those who had run the Resistance press of World War II set up a training center in 1946 to learn about the new values and skills needed to run a commercial newspaper. At *Le Monde*, established in 1945, journalists created a "Societé des Rédacteurs" ("Society of Journalists"), arguing that they had a moral right to safeguard the professional values of the newspaper by participating in its management. These groups prompted one of the earliest of modern qualitative studies of journalists.

By 1970, about 20% of French journalists had joined one of 33 such groups, producing enough anxiety to prompt a government commission on "problems posed by journalist societies." The commission argued against codifying the groups, and conflicts with national unions helped speed the decline of the movement, but the study was one of the earliest to examine closely the values and role of journalists (Lindon Commission 1970). A few years later, Freiberg (1981) also studied the associations of journalists as part of his qualitative inquiry into the continuing failed efforts of highly idealistic postwar journalists to rule a commercial press.

Meanwhile, French researchers had begun regular charting of the demographic profile of all holders of French journalists' cards, a broad population that included people in full-time newswork as well as others in related jobs (Centre d'Etudes et de Recherches sur les Qualifications 1974; Commission de la Carte d'Identité des Journalistes Professionels 1967, 1986 and 1995; Institut Français de la Presse 1991).

The 1980s saw several important qualitative studies of journalists. For his examination of journalists who produced the "elite" French news media, Rieffel (1984) interviewed 120 journalists at two national television channels, two major radio stations, three Paris dailies, and four news magazines. He concluded that his interviewees tended to support three roles for journalists: an explainer, an organizer of facts, and a teacher.

Voyenne (1985) provided a thorough, largely historical portrait of the changes in the working situation of French journalists. Padioleau (1985) offered a highly detailed comparison of journalists at *The Washington Post* and *Le Monde* and found that journalists in both places shared a strong sense of their newpaper's social and political mission, but that practices differed and notions of professional role at the Post were more clearly expressed and codified than at Le Monde. Balle (1987) used a historical perspective for most of his analysis and relied heavily on comparisons with the United States. He argued that the role of the journalist in France was limited by both an inability to breach highly suspicious public and private institutions and by the limited financing and audience of newspapers.

More recently, Charon (1993) argued that although they were more numerous and better trained, French news people had lost prestige and political clout and had also seen the conception of their role as key elements in the democratic process weaken. He argued that two less critical alternative roles were emerging with the journalist acting as the connector between a market society and its isolated consumers, or as a connector among individuals with common interests. He saw neither alternative as preferable to the classic role and called on journalists to engage in a thorough reexamination in search of a new unity and legitimacy for the profession.

METHODS

The goal of the author's study was to provide a systematic empirical analysis of a nationwide sample that allowed cross-country comparisons on both demographics and values of full-time news people. Such a study required a narrower definition of *journalist* than the one generally used by the French. Thus, the population of journalists for the author's study was 11,652 full-time French news people who fit the definition used in previous studies in other countries. That population of news people represented a subset of the 23,227 holders of journalists' cards, all of whom France considered to be "professional journalists." A commission representing journalists and publishers has been in charge of distributing the card and has given it annually to workers who earned at least minimum wage from journalistic activities. This included people who worked for print and broadcast news outlets, the specialized press (magazines other than news magazines), photographers, freelancers, part-time and unemployed journalists, and people who took dictated stories over the phone or who input a reporter's handwritten story into a computer.

This research replicated methods used in two previous U.S. studies (Johnstone, Slawski, and Bowman 1976; Weaver and Wilhoit 1986) by concentrating on full-time news people, that is, journalists at newspapers, news magazines, wire services, and broadcast news outlets. Most questions had been asked in the U.S. studies and in previous studies in Great Britain and what was then West Germany (Donsbach 1981; Köcher 1986).

At the time of the study, nearly half the 11,652 full-time news people in France worked for daily newspapers outside Paris, with broadcast ranking second, followed by Paris dailies, wire services and news magazines. The French journalists were selected through a two-step skip sampling procedure that called for random selection of 55 news organizations, then random selection of journalists within those organizations. Proportions of journalists in the sample working for each kind of organization closely matched statistics about card holders, with print journalists slightly overrepresented (five percentage points). During the spring of 1988, respondents in the sample completed a mailed or hand-delivered questionnaire that contained 72 questions. Starting early in the study, each respondent received a cookie to snack on while they did their work. A total of 484 usable surveys were completed, yielding a response rate of 70% (McMane 1989b). In this analysis the term *journalist* refers to full-time news people who participated in the survey.

BASIC CHARACTERISTICS

Age and Gender

The journalists had a mean age of 39.8 (median of 40), which closely matched the French labor force mean of 39. However, younger age groups were slightly underrepresented among journalists, with 31% of the sample aged 35 or under compared to 41% of the civilian workforce. With a mean age of 41 (median 39), male journalists tended to be older than their female colleagues, whose mean age was 37 (median 35).

Women made up 20% of the journalists. Although the proportion was lower than among full-time French workers (32% women), it reflected the situation among other white-collar workers (INSEE 1988). The proportion of women was the highest at newsmagazines (29%) and wire services (28%) and lowest in daily newspapers (16%). At the broadcast outlets, 24% of the journalists were women.

Background

The journalists in the study were more likely than the French labor force as a whole to come from a white-collar background. They were just as likely as workers in general to come from an artisan shopkeeper background, but far less likely to come from a family of laborers or farmers. The rate of occupational succession among the journalists, that is, the degree to which they followed in their parents' footsteps, was 6.5%, about the same as for teachers (5.5%).

Overall, 58% of the journalists were married with a substantial difference based on gender. Among the French population in general for the year of the study, 49% of men were married compared to 46% of women. Among the respondents, 63% of newsmen were married compared to 37% of newswomen.

Political Attitudes

Politics plays a large role in French society, and respondents answered two kinds of questions that addressed political views. First, they placed themselves and the editorial policies of their news organizations on a scale that ran from 0 (signifying extreme left) to 100 (signifying extreme right). Later, they were asked to fill in a label for their political tendency. As had been the case in previous studies of U.S., West German, and British journalists, on the numerical scale French journalists tended to place themselves both left of center (median 40) and to the left of their organization (which they put at median 51). Nearly two thirds of the French journalists placed themselves lower than 50. About 20% placed themselves at 50, and 15% placed themselves higher than 50.

Respondents were much less willing to give themselves a label. Although 10% of them declined to place themselves on a numerical scale, almost triple that number, 28.5%, left the political label blank. Journalists who were willing to answer were most likely to categorize themselves as "left" or "socialist," with these labels accounting for 53% of those who answered the question. Some variation of "center" accounted for 25%, "right" attracted 9.4%, and "apolitical" accounted for 12%.

Although exact comparisons with the French population were unavailable, a study done a few months before journalists were polled (Jeambar 1987), indicating that journalists and their audience were similarly reluctant to give themselves a label, and that journalists were less willing than the public to categorize themselves as of the right. That survey found 30% of the French adults unwilling to categorize themselves at all, with 55.4% of those willing to do so labeling themselves as on the left politically and 44.6% on the right. Center was not an option. Among the journalists who chose any version of the two possible options, 82.6% placed themselves on the left, with 17.4% on the right.

EDUCATION AND TRAINING OF JOURNALISTS

Among the journalists, 62% had a university degree, compared to 54% of all French white-collar workers. There was a small correlation between age and education, with younger journalists exhibiting a slight tendency to be more educated than their elders ($r = .17$, $p < .001$).

Gender and education showed a stronger correlation ($r = .35$, $p < .001$), indicating that female journalists tended to be more educated than males. Both tendencies were repeated in the French white-collar population (INSEE 1988).

Although only 15.5% of journalists in the study had diplomas in journalism, more than twice that number, 32%, had done some journalism study. Women were slightly more likely than men to have studied journalism, but not more likely to have a journalism degree. This portrait could soon change as the 1980s saw women for the first time gain parity, and even numerical dominance, at leading journalism schools.

In the study, four fifths of the respondents said they wanted to participate in continuing education. They most frequently mentioned journalistic topics (35%) followed by language (14.4%). Two fifths of the sample had participated in continuing education, with more than half of those people studying journalistic topics. Among journalistic topics, electronic editing—pagination and editing with a video display terminal—was mentioned most frequently (12% of those who mentioned a topic), with videotext journalism second with 11%.

For journalists and most other workers in France, continuing education became routine after 1971, when all workers got the legal right to continuing education paid by their employer. However, financing was limited, and although workers could request a topic of study, they ultimately had to abide by the employer's preference.

Working Conditions

Satisfaction. Eighty-five percent of the journalists said they were either somewhat satisfied (72%) or very satisfied (15%) with their jobs. Nine percent were somewhat dissatisfied, with 0.4% very dissatisfied and 3.5% undecided. As for the future, 77.5% of respondents expected to still be in journalism in five years, with 5% expecting to leave and 17.5% undecided.

Perceived autonomy. Respondents were asked to assess the importance of eight job factors that ranged from the material (such as salary and fringe benefits) to the less tangible (such as the political tendency of the organization and level of personal autonomy). The journalists' perceptions of their own level of independence were examined in another portion of the questionnaire that allowed comparison with a sample of the French population.

The notion of journalistic independence and personal autonomy has clearly been a revered ideal in France for a very long time. For example, the first successful editor, Theophrast Renaudot, produced his paper under the close scrutiny of the monarchy, but still declared in his first issue in 1632 that he would yield to no one in his search for the truth (Bailly 1987).

Thus, it is not surprising that among the eight job factor statements proposed, the two that addressed personal autonomy drew by far the highest support among French respondents (Table 11.1). However, while respondents were clearly strongly in favor of the ideal of journalistic autonomy, they were far less certain that journalists were actually independent. The journalists were asked to reply to a question that also had been asked of the French public a few months previously. The question asked if respondents believed that journalists were "independent," which was defined as resisting pressures of political parties, the powerful, or of money (Jaffré and Missika 1988; Missika 1989). The French public had become more pessimistic over time. In 1975, when the question was initially asked, 48% of the public sample saw journalists as succumbing to these pressures. The proportion rose to 58% in 1985 and to 63% in late 1987. Among journalists in early 1988, just over 33% agreed that journalists succumbed to such pressures, and only slightly more, 37%, saw journalists as resisting them. Another 29% were undecided. This mixed message could, in part, reflect a dislike among journalists for combining the notions of money, politics, and the powerful generally into one question. However, although they were clearly more divided than the public, journalists were also clearly less pessimistic than the public about this element of their autonomy.

Table 11.1. Job Aspects: Percentages of Those Saying "Very Important."

Freedom from supervision	84.8
Amount of personal autonomy	73.7
The chance to help people	37.5
The chance to get ahead in the organization	24.5
The editorial policies of the organization	24.1
The chance to develop a specialty	22.7
Job security	20.5
The pay	15.7
Fringe benefits	8.9
NUMBER OF RESPONDENTS	484

Gender influences. The female journalists in the survey were as likely as their male colleagues to note that they did reporting or editing "regularly," but males were far more likely, by nearly 3 to 1, to report that they "regularly" had influence in hiring and firing. The percentage of women who "sometimes or regularly" had some influence on hiring and firing was 12.4%, compared to 25.3% of the men.

French women also tended not to hold top jobs in French media organizations, according to a separate survey conducted by the journalists card commission (Commission de la Carte d'Identité des Journalistes Professionels 1995). The commission found that roughly 1 in 10 of directors at media operations in 1994 was a women (12%).

Although women were underrepresented at the top, other figures from that same demographic study of all holders of journalists cards indicated that women remained overrepresented in the margins and at the bottom of French journalism—those precarious and low-paying jobs. Women represented just under 37% of all card holders but a full 48% of all freelancers. An equally disturbing figure concerned women who had lost or left their journalism jobs. In 1994, nearly 45% of unemployed card holders were women.

Professionalism

Memberships and readership. Thirty-seven percent of respondents belonged to a union. French workers in general have been less unionized than other Western Europeans, although the general level of unionism in France had progressed until 1975. By the time of the study, fewer than 20% of all French workers were unionized (Mermet 1988). Although union membership had declined among journalists as well, the unions themselves continued to play a strong role in shaping the working conditions of all journalists. The French journalists' card commission was elected from slates of candidates provided by unions of journalists and of publishers. In addition, the national and regional contracts that set salary and vacation minimums were negotiated only between unions of owners and of journalists, but they applied to all journalists.

Twenty-three percent of respondents read at least one of the half dozen professional journalistic periodicals available. Such periodicals included a very expensive daily briefing about the day's press conferences and top media events, weekly trade magazines, and a scholarly journal.

Views on professional roles. French journalists professed a mix of journalistic roles that highlighted the increasing uncertainty in France over the role of interpretation and that did not often neatly fit patterns first established in U.S. research.

Respondents were asked to judge the importance of nine journalistic roles: "things the news media do or try to do today." In the 1982-83 Weaver and Wilhoit U.S. study (1986), 10 statements clustered together statistically to produce "disseminator values," "interpretive values," and "adversary values" (Table 11.2).

The two statements that had clustered together as disseminator values brought varied support from the French journalists. More than two thirds saw as "extremely important" the idea of speedy delivery of information to the public. However, the other statement in that cluster, concentrating on the widest possible audience, found strong support from only 8% of respondents.

Three statements that clustered together in the U.S. study as interpretive values received consistently low support, with 40% of French respondents considering as extremely important both the notions of "providing analysis and interpretation of complex problems" and of "investigating government claims." Only 30% of the French journalists gave strong support to the idea of a discussion of national policy.

The French survey included only one of the statements that loaded onto the U.S. adversarial values factor: the statement about being an adversary of public officials. Seventeen percent of respondents deemed this role "extremely important." There were no significant differences based on region.

The low support for the interpretive statements seems to be in harmony with a point of view that Rieffel (1984) found among journalists from leading news organizations. He reported that most were against the label of "commentator" and noted that it seemed as if the journalists felt that "the excessive growth of editorializing, of comment, was a defect that must be fought."

Additional analysis of findings also support a conjecture by Balle (1987: 99) that "by the force of ideas, [French] journalists continue to have an irresistible fascination for commentary and partisan interpretation, even as they more and more evoke the greatness of and reliance on American-style reporting."

Evidence supporting part of his conjecture arises from a limited but useful cross-cultural comparison of the newspaper journalists in the sample with a 1988 sample of newspaper journalists in the United States (Table 11.3). Even more so than for the overall sample, the French newspaper journalists expressed greater or equal support than the U.S. journalists for the statements that clustered in the U.S. sample as disseminator values.

However, there was no significant difference between the groups in the two countries on the one adversarial value included in both studies, and the French newspaper people were less likely than their U.S. counterparts to support the interpretive values or the notion of investigating government claims.

Table 11.2. Professional Values: Percentage of French Journalists Who See Media Roles as "Extremely Important" and Factor Loadings (>.200) on Nine Media Roles for Journalists in France (1988) and the U.S. (1982-83).

	"Extremely Important" (%)	French factor 1	French factor 2	French factor 3	French factor 4	U.S. factor 1	U.S. factor 2	U.S. factor 3
Get information to the public quickly.	69	—	.229	—	.813	—	.600	—
Provide analysis and interpretation of complex problems.	40	.224	—	.684	—	.652	—	—
Provide entertainment and relaxation.	8	—	.748	—	—	—	.688	—
Investigate claims and statements made by government.	40	.270	—	.486	.570	.641	—	—
Stay away from stories where content cannot be verified.	73	—	.349	.644	—	—	—	.924
Concentrate on news of interest to the widest possible audience.	28	—	.749	—	—	.301	.607	.287
Discuss national policy while it is still being developed.	30	.667	—	.313	—	.687	—	—
Develop cultural and intellectual interests of the public.	29	.751	—	—	—	.385	.469	—
Be an adversary of public officials by being constantly skeptical of their actions.	17	.706	—	.251	.335	.625	—	—
EIGENVALUES		2.021	.391	.061	.102	.101	.371	.01

Note: Number of French respondents = 484; number of U.S. respondents = 1,001

Table 11.3. Professional Values: Percentage of French and American Newspaper Journalists Who See News Media Roles as "Extremely Important" (1988).

	French Newspaper Sample (N = 310)	U.S. Newspaper Sample (N = 1,209)
Get information to the public quickly	69	66
Provide analysis and interpretation of complex problems	43	67
Provide entertainment and relaxation	8	19
Investigate claims and statements made by government	35	67
Stay away from stories where content cannot be verified	71	42
Concentrate on news of interest to the widest possible audience	29	18
Discuss national policy while it is still being developed	31	43
Develop cultural and intellectual interests of the public	28	—
Be an adversary of public officials by being constantly skeptical of their actions	14	20

The relative lack of support for investigation among the French newspaper people fits what appears to be an ambivalent attitude on the matter. Except for the regular efforts of the satirical weekly, *Le Canard Enchaîné*, investigation of government claims seems to remain a low priority among journalists in France, whether in or outside the capital. The *Canard* is hailed, but there appears to be little interest in copying it. For example, a two-part documentary on the paper consistently filled a Left Bank movie theater for several months, but when one of the paper's top investigative reporters offered a course in Paris at the Centre de Perfectionnement des Journalists training center on how to do investigative reporting, no one came.

Because one of the statements from the 1982-83 U.S. study was not included in the French survey (being an adversary of business), a new factor analysis was done on both sets of data using the nine statements included in both studies. The new analysis yielded different groupings for each country's sample. The U.S. data yielded three groupings with the one adversary of government role included in both studies loading onto a factor with the three interpretive roles. Quick information delivery and entertaining/relaxing the public created a second factor, and staying away from stories where facts could not be verified created a third factor. Among the French, the roles created four factors. However, six of the nine roles failed to load clearly onto only one factor. For example, the adversarial role loaded fairly strongly on a factor with discussion of national policy, but it also loaded with roles on two other factors (Table 11.2). The results support the idea that although two different cultures may each have a mix of role ideals, the nature of that mix can differ greatly.

Hypothetical situation. In an attempt to move from the ideal of abstract role statements toward the reality of the behavior of journalists, the previous studies in the United States, Britain, and what was then West Germany included hypothetical situations that called on journalists to choose from scenarios that described options for course of action. Although all the situations were simplistic, thus lacking in the nuances that would help a journalist decide on a course of action in a real setting, one situation produced large differences between British and German journalists in 1980 and was also used in the 1982-1983 U.S. study. In that hypothetical situation, respondents had been asked to agree with two approaches to covering the annual meeting of a political organization that had a "dangerous" policy. The approaches had called for "simply reporting the discussion and decisions" or "selecting and emphasizing the dangerous aspects." British journalists had highly supported the approach that called for straight reporting, West German journalists had leaned toward the warning approach, and U.S. journalists yielded a split response. Both the German and U.S. studies yielded more than 10% "undecided" responses.

Presented with the same situation, the French, too, were nearly evenly split, with 43% supporting the straight report and 47% supporting the warning. Ten percent of respondents were undecided. Anecdotal evidence from France suggests that the two approaches may not be mutually exclusive there, and that self-analysis of what is a "simple report" may be debatable. For example, for many observers in 1988, an existing political party fit the profile of a "dangerous" party: the xenophobic National Front of the presidential candidate Jean-Marie Le Pen. A political writer for a regional paper who had written about a Le Pen rally in Paris said his article was an example of straight reporting without commentary. The article ended with: "How many answered the call of Le Pen [to come to the Paris rally]? Certainly too many" (La Dépeche du Midi 1988).

Ethical standards. French journalists have dealt with ethical standards in a formal way for more than a half century. France's first journalism union, the Syndicat National des Journalistes, created an ethical code in 1918 that called on journalists to, among other things, refrain from seeking the position of a colleague such as by offering to work for less. The code also told journalists to keep professional secrets and to refrain from posing as someone else. The code retained those elements when it was revised in 1938, but lost bans on promoting "games of money" and on accepting appointments or gratifications that might present a conflict of interest. The later version also eliminated a threat of sanction by a union disciplinary council (Syndicat Nationale des Journalistes 1918; Friedman 1988).

The respondents were asked to describe the level of support they would give to eight controversial reporting practices. Seven statements, which had originated in U.S. studies and also been used in British and German studies, asked journalists to indicate whether each practice "may be justified" for an "important story" or whether it "would never be justified" (McMane 1989b). An additional question addressed passive deception. Consensus on the practices varied widely (Table 11.4).

Table 11.4. Standards of Reporting Practice: A Comparison of French Journalists and U.S. Newspaper Journalists.

	France ALL (%)	France Newspaper (%)	U.S. Newspaper (%)
Paying people for confidential information			
May be justified	36	32	17
Would never approve	49	54	72
Undecided	15	14	11
Using confidential business or government documents without authorization			
May be justified	69	68	69
Would never approve	20	18	22
Undecided	12	14	9
Claiming to be somebody else			
May be justified	40	39	1
Would never approve	48	47	70
Undecided	12	14	9

Table 11.4. Standards of Reporting Practice: A Comparison of French Journalists and U.S. Newspaper Journalists (con't.).

	France ALL (%)	France Newspaper (%)	U.S. Newspaper (%)
Just hiding your identity as a journalist			
May be justified	70	—	68
Would never approve	19	—	20
Undecided	12	—	12
Agreeing to protect confidentiality and not doing so			
May be justified	4	3	3
Would never approve	94	94	95
Undecided	2	3	2
Badgering unwilling informants to get a story			
May be justified	82	85	75
Would never approve	10	8	18
Undecided	8	7	6
Making use of personal documents such as letters and photographs without permission			
May be justified	12	13	34
Would never approve	73	71	51
Undecided	16	16	25
Getting employed in a firm or organization to gain inside information			
May be justified	56	56	63
Would never approve	25	25	24
Undecided	20	19	13
NUMBER OF RESPONDENTS	484	310	1206

As in the other countries that had been studied earlier, strongest agreement emerged on the question of breaking a promise to a source of confidentiality. In France, as elsewhere, fewer than 1 of 10 journalists said such a move could be justified. The other practice they most opposed was the use of personal documents or photographs, with fewer than 2 in 10 supporting the practice. Such disapproval fits traditional respect in France for the privacy of even the most notorious. For example, French law prohibits the publication of personal information dating from an "amnestied" period, such as the Nazi occupation during World War II.

Respondents gave highest support to the controversial practice of badgering an unwilling informant—82% said that might be justified for an important story. This finding was somewhat surprising in light of a tradition of deference toward sources. For example, one of France's top political journalists, Anne Sinclair, said she was an exception when it came to television's treatment of politicians because she tried to emulate U.S. journalists by diminishing the reverence she as a French journalist would naturally have toward such a source (Blume 1988). The finding also highlights the limitations of straight replication across cultures because the term *badgering* may indeed conjure up very different mental pictures. For example, although an extreme case of "badgering" in the experience of the French journalists may very likely recall a civilized but heated discussion with a source who agreed to be questioned, the extreme in the United States also includes a street chase or frontyard siege of an unwilling target by a flock of reporters.

Three other practices attracted support from more than half the sample—not revealing one's identity as a journalist, using confidential business or government documents without authorization, and getting employed to obtain inside information. The practices have continued to be used in France. The satirical weekly paper, *Le Canard Enchaîné*, often bases its stories on confidential government documents, with the mainstream press then using that paper as the source. A leading investigative reporter, Anne Tristain, first made her name in an investigation of the ultra-right National Front when she got a job as a secretary in the political party's office.

The statement that dealt with the passive form of hidden identity, which involved simply not saying one was a journalist, was added to remove the impersonation element from the single question in the original set that asked both about the justifiability of hiding one's identity and about posing as someone else. That original statement attracted support from 40% of the French journalists. When active impersonation—posing as someone else—was eliminated, the percentage supporting the practice rose to 70%.

Impact on public opinion. The French journalists assessed the news media's real and ideal levels of influence over public opinion using scales of 0 (signifying no influence) to 100 (very great influence). The mean for actual influence was 58.8, with the ideal at 47.1, indicating that French journalists believed media influence on public opinion was somewhat higher than it should be. This echoes earlier findings from Britain and the United States. The French have been particularly sensitive to this point during political campaigns when results of public opinion polls about candidates cannot be revealed after a certain date for fear that the outcome could be influenced.

CONCLUSIONS

This study indicates that French journalists who worked full time for news operations in 1988 tended to be predominantly male, with women overrepresented in younger age groups and underrepresented in management. They tended to be married if male and single if female. They were more likely than the French labor force in general to have college educations, to come from a white-collar background, and be members of a union. They tended to see themselves as slightly left of center and their organizations slightly right of center. They highly valued independence in their jobs but were not sure as a group that they were free from outside pressures. Most were satisfied with their work and expected to remain in journalism. They represented a mix of views on both professional roles and ethical standards and showed indications that they shared some beliefs with their colleagues in the United States, former West Germany, and Great Britain.

The findings of this study also suggest several areas for further research in France and elsewhere. The fundamental value of using questions that have been asked before is clear: We can compare people over time and place. Thus, it could be useful to ask these questions again of French journalists and to see how they have changed, or not, over time. Furthermore, in France and elsewhere researchers could enrich the portrait of the journalist by adding audience attitudinal data. Demographic data have begun to allow sorting out how journalists really differ or match their audiences, as well as each other, in basic characteristics. By asking a sample of citizens from each country the same questions posed of journalists, researchers could begin to gauge the difference between phenomena that apply only to journalists within or across cultures and those that permeate one or more cultures. For example, one of the most consistent findings across time and distance in Western industrialized democracies is that more than 9 out of 10 journalists think they should keep a promise of source confidentiality. However, we lack the data to sort out whether this is a journalistic attitude or a general part of the social code in those cultures that makes breaking such a promise unacceptable. Finally, because some attitudinal questions are culture-bound, it may be useful for researchers from several countries to try to formulate together a battery of basic questions and scenarios that have the same meaning in each place.

REFERENCES

Albert, Pierre and Fernand Terrou. 1985. *Histoire de la presse* [History of the press], 4th ed. Paris: Presses Universitaires de France.
American Society of Newspaper Editors (ASNE). 1989. *The changing face of the newsroom: A human resources report.* Reston, VA: Author.
Ardaugh, John. 1982. *France in the 1980s.* Harmondsworth, England: Penguin.
Arnould, Valerie. 1989, July 13. Existe-t-il encore un presse d'opinion en France? [Is there still a press of opinion in France?] *L'Echo de la Presse et de la Publicité*, 36.
Bailly, Christian. 1987. *Théophrast Renaudot.* Paris: Le Pré aux Clercs.
Balle, Francis. 1984, 1990. *Médias et société* [Media and society]. Paris: Presses Universitaires de France.
Balle, Francis. 1987. *Et si la presse n'existait pas* [And if the press never existed]. Paris: J.C. Lattés.
Balzac, Honoré. 1847, August 28. La Revue Parisienne [Paris review]. Quoted in Jean Daniel. *Le Quatriéme Pouvoir. Le Nouvel Observateur*, p. 22.
Bellanger, Claude, Jacques Godechot, Pierre Guiral, and Fernand Terrou, eds. 1976. *Histoire générale de la presse Française* [A general history of the French press]. Paris: Presses Universitaire de France.
Belot, Anne. 1988. *Le journal* [The newspaper]. Paris: Hachette.
Blume, Mary. 1988, March 14. The rising star of Anne Sinclair. *International Herald Tribune*, p. 20.
Bohére. G. 1984. *Profession journalist: A study on the working conditions of journalists.* Geneva: International Labour Office.
Bourdois, Jacques-Henri and Francis Balle. 1987, May 15. Les médias ont-ils les pleins pouvoirs? [Do the media have absolute power?] *L'Express*, pp. 100-112.
Caviglioli, François. 1989, May 18. Les nufragés de l'Iranglobe [The dustclouds of Iranglobe]. *Le Nouvel Observateur*, pp. 64-65.
Cazenave, François. 1995. *Les journalistes* [The journalists]. Paris: Hachette.
Centre d'Etudes et de Recherches sur les Qualifications. 1974. *Les Journalistes: Etude statistique et sociologique sur la profession* [Journalists: A sociological and statistical study of the profession]. Paris: La Documentation Française.
Charon, Jean-Marie. 1993. *Cartes de Presse: Enquête sur les Journalistes* [Press cards: A study of journalists]. Paris: Stock.
Comarin, Elio. 1989. L'Europe et ses journalistes [Europe and its journalists]. *Médiaspouvoirs* 13: 109-113.

Commission de la Carte d'Identité des Journalistes Professionels. 1967. *Enquête statistique et sociologique* [A statistical and sociological study]. Paris: Commission de la Carte d'Identité des Journalistes Professionels.

Commission de la Carte d'Identité des Journalistes Professionels. 1986. *50 ans de la carte professionnelle: Profil de la profession, enquête socioprofessionnelle* [Fifty years of the professional card: Profile of a profession and socioprofessional inquiry]. Paris: Commission de la Carte d'Identité des Journalistes Professionels.

Commission de la Carte d'Identité des Journalistes Professionels. 1995. *Chiffres de 1994* [Figures for 1995]. Paris: Commission de la Carte d'Identité des Journalistes Professionels.

Conseil, Odile. 1987. *Les métiers du journalisme* [Careers in journalism]. Paris: L'Etudiant/Bordas.

La Dépeche du Midi. 1988. Article describing Paris rally of Jean-Marie Le Pen, p. SP3.

Derieux, Emmanuel. 1975, May. La diffamation: Les limites de ce qu'il est permis de rendre public [Defamation: The limits on what can be made public]. *Press Actualité*, pp. 17-19.

Dobbs, Michael. 1986, June 3. French TV braced for another "reform." *International Herald Tribune*, p. 2.

Donsbach, Wolfgang. 1981. Legitimacy through competence rather than value judgments. *Gazette* 27: 47-67.

Eisenrath, Charles R. 1982. Press freedom in France: Private ownership and state controls. In *Press control around the world*, edited by Jane Leftwich Curry and Joan R. Dassin, pp. 62-84. New York: Praeger.

Escarpit, Robert. 1978. *Les reportages de Rouletabosse* [The reports of Rouletabosse]. Paris: Magnard Livre de Poche Jeunesse.

Freiberg, J.W. 1981. *The French press: Class, state and ideology.* Eastbourn, England: Holt-Sanders.

Friedman, Michel. 1988. *Libertés et responsabilités des journalistes et des auteurs* [The rights and responsibilities of journalists and authors]. Paris: Editions CFPJ.

Guery, Louis. 1987. *Le Quotidien Régional: Mon Journal* [The Regional Daily: My newspaper]. Paris: CFPJ/ARPEJ.

Guillaume, Yves. 1988. *La presse en France* [The press in France]. Paris: Editions de la Découverte.

Hazera, Jean-Claude. 1989. Projet d'une nouvelle charte pour les journalistes. *Médiaspouvoirs* 13: 128-132.

Hebarre, Jean-Louis. 1970. *Protection de la vie privée et la déontologie des journalistes* [Protection of private life and the ethics of journalists]. Paris: Institut International de la Presse.

Institut Français de Presse. 1991. *Les journalistes Francais en 1990: Radiographie d'une profession* [French journalists in 1990: X-ray of a profession]. Paris: La Documentation Française.

Institut National de la Statistique et des Etudes Economiques (INSEE). 1988, October. *Enquête sur l'emploi* [A study of employment]. No. D-128. Paris: INSEE.

Jaffré, Jerôme and Jean-Marie Missika. 1988. Les Français et leurs médias: Crise de confiance [The French and their media: A crisis in confidence]. *Mediaspouvoirs* 9: 5-15.

Jeambar, Denis. 1987, November 9. Le refus du clivage droite-gauche [The refusal of a left-right split]. *Le Point*, pp. 80-81.

Johnstone, John W.C., Edward J. Slawski, and William Bowman. 1976. *The news people: A sociological portrait of American journalists and their work*. Urbana: University of Illinois Press.

Jones, Clement. 1981. *Déontologie de l'information. Codes et conseils de presse. Etude comparative des regles de la morale pratique dans les métiers de l'information à travers le monde* [Ethics and information: Codes and guidelines of the press. A comparative study of the rules of moral practice in the information occupations throughout the world]. Paris: Editions de l'Unesco.

Köcher, Renate. 1986. Bloodhounds or missionaries: The role definitions of German and British journalists. *European Journal of Communication* 1: 43-64.

Lavoinne, Yves. 1988. *Journalistes et médiateurs* [Journalists and mediators]. Paper presented at colloquium on continuity and change in French journalism since the 1950s, University of Paris (IX), Nanterre, France.

Lindon Commission. 1970. *Rapport sur les problémes posés par les sociétés de rédacteurs* [Report on the problems posed by societies of reporters]. Paris: La Documentation Française.

Markham, James M. 1988, September 24. Can leftist pull French daily to center? *International Herald Tribune*, p. 2.

Martin-Lagardette, Jean-Luc. 1987. Informer, Convaincre: *Les secrets de l'écriture journalistique* [Inform, convince: The secrets of journalistic writing]. Paris: Syros.

Marzolf, Marion T. 1984. American "new journalism" takes root in Europe at the end of the 19th century. *Journalism Quarterly* 61: 529-535, 691.

Mathien, Michel. 1989. L'influence américaine sur la presse quotidenne régionale? [An American influence on the daily regional press?] In *Les médias Américains en France: Influence et pénétration*, edited by Jean-Claude Bertrand and Francis Bordat, pp. 42-48.

Mathien, Michel. 1992. *Les journalistes Français et le systéme médiathique* [French journalists and the media system]. Paris: Hachette.

Mathien, Michel. 1995. *Les journalistes* [French journalists]. Paris: Presses Universitaires de France.
McMane, Aralynn Abare. 1989a. *Les journalistes français et le perfectionnement* [French journalists and continuing education]. Advisory research report for the Centre de Perfectionnement des Journalistes, Paris. Described in La Lettre CPJ: Rue du Louvre, February.
McMane, Aralynn Abare. 1989b. *An empirical analysis of French journalists in comparison with journalists in Britain, West Germany and the United States*. Doctoral dissertation, School of Journalism, Indiana University, Bloomington, Indiana.
McMane, Aralynn Abare. 1992a. *Journalism and gender in France*. Paper presented at the annual meeting of Association for Education in Journalism and Mass Communication, Montreal, Canada.
McMane, Aralynn Abare. 1992b. Vers un profil du journalisme 'occidental': Analyse empirique et comparative des gens de presse en France, au Royaume-Uni, en Allemagne et aux Etats-Unis [Toward a profile of "Western" journalism: A comparative, empirical analysis of journalists in France, Great Britain, Germany and the United States]. *Reseaux* 51: 67-74.
McMane, Aralynn Abare. 1992c. L'indépendence et le journaliste: comparaison France et les Etats-Unis [Independence and the journalist: A France-U.S. comparison]. *Médiaspouvoirs* 26: 5-14.
McMane, Aralynn Abare. 1993. A comparative analysis of standards of reporting among French and U.S. newspaper journalists. *Journal of Mass Media Ethics* 8, 4: 207-218.
McMane, Aralynn Abare and M. Kent Sidel. 1995. Western Europe. In *Global journalism; Survey of international communication*, 3rd ed., pp. 123-152. New York: Longman.
Mermet, Gérard. 1988. *Francoscopie: Les Français, Qui Sont-Ils? Ou Vont-Ils?* [Francoscopie: The French, Who are they? Where are they going?] Paris: Larousse.
Missika, Jean-Louis. 1989. Les Français et leurs médias, la confiance limitée [The French and their media: A limited trust]. *Mediaspouvoirs* 13: 39-50.
Muller, Marie. 1987, August 28. Le pouvoir des journalistes [The power of journalists]. *Le Nouvel Observateur*, pp. 56-73.
Padioleau, Jean-Georges. 1983, February. Le journalisme politique et la Francaise: Regards etrangers [French political journalism: The foreigner's view]. *Esprit*, pp. 147-155.
Padioleau, Jean-Georges. 1985. *Le Monde et Le Washington Post*. Paris: Presses Universitaires de France.

Palmer, Michael B. 1983. *Des Journaux aux Grandes Agences: Naissance du Journalisme Moderne, 1863-1914* [From newspapers to wire services: The birth of modern journalism]. Paris: Aubier Montaigne.
Pinel, Delphine. 1983, June. Label pour une profession [Label for a profession]. *Presse Actualité*, pp. 12-13.
Rieffel, Rémy. 1984. *L'elite des journalistes* [The elite of journalism]. Paris: Presses Universitaires de France.
du Roy, Nicole. 1985, February 9. Les Français jugent les journalistes [The French judge their journalists]. *Télérama*, pp. 96-103.
du Roy, Nicole. 1988, May 18. Des chiffres et des rêves [Figures and dreams]. *Télérama*, pp. 74-75.
Sauvage, Christian. 1988. *Journaliste, une passion, des metiers* [Journalist, a passion, an occupation]. Paris: Editions CFPJ.
Sérieys, Gérard. 1985, April 4. *Le chômage des journalistes: Cruelles statistiques* [The unemployment of journalists: Cruel statistics]. Rue du Louvre.
Sicsic, Patrick. 1989, March 31. Statut fiscal du journaliste, frais professionnels, deduction supplementarie de 30% [The fiscal statute of journalists, professional charges and a 30 percent additional deduction]. *Echos de la Presse et de la Publicité*, p. 41.
Syndicat Nationale des Journalistes. 1918. Les devoirs et les droits professionnels [Professional duties and rights]. *Bulletin Mensuel* 1, December, 2.
de Tocqueville, Alexis. 1994. *La Démocracie en Amerique Tome I* [Democracy in American Volume 1). Paris: Gallimard. (Original work published 1935)
Vernier, Dominique. 1989. La Presse au tribunal [The press in court]. *Médiaspouvoirs* 13: 102-108.
Voisin, Bruno. 1984, November. Tous que vous avez toujours voulu savoir sur les journalistes [Everything you've ever wanted to know about journalists]. *Press Actualité*, pp. 19-33.
Voyenne, Bernard. 1963. La profession de journaliste [The profession of journalism]. *Informations Sociales* 5:15-24.
Voyenne, Bernard. 1985. *Les journalistes Français* [French journalists]. Paris: CFPJ.
Weaver, David H. and G. Cleveland Wilhoit. 1986. *The American journalist: A portrait of U.S. news people and their work.* Bloomington: Indiana University Press.
Wolton, Dominique. 1989. Le journaliste menacé par son succes [The journalist threatened by success]. *Mediaspouvoirs* 13: 51-53.

12

German Journalists in the Early 1990s: East and West

Klaus Schoenbach
Dieter Stuerzebecher
Beate Schneider
Institut fur Journalistik, Hannover

The decade between 1980 and 1990 brought about important changes in the German media system:

- In the mid-1980s, the exclusively public-service broadcast system in West Germany lost its monopoly. Commercial television and radio stations were established and expanded the electronic media offering. Thus, for instance, approximately 240 German radio stations were broadcasting in the early 1990s instead of about 40 at the beginning of the 1980s. This increase was particularly rapid at the end of the decade when terrestrial frequencies became available to the new stations, which subsequently did not have to rely solely on cable anymore. A similar expansion of the electronic media offerings could be found almost everywhere in the world at that time (see Becker and Schoenbach 1989).
- In West Germany, the press market also registered a dynamic development. Due to less expensive publishing and printing techniques, more, mostly highly specialized, print magazines

sprang up. In addition, a great number of weekly freesheets have been established, complementing the local information supply of daily newspapers.
- In 1990, reunification added five new states with about 16 million people to West Germany and introduced both freedom of expression and a market economy to the East German media.

These developments have certainly influenced journalism in Germany. The last time, however, that representative data had been collected at least on *West* German journalists' backgrounds, methods of work, job situations, attitudes, and motives was in 1980-81 (see, e.g., Koecher 1986). This was one of the reasons why, in 1992, the Press and Information Agency of the German federal government decided to fund a representative survey of almost 1,600 journalists in Germany. The study was mainly supposed to describe the working situations of East German journalists compared to the conditions of their colleagues in the West two years after the reunification of Germany (see Schneider, Schoenbach, and Stuerzebecher 1993a, 1993b, 1994).

METHODS

Due to the emphasis of the study on the social situation of journalists in the East, they were not simply included in a nationwide survey. Instead, two separate samples—one from the West and the East (the latter with a comparatively greater number of respondents)—were drawn (see Schoenbach 1992). In West Germany, 983 representatively selected journalists were interviewed by telephone between July 29 and September 29, 1992. A second telephone survey with a representative sample of 585 journalists working in East Germany was in the field between January 20 and February 4, 1993. Among the respondents in East Germany were 477 who had lived there already before the wall came down in 1989. Another 108 were "imports" from West Germany after November 1989.

Both samples were drawn from all permanently employed journalists in newspapers, broadcast organizations, news agencies, and print magazines. Among the latter, only those were excluded that were geared toward a specific expert audience or appeared less than once a month or were not sold but distributed for free. The number of employees in each enterprise was gauged by direct contacts with the employers or by using professional handbooks. As a first step of a stratified sampling procedure, we selected a representative sample of media enterprises. The number of persons to be interviewed in those organizations was determined in a second step. In the case of local and regional newspapers, we made sure that up to two thirds of the respondents worked for the local news sections of those papers. In a last step, several precautions were taken to ensure a random sample of the people to be interviewed by phone in each organization (for details see Schoenbach 1992; Schneider et al. 1993a).

The standardized questionnaires of the two surveys were not only nearly identical but also designed to be comparable with the last representative survey of West German journalists in 1980-81 (see Koecher 1986) and with the 1992 study of journalists in the United States (Weaver and Wilhoit 1996).

The social situation of journalists was a central issue in the interviews—particularly in the East. The questionnaires dealt with job security, the financial situation, the attractiveness of professional alternatives, unemployment and its causes, and the working situations of the respondents. Journalists were asked about their training for the profession, changes in their jobs, their career plans, job satisfaction, and about their information-seeking behavior.

Finally, a focal point of the study was the professional self-image of journalists: What were the important functions and tasks of journalistic work for them? Which advantages and/or disadvantages did journalists see in their profession? What did they think about their audience? How important was ethical behavior for them?

BASIC CHARACTERISTICS OF JOURNALISTS

Size of Journalistic Workforce

In 1992, about 30,000 permanently employed journalists (including those still in professional training) worked in Germany—serving a population of almost 80 million. Among them were 16% who were based in East Germany (with a population of about 16 million). Newspapers were still the most important employers: Half of all the journalists in Germany as a whole, and even two thirds of those in East Germany, worked for daily newspapers in 1992. Radio and television followed second with almost a third (30%) of all journalists in West Germany permanently employed by them. The respective figure for East Germany, however, was only 18%—due to the still small number of new (and commercial) radio stations in that part of the country two years after the introduction of a market economy and due to the traditional seats of television station headquarters. Most of these stations still serve a national audience instead of a regional one (there was no local East German television or local radio station at all in 1993) and broadcast from the West (Table 12.1).

Table 12.1. Media and the Journalistic Workforce, 1992.

	West Germany	East Germany
Newspapers	12,374	3,241
Magazines	4,681	403
News Agencies	789	295
Radio	4,509[a]	594[a]
Television	3,153[a]	244[a]
All (permanently employed) journalists	25,506	4,777

[a]Approximate figures: Journalists who worked for radio and those who worked for television could be only imperfectly discerned. The majority of broadcast journalists in training was still employed by the public-service stations, which—as a tradition in Germany—have produced both radio and television programs under the same roof. Therefore, those who want to enter broadcast journalism are still trained for both media.

Age and Gender

Compared to the early 1980s, West German journalists were younger in 1992: 38.5 years on average. Put differently, 61% of them were under 40, as opposed to 43% in 1980-81 (Koecher 1986). One has to be somewhat cautious about comparisons with the survey of 1980-81. Whereas large parts of the questionnaires were the same (see earlier discussion), the sampling procedures differed to some extent, and the earlier survey was based on face-to-face interviews instead of telephone ones. Nevertheless, the two studies proved to be similar enough to allow us to point out at least general tendencies (see the discussion in Schneider et al. 1993a).

East German journalists in 1993 who had lived in East Germany before the Wall came down were slightly younger than their West German colleagues: 37.2 years. The age bracket of the "30-somethings" is—particularly in West Germany—the largest (Table 12.2).

Three quarters of all journalists in West Germany in 1992 were male. This proportion, albeit still large, was obviously smaller than in the survey of 1980-81 for which Koecher (1985) did not even mention the proportion of women. Among East German journalists stemming from the German Democratic Republic (GDR), we found more women (36%) in 1993 than in the West. Particularly few women worked at West German news agencies, whereas noticeably more were employed at news magazines. In East Germany, the proportions of the female workforce were somewhat more equally distributed across the different media (Table 12.3).

Table 12.2. Age Structure.

	West Germany 1980-81 (N = 450) (%)	West Germany 1992 (N = 983) (%)	East Germany 1993 (N = 477) (%)
Under 30 years	12	19	25
30-39 years	31	42	36
40-49 years	27	22	30
50 years and older	30	17	10
Average age of all journalists	n/a	38.5	37.2

Table 12.3. Proportion of Women Working in Journalism.

	West Germany 1992 (%)	East Germany 1993 (%)
Newspapers	23 (N = 493)	35 (N = 341)
Magazines	35 (N = 170)	49 (N = 44)
News Agencies	19 (N = 32)	43 (N = 15)
Radio	22 (N = 171)	36 (N = 59)
Television	26 (N = 117)	28 (N = 18)
All journalists	25 (N = 983)	36 (N = 477)

The reason for the greater number of women in the East working as journalists is somewhat ambivalent: To be sure, the Communist government made a point of offering equal opportunities for men and women. However, it also reacted out of utter need: Women were forced to work in order to sustain the fragile and inefficient economic system of the GDR.

During the late 1980s, however, the number of female journalists entering the job market in West Germany was—in relative terms—even larger than in the East. In 1993, significantly more women still worked in East German media because, typically, the proportion of West German female journalists decreased with the duration of employment.

As many as 40% of the journalists in the West were female among those employed less than four years. Yet this proportion dropped to only 12% among those having worked for 24 years and more in journalism. In East Germany, however, even in this "veteran" group of journalists, the share of women was still 33% in 1993, only a little under the average female proportion in journalism of 36% (Table 12.4).

In West Germany, the income difference between men and women was particularly striking: 80% of the female journalists had a monthly net income of under 4,500 DM in 1992, whereas only half of the men (52%) were paid such a low salary. Put differently, women were, on average, paid only about 80% of the salary of their male colleagues. In East Germany, this was somewhat different: There were not only more female journalists in 1993, but they were also less likely to be underprivileged in terms of their wages. The average gender difference in income amounted to less than 10%.

Political Attitudes

German journalists in 1992-93 liked the Social Democratic Party and the Greens a little more than the conservative Christian Democrats and the strongly pro market-economy Free Democrats. The least sympathy—both in East and West Germany—was attributed to the socialists of the PDS (Party of Democratic Socialism) and the "Republikaner," an extreme right-wing party. This well-known "liberal bias" of journalists (see the discussion in Schoenbach, Stuerzebecher, and Schneider

Table 12.4. Proportion of Women in Journalism By Work Experience: Length of Employment as a Journalist at the Time of the Survey.

	West Germany 1992 (%)	East Germany 1993 (%)
Less than 4 years	40 (N = 156)	29 (N = 120)
4-8 years	33 (N = 271)	40 (N = 86)
9-13 years	22 (N = 179)	35 (N = 69)
14-23 years	17 (N = 195)	42 (N = 138)
24 years and more	12 (N = 178)	33 (N = 64)
All journalists	25 (N = 983)	36 (N = 477)

1994) was considerably stronger among East German journalists who had lived in the GDR before the wall came down. There, even the socialist PDS received scores only a little more negative than the ones for the Christian Democrats.

EDUCATION AND TRAINING

A university degree has become increasingly important in most German media. Almost half (45%) of all journalists in West Germany in 1992 had one, considerably more than at the beginning of the 1980s (34%) (Koecher 1985). Almost a fifth (19%) of all West German journalists in 1992 had studied mass communications or journalism as a major or minor—up from 6% in 1980-81 (Koecher 1986). For the East German journalists coming from the GDR, this figure was 48% in 1993—due to the strictly regulated access to the profession under the Communist regime. The most striking difference between East and West, though, is the proportion of the same East German journalists who—in 1993—did not have journalistic training at all—almost a fifth (18%). In the West, this figure was considerably lower—10%. All these results apply to women and men equally.

WORKING CONDITIONS

Communication with Other Journalists

Journalists have been called a particularly self-sufficient, "in-bred" group of people restricted even in their social contacts to friends and acquaintances involved in journalism or the media (see, e.g., Donsbach, 1982). Our results, however, do not support this view. In West Germany, the estimated average proportion of people "connected in some way with journalism or the communication field" among persons one sees socially was only 28% in 1992. For East German journalists having lived in the GDR before 1990, this figure was virtually the same, 27%.

Images of Audiences

"Self-confident," "open-minded," "interested in politics," "well informed," "critical, demanding"—these flattering attributes were used by the majority of German journalists in 1992-93 to describe their audiences. In West

Germany (where we have the opportunity to compare), media recipients were viewed even more positively than in 1980-81. In general, younger journalists were a little more critical than their older colleagues. However, compared to 1980-81, the differences between the age cohorts have greatly decreased. All journalists seemed to be more or less unified in the positive evaluation of their audience.

East German journalists who had lived in the GDR before 1989 had an even more positive image of their audience than their West German colleagues. Still, however, there were some striking differences between the two groups: More journalists in East Germany thought they worked for an "insecure" audience that was also "easily influenced." This image obviously mirrors the problems of East Germans finding their place in a unified Germany with a free market economy. Also interesting, journalists from East Germany more frequently assumed that their audience was "left wing," whereas those in West Germany more often believed that they worked for a "right-wing" public. Old differences between a formerly Communist and a capitalist society had obviously prevailed.

Job Satisfaction and the Attractiveness of Journalism

German journalists seem to have enjoyed their job in the early 1990s. We had asked them: "How satisfied are you, all in all, with your present job? Would you say 'very satisfied,' 'fairly satisfied,' 'fairly unsatisfied,' 'very unsatisfied'?" Ninety-six percent of the West German journalists and 94% of the East German journalists claimed to be at least "fairly satisfied." Another indicator of their job satisfaction was the answer to the question, "In sum: Have you advanced in your job as far as you had imagined, or is that rather not the case?" Eighty-seven percent of the West German journalists and 84% of those in the East said, "Yes, I have advanced as far as I had imagined."

What was it in particular that German journalists seemed so satisfied with? Almost half of the West German journalists (43%) and an even greater proportion of the East German journalists (73%) called their salaries "attractive." Surprisingly, more than two fifths of the East German journalists (42%) believed that, of all matters, their profession is held in high regard. In West Germany, only a tenth of our respondents said so. If one takes into account what the population generally thinks of journalists, the latter was certainly the more realistic assumption. Both answers were items on a list of "attractions" that working as a journalist may offer.

As in the early 1980s, an idealistic, "missionary" professional orientation aimed at stirring the audience up, enlightening it, and influencing it existed among West and East German journalists in 1992-93 (see

Koecher 1986). Common to East and West Germany, however, enjoying the journalistic work as such and the possibilities to pursue one's own interests were more important, and, at least for West Germany, this was increasingly so. The profession is exciting and eventful, one meets interesting people, one gets around a lot, the job offers many liberties because one can express oneself and can choose one's tasks autonomously—these comments reflect what journalists in both parts of Germany praised frequently. Of the "missionary" elements of the profession, only "the possibility to uncover and criticize grievances" received similarly strong agreement. Nevertheless, journalists who had lived in East Germany before the wall came down demonstrated more "idealism" compared to their Western colleagues—they more often liked the chances of "championing values and ideals" and "passing on my own convictions to many people."

A multivariate analysis of possible causes leading to a "mission-oriented" attractiveness of journalism revealed that only age contributed to its importance (Schoenbach et al. 1994). The older East and West German journalists were in 1992-93, the more often they found attractive "championing of values and ideals," "passing on my own convictions to many people," and "chances of influencing political decisions." All the other presumed causes for a missionary attitude that can be found in the literature (for a review see Schoenbach et al. 1994) did not play a significant role, such as being a member of the 1968 age cohort (the one leading the student rebellion in West Germany), being politically leftist, or being frustrated by an unsatisfactory career or "professionally deformed" by academic training, particularly in journalism and mass communication departments.

PROFESSIONALISM

Membership in Professional Organizations

Journalists in Germany are a well-organized professional group. In 1992, more than half (56%) of the West German respondents were members of a journalists union. In East Germany, the figure was even higher, at 69%.

Readerships of Professional Journals

Virtually the same proportion of East and West German journalists claimed to read at least one professional journal regularly: 72% in West Germany and 71% in East Germany. Readership was above average among men, people under 30, and again those over 50, and—not surprisingly—among members of professional organizations who usually get a journal as one of their membership benefits. In fact, only 52% of the nonmembers in the West and 43% in the East cared enough to read a professional journal regularly.

Views on Professional Roles

The rank order of the professional roles that journalists most identified with in 1992-93 was surprisingly similar among the respondents in the old and new states of Germany. At the top of the list we find "taking up grievances," "a proponent of new ideas," "a guardian of democracy," and "a neutral reporter of events." Only one of the roles offered in our interviews—the one of "neutral reporter"—was chosen by East German journalists a little less frequently than by their colleagues in the West. However, significantly more East German editors and reporters found the role of "somebody who advises and helps people" appropriate. In general, there was more readiness in the East to play an educational role than in the West: At least one of the items "instructor or educator" and "someone who exerts political influence" was mentioned by 39% of the East German journalists living in the GDR before 1989, but only by 20% of their West German colleagues. Compared to 1980-81, however, at least West German journalists were significantly more ready to "serve" in 1992. Roles implying a service orientation such as "somebody who entertains the public" and "mirroring what the public thinks" had become much more important than they were in the early 1980s (Table 12.5).

As for the attractiveness of "missionary" journalism (see earlier discussion), age was somewhat important also among the possible determinants for a more "missionary" professional role (instructor or educator, or someone who exerts political influence). A multivariate analysis demonstrated that again it was the group of older journalists that favored this role a little more, and those who sympathized either with extremely right-wing or left-wing parties. Also as before, all the other explanations, such as being frustrated by an unsatisfactory career or being "biased" by academic training or by "the spirit of 1968," did not explain why somebody tended to mention this journalistic role as a norm of the profession (Schoenbach et al. 1994).

Views on the Ethics of Journalistic Research

The proportion of West German journalists willing to say that "unusual" (i.e., illegitimate) research or reporting methods may be justified rose

Table 12.5. How Appropriate Are Journalistic Roles?

Question: "In your opinion, how should a journalist understand his/her task; how should a journalist see him-/herself? Please tell me whether you agree or disagree with the following descriptions."

Journalistic Roles	West Germany 1980-81 (N = 450) (%)	West Germany 1992 (N = 983) (%)	East Germany 1993 (N = 477) (%)
Taking up grievances	95	95	98
A neutral reporter of events	81	89	84
A guardian of democracy	79	81	87
A proponent of new ideas	72	87	94
A spokesman for the underdogs	70	74	84
Someone who advises and helps people	58	64	89
Someone who entertains the public	54	77	87
Mirroring what the public thinks	47	64	71
An instructor or educator	16	13	25
Someone who exerts political influence	12	11	25
Sum	584	655	744

from 1980-81 to 1992 for every one of the methods named in our questionnaires except for one: "badgering unwilling informants to get a story." The increase is especially striking for methods such as "using confidential business or government documents without authorization" and "getting employed to gain inside information." One may argue that at least West German journalists became particularly ready to cheat organizations. When a personal confrontation with individuals was involved, however, they agreed less often that "unusual" research techniques may be justified. In East Germany, justification for breaking norms of information gathering was still weaker for virtually all of the "unusual" practices (Table 12.6).

Readiness to use questionable research methods was definitely more widespread among the younger journalists in our surveys. Men and women did not differ in that respect. What made a difference, how-

Table 12.6. Journalists' Opinions on "Unusual" Research Methods.

Question: "Because it is often very difficult to get important information, journalists sometimes use unusual methods. Which of the following methods do you think may be justified and which would you not approve under any circumstances?" (Percentage who say may be justified).

Reporting Methods	West Germany 1980-81 (N = 450) (%)	West Germany 1992 (N = 983) (%)	East Germany 1993 (N = 477) (%)
Using confidential government documents without authorization	57	75	65
Getting employed to gain inside information	36	46	43
Paying people for confidential information	25	28	15
Pretending to have a specific opinion or attitude to get the trust of an informant	25	39	23
Claiming to be somebody else	22	28	27
Badgering unwilling informants to get a story	8	6	3
Making use of personal documents such as letters and photographs without permission	5	10	4
Agreeing to protect confidentiality and not doing so	1	3	1
Using hidden microphones or cameras	*	22	25
Sum	179	257	206

*not asked.

ever, is the media organization our respondents worked for: Both journalists in news agencies and in commercial radio and television stations were significantly more ready to justify dubious research techniques.

CONCLUSIONS

During the 1980s, journalism in West Germany experienced more professionalization, a considerable rejuvenation of the profession, and an increase in women's participation. Journalists from East Germany differed from their colleagues in West Germany in their sociodemographic structure: Editors and reporters in the East were even younger, the proportion of women was higher, their "liberal bias" was somewhat more distinct. The share of editors in East Germany without any prior journalistic training was considerably greater than in the West. Many of them had come into the profession through the back door—perhaps not surprisingly for a time when there were not enough professional journalists available for reestablishing the media in East Germany.

As to their professional attitudes, however, and their ideas about what their roles are, journalists in East and West Germany were less far apart from one another than one would have expected after the division of Germany for more than 40 years. In some cases, the kind of media organizations for which they worked seemed to stimulate greater differences in their opinions than an East or West German socialization.

In East Germany, journalists found their profession even more attractive than their already enthusiastic West German colleagues. The latter had shown significantly more job satisfaction in 1992 than at the beginning of the 1980s. The joys of journalism for them were obviously accompanied by a more favorable image of their audience—indicating that the reasons for job satisfaction may have changed somewhat, at least in the West. In 1992, the "expressive" elements of the profession—to be able to pass one's own opinion on to other people and to have a political impact—retreated in favor of intrinsic rewards, which manifested themselves more in the everyday work routines—in information gathering, writing, and conveying topical information. Also, a service orientation increased. More journalists were ready to offer something to the audience, and fewer of them wanted to stir it up, train it, or educate it. Only a small part of the German journalists felt legitimized to influence public opinion. Consequently, the often lamented self-sufficiency of journalists as a professional group was not found. Journalists at least claimed to be in touch with "ordinary people."

Parallel to this growing "craftsmanship" orientation of the profession, "bloodhound journalism" has spread—at least in West Germany. West German journalists were more willing in 1992 than a decade before to justify controversial methods of getting information for the sake of topical and interesting news for their audiences. Last but not least, our study puts legends to rest that had prevailed about West German journalism: The superiority of a "missionary" self-concept over a "bloodhound" one (Koecher, 1986) did not reflect the reality of Germany in the early 1990s. Only the East German journalists—mostly the older ones among them—seemed to lag somewhat behind their West German colleagues. They still felt more attracted to the advocatory-educational possibilities of their job, and they were less willing to justify dubious methods of information gathering.

REFERENCES

Becker, Lee B. and Klaus Schoenbach, eds. 1989. *Audience responses to media diversification: Coping with plenty.* Hillsdale, NJ: Erlbaum.

Donsbach, Wolfgang. 1982. *Legitimationsprobleme des Journalismus: Gesellschaftliche Rolle der Massenmedien und berufliche Einstellung von Journalisten* [Legitimation problems of journalism: The social role of the mass media and journalists' professional attitude]. Freiburg, Munich: Karl Alber.

Koecher, Renate. 1985. *Spuerhund und Missionar: Eine vergleichende Untersuchung über Berufsethik und Aufgabenverstaendnis britischer und deutscher Journalisten* [Bloodhound and missionary: A comparative study of professional ethics and role perceptions of British and German journalists]. Doctoral dissertation, University of Munich.

Koecher, Renate. 1986. Bloodhounds or missionaries: Role definitions of German and British journalists. *European Journal of Communication* 1: 43-64.

Schneider, Beate, Klaus Schoenbach, and Dieter Stuerzebecher. 1993a. Westdeutsche Journalisten im Vergleich: Jung, professionell und mit Spass an der Arbeit [Comparing West German journalists: Young, professional and liking their work]. *Publizistik* 38: 5-30

Schneider, Beate, Klaus Schoenbach, and Dieter Stuerzebecher. 1993b. Journalisten im vereinigten Deutschland: Strukturen, Arbeitsweisen und Einstellungen im Ost-West-Vergleich [Journalists in unified Germany: Structures, working conditions and attitudes in an East-West comparison]. *Publizistik* 38: 353-382.

Schneider, Beate, Klaus Schoenbach, and Dieter Stuerzebecher. 1994. Ergebnisse einer Repraesentativbefragung zur Struktur, sozialen Lage und zu den Einstellungen von Journalisten in den neuen Bundeslaendern [Results of a representative survey on the structure, the social situation and on the attitudes of journalists in the new states of Germany]. In *Journalismus in den neuen Laendern: Ein Berufsstand zwischen Aufbruch und Abwicklung*, edited by Frank Boeckelmann, Claudia Mast, and Beate Schneider, pp. 145-230. Konstanz, Germany: Universitaetsverlag.

Schoenbach, Klaus. 1992. Sozialenquête ostdeutscher Journalisten: Das Design der Journalistenbefragung [A social inquiry of East German journalists: The design of the journalists survey]. In *Pressemarkt Ost*, edited by Walter A. Mahle, pp. 131-196. Munich: Oelschlaeger.

Schoenbach, Klaus, Dieter Stuerzebecher, and Beate Schneider. 1994. Oberlehrer und Missionare? Das Selbstverstaendnis deutscher Journalisten [Educators and missionaries? The self-concept of German journalists]. In *Oeffentlichkeit, oeffentliche Meinung, soziale Bewegungen*, edited by Friedhelm Neidhardt, pp. 139-161. Opladen: Westdeutscher Verlag.

Weaver, David H. and G. Cleveland Wilhoit. 1996. *The American journalist in the 1990s: U.S. news people at the end of an era.* Mahwah, NJ: Erlbaum.

13

Journalism in Germany*

Siegfried Weischenberg
University of Munster
Martin Löffelholz
University of Leipzig
Armin Scholl
Free University of Berlin

Since the 1970s there have been various attempts in the Federal Republic of Germany to shed light on the processes of media content formation and especially to establish what factors affect journalistic work. In numerous empirical studies researchers have examined "what journalists think and how they work" (Kepplinger 1979). Research of the subjective dimension has included journalists' general professional mental structures (see Prott 1976; Zeiß 1981), their specific professional attitudes toward the public, and the perception of their own professional role (see Kepplinger and Vohl 1979; Donsbach 1982; Köcher 1985). Other topics included autonomy and socialization in media organizations (see Noelle-Neumann 1977; Gruber 1975; Gross 1981, Weischenberg 1977) and specific journalistic roles such as sports writer, local reporter, or editor-in-chief (see Weischenberg 1978; Mühlberger 1979; Jacobi, Nahr, Langenbucher, Roegele, and Schönhals-Abrahamson 1977).

---

*The research project on which this chapter is based, Journalismus in Deutschland, was funded by the Deutsche Forschungsgemeinschaft.

The research topics taking an objective approach include structures of organization and working conditions, for example, in the context of macro-media developments (see Rühl 1979; Dygutsch-Lorenz 1971; Langenbucher and Roegele 1976). The consequences of the introduction of new techniques for editorial work were also examined in this context (see Schütt 1981; Prott et al. 1983; Mast 1984; Hienzsch 1990). Finally, several empirical studies were carried out on the working situation of women in journalism since the end of the 1970s (see Freise and Drath 1977; Becker 1980; Neverla 1983; Neverla and Kanzleiter 1984).

Deficiencies of German journalism research have become evident regarding the state of basic statistical data. At present, it is not even possible to give the exact number of employees who work in journalism, because professional statistics on journalism in West-Germany combine different roles from numerous professional fields (see Weischenberg 1985; Medienbericht 1985; Mast 1987; Rühl 1987).

Furthermore, there are no current representative data about the characteristics, attitudes, and working conditions of this heterogeneous professional group. To describe the journalists' characteristics and attitudes, we still have to fall back on the secondary analysis of the Arbeitsgemeinschaft für Kommunikationsforschung (AfK) (see Weiß et al. 1977). Their results, based on surveys of journalists working for radio stations, daily or weekly newspapers, and local reporters of daily newspapers, are probably only very generally valid today.

In the empirical media research of the former socialist German Democratic Republic (GDR), as well as in West German surveys concerning the GDR, communicator research played only a marginal role. The few results are directly related to the functions and working methods of "socialistic journalism." After the political changes in the GDR and the changes in media and journalism, this research is rather outmoded for the journalism system in a unified Germany. As far as they exist at all, basic data on GDR journalism can only be regarded as partially valid, because the suspicion that they are politically and ideologically biased cannot be thoroughly invalidated (see Geserick 1989; Stiehler 1990).

Hypotheses about change within East German journalism and its consequences for journalism in the unified Germany must be based mainly on the analysis of the current situation of media and journalism in East Germany. The 1992 communicator study *Sozialenqete* conducted by Schönbach, Schneider and Stürzebecher (1994) presents new data. The main purpose of the *Sozialenquete* study is to compare East and West German journalists with regard to their social conditions as well as to their perceptions of role and autonomy (see Schneider, Schönbach and Stürzebecher 1993a, 1993b, 1994).

THEORETICAL FOUNDATIONS

The following study is based on a constructivist perspective and a system theoretical approach. What does this theoretical decision imply? What is its relevance for the interpretation of the empirical results?

The constructivist perspective avoids asking ill-posed questions such as "Do the mass media represent or bias reality?" Therefore, it is an instrumental or operative rather than an ontological view. The scientific demand that journalists should represent "reality" does not correspond with their actual professional demands. Indeed, objective reporting is a journalistic instrument and has nothing to do with an ontological representation of reality. The perception of reality in general, as well as the professional observation of reality (made by journalists, scientists, etc.), are both observer related (see von Foerster 1985).

The consequence of this way of thinking is the following: No institution or system is privileged to define what reality is and what it is not. To contrast mass media coverage with so-called "real world" data cannot be interpreted as a verification or falsification of journalistic objectivity. Extra-media statistics are more constructions of another reality by another system (e.g., by authorities) than an independent instance of reality itself.

The use of a system-theoretical frame for empirical research is due to the fact that journalism has been institutionalized. Journalists' formations of media content cannot be reduced to individual performances of single journalists because media organizations affect journalists' actions in advance. As a result, it is a risky attempt to infer the contents of mass media coverage (without content analyses of articles or programs) from the journalists' professional role perceptions. Organizational characteristics such as the size and differentiation of the media institution, its structure, and autonomy can be regarded as intervening variables.

Although we use social system theory, we prefer survey research to the observational method because the survey is the only way to do representative research. But how does one combine a nonpersonal system-theoretical approach with an instrument relying on individuals? After all, we cannot trace the social structures and social processes themselves by asking respondents. What we can do is gain information about the journalists' reflections on these structures and the effects on their (individual) behavior. This means that we have to bear in mind this shift of meaning when interpreting the data: The respondents' reports are no longer considered a genuine insight into the social system of journalism but a valid self-description of the individuals' motives and perceived system constraints.

METHOD

Population—Editorial Personnel in German Media Organizations

The population under study includes the editorial staff of daily, weekly and Sunday newspapers, news agencies and media service bureaus, freesheets, general-interest and special-interest magazines, alternative journals and magazines, supplements, radio and television stations under public law, and private radio and television stations. We used various source lists for media organizations such as *Stamm*, *Zimpel*, *IW-Dossier*, and *Redaktionsadreß*. For each type of media organization we drew up several criteria to define the universe of media organizations.

Newspapers selected had to have an editorial staff of their own. Local editions of a newspaper were not considered as separate units. The sample included all nationwide daily and weekly newspapers, all regional papers with a circulation of more than 100,000 copies, and every second newspaper up to 100,000 copies. We excluded official journals (published by government or authorities). Sunday papers were counted separately only if they had an editorial staff of their own with an editor-in-chief.

We included all news agencies, every second media service bureau, and every fifth freesheet. The media services had to fulfill the criteria of not being public relations organs. Often this could not be decided before the questionnaire was sent back. The freesheets without editorial content were excluded, as well as the official freesheets.

We included all general-interest magazines with 500,000 or more copies, and we selected every second magazine with a lower circulation. With regard to the special-interest magazines, the low-end limit taken into account was 10,000 copies. Again, we excluded public relations organs and official journals, as well as magazines for customers or those magazines published less often than monthly. Supplements had to have an editorial staff of their own to be included in the sample. All radio and television stations were included, except those which broadcast in a foreign language or from abroad (see Table 13.1).

The best method to gain information from an organization as a whole is to conduct a mail survey. In June 1992, we sent written questionnaires to the editor-in-chief or—in the case of the large organization of the public broadcast networks—to the personnel department. To increase the response rate, we phoned nonrespondents. This was necessary for East Germany more than for the Western regions because the media market in East Germany was changing rapidly at that time (reductions in staff, establishment of new media, and the shutdown of old media organizations).

Table 13.1. Universe and Sample of German Media.

Type of media organization	Universe	Sample	Response rate
National and regional (> 100,000 copies) daily newspapers	75	75	54 (72%)
Regional daily newspapers (< 100,000 copies)	276	138	97 (70%)
Sunday newspapers	4	4	3 (75%)
Weekly newspapers (> 100,000 copies)	7	7	5 (71%)
Weekly newspapers (< 100,000 copies)	84	42	25 (60%)
Freesheets	804	160	130 (81%)
News agencies	11	11	8 (73%)
Media services	122	61	38 (67%)
General-interest Magazines (> 500,000 copies)	54	54	36 (67%)
Other magazines (< 500,000 copies)	556	278	175 (63%)
Supplements	7	7	5 (71%)
Alternative magazines	136	68	41 (60%)
Public broadcast networks	18	18	14 (78%)
Private radio stations	147	147	112 (76%)
Private television stations	53	53	38 (72%)
Total/Average	2354	1123	781 (70%)

The questionnaire included the following variables: type of media organization, size of circulation (only print media), headquarters of the media organization (*Land* of the Federal Republic of Germany, which can be recoded in the dichotomous variable West and East Germany), gender, position (editor-in-chief, senior editor, ordinary journalist, trainee), contractual relationship (full-time vs. part-time salaried journalists and freelancers), department, and professional role (editor, reporter, correspondent, presenter, etc.).

Sampling

With the data from the media organizations we could estimate several parameters of the journalistic universe. We knew how many male and female journalists worked in East and West Germany in certain types of media organizations, in which departments, in which positions, and so on. These parameters could be used to divide the sample into strata. The net sample included 1,500 respondents. We had assumed a response rate of about 60%; therefore, we began with a gross sample of 2,500 journalists. For reasons of field organization, we split the total sample into two regional subgroups: East and West Germany. The gross sample consisted of 2,000 journalists from West Germany of 500 journalists from East Germany, which was disproportional to the total population of German journalists. This disproportion had to be accepted, however, because the variable "headquarters of media organization" is not a sufficient indicator of the journalist's regional origin. As many West German journalists have moved to Eastern regions, we had to oversample the journalists working in East Germany to get an adequate amount of original East German journalists.

The sampling was carried out in several steps: The first step consisted of the sampling of the media organizations. We fixed the number of the media organizations under study at 500 (that is, 64% of the 781 media organizations from which we gained information about the stratification variables). For the gross sample we had to get the average number of five journalists per media organization. However, we calculated an average number of journalists for each type of media organization. This kind of sampling only approximately represented the size of the single media organization but exactly represented the types of media organizations.

In a second step, for the bigger and more complex media organizations, we also categorized the departments. In the case of the media organizations with only one department we did not need this second step. The organizations with only few (up to five) departments were selected at random (probability according to their size). In bigger organizations the departments were summarized under two categories: "hard" and "soft" according to Tuchman's (1978) hard and soft news. From the first organization we selected the first "hard" and the first "soft" department (e.g., politics and culture); from the second organization we selected the second "hard" and the second "soft" department (e.g., economics and sports). The local and regional department was divided into the main edition or issue (located at the headquarters) and into local editions or issues (Bezirksausgaben), and it was alternately classified in the "hard" or the "soft" departments.

This method only worked for standardized structures, like those of newspapers. For other media organizations with other structures, we found a different method of sampling the departments: We took the complexity of the very big organizations (of public broadcast stations) and of a different structure (news agencies and magazines of general interest) into account by randomly selecting the departments without the combination described earlier.

Finally, there was another problem concerning the stratification of the sample that could not be solved in a satisfying way—the accounting for freelance journalists. The responses concerning the number of the freelancers were only vague and were probably based on overestimations of the respondents. Moreover, if we took into account that most of the freelancers work for two or more organizations, we had to reduce their number, without knowing how much. The gross sample of the freelancers therefore was fixed at only 20% ($n = 500$). Later interviews with journalists shed light on this matter, and we could better estimate the correct number of freelancers in Germany. Actually, one third of all journalists were freelancers, but the sample included only 20%. This disproportion could be corrected by weighting the sample.

In a third step we carried out the gross sampling of the journalists. We phoned the departments and asked for a list of all their journalists, even if we needed fewer respondents. We wanted to avoid having another selection of respondents than ours. Only in the case of big departments with more than 10 journalists, the journalists selected the names themselves: We asked for the names beginning with A to K or with L to Z to make sure that this selection was random.

Interviewing and Questionnaire

The study was conducted in the field from April to September 1993. The period lasted this long for two reasons: During the summer vacation many journalists were absent. Moreover, the interviews were conducted in person, which took longer than other ways of data collection. Although there is some research pointing out the advantages of telephone interviews (lower costs, practicability), we preferred the face-to-face interviews for two reasons: In the first place, the questionnaire was too long for a telephone interview. Using the telephone we would have risked that the interviews were interrupted too often or even broken off by the respondents. Second, we presented many of Likert scales instead of dichotomous scales, and we asked a question about the journalists' professional career that had to be self-administered by the respondents. This parallel survey on West German and East German journalists allowed us to follow different patterns of socialization in different social systems.

To make the results comparable with other work on journalism, we took several items from relevant studies (e.g., Weaver and Wilhoit 1986). Questions about professional status and career opened the questionnaire. The details of professional socialization were measured with regard to levels of education. The work of journalists was specified by describing what they do. We also asked for formal characteristics of their working conditions (number of employees, percentage of women) and for their subjective reflections on them (hierarchy, autonomy, satisfaction with the job). A special issue dealt with the use of technology. Following this, role perception was picked out as a central theme. Here, we focused on questions about the functions of the media and about the perceived role of the journalists, as well as on ethical positions concerning investigation procedures. In this context, we also examined the journalists' perceptions of their audiences. The relationship between the journalists' own political attitudes and the perceived political positions of the media they work for was considered another influential factor for journalistic communication intentions. The questionnaire ended with questions about sociodemographic characteristics.

BASIC CHARACTERISTICS OF JOURNALISTS

The typical German journalist in the early 1990s corresponds to ordinary images: He is male, married, has a university degree, and is 37 years old. For 10 years he has had a full-time job as a newspaper reporter in one of the traditional departments: politics, economics, culture, sports or local news, and has been permanently employed for eight years. His monthly net income is about $2,600 (DM 3,900), and he is a member of a journalistic union or association. Comparing the basic characteristics of U.S. journalists with this description of German journalists, there is much to be said for the hypothesis that the professional group of journalists is similar in industrial Western countries, regardless of the different political and social structures (see Table 13.2).

Table 13.2. Basic Characteristics of German and U.S. Journalists.

Characteristics	German Journalists 1993	U.S. Journalists 1992
Sex	69% male	66% male
Age (median)	35	36
Personal status	46% married	60% married
Has worked in journalism	10 years	12 years
Belongs to a journalism association	55%	36%
Yearly income (median)	$31,200 (net)	$31,300 (gross)
University study with (without) degree	65% (+ 18%)	82%
Works for daily newspapers	41%	55%
Works with a news staff (median)	70 journalists	42 journalists
Full time editorial workforce	36,000	122,000
Freelancers	18,000	(Not included)

Source: Based on data compiled from Weischenberg, Löffelholz, and Scholl (1994: 155), and Weaver and Wilhoit (1992: 3).

EDUCATION AND TRAINING

Journalists learn their roles in complex processes of professional socialization, which begin with training on the job and last for the whole professional career. About 60% had practical training before they were employed. Most of them started their journalistic careers as trainees at a newspaper. The other organizations offering posts for trainees—the public broadcast networks and the magazines—were far less important. Private radio and television stations, media services, and freesheets did not play a role in educating journalists.

To become a journalist, it is often necessary but not sufficient to do training on the job. Access to journalism requires the combination of several professional educations: Every fifth German journalist depended on practical training in a media organization as the only preparation for the job. Others studied special subjects at the university level (politics, economics, law or literature) or journalism. In sum, almost two thirds of the journalists studied—in addition to training on the job—journalism, mass communication, or a special subject. Eighteen percent left the university without a degree. This "successful failure" type was typical for the 1970s, when it was easier to become a journalist than it is in the 1990s. The high percentage of journalism students cannot be attributed only to the popularity of academic journalism. This was due also to the exceptional feature of the former East German journalists' education. Most of the "socialist" journalists had to pass examinations at the *Sektion für Journalistik* in Leipzig.

Every tenth journalist had no journalism-specific education at all (e.g., no practical training, no study in journalism or communication research, no journalism school). If you add the respondents who studied a special subject at the university with those who had no further journalistic education, about a quarter of the German journalists learned their journalistic skills outside a formal education for their profession.

WORKING CONDITIONS

Income

German journalists' median income was almost $2,600 monthly in the early 1990s. The journalists in lower income groups were trainees, reporters with few years of experience in journalism, and freelancers. We found journalists with management functions or many years experience in higher income groups. Almost 10% earned more than $4,000 monthly. Journalists working for public broadcast networks had the highest salaries ($3,000), followed by those employed by news agencies. Below average salaries were paid by the commercial radio stations ($2,250). The difference between public and private broadcast can be explained by history: The dual broadcasting system, which legally regulates the coexistence of public and private broadcasting, did not exist before 1984. As a consequence, young journalists with little experience in journalism worked for the recently developed private radio and television stations.

Overall median salaries for female journalists were lower than for their male colleagues. This gender gap can only partly be explained by the better paid management functions, which men held more often than women. The difference between male and female editors or reporters without management tasks was still $350 a month. Even if the correlation of gender and income is controlled by years of experience in journalism, the income gap remains notable. The lowest income was for female freelancers ($2,200). However, the overall median difference between permanently employed journalists and freelancers was less than expected ($200). We have to bear in mind, however, that only freelancers who mentioned journalism as their chief occupation were included in the sample.

Work

In general, the higher the journalists' positions in the hierarchy of the organization, the more hours they worked weekly. Editors-in-chief worked 54 hours, senior editors 48 hours, ordinary reporters 45 hours, and trainees almost 43 hours a week. The differences between the types of media organizations were marginal. The average weekly work time of the full-time staff hardly differed from the freelancers'—and this difference was due to the fact that freelancers have fewer management tasks.

In addition, we asked for the amount time spent on of certain types of work. Journalists spent most of their time investigating for their stories and writing. Other tasks included editing material from agencies, media services and public relations releases, as well as colleagues' texts. A notable amount of time was spent on administrative, management, and technical tasks. On average, journalists needed about two hours of their daily work time for the layout of newspapers, work on location, or participation in newsroom conferences.

The time spent collecting information is of particular interest because German journalists are sometimes blamed for neglecting the investigation of facts and for preferring to provide comment on their stories. Overall, about a quarter of the surveyed journalists did not use more than one hour a day for reporting. Almost a third needed one to two hours, a fifth two to three hours, and only a few needed three to four hours (12.5%) or more than four hours (8%) for reporting task. There are various subgroup differences: The average amount of time spent on reporting was lowest in broadcast stations and highest in freesheets (which correspond to the local newspaper journals). Another independent variable explaining the amount of time spent investigating stories was the position of the journalist in the media's organizational hierarchy: Editors-in-chief did reporting 80 minutes a day, ordinary journalists 150 minutes. More than half the senior editors did not have more than one hour a day at their disposal for investigation, compared to only a quarter of the ordinary journalists and even less than 15% of the trainees. As a matter of fact, this explains why freesheet journalists had so much time for reporting: Their organizational structures were very simple, and they did not have to assume the management functions that hinder the task of reporting.

The percentage of journalists who did no reporting at all was highest for broadcast stations (public: 19.5%; private: 14.5%) and for magazines (14.5%). We propose different reasons for these findings: The public broadcast networks as well as the larger private television stations have complex organizational structures with differentiated responsibilities for different types of work. Small private radio and television stations mainly carry entertainment programs, which do not afford much time for reporting. Magazines are a very heterogeneous type of media. Journalists of general-interest magazines did much more reporting than those of special-interest and special-issue magazines, who edited external authors' texts. In all the other types of media organizations, only 5% to 8% did no reporting at all.

Local reporters (155 minutes) and freelancers (176 minutes) took the most time daily to report. The full-time journalists—the senior as well as the ordinary editors—had to cope with management duties at the expense of investigative journalism.

The effects of the independent variables and covariates on the amount of reporting were documented with the help of analysis of variance statistics. The effects of type of media organization as described earlier were verified by the results, but they partly correlated with the effects of other independent variables and covariates. The public broadcast networks have complex structures. Many journalists worked in administrative departments and had administrative tasks that hindered them from reporting. However, administrative tasks were not only performed in administrative departments.

Local journalists and those who did not work in one specific department did much more reporting. The journalists who were not specialized worked for media organizations with small editorial workforces, which are similar to local news departments. We found these journalists to work especially for freesheets, in which they did more reporting. In sum, the journalism system was obviously not homogeneous but consisted of various subsystems, which had different functions and different focal points concerning the types of work done.

Job Satisfaction

Job satisfaction is often considered a result of the combination of subjective and objective aspects of editorial work: job-related expectations and demands that are obtained in processes of professional socialization and working conditions in media organizations, such as the type and size of media organization, position in hierarchy, employment terms, and department. We measured job satisfaction with several variables directly related to particular working conditions such as satisfaction with the following: income, daily workload, hierarchy, collegiality, promotion in the job, and so on.

As we expected, the overall means let us draw the conclusion that German journalists were very satisfied with their jobs. All means were above the theoretical mean of the scale (see Table 13.3). In particular, the collegiality and the atmosphere in the newsroom seemed to be regarded highly. However, there were some differences according to the hierarchical position: 90% of the senior editors were fairly or very satisfied with their inferiors, whereas only three quarters of the inferiors were fairly or very satisfied with their superiors. Job security was estimated rather skeptically by freelancers and trainees. Overall, the journalists' satisfaction was somewhat less favorable for the time spent reporting, daily workload, opportunities for further education, promotion, and pay.

Similar to the time spent on reporting, we tried to explain satisfaction with the time for reporting with an analysis of variance. The independent variables explained only 15% of the variance. The time a journalist has for the investigation of stories had only a slight, but significant,

Table 13.3. Job Satisfaction.

Dimension of Job Satisfaction	N	Means[a]
Relationship to inferiors[b]	227	1.77
Relationship to colleagues	1482	1.83
Relationship to superiors[c]	1299	2.11
Possibility to arrange work hours	1486	2.15
Quality of job education	1474	2.28
Editorial policies of the organization	1463	2.37
Job security	1486	2.58
Time spent on investigation	1471	2.67
Daily workload	1474	2.68
Opportunities for promotion in the job	1479	2.71
Pay	1486	2.73
Opportunities for further education	1477	2.77

[a]Ranking scale (1 = very satisfied, 5 = very dissatisfied).
[b]Only superiors were asked this question.
[c]Only inferiors were asked this question.

positive effect on satisfaction with time allotted for investigations. This means that some journalists were dissatisfied even if they had a lot of time to report, and others were satisfied even if they had little time. Other objective working conditions had no great effect, either, although time spent on administrative and management tasks did significantly predict less satisfaction with time for reporting.

PROFESSIONALISM

Professional Roles

Professional roles are related to the political functions of mass media as well as to the journalists' personal self-descriptions and perceptions. The notion "role perception" or "role conception" implies a self-referential framing, the observation of the attributed role to oneself, which need not be the same as the actual role enactment or role performance. The professional role perception may be an indicator or a condition for professional role acting. From this view, it is interesting to investigate whether concrete acting can be inferred from role conception. Only if journalists manage to apply their role conceptions to actual professional behavior are these role conceptions relevant for the construction of reality by the media. Unless this is the case, the journalists' descriptions of their roles are a kind of ideology about their jobs (even a misperception of self) or the public expression of socially desirable, but not actually performed, professional aims.

The connection between role conception or role perception and actual professional acting we call *relevance of action*. The relevance of action will be high if, for example, an advocacy journalist writes an article that stands up for disadvantaged groups in society. The relevance of role action may be affected by various independent variables: The journalist can only perform a certain role if the media organization provides editorial policies and material (financial) resources supporting the journalists' subjective role conceptions. Another condition is the journalist's sense of personal autonomy in the organization, which is often at odds with the elements of the media organization such as profit, technical routine, and so on. As a matter of fact, we do not believe role conception is a mere individual self-description but is a result of professional socialization processes. Journalistic role perception, therefore, develops in a social context with a certain degree of freedom of action.

The operationalization we used takes into consideration both aspects as a difference of professional aim (role aspect) and of actual performance (structural aspect). The journalists were therefore asked for various conceptions of their role (21 items), which they could answer with the help of a ranking scale (entirely agree, mainly agree, partly agree, less agree, do not agree at all). Moreover, they could estimate whether and to what degree they actually perform this aim in their daily jobs.

Most of the journalists approved of items describing their role as analyzers or disseminators of information, such as "providing analyses and interpretation of complex problems," "getting information to the public neutrally and precisely," "getting information to the public quickly," "presenting reality as it is," and "staying away from stories where factual content cannot be verified" (see Table 13.4).

Table 13.4. Professional Roles.

The following list contains a number of statements concerning the professional aims a journalist can pursue or the way a journalist perceives himself. Please tell me how strongly you agree with each statement.

Professional Role Items	N	Aimed Role[a] means	Realized Role[b] means
Provide analyses and interpretations of complex problems	1484	1.97	2.11
Get information to the public neutrally and precisely	1488	1.97	1.98
Get information to the public quickly	1479	2.01	1.89
Criticize bad states of affairs	1472	2.27	2.23
Present reality as it is	1464	2.30	2.10
Stay away from stories where factual content cannot be verified	1476	2.39	1.73
Develop intellectual and cultural interests of the public	1485	2.55	2.10
Present new trends and convey new ideas	1479	2.57	2.15
Concentrate on news which is of interest to widest possible public	1476	2.60	2.02
Provide entertainment and relaxation	1477	2.72	1.93
Stand up for the disadvantaged population	1477	2.74	2.50

Table 13.4. Professional Roles(con't.).

Professional Role Items	N	Aimed Role[a] means	Realized Role[b] means
Convey positive ideals	1472	2.84	2.30
Give ordinary people the chance to express their opinions about issues of public interest	1480	2.88	2.25
Help people in their everyday lives	1462	2.98	2.25
Be an adversary of public officials by being constantly skeptical of their actions	1479	3.05	2.23
Control politics, business, and society	1476	3.06	2.54
Present one's own opinion to the public	1476	3.20	1.99
Investigate claims and statements made by the government	1468	3.27	2.22
Be an adversary of business by being constantly skeptical of their actions	1472	3.36	2.22
Discuss national policy while it is still being developed	1463	3.43	2.21
Influence the political agenda and setting issues on the political agenda	1476	3.55	2.55

[a]Mean of a ranking scale (1 = entirely agree, 5 = do not agree at all)
[b]Mean of ranking scale (1 = realize entirely, 5 = do not realize at all)

The only item strongly agreed on that does not belong to a conception of passive, informative journalism was the aim to "criticize a bad state of affairs." However, this item is rather abstract. If we compare it to responses to more concrete items, such as "being an adversary of public affairs or of business by being constantly skeptical of their actions," "influencing the political agenda," and "controlling politics, business and society," journalists were much less likely to approve of an active and controlling role for journalism.

The respondents did approve of another kind of active, but not explicitly political or controlling, role for journalism. They responded positively to the aims of "developing intellectual and cultural interests of the public," "presenting new trends," "providing entertainment and relaxation," "giving ordinary people the chance to express their opinions" and "helping people in their everyday lives."

This description by single items can be consolidated with multivariate analysis. We are interested in grouping the journalists according to their role perceptions. An appropriate statistical method is cluster analysis. The cluster analysis used here is based on an iterative minimal distance algorithm. In the first step, the respondents are randomly sorted into a given number of clusters. Then the algorithm exchanges the cases iteratively to optimize the relationship of between variances, which must tend to a maximum, and within variances, that must be minimized. The solution which is mathematically and substantially most satisfying results in six clusters explaining 35% of the variance. Considering the high number of cases ($N = 1,498$) and variables (21 items) this solution can be accepted.

Cluster 1 consists of respondents who had no qualitative profile and who approved more than average of almost all of the presented items. We labeled this cluster "ambitious" journalists. In cluster 2, we built the opposite profile, that of "modest" journalists, who did not claim to belong to a "fourth estate." However, they did approve on average of aspects of informative journalism. This allows for a positive profile, as the average agreement to these items was rather high. The only group that refuted information journalism to a small extent were the "missionaries" (Köcher 1985). They wanted to present their own opinions to the public and to have an adversarial attitude toward the political and economic system. However, here the overall averages of the items in common were low, and the profile is not too salient.

A somewhat complementary journalist is the "monitor," who combined the aim of providing neutral, precise, and quick information to the public; the control of politics, economics, and society; the investigation of governmental claims; and the discussion of national policy. The profile of this cluster cannot be described as adversarial but as controlling and monitoring. The respondents rejected other kinds of active journalism such as presenting their own opinions, helping people in their everyday lives, or conveying new trends and ideas. Just one item—to provide entertainment and relaxation—characterized the "entertaining" journalists. They, too, rejected all kinds of active, political, or even information journalism. Finally, we have the cluster of "helpful" journalists: They were active but not political communicators, who wanted to give ordinary people a chance to express their views on public affairs, to convey positive ideals, to help people in their everyday lives, and to entertain. The six clusters presented give an idea of the different segments of journalism in Germany.

We can conclude that informative journalism seems to be a primary function of journalism in Germany overall because almost all the journalists strongly approved of it. German journalists differed according to secondary, but not less important, functions, including the political, monitoring, helping, and entertaining aims of journalism.

Knowing how journalists think about their roles does not predict whether they actually realize their intentions. Therefore, the respondents who entirely or mostly agreed with an item were also asked if they succeeded in performing this aim in their daily jobs. Overall, journalists were optimistic, but there were differences in their role as conceived and practiced (see Table 13.4). Advocacy and monitoring journalism were found more difficult to perform, whereas the realization of passive information journalism was prevalent.

These results obviously reflect rules of the media that are consensual such as providing (good) information for the public. Other professional aims are not supported by every media organization and do not belong to the primary functions of journalism such as missionary journalism. The less consensual a certain journalistic role is and the more ambitious the journalists' aims are, the less justified it is to infer the respondent's actual role directly from the reported role conception.

There is another condition that facilitates or complicates the relationship of the perception to the role actually played. This relationship is closer if the individual journalists' attitudes correspond to the editorial policies of their media organizations, or at least to that of the majority of the newsroom. As an indicator we used the comparison of the journalists' own political attitudes with the perceived political tendencies of their media organizations. Indeed, the majority of the journalists tended toward liberal political attitudes (slightly left oriented), but, significantly, the respondents also perceived their organizations in the middle of the political spectrum. This is another reason to believe that journalists are not free in realizing their professional aims easily, but are constrained by their media organizations.

ETHICS OF REPORTING

The journalists' job is to publish facts, even if sources do not want to provide information to the public. There exists in journalism no standard regarding which issues to publicize, although there are standards with regard to fact checking a story. There are numerous cases in which publicity is not desirable for ethical or moral reasons. Not only can the purpose of publicity be controversial, the means of getting information can also be subject to question. In many cases the best end does not justify the means. We simulated this double conflict by providing a situation in which, on the one hand, certain sources refused to provide information and, on the other hand, the means of obtaining information were either illegal or morally questionable.

The first glance shows the majority of the German journalists to be legally minded and of high moral integrity in their practice of reporting. They justified only very few morally controversial means of investigation. Comparing the items that were justified by a high number of respondents to those that were extensively rejected, the first group of items could be called "aggressive reporting practices," whereas most of the items of the second group could be classified "unscrupulous" (see Table 13.5).

Table 13.5. Approval of Unusual Reporting Practices.

Question: "It is often very difficult to obtain important information. Therefore, many journalists use unusual methods to get these information. Please tell me for each of the following means, whether you justify it, whether it depends on the situation or circumstances, or whether you do not justify it."

Means of Reporting/Investigation	Justify	Depends on Circumstances	Do not Justify
Using confidential government documents without authorization	26.4	27.4	46.2
Getting employed in a firm or organization to gain inside information	21.7	32.1	46.2
Pretending another opinion or attitude to inspire an informant's confidence	19.5	28.4	52.1
Paying people for confidential information	19.4	21.8	58.8
Claiming to be somebody else	18.9	26.3	54.8
Using hidden microphones or cameras	8.6	22.2	69.2
Badgering unwilling informants to get information	2.2	9.6	88.2
Making use of personal documents without permission	1.9	9.4	88.7
Agreeing to protect confidentiality and not doing so	1.5	8.3	90.2
Publishing the names of rape victims	1.1	3.0	95.9

Again, we tried to explain the variations in the several means of reporting practices with the independent variables used earlier in an analysis of variance. The results were somewhat disappointing: Only 7% to 13% of the variance was explained by the independent variables of gender, type of media organization, department, journalistic experience, and so on. In the first place, reporting with the help of "unusual means" seems to be a matter of individual ethics. However, there were a few variables that did slightly affect the reporting behavior. In some instances, women more than men tended to stay away from aggressive or unscrupulous reporting. Eastern and public broadcast journalists, too, were less likely to approve of unscrupulous practice than Western and private television or magazine journalists.

The younger and less experienced the journalists were, the more they justified certain unusual methods. Professional socialization not only brings an ethical maturity, but it also increases the journalist's routine so that he or she reports only to prove facts instead of investigating scandals. Finally, the journalists we call "missionaries" were more likely to justify the use of confidential government documents without authorization and the use of tactics such as claiming to be somebody else. This finding is a slight cue that the contrast of "missionaries" and "watchdog" (see Köcher 1985) may be an artificial result (see Schönbach et al. 1994).

REFERENCES AND SELF-REFERENCES IN JOURNALISM

Influences on Journalism

The relation between journalism and its environment can be operationalized in various ways. A rather general indicator is the influence of several reference groups or instances on journalistic work. More specifically, we looked for concrete feedback from certain systems in the journalistic environment. Altogether, the journalists did not report large effects caused by any reference group, but there was a difference between the amount of interior and exterior influence. The newsroom itself—superiors as well as colleagues—defined the limits of the coverage. The only exterior variable to which the journalists attributed a comparable influence was the readership or the audience. Somewhat less influential seemed to be public relations, publishers or broadcast supervisors, the journalists' friends and family, business, political parties, trade unions, sport associations, and churches.

These results could suggest that journalists' work primarily relies on their colleagues and on their peer groups' consensual professional views. There are two reasons that lead us to favor another perspective: (a) the main influence on journalistic work was an interior but hierarchical one; and (b) the journalists attributed a major influence to the readership or audience, in addition to these interior references. A system-theoretical approach, rather than the teleological assumption that journalists intend to establish a fourth estate, can explain this finding. On the one hand, the newsroom is an organization with hierarchical structures. On the other hand, the audience is the main (exterior) reference for journalism overall. The journalists' role as providers of media coverage immediately depends on the audience's role as customer and recipient.

There are other indicators supporting the hypothesis that journalists' work is self-referential: More than 80% of the journalists reported that at least some of their acquaintances and friends were also journalists. Asked for their professional reading habits, more than two thirds of the respondents mentioned the most important news magazine in Germany, *Spiegel* (mirror), followed by the public news telecasts (between 55% and 62%), the national quality newspapers (between 22% and 47%) and the tabloid *Bild* (22%). Again, we prefer to interpret this finding in a system-theoretical sense as a reflection of the media system's self-organization rather than to consider it a result of individual influences on individual journalists' work.

Influence of Public Relations

In addition to these global descriptions, we have taken a closer and more specific look at the (estimated) influence or the importance of public relations on journalism. Public relations can be modeled as an intersection of several systems such as politics, business, and journalism. Via public relations and press releases the environmental systems try to transfer their images and information into the journalistic system and mass media. However, for journalists as well, press releases worked out by public relations organizations have become more and more important as information sources.

We asked the respondents to estimate different dimensions of the quality of the press releases they get in their day-to-day job. In general, the journalists rated press releases rather positively. More than half of them believed that they were important and that they suggested issues for new stories and saved time during reporting and investigation. However, 40% thought that there were too many press releases. Other negative aspects included the following: Only one third of the respondents approved of the statement that press releases are well prepared, almost one third suspected that they tempt coverage that is too uncritical, and a quarter regarded them as substitutions of their own (critical) reporting.

These aspects of press releases suggest that journalism depends on the information disseminated by public relations. However, journalists processed this information critically, according to their reports. Content analyses will have to inquire how much and to what degree information presented in press releases enters mass media coverage in order to evaluate the actual influence of public relations on journalism (see Schweda and Opherden 1995).

Images of the Audience

From a system-theoretical perspective, the audience is a central part of the mass communication system and not only a variable affected by journalists' professional intentions. Mass communication research dealing with the audience often explores the effects of media content on its recipients or, even further, the nature of the audience as active recipients. In journalism research, however, the audience is a reference instance that is important for the journalist's permanent observation and management of his or her own work.

Journalists are often blamed for having a negative image of the audience. They are said to despise their audiences and to regard them as narrow-minded. These images are the reason why journalists want to educate and influence the public, instead of merely serving as moderators in society. Our findings do not support such charges because 40% to 50% of the journalists regarded their audiences as open-minded, well informed, critical, politically interested, and educated. Only 10% to 25% ranked their audiences negatively and rarely in an extremely negative way. Descriptive characteristics, rather than those offering a clear assessment, tended to be ranked in the middle of the scale. A more detailed analysis will have to test the correlations of the journalists' images of the audience and their role conceptions, as well as other basic variables such as media type, department, hierarchical position, journalistic experience, and so on (see Weischenberg, Löffelholz, and Scholl 1997).

To summarize the results at this level of analysis, we have good reason to describe journalism as a self-referential system. That does not imply that journalism has no contacts with its environment. On the contrary, these contacts are necessary, complex, and detailed. However, there are no direct effects from the environment on the system's structure. Nevertheless, the journalists' objectives are not self-directed but directed toward their audiences. We know this from their reports on what constituted influences on their work. As a consequence, journalists' perceptions of their audiences take this into consideration. According to the journalists' answers to our questions, the audience is able to respond to the media coverage critically and conscientiously. This rather positive image makes sense if we are to understand how journalists create self-esteem within their own profession.

SUMMARY AND CONCLUSIONS

The method of this study is somewhat different from that of other comparable studies. The universe is not confined to full-time news people but also includes entertainment journalists, journalists working for freesheets and special-interest or special-issues magazines, as well as freelancers. The universe could be described with regard to central characteristics that were used to stratify the sample. Disproportions in the sample, either those from oversampling small subgroups or those from the field, were equalized by weighting according to the proportions of the universe. The process of sampling was strictly random. The sample consisted of 1,498 respondents representing the various fields in journalism. The questionnaire covered central issues confronting journalism research.

With the results of this representative study, we were able to test the central hypotheses that have arisen since the 1970s. Thus far, these hypotheses were empirically tested only with the help of case studies or of studies within certain subgroups in journalism. Although their results were methodologically rather weak, they affected political discussion enormously. German journalists were said to constitute an autonomous class in society, who do not orient themselves to their audience, to whom they attach little value, but to their colleagues. According to such studies, there were serious discrepancies between the politically leftist journalists and the "public," who perceived problems in society in a different way (see Kepplinger and Vohl 1979). Political and professional attitudes are directly relevant for the day-to-day job because journalists manage to translate them—deliberately against the public opinion—into media coverage. They do not perceive themselves as neutral moderators of events and processes in society but as critics, controllers, and advocates. The consequences are problems of journalism's legitimation (see Donsbach 1982).

Such gross and weakly proved findings and interpretations can now be rejected; there is no empirical evidence for them. For economic, technological, and educational reasons, there has been a convergence in journalism in the Western democratic countries. The formation of media content is the result of a process with high complexity. The journalists' communication intentions are based on permanent observations of their own professional aims and of their effects. Furthermore, the aims only find expression in media coverage under certain conditions. It is not adequate to model the journalists' attitudes in a simple causal connection as an independent variable. Instead, we have to consider organizational constraints and complex interactions of journalism, mass media, mass communication, and their relations to other systems in society.

REFERENCES

Becker, Barbara von. 1980. *Berufssituation der Journalistin: Eine Untersuchung der Arbeitsbedingungen und Handlungsorientierungen von Redakteurinnen bei einer Tageszeitung* [The professional situation of female journalists: An inquiry into the working conditions and behavioral orientations of female journalists at a daily newspaper]. Freiburg, München: Minerva Publikation.

Donsbach, Wolfgang. 1982. *Legitimationsprobleme des Journalismus: Gesellschaftliche Rolle der Massenmedien und berufliche Einstellung von Journalisten* [Problems of legitimation in journalism: The societal role of mass media and professional attitudes of journalists]. Freiburg, München: Verlag Karl Alber.

Dygutsch-Lorenz, Ilse. 1971. *Die Rundfunkanstalt als Organisationsproblem: Ausgewählte Organisationseinheiten in Beschreibung und Analyse* [The broadcast station as an organizational problem: Description and analysis of selected organizational units]. Düsseldorf: Bertelsmann Universitätsverlag.

Foerster, Heinz von. 1985. *Sicht und Einsicht: Versuche zu einer operativen Erkenntnistheorie* [Sight and insight: Essays on an operative epistemology]. Braunschweig, Wiesbaden: Vieweg.

Freise, Heinrich and Jochen Drath. 1977. *Die Rundfunkjournalistin* [The female broadcast journalist]. Berlin: Verlag Volker Spiess.

Geserick, Rolf. 1989. *40 Jahre Presse, Rundfunk und Kommunikationspolitik in der DDR* [40 years of press, broadcast and communications policy in the GDR]. München: Minerva.

Gross, Bernd. 1981. *Journalisten—Freunde des Hauses? Zur Problematik von Autonomie und Anpassung im Bereich der Massenmedien* [Journalists—partial observers? On the problem of autonomy and accommodation in the field of mass media]. Saarbrücken: Verlag "Die Mitte."

Gruber, Thomas. 1975. *Die Übernahme der journalistischen Berufsrolle* [Adapting the professional role of journalists]. Nürnberger: Verlag der Nürnberger Forschungsvereinigung.

Hienzsch, Ulrich. 1990. *Journalismus als Restgrösse: Redaktionelle Rationalisierung und publizistischer Leistungsverlust* [Journalism as a remainder: Editorial rationalisation in the newsroom and the waste of journalistic potential]. Wiesbaden: Deutscher Universitäts-Verlag.

Jacobi, Ursula, Günter Nahr, Wolfgang R. Langenbucher, Otto B. Roegele, and Marta Schönhals-Abrahamson. 1977. *Manager der Kommunikation* [Manager of communication]. Berlin: Verlag Volker Spiess.

Kepplinger, Hans Mathias and Inge Vohl. 1979. Mit beschränkter Haftung: Zum verantwortungsbewusstsein von Fernsehredakteuren [With limited liability: On TV journalists' sense of responsibility]. In *Angepasste Aussenseiter: Was Journalisten denken und wie sie arbeiten* [Conforming outsiders: What journalists think and how they work], edited by Hans Mathias Kepplinger, pp. 223-259. Freiburg, München: Verlag Karl Alber.

Köcher, Renate. 1985. *Spürhund und Missionar: Eine vergleichende Untersuchung über Berufsethik und Aufgabenverständnis britischer und deutscher Journalisten* [Bloodhound and missionary: A comparative inquiry into professional ethics and role perceptions of british and German journalists]. Dissertation Thesis, München.

Langenbucher, Wolfgang R. and Otto B. Roegele. 1976. Pressekonzentration und Journalistenfreiheit [Press concentration and journalists freedom]. Teil A: Untersuchungszeitraum 1961 bis 1971. In *Pressekonzentration und Journalistenfreiheit. Zur entwicklung der Arbeits- und Beschäftigungssituation von Journalisten der Tageszeitungen in der Bundesrepublik Deutschland* [Press concentration and journalists freedom: On the development of the working and employment conditions of journalists in German daily newspapers], edited by Wolfgang R. Langenbucher, Otto B. Roegele, and Frank Schumacher, pp. 11-133. Berlin: Verlag Volker Spiess.

Mast, Claudia. 1984. *Der Redakteur am Bildschirm: Auswirkungen modernerer Technologien auf Arbeit und Berufsbild des Journalisten* [The editor at the computer: The effects of modern technology on journalists work and professional image]. Konstanz: Universitätsverlag Konstanz.

Mast, Claudia. 1987. Anforderungen an den Journalismus und die Journalistenausbildung angesichts des Strukturwandels des Mediensystems [Requirements of journalism and journalistic education in view of the structural change in the mass media system]. In *Zwischenbilanz der Journalistenausbildung* [Summary of journalistic education), edited by Jürgen Wilke, pp. 217-232. Freiburg, München: Verlag Ölschläger.

Medienbericht. 1985. *Bericht der Bundesregierung über die Lage der Medien in der Bundesrepublik Deutschland* [Federal government report on the situation of mass media in the Federal Republic of Germany]. Bonn: Bundespresseamt.

Mühlberger, Holger. 1979. Stille Teilhaber: Zur gesellschaftlichen Integration von Lokaljournalisten [Silent partners: On the societal integration of local journalists]. In *Angepasste Aussenseiter. Was Journalisten denken und wie sie arbeiten* [Conforming Outsiders: What journalists think and how they work], edited by Hans Mathias Kepplinger, pp. 97-114. Freiburg, München: Verlag Karl Alber.

Neverla, Irene. 1983. Arbeitsmarktsegmentation im journalistischen Beruf [Segmentation of the labor market in the profession of journalism]. *Publizistik* 28, 3: 343-362.

Neverla, Irene and Gerda Kanzleiter. 1984. *Journalistinnen: Frauen in einem Männerberuf* [Female journalists: Women in a male profession]. Frankfurt/Main, New York: Campus Verlag.

Noelle-Neumann, Elisabeth. 1977. *Umfragen zur inneren Pressefreiheit: Das Verhältnis Verlag-Redaktion* [Polls on internal press freedom: The relationship between publishers and editors]. Düsseldorf: Droste Verlag.

Prott, Jürgen. 1976. *Bewusstsein von Journalisten: Standesdenken oder gewerkschaftliche Solidarisierung?* [Journalists' consciousness: Professional orientation or unionist solidarity?]. Frankfurt/Main, Köln: Europäische Verlagsanstalt.

Prott, Jürgen et al. 1983. *Berufsbild der Journalisten im Wandel? Zeitungsredakteure unter den Bedingungen der Bildschirmarbeit* [The professional image of journalists in change? Newspaper editors working under conditions of computer work]. Frankfurt/Main: R.G. Fischer Verlag.

Rühl, Manfred. 1979. *Die Zeitungsredaktion als organisiertes soziales System* [The newspaper newsroom as an organized social system]. Second edition, Fribourg: Universitätsverlag.

Rühl, Manfred. 1987. Journalistenschwemme in einer Kommunikatorendürre: Anmerkungen zur Steuerungsproblematik in der Ausbildung von Berufskommunikatoren [The flood of journalists in a communicator drought: Notes on the problem of steering the course of professional communicators education]. In *Zwischenbilanz der Journalistenausbildung* [Summary of journalistic education], edited by Jürgen Wilke, pp. 65-88. Freiburg, München: Verlag Ölschläger.

Schneider, Beate, Klaus Schönbach, and Dieter Stürzebecher. 1993a. Westdeutsche Journalisten im vergleich: Jung, professionell und mit Spass an der Arbeit [West German journalists in comparison: Young, professional and enjoying their jobs]. *Publizistik* 38, 1: 5-30.

Schneider, Beate, Klaus Schönbach, and Dieter Stürzebecher. 1993b. Journalisten im vereinigten Deutschland: Strukturen, Arbeitsweisen und Einstellungen im Ost-West-Vergleich [Journalists in the unified Germany: Structures, working practices and attitudes in east-west comparison]. *Publizistik* 38, 3: 353-382.

Schneider, Beate, Klaus Schönbach, and Dieter Stürzebecher. 1994. Ergebnisse einer Repräsentativbefragung zur Struktur, sozialen Lage und zu den Einstellungen von Journalisten in den neuen Bundesländern [Results of a representative survey on the structure, social situation and attitudes of journalists in the new federal states]. In *Journalismus in den neuen Ländern: Ein Berufsstand zwischen Aufbruch und Anpassung* (Journalism in the new federal states: A profession between emergence and accommodation), edited by Frank Böckelmann, Claudia Mast, and Beate Schneider, pp. 145-230 and 460-497 (appendix). Konstanz: Universitätsverlag Konstanz.

Schönbach, Klaus, Beate Schneider, and Dieter Stürzebecher. 1994. Oberlehrer und Missionare? Das Selbstverständnis Deutscher Journalisten [Educationalists and missionaries? The self-perception of German journalists]. In *Öffentlichkeit, öffentliche Meinung, soziale Bewegungen* [Public sphere, public opinion, social movements]. Sonderheft 34 der Kölner Zeitschrift für Soziologie und Sozialpsychologie, edited by Friedhelm Neidhart, pp. 139-161. Opladen: Westdeutscher Verlag.

Schütt, Bernd. 1981. *Vom Tagesschriftsteller zum technischen Redakteur? Versuch einer logisch-historischen und empirischen Analyse journalistischer Tätigkeit* [From daily essayist to technical editor? An essay on a logical-historical and empirical analysis of journalist work]. Frankfurt/Main: Haag & Herchen Verlag.

Schweda, Claudia and Rainer Opherden. 1995. *Journalismus und Public Relations: Grenzbeziehungen im System lokaler politischer Kommunikation* [Journalism and public relations: Bordering relations in the system of local political communication]. Wiesbaden: Deutscher Universitäts-Verlag.

Stiehler, Hans-Jörg. 1990. Medienwelt im Umbruch: Ansätze und Ergebnisse empirischer Medienforschung in der DDR [Media world in change: Approaches and results of empirical media research in the GDR]. *Media Perspektiven* 2: 91-103.

Tuchman, Gaye. 1978. *Making news: A study in the construction of reality*. New York: The Free Press.

Weaver, David and G. Cleveland Wilhoit. 1986. *The American journalist: A portrait of U.S. news people and their work*. Bloomington: Indiana University Press.

Weaver, David H. and G. Cleveland Wilhoit. 1992, November. *The American journalist in the 1990s: A preliminary report of key findings from a 1992 national survey of U.S. journalists*. Arlington, VA: The Freedom Forum.

Weischenberg, Siegfried. 1977. Berufliche Autonomie und journalistisches Selbstverständnis [Professional autonomy and journalistic self-perception]. *Publizistik* 22, 2: 150-158.

Weischenberg, Siegfried. 1978. *Die Aussenseiter der Redaktion. Struktur, Funktion und Bedingungen des Sportjournalismus: Theorie und Analyse im Rahmen eines allgemeinen Konzepts komplexer Kommunikationsforschung* [Outsiders in the newsroom. Structure, function, and conditions of sports journalism: Theory and analysis in the framework of a general concept of complex communication research]. 2nd ed. Bochum: Studienverlag Dr. N. Brockmeyer.

Weischenberg, Siegfried. 1985. Die Unberechenbarkeit des Gatekeepers: Zur Zukunft professioneller Informationsvermittlung im Prozess technisch-ökonomischen Wandels [The unpredictability of gatekeepers: On the future of professional information delivery in the process of technical and economical transformation]. *Rundfunk und Fernsehen* 33, 2: 187-201.

Weischenberg, Siegfried. 1992. *Journalistik. Band 1: Mediensysteme, Medienethik, Medieninstitutionen* [Journalism. Volume 1: Media systems, media ethics, media institutions]. Opladen: Westdeutscher Verlag.

Weischenberg, Siegfried. 1995. *Journalistik. Band 2: Medientechnik, Medienfunktionen, Medienakteure* [Journalism. Volume 2: Media technology, media functions, media actors]. Opladen: Westdeutscher Verlag.

Weischenberg, Siegfried, Martin Löffelholz, and Armin Scholl. 1993. Profile der Aussagenentstehung. Journalismus in Deutschland: Design und erste Befunde der Kommunikatorstudie [Profiles of content formation. Journalism in Germany: The design and early results of a communicator study]. *Media Perspektiven* 1: 21-33.

Weischenberg, Siegfried, Martin Löffelholz, and Armin Scholl. 1994. Merkmale und einstellungen von journalisten: Journalismus in Deutschland II [Characteristics and attitudes of journalists: Journalism in Germany II). *Media Perspektiven* 4: 154-167.

Weischenberg, Siegfried, Martin Löffelholz, and Armin Scholl. 1997. *Journalismus im der Gesellschaft* [Journalism in society]. Opladen: Westdeutscher Verlag (in preparation).

Weiss, Hans-Jürgen et al. 1977. *Schlussbericht Synopse Journalismus als Beruf: Forschungssynopse* [Final report on the synopsis of research on journalism as a profession]. Unpublished report: Freiburg, München.

Zeiss, Michael. 1981. *Bewusstsein von Tageszeitungsredakteuren: Eine Studie über Bedingungen, Struktur und Folgen journalistischen Berufsverständnisses* [Consciousness of daily newspaper journalists: A study on conditions, structure and consequences of journalistic role interpretations]. Berlin: Verlag Volker Spiess.

14

Hungarian Journalists

Ildiko Kovats
Hungarian Academy of Sciences

The first significant professional association of Hungarian journalists was founded in 1896. So if we accept that one of the most important steps in the development of a profession is the formation of a professional association with its own special value system and protection of interests, the beginning of the journalists' profession in Hungary can be construed as such an event. It was at the end of the last century that the commercial press began to develop in the capital (Budapest), and this made it possible for the best journalists to earn their living exclusively from writing for newspapers and journals. The association had double aims: First, it protected the journalists from the growing attacks of the politicians by elaborating professional norms, and second, it was a charitable institute for its members, which supported journalists' independence and limited attempts to corrupt journalists.

During the next decades, some other associations were formed on a more general basis such as for commercial and noncommercial journalism. The journalists of the capital and of the rural areas associated separately for a long time because of the big differences in the character of the papers (urban versus rural). It was not obligatory for working journalists to belong to any professional association until the 1940s. At that time, the Ministry of Home Affairs founded the Chamber of the Hungarian Journalists. Its aim was to strictly control the ideology of journalists in the prewar period. At that time only the registered members of the Chamber could work at newspapers and journals or could write for them as freelancers or part-time employees.

During the 45 years of the communist period, there was only one professional association for journalists, and those working at different papers had to join it. The association was a peculiar mixture of a professional trade union, a bureaucratic controlling body of the professionals, a training center, and an essential part of the communist party's information system. This situation changed only in the late 1980s, coinciding with the political changes in the country. The journalists' "palace revolution" removed the ideologically compromised leadership, and the journalists took the direction of the professional association into their own hands. The new leadership supported the "negotiated revolution" but, at the same time, they emphasized the association's political independence. As a consequence, they had to give up the financial support of the state.

To now work as a journalist or simply to write regularly for journals or newspapers does not require any permission, registration anywhere, or membership in professional associations in Hungary, so it is hard to say how big the journalistic workforce is in this country. The number of those engaged in journalistic activities can be estimated on the basis of membership in professional associations and the information of a media marketing and public relations firm. According to the Index of Hungarian Journalists (1993), there were 8,870 journalists in Hungary who wanted their names to be published in the index at the end of 1993. At that time the overwhelming majority—about 80% to 85%—were members of the Hungarian Association of Journalists. The preconditions of membership were and are the presentation of 10 articles published in newspapers or journals and recommendations of two members of high reputation.

As for as the characteristics and structure of the Hungarian journalists' workforce, there are data available only about the members of the Association, who represent about 80% to 85% of all Hungarian journalists. The information in this chapter comes from the database of the Association (Kovats and Tolgyesi 1994).

At the end of 1994 the Association had 7,140 journalist members and 111 supporting members. Among the journalist members 82% were active and 18% received pensions. In Hungary the retirement age is 60 years for men and 55 years for women. The majority of journalists do not go on pension, or they do but continue to work. It is hard to say when a journalist is "too old" to write. This is why it makes no sense to separate the active and retired journalists in an analysis of the characteristics of the journalists' society.

BASIC CHARACTERISTICS

The profession of journalists in Hungary seems to become more and more closed. In 1981, the percentage of those who came from a family in which the father was an intellectual was 35%—in 1992, 53%. In 1992, 46% of journalists were born in Budapest, 31% in other towns, and 15% in villages. In 1981, 43% were born in Budapest, 31% in other towns, and 27% in villages.

Two thirds of the journalists started their careers not as journalists and only later found their way to this profession. Forty percent of those interviewed said that they had consciously chosen the profession. The rest said that they became journalists as a result of circumstances. Especially among the younger journalists, we can find more who consciously chose this profession (Vasarhelyi 1992).

In 1994, 8% of the members of the Association of Journalists were younger than 29 years of age, 19% belonged to the 30-39 age group, 32% to the 40-49 age group, 16% to the 50-59 age group, and 25% were older than 60 years of age. Two-thirds (67%) of the journalists were male, and 33% female. Among the 82% active journalists, 71% were employed, 7% were freelancers, and 4% worked for papers regularly on the basis of contracts. Nearly three fourths (72%) of the journalists worked in the capital, Budapest, and 28% in the provinces. About two thirds (68%) of the journalists had a degree from a college or high school, and half of the journalists said that they were familiar, or more or less could understand, at least one foreign language. Seven percent had a good command of English, 7% Russian, 5% German, and 4% French. The percentage of those who entered the Association following the change of the regime between 1990 and 1994 was 29% of the total membership.

Age

It may be debated whether it is favorable in a period of sharp social and political changes to have almost half—48%—of the journalists belonging to the age group of 40- to 59-year-olds, 25% older than 60, and only 27% younger than 40 years of age. It was an encouraging sign, however, that fresh blood entered the veins of journalism: The percentage of journalists younger than 40 entering the Association was 55% following the change of the regime in 1990-1993, so the membership of the Association became younger. However, there was another peculiarity of the newcomers—not only their age, but their education level as well was lower than that of those joining the profession in the years before. The new tabloid papers that appeared with the commercialization of the press did not really take journalists with high education. The overwhelming majority of these new recruits did not have any journalist's education—only 16% of them had attended courses of journalism at the Journalists' Association as opposed to 43% of the "old journalists," who had worked before the change of the regime.

There are differences between the journalists belonging to different age groups. For example, the proportion of those who had only secondary education decreases with age—but only until 60 years old. The proportion of journalists who received no tertiary education was lowest in the age group comprising 20- to 29-year-olds—about 50%. At the other end of the demographic tree, the journalists older than 60 had lower qualifications (29% had only secondary education) compared to the age group of the 30-59 (22% to 26% with only secondary education). This is explained by the fact that 40 or 50 years ago, when the elderly age group began to work, no certification was needed for a person to become a journalist. Later, in general, it was required and could be avoided only in two periods following great political changes—the period following 1948, when the communist party took over in the country, and the period after the defeat of the 1956 revolution.

In these times, a large number of journalists were disqualified, and the new holders of power, the communists, filled up the vacant state-owned editorial offices "with highly committed young workers and peasants." These same workers later received the job as a "party obligation," knowing nothing about the profession. A party leader in high rank said in 1948: "We have two kinds of journalists: those who are good journalists but are bad communists, and those who are good communists, but are bad journalists" (Kovats 1996: 38). During and after such periods, the special training of the newcomers and the ideological brainwashing of the old staff was part of the agenda. The specificity of these courses was such that they could not be integrated into the system of formal education but belonged to the competence of the special party education organizations and the professional association.

With the exception of a short time in the 1950s there was no journalism education at the colleges or universities in Hungary before 1993. Journalists older than 60—if they had any degree—were more likely than others to have degrees from faculties of law or some "other kinds of paper," including the diploma of the Party Academy or some special prewar educational form. Among every age group, the teacher's degree is the most common. The proportion with diplomas from foreign universities is low but more frequent (6% to 7%) among the two youngest age groups.

The youngest and the oldest of the journalists have something in common, namely, their deficient professional education. In both groups the proportion of those who attended journalists' courses organized by the Association of Journalists or the media institutions is much lower than in the middle-aged category. Among those younger than 29 years of age, this percentage is 27, among those older than 60 it is 21%, and between the two age groups the percentage of those who attended journalists' courses increases gradually up to 43.

There is an age-related peculiarity in the knowledge of languages—the knowledge or understanding of German characterizes the elderly. Among those older than 60, the percentage is 46, whereas among those 20 to 29 years of age it is only 14%. The opposite is true for the English language—40% of the youngest age group said that they knew or at least understood English, but among those older than 50 this proportion is about 28%. The knowledge of Russian was more often mentioned among those 30 to 50 years of age, whereas those younger or older mentioned it more rarely.

Gender

What is the difference between male and female journalists' careers? The data show that the profession opened later for women than for men. More women are to be found in the younger age groups than in the older ones. Two thirds (67%) of the female journalists are younger than 40 years of age, compared to 57% of the male journalists. Only 18% of the women are older than 60, compared to 26% of the men. There is no difference in the levels of education between female and male journalists, but there are differences in subject matter. In comparison with men, there are many more women with degrees from teacher-training colleges or universities and fewer with degrees from universities and colleges of law, technology, and agriculture. The percentage of those who graduated from schools of journalism is higher among women (39) than men (33). The knowledge of at least one foreign language among female journalists is also higher (62%) than among males (57%). Despite a higher educational level, female journalists' earnings are much lower than those of males.

The capital city offers more opportunities to women in journalism—77% of them work in Budapest as opposed to 70% of men. One negative fact deserves mentioning when evaluating the social situation of the female journalist: This demanding profession with the special way of life it requires is not conducive to good family life for a woman journalist. The proportion of divorce is twice as high among female journalists as among males, and the number of children is much smaller with female journalists than with males.

Religious and Ethnic Origins

There are no data available about the ethnic and religious orientations of the Hungarian journalists, and this is not an accident. Any information on religious or ethnic origins is considered to be a delicate issue in Hungary, although the latter is less sensitive. During the communist era, there was an anti-nationalist and anti-religious atmosphere, although not so marked as in the 1980s. Even so, it continued to influence people's way of thinking for a while.

The Roman Catholic Church has a dominant role in Hungary. In spite of the secularization tendencies of the communist era, 69% of the people older than 15 were baptized in this church, and 24% in one of the reformed churches. A third of 1% identified themselves as Jewish, 0.1% belonged to other little religious communities, and 5.4% were not baptized at all.[1] In spite of these high percentages, the percentage of those identifying themselves as believers is about 60%, with 40% nonbelievers or atheists. The percentage of regular church-goers is 11%.

Two conflicts must be mentioned concerning the question of religion: the tension between believers and nonbelievers, and the digging up of the so-called Jewish problem. This "problem" was used by certain political forces, attaching the Jewish faith to liberal and communist orientations, cosmopolitism, and nonunpatriotism. In the new era of pluralism and free speech, anti-Semitic voices have grown louder. These questions have a special connection to journalism and explain the sensitivity of ethnic and religious identification. The professionals still remember the anti-Semitic and fascist restrictive measures in the 1940s in Hungary before and during World War II. These measures included the Jewish laws, which limited the proportion of Jews in journalism to 6% and dismissed hundreds of journalists from their jobs. When applying for membership in the Journalists' Chamber (which was a precondition for working journalists at that time), candidates had to present documents certifying that they were not Jewish. Those in power at that time combined religion with ethnicity, saying Jews were not true Hungarians; they had no genuine nationalist feelings and their activities in the ideological sphere

---

[1] In Hungary the overwhelming majority of people (70 %) were christened to be Catholic or belong to the reformed churches (20% Calvinist and 5% Lutheran). The percentage of nonpracticing believers is 51, but the percentage of church-going worshippers is only 11. Of the 60% of respondents in a 1993 survey who said they were "religious," many were not attached to specific churches. The proportion of nonbelievers among leaders was higher (36%) than among the adult population of Hungary in 1992 (24%), according to the Hungarian Statistical Office, and is probably higher for journalists as well.

were dangerous in wartime.[2] From then on, the religion of journalists was an especially sensitive question.

The long period of communism resulted in a relatively high level of atheism and secularization of the social, political, and cultural life. Those especially attached to the ideological sphere such as journalists and the majority of the intelligentsia became alienated from religion. Following the system change, many of them perceived the return of the churches into the social life and public sphere with strong suspicion, remembering the prewar interweaving of the Roman Catholic Church and the State. However, some of the representatives of the religious orders accused the nonbeliever journalists of communist orientation, moral insufficiencies, and liberal manipulation of the society.

Two more facts should be noted concerning the relationship of religion and journalists. First, not unparalleled in the history of the Hungarian journalists' community, Catholic journalists felt they had to express their particular interests and established their special association in 1990. (The first Catholic association of journalists was formed in 1898.) The membership of the Association consisted of about 160 members in 1995, but this total included members from abroad and the technical staff of the religious publishing houses as well. The second fact is the number—43—of journalists who indicated religion and worship as their special field of competence in the list of journalists (*Journalists' Yearbook* 1996).

Concerning the ethnic characteristics of the country, two specifics of the situation should be emphasized. First, as a consequence of historical events and agreements, in Hungary the overwhelming majority of the population is Hungarian. When using the word *minority* or *minority problem*, the Hungarians first think about the Hungarian minorities of 3.5 million people living in neighboring countries as a result of the peace agreements changing the borders of the country after the first and second World Wars.

Second, an important aspect of the communist/socialist ideology was an emphasis on its international character. The suppression of nationalist feelings and ethnic affiliation, and at the same time the negation of the ethnic tension, swept the problem under the carpet. In reality, this contributed to the assimilation or quasi-assimilation of minorities.

The percentage of ethnic minorities in Hungary is low. According to the 1990 national census, it is between 2% and 3%. According to the estimates of the ethnic associations applying for state support in 1993, however, that total is about 10%. Half are gypsies, a fifth are German, about one tenth Slovakian, one tenth Croatian, and the others belong to nine other small ethnic minorities.

---

[2]The president of the Chamber of the Hungarian Journalists was executed after the war for upholding the idea of fascism (Kovats 1996).

A new minority law was passed, and under it a system of self-government for minorities was created. Under the law, ethnic minorities are a constructive part of the Hungarian state, and everybody has the right to decide to which ethnic group they belong. However this is not registered officially because of the historically sensitive character of the question in East and Central Europe.

When speaking about the ethnic minority in the country, the people mean, in general, the Gypsy problem because of their relative significant number (500 to 600 thousand from the 10 million inhabitants of Hungary), their strong visibility, and their economically and culturally disadvantageous situation. After the political changes, they started to organize themselves. There are very few Gypsy journalists, but in 1992 the School of Journalism of the Hungarian Association of Journalists supported them in organizing a special course in journalism.

Otherwise, there is no registration of journalists belonging to particular minorities. The only thing we know is that 48 journalists mentioned ethnic minorities as one of their main fields of competence in 1995 (*Journalists' Yearbook* 1996). Ethnic minorities have newspapers and radio and television programs on central and local stations, but we have no data concerning their staffs.

Political Attitudes

In 1990, with the change of the social-political regime, the political palette of Hungary changed drastically. Instead of the one-party communist system, a multiparty parliamentary system developed. New parties mushroomed very quickly, and the different groups of the intelligentsia played a decisive role in this development. The regime change was peaceful in Hungary, a bloodless "negotiated revolution."[3] The newspapers and journalists played an important role in the "negotiated revolution"—they contributed to the situation, when the political battles were fought on a symbolic level, in the pages of newspapers and on the screen. They got rid of self-censorship, criticized the former administration, and introduced the representatives of the opposition, the emerging new political forces into the public sphere. In a period of a political vacuum they played the role of nonexistent democratic institutions and were politically active in helping the changes. After the first free elections the new political administration questioned the active political role of journalists especially because they did not seem to be ready to serve the new

---

[3]In 1989, the communist party, which had lost its strength and legitimacy in the country by that time, was willing to discuss the conditions of peaceful transition and the circumstances of the first multiparty elections with the different opposition groups.

political elite. In the name of freedom of the press and freedom of opinion, journalists continued to push their own political priorities. As a result, they were accused by the nationalist-Christian-traditionalist governing coalition of having remained communists or being former communists turned liberal.

In 1992, there was a survey of 400 journalists initiated by the Journalists' Association into the situation, attitudes, and opinions of Hungarian journalists (Vasarhelyi 1992), including their party preferences (see Table 14.1).[4]

Table 14.1. Political Party Preferences of Journalists and of the Adult Population in Hungary, Fall 1992.

Party Preferences	Journalists ($N = 400$) (%)	Adult Population (N = 1,000) (%)
Young Democrats (radical, liberal, national orientation)	34	28
Hungarian Socialist Party (reform wing of the former communist party, soc.dem. orient.)	11	6
Alliance of Free Democrats (liberal democratic party)	10	7
Hungarian Democratic Forum (traditionalist, nationalist)	9	8
Christian Democratic Party	2	4
Little Holders' Party (traditionalist, populist party)	0	6
Other parties	0	6
Have no party preferences or do not know	30	35
Total	96	100

Source: From The Situation, Ways of Thinking and Involvement of Journalists—1992 by M. Vasarhelyi, 1992, Budapest: MUOSZ [Hungarian Association of Journalists].

[4]The study contains the results of a survey of a representative sample of journalists (400 persons) sponsored by the Association of Journalists about the situation, standpoints, and role images of journalists. The survey was carried out in 1992 by Maria Vasarhelyi, researcher of the Research Group for Communication Studies at the Hungarian Academy of Sciences.

Journalists were asked to choose between different ways of thinking, social philosophies, and ideologies and to decide which two they could take on themselves. The offer was: liberal, democratic, reformist, leftist, adherent of order and stability, nationalist, conservative, traditional, radical, and rightist. Slightly more than one third (35%) chose the combination "liberal, democratic"; 13% considered themselves "reformist, democratic"; 11% as "leftist, democratic"; 10% said they were "adherent of the order and stability, democratic"; 6% "nationalist, democratic"; 5% "conservative, traditional"; 3% "radical"; and 1% "rightist."

A special set of questions was asked to discover the relationship of journalists' views to national values and to the question of whether the country has to develop "in its own way" or to follow Western countries. More than one third of those interviewed shared the opinion that Hungary has to develop "in its own way," taking into consideration the special circumstances of its development and protecting its own cultural values. Fifteen percent of the journalists held a similar opinion, although they were a little less nationalistic and did not emphasize that national values would be in danger. About 15% of journalists said that the best conditions for development would be complete openness and imitation of the Western example.

Although the majority of the journalists had strong opinions and affiliations to the different parties, 30% of the respondents said that they had no party preferences in 1992. In 1990 the winner of the first free elections in Hungary was the Hungarian Democratic Forum supporting nationalist, traditionalist, Christian ideas that promised gradual development as opposed to the shock therapy of the liberal parties. They formed a coalition with the Christian Democratic Party and the Small Holders' Party, a populist party with the slogan "God, fatherland, family." Only 15% of the journalists supported the governing coalition at the time—9% supported the Hungarian Democratic Forum, 2% supported the Christian Democrats, and 4% mentioned other non-parliamentary parties. The Small Holders' Party was not mentioned by the journalists interviewed.

At the same time, 34% of the journalists interviewed supported the Young Democrats as being in opposition—an interesting party of the younger generation, which at that time seemed to be radical, liberal, and somewhat nationalist.[5] At that time, 11% of the journalists supported the Hungarian Socialist Party—the surviving reform communists, who aimed to transfer their party into a social democratic body. Ten percent shared the ideas of the Alliance of Free Democrats, a liberal party with a social-

---

[5]Before the election, the party changed sharply. It turned to traditionalist and nationalist values, rejecting the possibility of any cooperation with the leftist, social democratically oriented Hungarian Socialist Party. The popularity of the Young Democrats fell swiftly among the journalists and the population as well.

liberal and a conservative-liberal wing, and 30% of the respondents could not name any party they wanted to support.

Since 1992, there has been no research into the political attitudes of journalists. In 1994, the winner of the second free elections was the Socialist Party with more than 50% of the votes, and the second most successful party was the Alliance of Free Democrats. The two parties formed a coalition, and the former governing parties went into opposition. The Young Democrats changed into a more conservative nationalist party.

After the second election, the percentage of journalists who considered themselves as supporters of a nationalist-traditionalist-Christian orientation, even after it was ousted from power, could be estimated at 5 to 10.[6] In 1995, the rest of the journalists seemed not to have taken sides, gently criticizing the restrictive policies of the socialist-liberal coalition or supporting them.

EDUCATION AND TRAINING

Until 1990, when the social-political regime changed, there had been only two forms of professional education in Hungary: the School of Journalism of the Hungarian Association of Journalists, and the professional courses organized by the Hungarian Radio and the Hungarian Television from time to time to cover the special needs of these institutions, which had a monopoly on broadcasting. In the early 1950s, there was journalism education at the university level, but the political leadership, which suppressed the 1956 revolution in Hungary, noted that the students in the course on journalism were too active during the revolution (counterrevolution in their terms) and did not want to maintain this vipers' den anymore, so it was closed down. From that time on, the journalism courses organized by the Journalists' Association were the only form of education for journalists. As time passed, the length of the courses came to vary between three months and two years. There was double screening of the candidates who wanted to learn there—only those working for a newspaper could apply for enrollment with the support of the general editor, and they had to pass an entrance examination of political, cultural, and professional knowledge.

This education consisted of two parts. The more important one was to familiarize the students with the expectations of the political lead-

---

[6]This is the percentage of the estimated membership of the Hungarian Journalists' Community, an association of journalists formed on the basis of nationalist-traditionalist-Christian ideology.

ership, with the essence of so-called politically committed journalism, and with the political limitations of journalism. The less important part was the professional education, but the students thought more higher of this part and considered it more useful. However, the insight into the devil's kitchen of the establishment was not useless either, although it often led to conclusions by the students different from the ones expected.

The precondition for applying for admission to a course on journalism was a degree, or at least a promise that the candidate would complete his or her tertiary education. According to an order of the Information Office, every young journalist employed at a newspaper's editorial office had to complete a course on journalism within a given interval. In 1981, 80% of the youngest age group—those younger than 29 years of age—had completed the course. With the progress of time, however, the general editors did not feel this central order was obligatory any more, and the percentage of those who completed the course became lower.

At the same time, a degree was needed if a journalist were to receive a job at a "good" newspaper or journal. In 1968, 46% of the journalists had a degree; in 1981, 64% and in 1994, 68%. According to the database of the Journalists Association in 1994, half the journalists who had degrees had received them in teachers' training colleges or universities, 10% had attended business schools or universities of economics, 6% had received technical degrees, 6% had graduated from universities of law, 4% had received their degrees abroad, and the degrees of 23% came from some other kind of college. The results of the research launched by the Association of Journalists (Vasarhelyi 1992) showed that those who had degrees from universities of economics or technology had much better chances than their colleagues in their professional careers.

After the change of the regime in 1990, the picture of journalists' education changed drastically. There was a boom in the press and the media due to the arrival of freedom of the press and the appearance of new communication technology in Hungary. A lot of specialists were needed, and this led to a boom in the different areas of professional education. The School of Journalism run by the Association woke up first, reorganizing its courses and adapting them to the new professional and political requirements and offering paid courses. First the editorial offices covered their delegates' tuition fees, but later on it became clear that the students themselves were ready to pay in the hopes of getting a good professional job.

An oversupply of different private "professional" training courses appeared in the educational market, with varying levels and curricula. These courses generally offered practical knowledge and developed the students' communication skills. After the privatization of newspapers and journals, the new owners—especially the foreign ones—devoted much attention to the training of their staffs, first in the use of new technology, and tried to teach them the requirements of the Western-style journalism of the mother enterprises. In addition, the dailies of big circulation started to offer training courses to future journalists. They made the participants pay for these courses, but at the same time they chose the most promising ones for their own newspaper staffs.

In 1993, education for journalists appeared again in the offerings of the Budapest ELTE University, and several other universities and colleges followed suit. These schools wanted to attract more students, offering them journalism as a minor in addition to their majors. The teacher-training faculties especially wanted to improve their enrollments because the situation of the schools and teachers had became unstable due to the withdrawal of the state from the financing of education.

In May 1995, there was a conference for the organizers of communication education in Hungarian colleges and universities. It was there that it became clear that there were courses on media, communication, and journalism at 12 universities and colleges in Hungary. The number of applicants were three to four times larger than there were places available at these courses. All these schools had some common problems—everywhere there were great restrictions in the budget, and in such circumstances it was very hard to start a new specialty. The contents and methods of the courses were very different, and there was a shortage of competent teaching staffs and a lack of expensive media technology needed for educational purposes.

In accordance with the competence and aspirations of the professors, there were very different types of courses, but the representatives of all the schools said that there was a demand for their graduates in the media sphere. Almost nowhere was the training of journalists introduced as a major. It meant special studies leading to a second degree, or it was a minor, or it was not journalism as such, but it appeared in the broader context of mass or public communications. Cooperation existed only on a very low level among these schools because of the competition incited by financial restrictions, the reduction of teaching staffs, and the reluctance of the professors to be tested by their fellow professionals.

The Budapest ELTE University provides classical training in journalism at the Faculty of Liberal Arts and offers a second degree to top it. They invited well-known journalists to develop their students' creativity and communication skills, and teach communication theory and freedom of the press. The lecturers focus on the cultural and aesthetic aspects of the modern mass media. The Department of Sociology developed a specialty in communication research. There is a third, postgraduate course on journalism for those working for the papers and the electronic media.

The education in communication at the University of Pecs concentrates on theoretical questions of the media and communication, especially from an anthropological and etiological point of view. The University of Szeged specializes in training journalists for local radio, television, and the printed press. The Faculty of Social Sciences at the University of Economic Sciences is developing journalists' training in the broader context of public communication, offering parallel courses on persuasive rhetoric, public relations, the uses of new communication technologies, and international communication. All these subjects are rooted in the foundation subjects of theory and research methods of public opinion and mass communication, the peculiarities and rules of functioning of the media market, and the legal and ethical regulation of these fields. The subjects offered by other faculties—especially marketing communication, advertising and negotiating techniques—broaden the scale of choices for the students.

The religious colleges and universities are aiming at developing communication between the churches and society, paying great attention to the ethical and psychological aspects of communication, and adding some special religious studies to the curriculum. Redetermining and extending the role of teachers in the small local communities as mediators and organizers of the local public sphere, with the help of the local press and perhaps the new communication technology, is a challenge at the teacher- training faculties.

Following the change of the regime in 1990, Hungarian journalists benefited from the professional tradeoff with U.S. journalism in different forms. Scholarships were offered to well-known Hungarian journalists so they could master U.S.-style liberal, fact-based, and investigative journalism in the states, and a journalism center was opened in Budapest financed by the International Media Foundation. However, the Center's functioning was not entirely successful. In the hope of quick results it targeted midcareer education for journalists on the assumption that Hungarian journalists did not know what true journalism is because they were not professional. However, the Hungarian journalists had no time to join these courses to develop themselves because of the pressures of work. In addition, the professional criteria set by U.S. journalism and those required by the local market are not necessarily the same.

Quite often the U.S. specialists were frustrated because they thought they had brought the torch of enlightenment to Hungary in vain—their good intentions were not acknowledged. This was caused by two factors: They did not find good target groups for their courses, and they tried to plant U.S. ideas and practices directly into the Hungarian field, without any willingness to get acquainted with the local circumstances. More successful were the U.S. professors who taught students at the various colleges or universities under long-term contracts and not as envoys of shuttle cultural exchanges, and who were interested in Hungary from a professional point of view or wanted to do communication research.

PERCEIVED AUTONOMY OR FREEDOM

The research initiated by the Association of Journalists in 1992 inquired about the perception of autonomy of journalists in the course of their work (Vasarhelyi 1992). Nearly half (45%) of the journalists responding said that there was total freedom of the press, 50% felt that the freedom of the press was partial, and 4% held the opinion that there was no such freedom in Hungary (see Table 14.2). Those who evaluated the situation of freedom of the press as partial mainly referred to the pressures from the government (30%) or those exercised by the owners of newspapers (39%), or they mentioned the lack of legal regulations for the media (29%). Even among those who said that there was total freedom of the press in Hungary, 35% said that there were taboos restricting journalists, especially in the field of politics.

Table 14.2. Opinions of Journalists and Adult Population About the Situation of the Freedom of the Press in Hungary, 1992.

	Journalists (N = 400) (%)	Adult Population (N = 1,000) (%)
There is total press freedom	45	35
There is partial press freedom	51	52
There is not press freedom	4	2
Do not know	0	11
Total	100	100

Source: Vasarhelyi, 1992.

Note: The evaluation of the situation of press freedom correlates with some social characteristics of the journalists. Men, those in higher positions, those having sympathy for the governing parties and the youngest (under 30 years) and oldest age groups (older than 50 years—and with the lowest education level) perceive the situation better than women, those in lower positions, supporters of the parties in opposition, and age groups between 31-50 years.

As for personal autonomy, journalists thought that they were a little freer in the selection of their subject than in its evaluation or interpretation (see Table 14.3). About half (51%) of the journalists rated their independence in selection of stories as "very high," and 29% as "high." As for interpretation and comments on the events, 46 percent said their autonomy was "very high," and 32% said that it was "high." Senior, more qualified male journalists living in the capital and earning more evaluated their freedom higher than the others.

The journalists were also asked about whose expectations were more important for them from a list enumerating the audience, the general editor, the characters they deal with in their articles, their columnists, or their colleagues. Rated most important were the expectations of audiences, followed by the characters in the articles, the evaluation of the colleagues, the columnists, and the general editor (Vasarhelyi 1992).

Journalists were also asked to evaluate their working conditions, the content of their work, and their workload. Of 12 choices offered, they were most content with the interesting character of their jobs and next with their colleagues. The rest of the choices, in an order of decreasing satisfaction, were as follows: democracy in the editorial office, the personal characteristics of the immediate boss, the atmosphere in the

Table 14.3. Freedom in the Selection of Subjects and in the Interpretation and Comment in 1981 and 1992 (N = 400).

	In the Selection of Subjects		Interpretation and Comments	
	1981 (%)	1992 (%)	1981 (%)	1982 (%)
Very high	10	51	22	46
High	32	29	38	32
Fair (medium)	47	15	30	18
Low	10	5	10	4
Total	100	100	100	100

Source: Vasarhelyi, 1992.

Note: The simple comparison of the data over time can be misleading because of big changes in the circumstances. In 1981, journalists could compare the situation to their earlier experience and its relative improvement. However, there is no doubt about the tendency of the changes from 1981 to 1992.

newsroom, the competence of the immediate boss, the assets of the working environment, income, the material conditions of work, the chances of promotion, the strength of the assistant workforce in the editorial office, and the opportunity to travel abroad.

Forty-one percent of the journalists said that they have to work too much, 49% said that their workload was just right, 7% found their work too little, and 3% gave other answers. Those working for local newspapers in the countryside were most likely to say that they had too much work to do. On the average journalists worked 9.4 hours on weekdays and 6.5 hours on weekends.

Two fifths of the journalists thought about changing their workplace. The majority mentioned problems of professional character. The next reason mentioned was income followed by dissatisfaction with the atmosphere at the editorial office and the problems caused by differences between their political views and those held by the editors. Although the level of the unemployment among journalists was about 4% in Hungary in 1992, journalists were afraid of it. Young journalists, women, and those working for local dailies were most worried.

MEMBERSHIP IN PROFESSIONAL ORGANIZATIONS

The main professional organization of the journalists, the Hungarian Association of Journalists, celebrated its 100-year anniversary in 1996, although up to 1920 it included only the professional journalists of Budapest. As was noted at the beginning of this study, the number of its members is now larger than 7,000. The two other associations are the Community of the Hungarian Journalists, which was founded in 1992, and the Association of the Hungarian Catholic Journalists, founded in 1990. The estimated maximum of the membership of the former organization is about 600, whereas that of the latter is 160. In both organizations half the journalists have double membership—they are also members of the Hungarian Association of Journalists. As discussed earlier, membership in the new associations demonstrates political convictions (e.g., nationalist) or a special view of life (religious) rather than being of practical significance.

Although the Association of Hungarian Journalists declared itself a politically free professional organization, this means only that it is not ready to deal with or judge the political convictions or activities of its members. It does not mean that the Association does not have a political profile. As a professional association, it acknowledges the liberal criteria of professional journalism and the liberal understanding of press freedom. This is why the association had many conflicts with the new political elites in power, especially during the first period of the new social-political system following the elections of 1990, when the coalition in government could be characterized as supporting traditionalist, nationalist, and Christian values claiming the respect of the new and freely elected authority.

CONCLUSIONS

The radical change of the social-political systems in 1989-1990 and the "revolutions with different attributes" in Eastern and Central Europe brought big changes in the public sphere and in mass communication as well. More exactly, the change of these spheres was part of the broader social-political changes, and it would be very hard to say what was the cause and what was the result of these interconnections.

Immediately after the changes, Western specialists arrived in these countries to teach the formation of new democratic institutions and to help develop the new roles and behaviors needed in the everyday functioning of democracy. Special emphases were given to the public sphere, to mass communication, and to journalists as professionals. The commercial, privately owned press and electronic media were novelties in this part of the world.

The liberal model of journalism became an ideal here as well, although not without contradictions. The majority of Western specialists thought that the journalists who worked within the former social-political systems—communism or socialism—could not acquire and practice genuine professional (commercial, liberal) journalism. The journalists were supposed to start to learn the impartial, objective journalism based on facts, to put the emphasis on the news and not on opinion and personal convictions (or at least to separate them). However, these efforts and the arrival of the commercial press and media system were not met with unanimous zeal on the part of the journalists.

The larger press freedom and the higher salaries offered by the new commercial media were accepted with appreciation. Meanwhile, the growing level of stress caused by the clashes in the pluralistic political system and the conflicts of economic reorganization resulting in big social suffering shook the journalists. This induced them to take a stand and to express their own opinions about the change in their environment.

In this time of social upheaval, the journalists were confused between their different roles: the role of professional, the role of intellectual, and the role of citizen. As professionals, they were supposed to be objective, impartial, and outside mediators. As intellectuals, they wanted to express themselves, their views, and affect the development toward specific orientations, including democracy. The journalists were in permanent opposition to those in power. Finally, as citizens, they wanted to participate, to take an active part in the big social-political changes, and to support the political aims they considered important.

It is clear that there is no other choice for the Hungarian journalists than to join the world-wide successful liberal model under the circumstances of growing internationalization of the media industry. Yet it is not clear what kind of society this helps to build.

As far as the question of professionalism is concerned, it must not be forgotten that there were a lot of newspapers and journals read by a large readership, and the electronic media also had a large audience. One surprise for the Western specialists was that the biggest newspapers inherited from the previous political system and written by the same journalists survived and, what is more, remained successful. Does this mean that the brilliant Hungarian journalists could adapt themselves very quickly to the changing requirements of the competitive situation? Or does this mean that the professionals did not have to undergo such monumental changes as were supposed by the Western specialists? Or maybe, there was not a big change, but the Hungarian audience was conservative and appreciated the nonprofessional journalism? These questions have yet to be answered.

The Western specialists—and together with them many members of the new political elite in the country—were convinced that the majority of journalists morally and politically compromised themselves by "serving the communists" and expected big changes in the editorial staffs (like in the Eastern part of the newly united Germany), or at least public apology. The most radical elements of the new political parties demanded that the Association of Hungarian Journalists exclude its "most compromised members." However, this would be a hard task because the destiny of the journalists was varying like that of the other social strata. Few of them were and remained communists. Others joined one of the new political forces. Some of them, for the first time in their lives, were involved in political activity. Some were politically active during the previous system and arrived "on the road to Damascus, transforming Saul into Paul," and, finally, many of the journalists had enough of the political games and decided to remain far removed from these processes.

In the past hundred years, there were at least six significant breaks in the social-political development of Hungary, and all these had large effects on the journalists: the First World War with its tragic results, the Soviet type Conseils' Republic of 1919 and its failure, the Second World War with its prewar horrors and the communist takeover in 1948, the revolution of 1956, and finally the peaceful but radical change of the political regime in 1989-1990. The journalists were involved in each of these changes, both pro and against, and were whipping posts and punished when the changes turned in the opposing direction. The normal functioning of democratic systems assumes the rotation of the different political forces, which makes the journalist witch hunts suspect. This is why the Association of Hungarian Journalists did not take any measures against any of its members but left the question to them to decide on the basis of conscience.

At the end of 1995, the Association of Hungarian Journalists ordered an analysis of its old and new members and of the balance these changes produced in the membership (Kovats 1996). It became clear that 32% of the membership joined the Association between 1990 and 1995, after the change of the political regime. Those who declared withdrawal from the Association as a form of protest against its decisions were rare, no more than 125 members. Passive resistance was more typical such as nonpayment of the membership fee, which resulted in their expulsion. The big turmoil characteristic of the Hungarian press system had its effects on the Association's membership—there were many newcomers but more than 10% of them disappeared and were not among the members in 1995.

These contradicting processes did not change significantly the structure of the membership. Hardly perceptible changes included the relatively higher proportion of women and young people among the newcomers. It seems that the genuine changes in the Hungarian journalists' society took place in other dimensions waiting for disclosure. Their character is rather qualitative than quantitative and must be linked to the changes in the media system and the communication policy of the country. The research concerning the situation and role perceptions of Hungarian journalists has only begun in Hungary, and that is why our knowledge in this sphere is very limited for now.

REFERENCES

Index of Hungarian Journalists. 1993. Budapest: INFO and PR Services Lc.
Journalists' Yearbook. 1996. Budapest, Hungary: Magyar Ujsagirok Orszagos Szovetsege [Hungarian Association of Journalists].
Kovats, Ildiko. 1996. The association life of the Hungarian journalists—1896-1996. In *Year Book of the Hungarian Association of Journalists*, pp. 7-63. Budapest: MUOSZ [Hungarian Association of Journalists].
Kovats, Ildiko and Janos Tolgyesi. 1994. The characteristics of the membership of the Association of Hungarian Journalists. *Magyar Sajto*, No. 16-17. Budapest: Hungary MUOSZ [Hungarian Association of Journalists].
Vasarhelyi, Maria. 1992. *The situation, ways of thinking and involvement of journalists—1992.* Budapest: MUOSZ [Hungarian Association of Journalists].

15

Polish Journalists: Professionals or Not?

Jerzy Oledzki
University of Warsaw

More and more Polish journalists are worrying about the increasing deficit of social respect shown toward the practice of their occupation. It appears that journalists would like to gain respect for their work not through increased knowledge and greater self-discipline in ethical behavior and improved skill, but through, first and foremost, shallow entertainment and quests after scandals and corruption, sensational descriptions of which are meant to attract the attention of readers and to increase the circulation of newspapers.

In the materials that follow, I show the need for special attention to the journalistic environment in the formation of professionalism as the proper antidote to the previously mentioned "deficit of social respect." I draw, among other things, on the findings of the first stage of research that I conducted among 238 journalists who worked on 48 daily papers in Poland[1] and also on interviews with 38 journalists that were carried out by students of the Institute of Journalism at the University of Warsaw in 1994.

---

[1]Two hundred thirty-eight journalists from 48 daily presses took part in the face-to-face, questionnaire-type research. They came from the following cities: Bialystok, Gdansk, Katowice, Krakow, Lublin, Lodz, Olsztyn, Poznan, Szczecin, Warsaw, and Wroclaw.

DEFINITIONS OF PROFESSIONALISM

What is professionalism? This notion is defined in dictionaries as "professional practice in such fields as the arts, athletic disciplines, etc." A *professional* is defined as "a specialist, an expert in some field, a person well acquainted with his or her own occupation." Colloquially, when we hear the word *professionalism*, we understand mastery, in other words, an exemplary, faultless (conscientious, honest, etc.) execution of one's occupation. Do journalists have, in general, something in common with professionalism? Can they be professionals? On that score such famous U.S. sociologists of mass communication as Wilbur Schramm or Penn Kimball have a range of doubts (Singletary 1982).

The latter, for example, stated: "So long as admission to a journalistic career is not conditioned by an obligatory period of specialist training, and there is not a test of skill to authorize the assumption of the practice, journalists will not be able to count their occupation as having something officially in common with professionalism" (Singletary 1982:75). From my point of view, the previously mentioned stipulations have a character that is more formal than substantial. The term professionalism originates from the Latin *profesio*, meaning, among other things, craft, profession, as well as testimony or declaration, and it indicates an occupation into which one may enter if having a closely defined and demanded stock of knowledge that is pointed to and confirmed by the suitable certificate. Under this notion are included the so-called closed professions such as the practice of medicine or law. Professionals create their own frameworks with norms of behavior and ethical values specific only to their occupations. Externally, they are represented through formally qualified professional organizations that operate autonomously in their countries.

Professionalism, in this context, is a narrowly defined and expected group of behaviors of people who, given their title of specialist education and the execution of their work, give a guarantee that they will properly represent their clients/patients and not, on any score, harm them. Situations in which an individual who is acknowledged as a professional breaks out of the defined professional frame, and, as a consequence, is removed from his or her professional organization are received with extreme social disapproval. Professionalism indicates, therefore, behavior that agrees with the standards and ethics of the profession. Journalism is an open profession; a special exam is not necessary, and no precise, well-defined stock of knowledge and skill is needed to possess in order to carry out this occupation. The inference is that journalism is not a profession.

Advocates of the opinion that journalism is a profession assert that it is required, among other things, that media workers' behavior be in accord with ethical standards of the occupation. They also advance an additional argument that with the determination of professionalization of an occupation comes the possibility of the attainment of an assured degree of autonomy in a red-tape social system (Curry 1990). This autonomy expresses itself through the stabilized position of an organized, occupational structure that is officially independent.

At the individual level, four elements are necessary in transforming a given individual into a professional: (a) a well-defined system of recruiting candidates and their subsequent instruction, (b) a period of special occupational training and the possibility of reciprocal interaction of the members of this group, (c) a fully elaborated collection of principles of behavior for the members of this group and a system of checking up on compliance with these principles, and (d) influence on the social opinion of this professional group.

Each of these elements is equally essential and plays an important role in the creation of a system of professional values, eventually fashioning a separate subculture. If we take into consideration the real state of preparation for the occupation, existing codes of behavior, and activity of journalistic organizations, we might agree with the statement that journalism is a profession. Therefore, we have all the more right to expect that journalists have the duty to be professionals.

JOURNALISTS' OPINIONS ON PROFESSIONALISM

There will be no further theoretical discussion; this chapter now turns to the opinions of Polish journalists themselves on the theme of professionalism. How do they understand the idea? Do they perceive a need for the betterment of their occupation? Among 38 interviewed journalists of many years of professional practice there was not one person who thought that in the occupation of journalism there was no place for professionalism. The notion was defined variously, but the idea of occupational excellence was always retained. The following are various comments from journalists on the subject (roman numerals in parentheses indicate the catalogue number of each journalist's statements that can be found in the author's archive):

> Journalistic professionalism is, most simply, the maximum honesty in the presentation of information. In preparing information we must always think of the recipient. What interests the reader is the only important thing. We are in service to society and we must think of those for whom we work. (XXXVII)

Full professionalism consists in absolute compliance with the principle, "The customer is our master." It must be complied with because no one other than the customer, in such a more or less direct manner, finances the media. Anyway, here in a certain fashion the circle is closed because respect for customers, who, in the instance of media, are viewers, hearers, readers, and advertisers, is not only an indication of professionalism, but a necessary requirement for the functioning of the means of transmission and consequently the upkeep of the places of employment for journalists. (XXXI)

Professionalism to me is exact, precise preparation of oneself for every program. Respect for the listener. But, above all, all the time, self-improvement in the profession—through reading, extending the workshop, not locking oneself in one's narrow specialty, skill bound with contact with the listener, with the reader, and humility—a very important matter. Giving a ready ear to remarks, entertaining and analyzing them, from each. And, of course, self-criticism, honesty, objectivity. Also, this is very important, that one should be oneself. Always! (XXVIII)

For me, the professionalism of a journalist means that you do your own work, independently of whatever else is happening, independently of pressures, such as when someone attempts to exert influence on you, and independently of the outside world. To put it simply, you have your own plot of ground to work, and you do that the best you are able. (XXV)

I understand professionalism as a constant need for improvement of one's own occupation, a continuous thirst to be still better. He who, for example, provokes conflicts using racial or nationalistic pretexts to attain his own ends—riots breaking out—for me that is not a journalist. That is exclusively a provocateur, whose tools of the trade are paper and pen. A journalist must have an awareness of the strength of the written word and a feeling of social sensitivity and responsibility. Victor Hugo said that "the pen has the lightness of wind and the strength of a thunderbolt." One must know how to direct that power. (XXI)

If someone has an awareness of the tools which are necessary for the execution of a particular occupation, if he puts these tools to work for him, that means that that person is a professional. Skill often is connected with tools—know how—I know how to conduct myself in a particular situation, I know what to do, I know which tools to take to work. What, for me, is professionalism, I would stipulate in the following words: Professionalism is the guarantee of occupational security. It gives me psychic comfort, that I won't make myself ridiculous, I won't make a fool of myself, I won't let people down. I don't know of such an instance in which professional behavior has resulted in a taint on a professional's character. (XVII)

Professionalism is competence in form and content. In other words, a certain store of knowledge and indispensable workshop preparation for the "sale" of acquired and possessed knowledge. (XVI)

Professionalism in journalism is the skill of connecting facts with the mind of the reader, erecting a footbridge between that which happens where we were and where the reader was not, and his possibilities, knowledge, perception, because each press has its own customers, it adapts to his language, its own way of elaborating, it measures out information in a way appropriate to it, appropriately describes facts, etc. Each newspaper or radio station is building bridges between a reality happening without the participation of the readers and us. This is the metaphor for professionalism: a bridge between described facts and readers. (XIV)

A journalist is not a professional. A journalist knows a lot but only so much, and is able to exploit knowledge and experience and transmit it in an interesting manner to readers, listeners, or television viewers. People don't require a teacher in the person of the journalist. They want only to get an honest picture of events, not to be tutored by a bad humored, overwise journalist. (XIII)

Professionalism in the occupation of journalism is, for me, comprised of many elements. First, journalistic honesty, an honest approach to the subject matter, integrity, ethics, which is sometimes hard, when, for example, we speak about the particular people's tragedy. The next element is self-preparation for the subject matter which is being written about. The element that testifies to the rank of a journalist is, furthermore, his ability to enlarge his net of informants. Workshop skills are of course important. Maximum communication using the minimum of words. (XII)

Each journalistic work, each item, must be professional; professional meaning good, well shaped, comprehensible, clear, up to date, etc. This house must be built in order that it not collapse, and furthermore that it be pretty and functional. (X)

I am a professional, because I can write quickly and well. I write about various subject matters, and the bulk of these texts please the readers. (V)

A professional journalist should be able to write each text required of him; not all his works, however, will be "gems," of course. This distinguishes the professional from the amateur, who can write even good texts, but only when they concern the sphere in which he works. Information is a commodity and in order for it to be possible to sell it, it must be of the highest quality and have the most attractive packaging. It is necessary to dig it out from under the earth, to out pace the competition. (IV)

> The most important principle is a faithful representation of a picture of reality, just like it is. Secondly, all information must be adequately checked; the best way to do this is to check from two sources. It is necessary to try to be the most objective, and not select news according to what pleases us, and what doesn't. Our assignment is being a mirror. On the other hand, our assignment is the extraction of that which is the most important. Furthermore, we should write in order that the reader, as well, who is not steeped in the particulars of a matter as we are, understands what's going on. The next rule—always separate news from commentary. The citing of sources of information is a very important element of professionalism. Compliance with the rule of "off the record," meaning, "not for publication," is essential. And so-called "background" and the maintenance of the anonymity of the informant according to his wishes, are also very important. (XXXV)

> I repeat, the requirement of good, professional journalism is the separation of commentary from information. (XXXIV)

> Professionalism is a state to which one constantly strives. It's an ideal. It's a synonym of the word *perfectionism*. Occupational excellence. If you acknowledge that you are a professional, that's the end of fun and games. At all times one must assume an attitude of distance to what one is doing, and evaluate it critically. If criticism stops, that's the end of the growth of the profession. (XXVII)

THE PROFESSIONAL JOURNALIST

These opinions demonstrate how people working in mass media make use of a socially keen and important instrument and simultaneously demonstrate the importance of access to these means for persons for whom media is their professional work. Users of the media have the right to expect that they are not led astray, are not manipulated, and are not exploited. They want to trust journalists. Do the journalists who took part in our study also have such a vision of their profession? Among the most characteristic statements I counted the following:

> A professional journalist always strives for objectivity. He doesn't write biased material; he doesn't agree with the proposition that a sufficient version covers one side. A journalist feels responsible to his customers. He always gathers complete material; he can ask every indispensable question. His articles don't have any gaps. Such a journalist pounces on material, whose capture is difficult or almost borders on impossibility. He absolutely never betrays his sources,

and if it is necessary to go to jail in doing so, he goes. A professional journalist never mixes classes of information. He distinguishes informational writing and opinion, commentary. It is well if, at the same time in his career, he doesn't do both things simultaneously. They are physically distinct parts of the paper. (XIX)

A journalist is such a person, for whom such terms as impartiality, objectivity, honesty, integrity, exactitude, compactness are familiar. A journalist frequently stands at the crossroads of whether to choose loyalty to the editorial staff or loyalty to the reader. At times it is hard to reconcile the two. I, however, am of the opinion that since we write for people, it is to them that we should be loyal. (XIII)

A journalist is a press spokesperson for his newspaper and editor-in-chief. That's why, unfortunately, he must repeatedly deeply conceal his opinions and write as instructed. Journalism is one big compromise! (XXIII)

Journalism is not for people who can only consider behavior with which they are comfortable as ethical. In all journalism is embedded a little cynicism in view of the fact that the journalist executes orders of the establishment for which he works. You can never be in a situation of such moral comfort that what the paper publishes always suits you. History trained my generation of journalists to be very cynical because we frequently wrote of things with which we did not agree. (XXXII)

The most important thing is integrity, even unthinking integrity, even when it proves to be unpleasant or painful. Secondly, one must be, simply, curious, a person who is interested by everything. When something happens you feel sort of like a craving to see it, to question, to understand. The third feature, without which I couldn't imagine a professional journalist, is independence. If you're thinking of going in for journalism, you must be conscious of the fact that you are forbidden to get stuck in any ideology whatsoever. There is a border, which you yourself must feel, and beyond which you feel that you are already too emotionally engaged in order to, in that field, cultivate journalism. (XXXVI)

A professional journalist must remember that he's not practicing art for art's sake, and all elements which he employs have their goal, which is to reach the viewer or listener. I'm of the opinion that journalistic information must be made in such a way that our sympathy is illegible, that the viewer could not be able to say that I like politician X and that I don't like politician Y. That is extremely hard, but that's how it must be done.(VII)

There's no such thing as objective journalistic information—you look at the world with your own eyes, which will not be free from subjectivity. It is not possible to free oneself of that, but it is possible to try to maintain a certain distance from what you're working on, to look at it from another angle. Fine journalistic work was, for example, provoked by German journalists on the selling of uranium by Polish civil servants. It is possible to reflect on this, on whether it was ethical. The problem was announced publicly—in Poland it is possible to buy fissionable material. A journalist acted here on behalf of good people. The disclosure of matters depends on his professional obligation. The dilemma can be just that, do you exhibit a victim, or the negative action of a hero, or is it enough to show the problem. That was the case in that vote in the Parliament where few deputies were voting for themselves and their absent fellows. I formulated those voting from behind, without seeing their faces. Anyway, only like that could we register them. I knew who they were, but I didn't expose them—then I would be taking on the role of prosecutor. My assignment was to draw attention to the problem and I was successful—votes are not done that way now. Such is the aim of the work of a journalist. (XXV)

Provoking events, in order to describe them, is dishonest because you don't describe the truth but facts you have created. The most important thing is, that what's written is genuine. (V)

A good, professional journalist is some one who has individuality, is someone individual, distinct, who can come into contact with surrounding reality. He must have an ear for people and social sensibility. A good journalist should also possess solid knowledge, at least in one sphere. Even let it be beekeeping and let the journalist handle the daily sports column. On the face of it these subjects don't have anything in common. That is reality, but someone who has such extensive knowledge has respect for the knowledge and skill of others. A dilettante, who doesn't know anything about anything, doesn't appreciate the worth of expertise; he will not listen to that which others say because to him it will always seem that he knows everything better. (XXX)

Journalistic information cannot be biased in any instance. It must relate and reflect reality like it is—not colored with a mix of subjectivity. (XXII)

It is necessary to be the ears and eyes of the reader. For me journalism was always the possibility of helping people in various, even the smallest of, matters. The essence of this profession is not the observation of my own insides. That people simply aren't interested in. My assignment is the elucidation of the mechanisms of power, service in concrete matters. (XX)

It is requisite that a good journalist is able to achieve a synthesis, to quickly gather the building blocks of various elements. It's a question of speed in work, skill in completing a summary. This particularly applies to radio and television. When I was a foreign correspondent, a report could only be about 40 seconds. And here I am reminded of the words, which, unless I am mistaken, Hemingway wrote to someone, "I apologize for writing at such length, but I didn't have time." Skill in presenting a short transmission of one's thoughts is essential. Language is also important, the qualities of language, wealth, the skill of an accurate formulation of thoughts, because all journalism is based on written journalism. (I)

In the instances which involve human life, human fates, self censorship must exist. That's how it was in the instance of the scandal connected with the money of the Foundation for the Matter of Polish German Reconciliation for victims of the war, with which Mr. Wilk transacted a business deal for himself. From the point of view of professionalism it would have been appropriate to amplify the matter, because actually, it was scandalous. I tried, however, to write little about the matter because I could seriously hurt Polish Germans relations. I didn't want all Germany to resound, "We give them money, and they arrange personal business deals for themselves with it." In such an event, the choice whether to be a professional and do harm, or to not be a professional, is very hard. (XXXV)

More and more frequently it is often thus that we sell out our own ideals, opinions, values. Words: truth, honesty, objectivity, in other words, common journalistic integrity, have lost their primary meaning. I understand that since it has come to us to live in such crazy times, it is possible that we share some of the madness. But we mustn't give in to madness. A journalist aspiring to the appellation professional must be a person of honor, otherwise he would be an ordinary impostor. Fortunately a decent-sized group of colleagues still think this way. I hope that we never will never have to feel shame that we practice this profession. (XXVII).

I must not cross the border beyond which I begin to cause harm to people; however, there are such types, who dream of this daily—crossing that border, to bring out a terrible reaction, in order to create some stir. A journalist is, at this moment, a kind of source of light, showing, leading the way, and also steering the way. One ought to remember that it is possible to draw people with your own style, and from that it's just one step to being a politician. (XXIV)

People with an ideological taint lead a paper into degeneration. This phenomenon in our situation is very dangerous because our politicians are betraying desires to take control of the media. And, conversely, our colleagues mix political activity with their work. When a politician is a good columnist, the situation is permissible, but it is impossible to carry out these functions at the same time. (XXIX)

With time I became aware that it is possible to learn the use of the pen, but that in itself is too little to make one a journalist. Genuine journalism is a passion, which one may link with hard work.

Sometimes someone will work hard and attain some success, some satisfaction with what he does, and make a name, but without passion, without journalistic bite. He performs the function of a journalist, and it's not really the same. (II)

THE TRIAD OF PROFESSIONALISM

The opinions represented here in each instance underline the significance of professionalism in journalistic work. The concept of *professionalism* is appraised in various ways, but professionalism is always seen as an occupational problem worthy of realization or as an ideal worthy of attainment. If we were only quoting opinions acknowledged as typical for the entire journalistic environment in Poland, then surely we might wonder from whence instances of journalistic slovenliness spring, or whether these rare bad journalists are only undereducated or just amateurs. Unfortunately the quoted opinions are not representative of several thousand environments. Those journalists quoted were selected by students of the Institute of Journalism as professional journalists, experienced people of the pen, microphone, and camera who could serve as examples to these young pupils.

It can therefore only be ascertained that the presented opinions suggest that representatives of the Polish journalistic elite consider professionalism as a requirement in the practice of journalism, which their own work must execute honestly, in agreement with principles of art, in order to deserve the appellation of a person of public trust. According to these opinions journalists are responsible for delivering information; they must be conscious of their role in society. They must be able to find information suitable for the news, meaning that which concerns readers and is useful to them. They have to be at the same time honest, conscientious, objective, inquisitive, courageous, and so on. I do not suppose that it would be possible anywhere in the world to find such a journalist, but, as the quoted material reflects, the aspiration for professionalism is a duty of all qualified journalists and not just ideal individuals.

Such basic canons of journalism as truth, impartiality, integrity, and exactitude are the standards of the profession, compliance with which every reader, radio listener, and television viewer has the right not only to expect but to demand. Journalists who are mindful of these canons are called professionals, and they decide the credibility of media, which is an essential condition for the existence of these media.

Compliance with the principles of objectivity and impartiality appears as one of the leading injunctions. One of the heroes of the student interviews said:

A journalist must not stand on any side of a conflict. Whenever I look at our beloved television, I read our press or listen to the radio, I see that for many journalists their work is a question of that about which we are struggling, what we're striving towards and where we are. It's not about how to write in order not to offend anyone. A journalist simply cannot show his sympathies in his work. That's an error, which many people make. They form ranks on one side or another of some issue. We don't have real impartiality in journalism as long as in order to be well informed it is necessary to read several newspapers: *Zycie Warszawy, Gazeta Polska, Gazeta Wyborcza, Trybuna*, and maybe *Rzeczpospolita*. Only then will you have some kind of a picture of what's going on. On the other hand, if we're talking about such media as public television, there is absolutely no right to sympathize with any side whatsoever, regardless of what we're talking about. (X)

A journalist who takes a stand loses authority. One of the interviewees specified outright the following reminder: "It is always necessary in this occupation to remember one thing: It is an occupation in which you have one name, one voice, one face, and one reputation. You work on those for twenty years and lose them in a second" (X).

It is worthwhile at this point to consider that everything in our consideration thus far refers to informational journalism, not to journalists who write commentary, from whom it would be difficult to demand impartiality (impartiality is however absolutely demanded and expected in all material broadcast through public radio and television). Hence, the separation in the press of news from commentary is important. It is a cardinal rule of journalism in fully developed democratic countries. There is a clear differentiation between journalists/reporters and journalists/commentators or columnists. In order to illustrate this difference I reworded a statement of the Russian prose writer Wladimir Wojnowicz about reporters and the writers whom we call columnists: "A reporter relates events even seated on board a sinking ship: 'We are sinking, the water level is rising. . . .' A columnist in such a situation must gather manuscripts and jump into a life boat. Only later will he analyze the catastrophe" (Zebrowska 1994: 12).

Professionalism in journalism contains within itself the idea of a service to society. It embraces three areas: technical/workshop, professional qualifications, and ethics. The area of technical-occupational consists of a correct skill in the use of appropriate language for each journalistic statement, the exercise of technical equipment, the collection and documentation of information, the duty of attaining the primary source of information (if that is impossible, the verification of information and the cross-checking of sources), and the speed of work. We can call this whole technical area workshop skills, or, for short, "workshop."

The second decisive area of professionalism is occupational "ethics," which means, above all, integrity, honesty, impartiality in the presentation of facts, not exposing sources of information, and respect for the reader. It is worthwhile at this point to remember the words of the sociology professor Czarnowski (1956: 124): "Journalism without ethics is a fraud." Equally important, if not fundamental in journalism, is the third area, which we designated with the catchword "knowledge." A journalist must have the appropriate scope of knowledge; in other words, he or she must possess sufficient qualifications of the subject matter in order to write on a particular subject. This is not just the formal requirement of possession of an appropriate diploma, but the necessity of the acquisition of knowledge helpful in the preparation of the journalistic material, the acquisition of information about the subject matter on which one is writing, and the introduction of the material in a competent manner.

Finally, professionalism in the occupation of journalism is made up of three determinants, which in sum create the triad of professionalism. Graphically, they create an isosceles triangle: workshop/ethics/knowledge (See Figure 15.1). Some journalists are more professional than others. Professionalism doubtlessly influences the quality of completed work. Research suggests that journalists of a pro-professional orientation (that is, journalists who acknowledge that professionalism in journalism is of a special occupational value, worthy of attainment) distinguish themselves with many feelings of responsibility and impartiality. They are characterized by constant aspiration for profes-

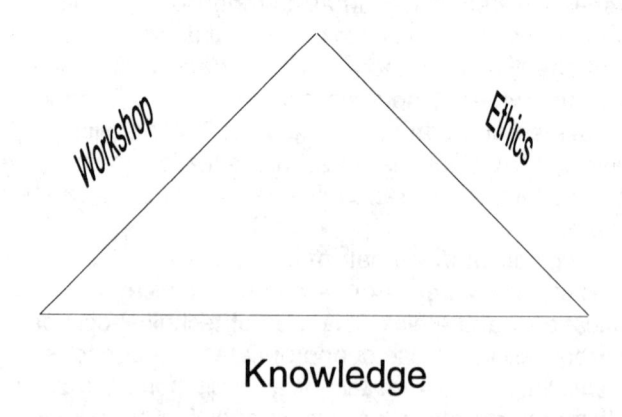

Figure 15.1. Three determinants of professionalism

sional and personal perfection, as well as the improvement of the entire medium in which they work, whose fate and good name is not a matter of indifference to them. Finally, they are very critical of their occupational environment and employers, and their occupational aspirations and dreams of work in an ideal newspaper, radio, or TV station are very high.

PROFESSIONALISM IN A TIME OF TRANSFORMATION

The change of the political system in Poland, the liquidation of censorship and the party monopoly of the RSW "Prasa Ksiazka Ruch" (RSW stands for Robotnicza Spoldzielnia Wydawnicza—communist party organs for publishing the press, books, and for the distribution of them), the disappearance of the communist party, and the party practice of steering the press, all played a part in Polish journalism and the whole press system. The appearance of private media in Poland, full freedom in the publication of press titles, the wane of structural dependence on political power, and the occurrence of a pluralism of ideas endowed journalists with completely different conditions of work. These conditions provided a natural opportunity to perfect the occupation of journalism and also the cultivation of the principles of professionalism. One might be lead to the hypothesis, on the basis of these study results, that with the coming of a free market, the fate of each individual medium would be decided now not by the governing political party but by newly established capital, advertisements, and the reader, viewer, and listener. However, professionalism would be demanded of journalists. Frankly, there emerged the supposition that the professionalism of journalists and editors would decide, to a greater degree, the future of newspapers.

How did journalists perceive the meaning of the new changes and their influence on the function of the press? How did they appraise the meaning of professionalism for the future of the news media for which they work?[2] Answers to these questions came from a questionnaire conducted among journalists on daily papers in Poland. The first stage of research was carried out in 1992; the second I hope to conduct after the passage of five years, in 1997, with the goal of grasping the changes and analyzing the observed transformational processes and trends. I pre-

---

[2] It would be worthwhile here to mention that thanks to the effort undertaken by the Polish journalistic associations, in March 1995, a "Charter of Media Ethics" was prepared. In just the first week after its publication, the charter was signed (voluntarily, because there was no obligation) by several score of Polish publishers and owners of radio and TV stations. Journalistic occupational organizations began creating a Press Council, whose assignment would be the appraisal of compliance with Charter principles by the signatories.

pared six-page questionnaires for the face-to-face interviews with 240 journalists. From all about 100 daily newspapers in Poland in 1992, 48 dailies with the highest circulation, were chosen in 11 biggest cities around the country. It was decided to take any five persons (two editors from the top executive and three journalists from the staff) from each newspaper for interviews conducted by the researcher at the newspaper. All interviews were conducted during two months in the spring 1992. From the 240 questionnaires completed, two were lost before the final computing. Results of the first round permit, thus far, the ascertainment of the state of journalistic opinion about the role of media and journalists.

First, as Table 15.1 indicates, there was a general convergence of opinions of Polish and U.S. journalists on the most important functions of the press.[3] This reflects the change in the political system of Poland. It would have been impossible to expect 8 to 10 years earlier that Polish journalists would acknowledge popularizing the politics of the government and the mobilization and organization of public opinion as unimportant functions of the press (see Table 15.2), and—similar to U.S. journalists—that they would identify as most important among their assignments informing and criticizing as well as uncovering "dark matters" (see Table 15.1).

Table 15.1. Very Important Function of the Press.

Function	Polish journalists ($N = 238$) (%)	"U.S. journalists ($N = 301$) (%)
To inform	95.8	99.3
To criticize and monitor	60.1	69.1
To expose "dark matters"	44.9	48.5
To intervene	43.7	—

---

[3]In 1986, thanks to the E.W. Scripps School of Journalism, Ohio University in Athens, and the Scripps Foundation, I conducted questionnaire-type research among the press journalists and students from the schools of journalism in Athens, OH; University of North Carolina in Chapel Hill, and University of Iowa in Iowa City. Research was devoted to the meaning of the First Amendment and functions of the U.S. media understood by media people in the United States. Working journalist samples were drawn from 13 newspapers in Iowa, 12 in North Carolina, and 22 in Ohio. I got 301 completed questionnaires back, of which 161 were completed by the journalists (62% of the sample) and 140 by the students of the previously mentioned schools of journalism (100% rate because questionnaires were given in the classes). The details of this research can be found in Oledzki (1992).

In 1992 (the third year of the political transformation in the country), Polish journalists' views about occupational impartiality were ambivalent, as Table 15.3 indicates. The bulk of them still did not perceive a danger to impartiality from a journalist's engagement in political and economic activity or the assumption of public functions. Combining journalistic work with other duties is, in many fully developed democratic countries, considered inadvisable because of the danger it poses to the

Table 15.2. Dispensable Functions.

Function	Polish journalists (N = 238) (%)	"U.S. journalists (N = 301) (%)
To propagate the politics of the government or the president	62.6	38.7
To mobilize and organize	58.4	39.5
To influence opinions	23.9	23.9

Table 15.3. Professional Impartiality: Can Journalists Take on Other Activities? (N = 238).

Statement	Agree (%)	Don't agree (%)	No opinion (%)
It would be appropriate to forbid journalists any kind of economic activity or memberships on boards of directors, in the same way that other people who are fulfilling a public function are so forbidden	32.3	47.5	20.2
Journalists must not become engaged in the political activity of any political party	50.0	40.8	9.2
Journalists may take on public functions on the condition that they resign from their work in journalism	44.5	42.9	12.2

principle of objectivity. Some Polish journalists seem to perceive the pitfalls of such double employment (see Table 15.3), but, as they explained to me in direct conversations, "livelihood defines consciousness, and the cash box defines loyalty." The chase after money is necessary to make possible a relatively decent life for their families.

One may designate Polish journalists as liberal because of their preference for individual freedom over the value of social equality (Table 15.4), and because their political orientation leaned more toward the leftist view (Figure 15.1). Yet Polish journalists were not convinced that the mass media in Poland should try to fulfill the role of a "fourth estate" in the country (see Table 15.5). They appeared to assume that journalists in Poland were not yet a strong, privileged, and active elite, which would enable the fulfilling of such a function. However, the majority of Polish journalists agreed with the duty to explain to the readers their surrounding reality and to detect scandals and corruption (see Table 15.6). When it comes to ethics, Polish journalists evaluated themselves slightly lower than lawyers but decidedly better than politicians, businessmen, and civil servants (see Table 15.7).

Table 15.4. Liberal Tendencies among Journalists (N = 238).

Question: What is more important: freedom or equality?

Statement	Agree (%)	Don't agree (%)	No opinion (%)
A. I think that both freedom and equality are similarly important. If, however, I had to pick just one of the two, I think that personal freedom is more important because each person must profit from freedom and develop without obstacles	75.6	(Neither A nor B)	
B. Of course, both freedom and equality are important. If, however, I had to pick only one of the two, I think that equality is more important since no one should live with discrimination, and differences between individual social classes must not be too large	7.6	15.1	1.7

Table 15.5. Should the Polish Media Be a "Fourth Estate?" (N = 238).

	Yes (%)	No (%)	Don't know (%)
In your opinion, should the mass media in Poland fill the role of a "fourth estate" in the country?	55.9	34.4	9.7

Table 15.6. Professional Self Appraisal: The Journalists' Opinion of the Occupation of Journalism (N = 238).

	Agree (%)	Don't agree (%)	No opinion (%)
Journalism is a transmission of information to people connected with opinions such that the customers understood their meaning	78.1	16.4	5.0
Journalism is the procurement of information hidden by the authorities and corrupted people	68.5	21.8	8.4
Journalism is a social service and one should be mindful only of the welfare of the reader	61.8	25.2	12.6
Journalism is the informing of people of how they are and how they ought to be	33.6	55.5	10.5
Journalism is just an interesting way of earning a living	17.2	74.8	10.5
Journalism is always the propagation of definite political opinions and the maintenance of loyalty to one's employer	7.1	87.8	4.6
Journalists are just people to hire: They write everything.	5.0	91.2	3.8

Table 15.7. Evaluation of Ethical Norms (N = 238).

Question: In which mentioned group, in your opinion, are ethical norms the lowest in present day Poland?

	(%)
Politician	47.1
Businessmen	26.9
Civil servants	21.0
Journalists	2.9
Lawyers	1.3

As a supplement to the results of the survey research, the following are statements taken from selected Warsaw journalists. Questions touched on their assessment of their working environment, among other topics:

> A premium has never been placed on knowledge and professionalism in Polish journalism. "Plebeian" journalism never attached importance to the development of one's own individuality. It was generally accepted that the journalist reads only his own text, and that, too, inaccurately. That was the characteristic feature of Polish journalism, and it is still in force in a large degree as in the past. (VI).

> The majority of young people who come from the underground press treat the press exclusively as a means of transmitting self-expression and one's own opinions. It wasn't necessary to do anything more than to slap the reds. In the underground press the selection of information didn't come into consideration. The young don't know how to listen to anyone else. The young generation lives only for itself and it doesn't listen; it is physically incapable of listening. (XXIX).

> Polish journalism, particularly young, is very aggressive. Self-confidence and, at times, outright boorishness try to make up for the lack of competence and expertise. Professionalism, therefore, is understood by the young as bad. They think that journalism is privileged, and a journalist may do as he likes. (XIII)

> In my opinion, unfortunately, the environment, taken as a whole, is professionally weak. Many journalists have taken a little bit of a "short cut" to the occupation; they entered therein without the humility appropriate to every occupation. Many of these amateurs, convinced of their own infallibility, came from the underground press; the result is probably at this time a more politicized profession. The old media system broke down; journalistic authority collapsed. Each is creating his own school of journalism. (IV)

My generation, and maybe even the young generation, is partly corrupted. I imagine that very good journalists in the democratic system, which now is beginning to sprout among us, will be people who, at the present moment, are either in kindergarten or just being born. That will be the generation which doesn't know the existing state. All these bloody scandals will be behind them, I hope. This taking advantage of various situations and stands and functions will be, I am an optimist, also behind us. I think that we must reach this. And only then will they be different journalists. (XXVIII)

Now journalists can show reality impartially, and what they do is better and better. It is very big progress, but, of course, there is no way to learn in four years everything that in other countries was learned through decades. The main fault of our journalism is the constant preponderance of commentary over information. Journalists, chiefly inexperienced, want to speak their own minds on some subject matter, and the reader would like rather to find out what, not what the journalist, but, for example, a politician or a learned or famous artist has to say about a given matter. (III)

After 1989, many newspapers had a very distinct political line and identified themselves with various political groups. Journalists and editors were inclined to reflect upon whether or not to publish a given article because maybe it would harm their side or somehow help a second side. That is a way of thinking which should not exist in journalism in a genuine democracy. Presently I feel there's been much progress on this score. People who conduct political journalism understood that it is possible to write a lot about politics, but in ways that they serve the reader and not some political group. I appraise it as very positive that newspapers are trying to be objective and are able to critically describe the whole political and economic scene, but it is a process which goes on still. (XXXVIII)

The presented materials, besides indicating that we may have hope, provoke discussion on the subject of journalistic work in the new democratic Poland and permit also the extrication of very general deductions.

CONCLUSIONS

The change of the one-party political system, which availed itself of the means of transmission as an instrument of political warfare and as a handy tool for propaganda serving the retention of authority, to a multi-party democratic system, which, among other things, enables a free activity of the public and private media, brought about a rivalry of the newly created market of reader customer/client and not broadcaster/political administrator. This contributed to the growth of the meaning of professionalism in the occupation of journalism. Both journalists and users of media concur in a positive assessment of professionalism. Journalists perceive the concrete value of professionalism for the credibility of media among their users; users of media want to avail themselves of only such media which, in their opinion, present professionally prepared materials.

Is full professionalism possible? In Poland the title *professional journalist* is not acknowledged. The fact is that we already have, however, many winners of prestigious journalistic prizes who would confirm the opinion that achieving an above-average level of occupational excellence is possible. The aspiration for perfection is, after all, an inherent feature of human nature; similarly to err is human. Particularly in the profession of journalism it is not possible, from all accounts, to find a journalist of long standing who with a clear conscience would positively estimate his or her behavior during every day of his or her career. It is said, as well, that journalists and angels have only one thing in common—the feathers of the angels' wings and the feathers on a quill pen.

After several dozen years of work, after he was already retired, Henryk Korotynski (1987: 380-381), winner of many all-Poland journalistic prizes, wrote:

> In these my memoirs and settlement of accounts, I cannot not confess that. . . . I look upon my own journalism as on a defeat in a great love. So many flaws, so many shadows, so much walking the high wire and falling from the wire. In this profession (if one is not going to stand on the sidelines), I don't believe that one could completely maintain moral purity, and, so, what is stable, always, in each writing and editing, is consistence with my own views with that which has gone to print or to broadcast.

A sad final point, not to say a desperate one, is made by Aleksander Fredro (Polish poet living in 1793-1876):

> Like a chimney sweep,
> so is a journalist
> A devilishly hard job.
> he cleans, and gets himself dirty.

That confession from an old journalist and his characteristic sarcasm does not repudiate our consideration of professionalism. On the contrary, it proves only that maybe later will we take care of the problem of the formation of occupational consciousness among all media workers, for whom the problem of professionalism does not as yet exist. Consequently we have such journalism and media. For the consumers of the contents of media it is important that there will be fewer of the kinds of reporters who complained that "people demand too much of journalists. Not just to be interesting, but to be true."

REFERENCES

Curry, J. Leftwich. 1990. *Poland's journalists; Professionalism and politics.* Cambridge: Cambridge University Press.

Czarnowski, S. 1956. *Dziela (Vol. 5).* Warsaw: Panstwowe Wydawnictwo Naukowe.

Korotynski, H. 1987. *Three quarters true. Reminiscences.* Warsaw: State Publishing Institute.

Oledzki, J. 1992. The American conception of the freedom of the press. In *International circulation of information,* edited by J. Oledski, pp. 92-116. Warsaw: The Publishing House of the University of Warsaw.

Singletary, M.W. 1982. Commentary: Are journalists "professionals"? *Newspaper Research Journal* 3, 2: 75-87.

Zebrowska, A. 1994, October 12-13."Uncompromising. Anna Zebrowska Converses with Wlodzimierz Wojnowicz. *Gazeta Wyborcza,* p. 12.

16

Journalists in Emerging Democracies: The Case of Spain*

María José Canel
Antoni M. Piqué
University of Navarra

It is commonly accepted that real democracy is participatory. Studies in politics and social science argue that, in democracy, people are to play an active part in public affairs. Therefore, participatory democracy relies on the ability of citizens to make informed decisions. Among other alternatives for obtaining information, the news media are important channels to make the individual aware of the society in which he or she lives (Semetko, Blumler, Gurevich, and Weaver 1991). Communication is therefore essential to the democratization of societies (Hagen 1992; Wasko 1993). To enable the citizen to participate in political affairs is seen as part of the mission of the news media.

If real democracy is a participatory one in nature, the shaping of professional attitudes of journalists is crucial for the system to work properly. It is not enough that free access to the media is guaranteed by law; it is also necessary that journalists think of their audiences as active participants in the public sphere.

---

*The authors gratefully acknowledge the data given by Professors Manuel Martín (University of Vigo, Galicia) and Norberto González (University of La Laguna, Tenerife, Canary Islands), and also David Carradini for his help in the translation.

Spain is an interesting case study. It has evolved from authoritarianism to democracy in a way quite admired around the world. Between 1975, the time of General Franco's death, and 1978 a democratic system was established, even after 40 years of strong dictatorship. A full, democratic Constitution was passed in 1978, and proper national, regional, local, and—since 1989—European free elections have been conducted since then. In 1995, the whole evolutionary process, properly called *The Transition*, has been regarded as complete with democracy truly established in Spain.

Have professional attitudes of Spanish journalists evolved at the same pace as the political system? This was our main research interest in depicting the profile of Spanish journalists. If the country has progressed to democracy, shifts in journalists' professional attitudes should be prominent, and that shifting paradigm may suggest a model that would be helpful for other emerging democracies such as those in Eastern Europe.

Our initial hypothesis was that there has to be an age at which professional attitudes start to change. Attitudes among young journalists—because they have been brought up in a democratic system—should contrast with those of older journalists, whose main professional routines were established during an authoritarian regime.

First we focus on basic characteristics of Spanish journalists, and then we closely examine our hypothesis.

METHODS

Data used for our article were taken from a 1991 mail survey conducted for the project "Media and Democracy," a study of the professional values among journalists from seven countries. A random sample in all the countries was composed of 600 journalists working in print media, radio, and television. Journalists working in other media or jobs were excluded. The sampling error is ±4 percentage points.[1]

---

[1] The reply rate in Spain was the lowest, maybe because studies of this kind are not common. There is a previous survey published in December 1990 in Periodistas, the journal of the Federación de Asociaciones de la Prensa, which concentrated more on habits of life, consumption, and social status than on professional values and job conditions (The Spanish Journalist Profile). La élite de los periodistas (The Elite of Journalists) is another study that just focused on management-level journalists (see Diezhandino and Bezurartea, 1994). The prominent role the media are taking in political changes in Spain deserves new studies. A further and more detailed project is being prepared at the School of Journalism of the University of Navarra. It will concentrate on how professional attitudes are being changed as a result of the present increase of investigative journalism.

In order to test our hypothesis, we regarded age as an important variable in our measurements. We found that at 45 years old role perceptions and other variables start to change direction. Two age groups were constructed—the first, made up of those up to 45 years old, was called the Democracy Group, and the second, comprising those over age 45, was called the Transition Group.

People aged 45 at the time of the survey (September and October 1991) were 29 at the time of Franco's death. Therefore, people over 45 in the survey had been working at least six years under Franco's regime. People under 45 in the survey had not had much time to work during Franco's regime.

BASIC CHARACTERISTICS OF JOURNALISTS

It is clear from Table 16.1 that journalism is a younger person's occupation in Spain, with a very high proportion of journalists under 45 (87%). This may be an indicator of a very high departure rate among older journalists—those who came to age professionally during the old regime.

Although the overall proportion of women journalists is relatively small (25%), data allow us to say that in Spain journalism will no longer be such a male profession. Table 16.2 shows how strongly women have emerged in the journalistic workforce in recent years. Whereas in the 36 to 40 age group of the sample there are only 9% women, in the 20 to 30 age group the proportion surges to 47%.

According to the distribution of women students in communication schools (64% opposed to 36% men), in less than five years there will be more women than men entering professional journalism, if most of them take jobs in the field. Most of the women—84% in our sample—

Table 16.1 Age (N = 149).

Age	Valid (%)	Cum. (%)
22-30	20.1	20.1
31-35	30.9	51.0
36-40	22.1	73.1
41-45	14.1	87.2
46-50	5.4	92.6
50-55	5.4	98.0
56-60	2.0	100.0

Table 16.2. Gender by Age (N = 149).

Age	Women	Men	Percent of Sample
22-30	46.7	53.3	20.1
31-35	32.6	67.4	30.9
36-40	9.1	90.9	22.1
41-45	14.3	85.7	14.1
46-50	25.0	75.0	5.4
50-55	0.0	100.0	5.4
56-60	0.0	100.0	2.0
Total	24.8	75.2	100.0

have gained access to journalism jobs in the last 20 years. All of them have a proper degree in communication, so all of them have succeeded in college, compared to the 13% of men who have not finished their degree.

Political Attitudes

Journalists in Spain tend not to be identified with a party. More than half of our sample (57%) chose "none" in response to the party identification question.

Among those who did choose a party, a majority are left-wing—one third chose PSOE (Socialist Workers' Party—social-democrat) and one fourth IU (United Left—communists and the like). About 14% chose chose PP (Popular Party—conservative) and 11% depicted themselves as centrists such as CDS or regional lists such as Catalan nationalists of *Convergència i Uni*—and the Basques from *Partido Nacionalista Vasco*.

Even more significant than party identification is ideological positioning. Journalists were asked to identify their political leaning on a left-right scale, with 1 being the extreme left and 7 the extreme right. The average is 3.16, or center-left. Percentages are 27% for values 1-2 (left) and 23.5% for value 3 (center-left). The central value was chosen by 22%, whereas values in the right are never over 12%.

Thus, our study suggests that there is a left-wing positioning among Spanish journalists. This is not surprising. The process of transition to democracy was dominated by centrist-leftist parties. Right and center-right parties were born from the ruins of the old regime and from some "soft reformists" and technocrats hidden behind the regime's curtains. It is not surprising that media professionals look at them and their parties as those who had kept—or helped to keep—journalists under strict censorship. Among media professionals, freedom of expression was seen to be a leftist achievement, and so liberalism was seen to be a reaction to Franco's extreme right-wing authoritarianism.

It is interesting to see that media professionals are more to the left than voters. If we compare journalists' party identification with the popular vote there is an interesting gap. In the last national elections (May 1993), 48% of voters chose a left-wing party, compared to 59% of journalists' party identification, an 11-point difference; conversely, 35% of the public voted for right-wing parties, compared to 14% of journalists' party identification.

Journalists are even more to the left than they perceive their audience to be. On a scale from 1 to 7, journalists think their audience is at 3.88, a center position leaning very slightly to the left. Journalists' perception of their audiences' political leanings matches the electoral results.

Available data allow us to conclude that journalists are more progressive than the average citizen, but they try to adjust their message to their perceived audience's political leaning. In fact, "to catch audience's attention" is regarded as a very important "constraint" in news processing work; the fifth among a list of 11 (see Table 16.4). Strikingly, it appears that catching the public interest is a professional struggle for journalists. This is all the more surprising, given that public interest is not necessarily seen in Spain as a usual criterion in gathering and processing news. However, the definition of good journalism as avoiding personal ideological preferences from biasing their work is quoted by a high rate of the sample, especially among the younger journalists.

There are interesting findings in this field when comparing the Democracy Group with the Transition Group. First, there is a high difference in party identification between both groups. Whereas 40% of the Transition Group (older journalists) say they do not identify with any party, 60% of the Democracy Group (younger journalists) do.

Even more interesting is Figure 16.1. It shows for both the Democracy Group and the Transition Group the political leanings and the perception of news and op-ed lines of the media they work for, of their audience, and of themselves. Journalists from the Democracy Group are more to the left than the older ones. Whereas younger journalists see their audience leaning quite closely to the news and opinion lines of their media, older journalists say their audience is more to the right than their news and opinion line—even though these older professionals perceive their media as slightly more to the left. It can be said that younger journalists adjust their work more to the perceived audience's preferences than do older journalists. In fact, as will be seen later, younger journalists are more likely to avoid their ideological preferences in order not to bias their work.

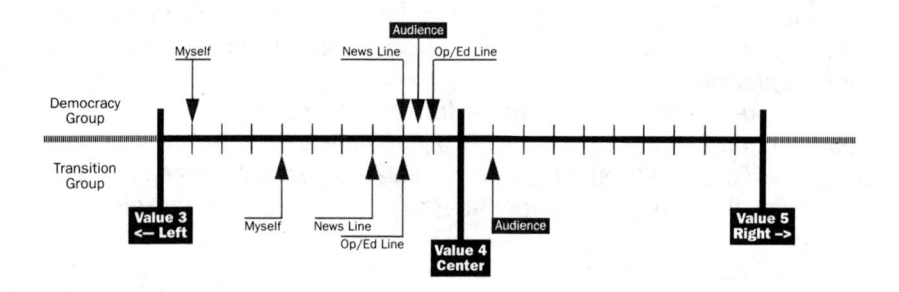

Figure 16.1. Compared political leanings
(Journalists' perception of the self-political leanings and that of the audience, the news line and op-ed line of the media they work for)

EDUCATION AND TRAINING

Nearly 99% of our sample claim to have studied at the university level, and 84% claim a proper degree (72% undergraduate and 12% graduate). The gap is due to journalists who have some unfinished course work. Since the early 1980s, it is quite common in Spain that students are hired as interns before getting their degrees. These people usually combine study and work. Because the degree is not required for a full job contract, some journalists do not complete their degrees. In fact, more than half of the people (58%) who have not gotten their degrees are between 23 and 35 years old.

The high proportion of journalists who majored in communication (87%) shows that this degree, although a relatively recent addition to the university curriculum, is already well established. Journalism was not in fact established as a university degree until 1972. To that point, schools of journalism were under the control of the Minister of Information and Tourism, which is why 15% of the Spanish journalists have a three-year certificate from a nonuniversity school of journalism, and 69% have a five-year university degree from a university journalism school. The remaining 3 percent hold a master's or PhD in journalism or communication.

All in all, it is not common nowadays that the media hire people without a proper degree in communication, or that people with other degrees look for a job in the media. Yet since 1992, press associations do not grant membership to people without a degree in communication. A previously accepted condition for membership in these associations, that of five years of media work experience, was suppressed. This decision was not controversial, although it had been so in previous attempts.

The number of people who have no communication education whatsoever is quite low: two radio broadcasters under age 35. Radio is the most amateur medium; it is also easier to be hired in radio broadcasting than in television or print without a degree in communication. Radio is the medium in which professionals have the lowest academic qualifications.

PROFESSIONALISM

Some authors argue that professionalism refers to the adoption of, and training in, job performance standards in news gathering and news processing. Professionalism implies that the process of adopting norms is dominated by reporters, editors, and producers who are directly involved in news gathering and processing, and that adopted norms become common guides for the news work. The strength of these norms relies on them being shared. The more highly shared the professional values, the easier is the work within the newsroom because uncertainty over news and its treatment and internal disputes are minimized with adherence to broadly accepted norms. Professionalism is thus measured by the existence of shared values and procedures (Sigal 1973; Tuchman 1978; Fishman 1980; Gans 1980; Shoemaker and Reese 1991).

Studies have also shown that there is a higher pluralism in role perceptions in journalism than in other professions. The "modern journalist attempts to blend the classical critical role of the journalist—as interpreter or contemporary historian—with the technical requirements of disseminating great volumes of *descriptive* information" (Weaver and Wilhoit 1991: 144). Therefore, along with almost universal perceptions of journalist roles, there are slight differences among certain types of journalists (Weaver and Wilhoit 1991). Our results confirm both ideas and suggest that there is an emerging consensus on professionalism among Spanish journalists.

The Professional Community

If the professionalism of Spanish journalists were measured only by association membership, results would be disappointing. Rates of professional society membership are low, with nearly one third of all journalists not belonging to any professional group. However, one should take into account that association membership in Spain has political strains inherited from Franco's era.

The professional journalist society par excellence is the *Federación de Asociaciones de la Prensa de España* (FAPE; Spanish Press Societies Federation), which includes 43 regional associations plus the *Collegi de Periodistes de Catalunya*. They are corporate entities with little relevance to labor policies. With the exception of some of them such as those of Madrid, the Basque Country, Sevilla, and the *Collegi*, these societies offer no professional activities, and their services are mainly social.

Among the Spanish journalists, 61% belong to FAPE. Up to late 1970s, membership in press associations was required for employment—another political toll imposed by the old regime in order to control journalists. Nowadays FAPE membership is just a matter of tradition.

Just 4% of our sample belong to a union. The main reason for this low figure can be found in the partisanship of unions in Spain. Although they are lately gaining more independence, the two major unions are sponsored by parties, one by the Socialist Party and the other by the Communist Party. Journalists are reluctant to become members of a union that could add political constraints to their work. They are also reluctant to be regarded as labor-wage workers as the Spanish unions qualify them. They are looking for more professional associations.

It is noteworthy that the first professional union, the *Sindicat de Periodistes de Catalunya* [Catalonian Union of Journalists], has attracted 20% of Catalan professionals since it was created in 1993, whereas before only 6% of Catalan journalists were unionized. Outside Catalunya, it is also significant that almost all journalists' representatives in the committees that deal with salaries and working conditions in each medium are absolutely independent of unions.

Radio journalists have the lowest rate of membership in associations, just 55%, compared to the 68% among print media journalists and 74% among those in television. However, radio rates the highest in union membership—11% as opposed to 2% of the print media and 6.5% of television. This is not surprising, considering that some radio journalists started working in the technical field, in which union membership rates are higher. The same reason also holds for the television union figure.

Association rates are higher in the Transition Group than in the Democracy Group. Differences increase in the extremes—among journalists under 30, 57% do not belong to a professional association or to a labor union, compared to 25% for the 51 to 55 age group.

Role Conceptions

Debate about the role of the press is not common among Spanish journalists, nor among scholars, as the few studies suggest. Nevertheless, it is generally perceived that there is a changing role of the press, especially in discovering affairs of political corruption that have, at least, led the government to call for earlier elections (held in March 1996). This fact calls for studies to measure this shift accurately.

Earlier studies of journalists include a wide variety of role conceptions. Cohen (1963) was one of the first scholars to propose a typology, distinguishing between the "neutral" and "participant" roles of U.S. journalists. Johnstone et al. (1976) applied this typology in a survey of U.S. journalists and found evidence of those two purely ideological types among working journalists in the early 1970s. Extending this typology, Weaver and Wilhoit (1991) suggested that three, rather than two, relatively distinct belief systems dominate journalists' attitudes about press functions: adversarial, interpretive, and disseminator.

Designers of the survey we used employed two basic dimensions: the passive-active and the advocate-neutral. The first refers to the journalist's autonomy as a political actor and the second to the journalist's positioning as a political actor. We did not use scales for these dimensions because the research results have yet to be published. Instead, we used the three-dimensional approach.

Journalists in our sample were asked to assess—from 1 (very) to 4 (not at all important)—the importance of several aspects of their work such as "giving information to others." They were also asked to rate their understanding of news reporting on 7-point scales, in which the extremes were factual-interpretive, advocate-impartial, critical-constructive, and informative-entertaining.[2]

---

[2]The following items were measured on a 7-point scale:
 1. In making decisions, journalists have to choose among different forms of news reporting. One possible choice is to let the facts speak on their own or to give the audience some interpretation of the facts. To what extent is a factual or interpretive style typical of your work? (1 was factual, 7 interpretive).

We tried to match these questions with the disseminator, adversarial, and interpretive roles. The "importance of giving information to others" and "making public problems" were taken to define the *disseminator* role. The *adversarial* role was defined by the critical-constructive scale of news reporting and a question about how journalists relied on official sources. The *interpretive* model was defined by the "importance of influencing the public," "championing values and ideas," and the factual-interpretive and advocate-impartial scales.

Table 16.3 shows that a very large majority of journalists fulfill the disseminator role of the press: 93% think it "very" or "highly" important to give information to others and to cover public problems. Strikingly, only 64% regard as very important being the first to know of an event. The cross-tabulation by medium helps to clarify this: Radio is the medium for informing people, television for entertaining them, and the press for helping them interpret events.

The adversarial model is endorsed by a high percentage: Nearly 99% agree (give values 1 to 3 on a 7-point scale) with the idea that journalists should conduct their own inquiries rather than relying on close or routine associations with official sources. Values on the scale critical-

Table 16.3. Importance of Journalistic Roles (Percentages of the sample who answered "very" or "highly important").

Journalistic Roles	%	N
Give information to others	93.2	138
Publicize public problems	93.2	138
Be the first in knowing of the event	64.2	95
Influence the public	44.4	63
Champion values and ideas	42.8	62

2. Another choice could be between news reporting that defends a particular point of view and news reporting that presents impartial factual writing. To what extent is advocate or impartial typical of your work? (1 was advocate, 7 impartial).

3. Another choice is between news reporting that takes a critical posture toward political leaders in order to protect the public from abuse of power and news reporting that takes a constructive posture toward political leaders in order to help them communicate with the public. To what extent is a critical or constructive posture typical of your work? (1 was critical, 7 constructive).

4. Finally, you can choose between news reporting to catch large audiences and news reporting to merely keep people informed. To what extent is an informative or entertaining posture typical of your work? (1 was informative, 7 entertaining).

constructive are more in the center, with 37% giving a medium value, but 54.5% are critical as compared with 7% who claim to be constructive. The high number of middle-of-the-road values in this scale could be explained by those journalists who are reluctant to assume an adversarial role, but even more reluctant to support political leaders.

There are interesting results for the interpretive model. A significant 44% and 43% give importance to influencing the public and to championing values and ideas (Table 16.3). Looking at news reporting style, only 14% agree with an advocacy writing style, whereas a majority (61%) claim to be impartial. More than half (55%) give values 1 to 3, agreeing with the factual news reporting style, but 26.5% tend to lean more to the interpretive side.

It is clear that a majority of Spanish journalists agree with the idea that journalism is more a task of disseminating information and factual writing than interpretation. A majority tend to be impartial, but there are important figures supporting the interpretative role. These inconsistencies are of great interest to this study. Why is it that journalists favor impartial and factual writing while at the same time they regard influencing the public and promoting values and ideas as important? Is there any variable that could help us to understand this pattern? Following our hypothesis, we used age, and interesting results, explained in the next major section, confirmed our intuitions.

Professional Values by Medium

When analyzed by medium, the interpretive function is more salient for print journalists (Figure 16.2). Although 33% of the print journalists give values 5 to 7 on the factual-interpretive scale, just 17% of radio and 12% of television journalists favor an interpretive style. This result is not surprising, considering the greater possibilities for interpretive writing in the press as compared with radio and television newscasts.

Print journalists also are more in favor of conducting their own inquiries rather than relying on close or routine associations with official sources. This has to do with the particular situation of the press in Spain.

Although main political corruption affairs were uncovered by the press after the survey was conducted, by that time a new newspaper, *El Mundo*, had already been founded with a determined adversarial role. The paper based its huge success—in just six years it climbed to the second best-selling paper—on investigative journalism. As has been shown afterward, that particular newspaper and the press in general have developed investigative attitudes that are accepted by public opinion. Regarding political affairs, the newspaper press is more proactive in its adversarial role than radio and television press.

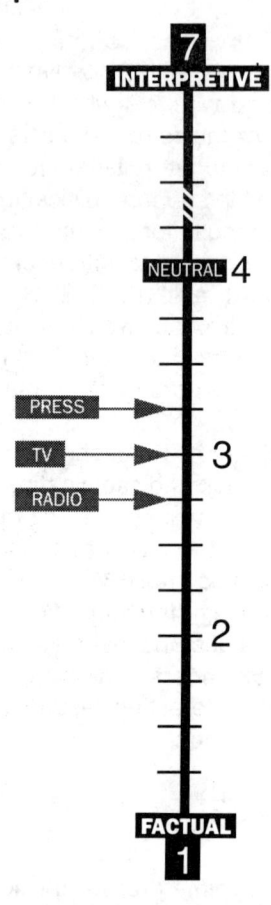

Figure 16.2. Factual/interpretive style by media

The informative-entertaining scale analyzed by medium yielded expected results—the range of values were wider for television journalists, who are closer to the entertaining role, than their colleagues in the print media.

THE TRANSITION GROUP VERSUS THE DEMOCRACY GROUP

Professional Roles

The 45 to 49 age group show changing professional attitudes and perceptions. Therefore, we fixed 45 as the age cutting point between the Democracy Group (younger) and the Transition Group (older than 45).

Our initial perception was that although the Democracy Group had not started working during Franco's regime, the Transition Group had established their professional routines under that regime. If this is so, the second group might have inherited some professional norms more appropriate to a regime in which watchwords and strict previous censorship were legal practice. The older journalists might also be more committed to political beliefs and to the need for reforms because they tried to maintain a free information flow, using a writing style that allowed readers to read real facts between the lines or running lots of stories about elections in foreign democracies in the international section. Therefore, in our sample, the Transition Group might be more for an advocacy and interpretive journalism than the Democracy Group. Because the latter group has been trained under a regime of freedom of information, impartiality and adversarialism should be more highly rated values than advocacy and interpretation.

Findings partially confirm our hypothesis. Figure 16.3 displays news reporting-style scales by age groups. The first three age groups (ranging from 30 to 44 years) favor more factual news reporting than interpretive, more critical than constructive, and more impartial than advocacy news reporting. In the last two age groups (those ranging from 45 to 54), trends change to more interpretive and more advocacy styles (for those 45 to 49).

Some trends deserve more discussion. The Transition Group (older) leans clearly to the interpretive versus the factual side. Not only do a majority give 6 and 7 values, but none of them give 1 and 2 values. They do not agree at all with a merely factual writing style. The Democracy Group (younger) is clearly inclined to the factual type.

The same happens, although less strongly, with the critical-constructive scale. None of the Transition Group give a 1 value, although it is true they do not give either extreme values for the constructive side. Comparatively, the Democracy Group are more adversarial, and some values are quite widespread.

Asked about assessing the importance of influencing the public, the younger journalists tend to assign no importance, but the older journalists tend to assign more. The same happens to the importance given to championing values and ideas—most of the younger journalists say some or none, whereas most of older journalists say much and a lot.

Both groups behave quite similarly with regard to the "disseminator" role. Both regard it very important to give information to others and to publicize public problems (an average of 80% give a value of 1—very important—in all age groups).

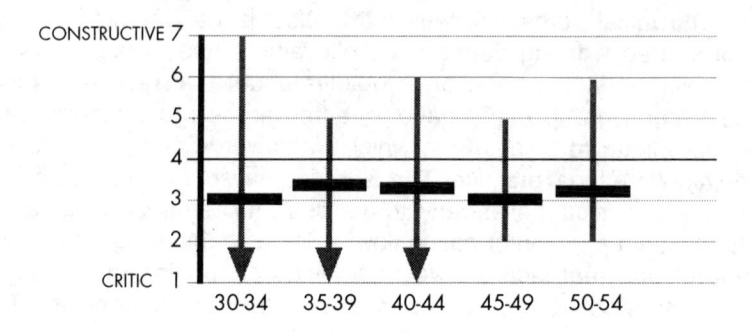

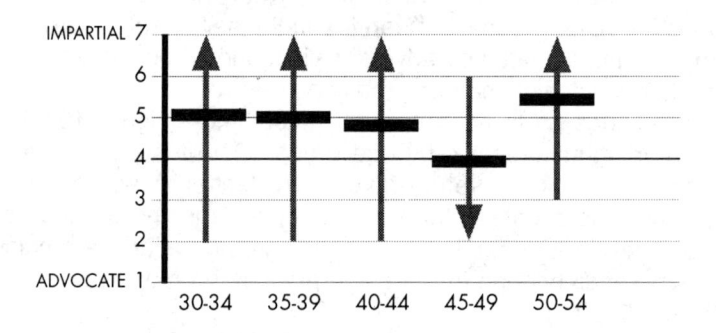

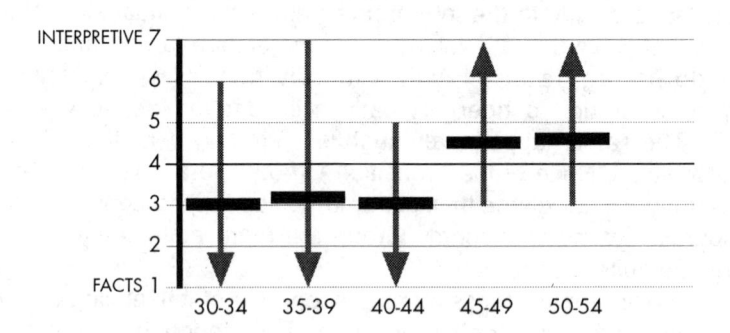

Figure 16.3. Professional roles by age groups

Perceived Autonomy

To measure perceived freedom, journalists were questioned about what they thought were the main constraints on their work. Findings shown in Table 16.4 suggest that journalists claim to be more constrained by factors of a technical or institutional sort than by professional or labor ones.

Table 16.4. Main Constraints at Work (Percentage selecting "very important" and "important").

Constraints	%	N
Lack of space	75.0	111
Deadline pressures	72.5	108
Lack of investigative resources	60.3	88
Restrictions on government documents	56.5	83
Need to catch audience's interest	53.4	78
Difficult access to personalities	44.1	64
Difficult access to the powerful	42.4	61
Ignorance of the issues covered	32.2	47
Pressures from my boss	21.9	32
Avoiding personal bias	6.2	9
Pressures from the publisher/owner	4.9	7

Three of four journalists say that scarcity of time and space are factors that constrain their work much or a lot. The same applies to deadlines. Lack of resources for investigation is claimed by three of five journalists. More than half selected an official constraint—difficulties of access to government documents—and the "need to catch the audience's attention" is seen as a work hurdle by slightly more than half of the sample.

It is interesting to see that only 1 in 20 journalists select pressure from the owner as an important constraint. This could be an indicator of media owners' fair play—journalists do not perceive publishers or owners to be controlling their work and feel their jobs are quite independent of that dominance. Accordingly, it could be said that owners rely on journalists' professionalism. Pressures from immediate superiors were also selected by a low proportion of the sample.

These data are consistent with what journalists point out as the main reason for editors to strongly edit their work. The people who said that others in the newsroom change their story in order to balance it— either to increase its neutrality in a political conflict or to tilt the story to a political side—never exceeded 9%. However, the percentage of people who said their reporting was changed in order to catch the audience's interest was much higher (29%).

In general, conflict between news processors (editors) and news gatherers (reporters) seems to be low. Most of the modifications of stories were reported to be done to hook the audience and not to adjust the copy to a political authority, owner preferences, or such other criteria. In any event, a more accurate study on the meaning of such editing styles is needed to make strong assertions about the supervisors' work on reporters' copy.

There is an expected difference between the Transition Group and the Democracy Group. The least autonomy is claimed by the latter, the young journalists. Among them, 24% say pressure from the immediate superior in the newsroom is an important constraint, whereas just 11% of older journalists claim this. Among older journalists, 63% say that immediate superiors are not at all a constraint, whereas 38% of young journalists agree to that. This is obviously understandable: Young people are not in high positions, therefore, they are less able to interpret and portray their beliefs in their reporting. They need to keep to the facts. That might be part of the explanation for why young journalists have a more impartial profile, favoring neutral and factual journalism.

Views about News Values

As was pointed out when dealing with professional values, professionalism implies that journalists have the dominant role in establishing professional values, particularly news values. Journalists are the main decision makers in defining what is news.

Perceptions of journalists in our sample confirm this idea. They were asked about the main sources in deciding what's news—wire services, national media, journalists from your own newsroom, or your main competitors. Every source was to be measured on a 4-point scale, with 1 being very important and 4 not important at all.

Journalists think they are the main sources in deciding what is news. "Other journalists in my newsroom" is claimed by the majority to be the main source for deciding what is news (74% chose value 1 or 2). More than two thirds (68%) say wire services are very important or important, about half of the sample say national media are, and only 23% say main competitors are.

Analyses by age groups are consistent with previous findings. Comparing both groups, journalists from the Transition Group claim to be more independent of external sources such as wire services and national media. These older journalists tend to think that wire services, national media, and main competitors are just somewhat or not at all important, with a difference of 15 points over young journalists.[3]

---

[3]Some data, which have not been analyzed here because they are part of future research, deserve a short discussion. Young journalists tend to use more visual material such as pictures or infographics. There is also a higher visual culture among young journalists than among older ones.

There is another point that deserves comment. Comparative electoral studies have shown that Spanish journalists behave according to partisan-ideological paradigms. They fulfill the "servant" model: They feel that politicians need the media to communicate with the public. In electoral campaigns, government and official stories get more chances in a news value competition. As a result, the party in government receives more and better coverage than opposition parties, in part because journalists seem to make no distinctions between government news and campaign news from the incumbent government party. In the last 1993 national elections, PSOE, the incumbent party, received more and better coverage on all television networks. Conversations with some journalists showed that the message from the party in government was considered more newsworthy than the messages from other parties, no matter whether these messages were related to governance or mere electoral strategy.[4]

Although our questionnaire did not refer to electoral coverage, results confirm in part these perceptions. In our sample, two thirds think journalists should report on information about parties as it is given, implying that no analysis or background should be added to it. Moreover, when asked to rate the importance of party information and governmental information, 51% gave more importance to the governmental information, whereas just 21% did for party content.

The previously mentioned successful results of Spanish investigative journalism might modify this attitude. It seems that there is an increased belief in the need for independent journalism, based on recent experience that only this can reveal political failures about which people should know and which should not be allowed to be kept secret. Perhaps there is also a growing partisan or ideological disenchantment among young journalists who think the current government or party has done such a poor job that it no longer deserves support. Research based on newsroom observation during the March 1996 elections will test these hypotheses.

Views on What Is Good or Bad Journalism

In order to measure journalists' views of what is good and bad journalism, we asked them about what they regard as good informative work. Several statements were given using a 7-point scale, with 1 being "agreement" and 7 "disagreement." Most of the statements were related to the concept of objectivity.

---

[4]Results of the research conducted by Holli Semetko and Juan Díez Nicolás can be found in Nicolás and Semetko (1995).

None of the options were chosen by a majority. Not quite one third (30%) say that good journalism is based on equal and balanced examination of both sides in a political conflict. However, another 30% agree that good journalism is something more than gathering statements of different parties about political affairs. Only 15% agree that good journalism expresses every position of parties in equal terms, and not quite one fourth (23%) agree that the good journalist avoids his or her personal beliefs so as not to bias news reporting.

Almost all (99%) say that to be objective is very important. However, when asked to choose statements that define their concept of objectivity, interesting inconsistencies resulted. The most frequently chosen option (30%) for objectivity—"Good journalism is something more than gathering statements from different parties about public affairs"—is not the most factual one. Interestingly, it is the most "objectivist" choice—"Good journalism gives equal chance to both sides in a political conflict"—which gets less support (15%; see Table 16.5). Yet "equal and balanced examination of both sides in a political conflict" gets twice as much support (30%).

Previous interpretation of these data conducted by Martín and González suggests that there is a gap between what journalists think is best—factual journalism—and what they practice: a nuanced version of factual journalism. It seems, according to both authors, that there is no consensus among journalists on what is objectivity. Journalists agree on some basic principles that guide their activities but disagree when defining them.

Table 16.5. Objectivity by Group (N = 145).

	Democracy Group (younger) (%)	Transition Group (%)	Total (%)	(N)
Equal and balanced examination of both sides in a political conflict	27.8	47.4	30.3	44
Something more than gathering statements on public affairs from different parties	30.2	31.6	30.3	44
Gives equal chance to both sides in a political conflict	15.9	10.5	15.2	22
Shows what party is right	0.8	–	0.7	1
Avoiding personal opinions in reporting	25.4	10.5	23.4	34
TOTAL				145

There are also interesting differences noted by age groups. Whereas 47% of the Transition Group (older journalists) chose the more factual statement ("equal and balanced examination of both sides in a political conflict"), just 28% of the Democracy Group did so. It seems that older journalists follow the "objectivistic theory" (close to the fairness theory), whereas younger journalists understand that if guided by facts, there is more to reporting—equal sides do not always conform with reality (Table 16.5).

CONCLUSIONS

The tendencies for professional journalism in Spain are toward requiring a complete degree in communication, an increasing number of women in the profession, a high degree of nonpartisanship, and a lower importance for ideologically based reporting and editing and fewer members in professional associations. Spanish journalists seem to have pluralistic values—a majority embrace both the "disseminator" and the "adversarial" role models—in the sense of less reliance on official sources.

However, different trends, started during the 1975-1978 transition to democracy, were detected. Journalists who have undergone the process to democracy fully established as professionals are more advocate than impartial, interpretive than factual, and more supportive than critical. They are also more likely to identify with a party than young journalists and to be committed to certain beliefs. They regard as important influencing the public and championing ideas and values.

Journalists who established a full career under the current democracy are, compared to the older group, more impartial than advocate, more factual news reporter than interpretive, and more critical than constructive. They are also less likely to identify with a party and to feel their work to be committed to values and ideas. Moreover, although they are more to the left than their audiences, they seem more attuned to their audiences' political preferences than their older colleagues.

Both groups highly agree on giving "objectivity" a high value. Yet whereas older journalists are more likely to support an objectivistic theory (equal examinations of both sides), younger journalists are less likely to do so. There is something more than balance and equal terms if facts are followed. This difference in age group profiles is a consequence of the political events and social evolution that fueled—and were caused by—the transition to democracy. During the last years of Franco's regime and the first years of the transition to democracy, journalists who are now in managing positions were then allies of the democratic politicians opposing the dictatorship, so they were, and are, more partisan.

Once in democracy, the news media were seen as important means to teach people "how to be democratic" and to spread respect toward institutions such as the monarchy and the government. The media were managed by these journalists like servants of the system. Journalists understood that politicians and institutions needed coverage to communicate with citizens to attach them to the newborn democracy. At that time, news was not what had happened but what officials said had happened. That is why, for most of the older "transition journalists," unveiling scandals or putting politicians under criticism is regarded as attacking the democracy, built with their help and resistance during the late years of Franco's dictatorship.

There is an emerging concept of the journalist role among younger journalists. This new concept means being close to facts and free of ideological prejudices—far from championing beliefs. However, they are committed to action, and a more critical role is endorsed. Due to political scandals and as a reaction to the reluctance of the socialist party to resign power (as of this writing, PSOE has been in power since 1982), the press is starting to develop a more detached position toward authority. As a consequence, journalists are more distant, reactive to official sources, and proactive in analyzing the political messages.

Our study gives support to the idea that Spanish journalists' role orientations are changing along with the evolution of the system. They are moving from the traditional partisan-ideological paradigm toward a more adversarial-nonpartisan one. However, it is hardly believable that the next step in this evolution will be like what has been criticized in Watergate's aftermath—an innocuous equal-sided journalism resulting from skepticism toward politicians and public affairs by the media.

There is not enough evidence to add fully to the changing paradigm of the audience-serving category. However, present actions of the press against political corruption, along with the increasing special interests coverage—all surrounded by a heavy competition for audiences—lead one to think that there is a growing belief in the need for a more independent journalism, based on the assumption that only this type of journalism can uncover and publicize political failures and flaws about which people should know and which should not be allowed to continue. Journalists feel themselves committed to enabling their audiences to participate in public affairs, but these are intuitions that require further research.

REFERENCES

Cohen, Bernard C. 1963. *The press and foreign policy.* Princeton, NJ: Princeton University Press.
Diezhandino, Pilar and Cesar Coca y Ofa Bezunartea. 1994. La élite de los periodistas [The elite of journalists]. In *Serie de Comunicación No. 2.* Universidad del País Vasco.
Fishman, Mark. 1980 *Manufacturing the news.* Austin: University of Texas Press.
Gans, Herbert. 1980. *Deciding what's news.* New York: Vintage.
Hagen, Ingunn. 1992. Democratic communication. Media and social participation. In *Democratic communications in the information age,* edited by Janet Wasko and Vincent Mosco, pp. 16-27. Toronto, Canada: Garamond Press.
Johnstone, John W.C., Edward J. Slawski, and William W. Bowman. 1976. *The news people: A sociological portrait of American journalists and their work.* Urbana: University of Illinois Press.
Nicolás, Juan Díez and Holli A. Semetko. 1995. La televisión y las elecciones de 1993 [Television and the 1993 elections]. In *Comunicación Política,* pp. 243-304. Madrid: Editorial Universitas.
Semetko, Holli, Jay Blumler, Michael Gurevich, and David H. Weaver. 1991. *The formation of campaign agendas.* Hillsdale, NJ: Erlbaum.
Shoemaker, Pamela and Stephen D. Reese. 1991. *Mediating the message.* New York: Longman.
Sigal, Leon V. 1973. *Journalists and officials.* Lexington: DC Heath.
Tuchman, Gaye. 1978. *Making news.* New York: Free Press.
Wasko, Janet. 1993. Studies in communication and democracy. In *Communication and democracy,* edited by Slavko Splichal and Janet Wasko, pp. 163-167. Norwood, NJ: Ablex.
Weaver, David and G. Cleveland Wilhoit. 1991. *The American journalist: A portrait of U.S. news people and their work.* 2nd ed. Bloomington: Indiana University Press.

IV

NORTH AFRICA

17

Algerian Journalists and Their World*

Mohamed Kirat
United Arab Emirates University

The media system in Algeria has been strongly influenced by the history of the country, mainly the French colonialism that lasted more than 130 years. Algeria received its independence in 1962 and adopted a socialist one-party political system. From 1962 until 1989,[1] the press was govern-

---

*The author wishes to express his respect to the souls of the 50 journalists—as of October 15, 1995—who were assassinated in the ongoing conflict between the backed military regime and the Islamic Salvation Front. Some of them were interviewed by the author and filled out the questionnaire for this study. Heartfelt sympathy and sincere condolences to their families, friends, and loved ones.

[1]The popular riots of October 5, 1988 were a turning point in the history of modern Algeria. The regime was obliged to start a new era of multipartisanship and therefore a more open press system with an independent press, a partisan press, and the old government and state press. A new constitution was adopted on February 23, 1989. On April 3, 1990, a new law of information (*code de l'information*) was adopted, thus eliminating the 1982 law described by journalists as repressive and penal. These changes transformed the media scene in Algeria to a large extent. Newspapers, magazines, and periodicals mushroomed. By June 1990, more than 30 publications were created, and newspaper circulation jumped

ment-owned and orchestrated by the Front de Liberation National (FLN) party. Inevitably the Algerian press during this period was a docile mouthpiece of the system. A one-way communication was established from the rulers to the populace.

By 1986, the number of journalists in the country did not exceed 800[2] for a population of 24 million inhabitants, and the number of daily newspapers was only six. These numbers suggest that the FLN information network could not reflect the aspirations of the masses; rather, it was a mere reflection of the party's contradictions and anomalies.[3] Unfortunately, the mass media in Algeria were not used to integrating the masses into the development process but to consolidating the privileges of the nomenclature and the military power elite.[4] It is to be noted here that the power struggle in Algeria after independence has not been a conflict between the bourgeoisie and the peasants but "rather, it has been the contest for power among dozens of groups and clans. This continuing struggle of clans has also been the source of the country's political instability." (Ottaway and Ottaway 1970: 5).

Unlike many socialist and communist countries—in which the party controls the press—the state in Algeria, through the Ministry of Information, controls most of the news organizations. The FLN became an institution of management and administration and was neutralized as a strong political institution. This phenomenon has had severe repercussions on the organization, management, and operations of the media in independent Algeria. The press did not have a clear legal framework in which it could find its prerogatives, roles, rights, and duties. This confus-

---

from 500,000 to 1.2 million a day. The creation of more than 60 political parties opened a new era for the Algerian press. In addition to daily publications, a regional press, a specialized press, and a feminist press were established to fill the wide vacuum that was intentionally created by the one-party system.

[2]The number of journalists was estimated at 1,500 in 1990 and at about 2,500 in 1992. Official statistics were never available at the Ministry of Information.

[3]The FLN (Front de Liberation National), the unique party in the country, is theoretically supposed to be the cornerstone of Algeria's political and information system. This is what the literature of socialism and communism reports. Even in most of the socialist countries the unique party is the architect of politics and information. In Algeria, however, the FLN was used from the independence of the country until 1988 as a Trojan Horse by various factions—military, political and financial—to serve their own interests.

[4]The news organizations of Algeria were used and exploited most by a handful of politicians to serve their interests and those who backed them—military and economic powers. The masses were never integrated, and they were used only as subjects for the political propaganda of the system—Socialism, Panafricanism, Non-Aligned Movement, cultural, industrial and agrarian revolutions, and so on.

ing situation has killed the sense of criticism, investigation, and development journalism in the Algerian press. Insecure and unprotected, Algerian journalists were transformed into government secretaries.[5]

After 20 years of independence, the media scene in Algeria has been characterized by a score of problems, contradictions, and anomalies. The media system has suffered from poor diffusion and distribution of print—almost 40% of the counties (communes) in the country do not receive any kind of publication. Algiers and the large urban centers monopolize both the media and journalists. Consequently, the masses in the rural areas are left out and alienated by the media system that is supposed to integrate them.

The media system in Algeria has also lacked a clear communication policy and a precise communication law. Until 1982, Algeria did not have an information act or a communication law. This automatically led to an absence of statutes for both the profession and the journalist. A kind of dualism—party press and government press—characterized the Algerian media. This dualism reflected the absence of a clear communication policy in Algeria. Some news organizations are controlled by the party, whereas the rest are controlled by the Ministry of Information. This contradicts the principles of socialism in Algeria and reflects the marginalization of the party by the state.

Another dualism reflected the contradictions of the system. The bilingualism of the Algerian media is in a way a healthy sign, but in the case of Algeria and because of the politicization of the language it has had many drawbacks for the media. Although the majority of the Algerian population reads and understands Arabic better than French, the French press in Algeria has always been stronger, more critical, and more credible than its counterpart in Arabic. The French language has always been the language of the nomenclature and those who have the decision-making power.

It is worth noting that the communication system of a society reflects and mirrors its economic, political, and bureaucratic institutions. Algeria is no exception. The establishment of bureaucratic state capitalism in Algeria with a capital-intensive approach to economic development neutralized the possibilities of integrating the masses into the communication process. As Yu put it: "What goes on and comes out of a mass communication system reflects what basic beliefs a country holds about the nature of man, the nature of society, and the relation of man to society and the state" (Yu 1977: 174).

---

[5]With a lack of a defined policy of information, a lack of professionalism, a lack of a rational law, and an absence of any protection, the Algerian journalist was obliged to avoid problems with the rulers by self-censorship and by avoiding sensitive issues and investigative journalism.

METHODS

The main research method employed in this study is the survey. An 88-item questionnaire was administered to journalists in early 1986. The second method used was interviews with officials in the Ministry of information, media managers, editors, reporters, professors, researchers, and students at the Institute of Information and Communication sciences in Algiers. On-site observation in the newsroom was also used by the researcher to assess the mechanisms of news operations.

Sampling

No sampling procedure was undertaken in this study. The research was intended to cover the whole journalistic workforce of Algeria because of the relatively small number (800).

The News Organizations

This study covered the daily press, the radio and television networks, and their affiliates in Oran and Constantine, as well as their various divisions (Arabic, French, Tamazight, international), the national news agency (APS, Algerie Presse Service), the nonspecialized magazines, weeklies, and the mass organizations' papers (youth, women, workers, war veterans, and peasants). Specialized magazines and news publications that are oriented to a very special audience were not included in this study.

Definition of a Journalist

Journalists as used here refers to full-time reporters, correspondents, columnists, newsmen, editors, and writers; in other words, the editorial staff of a news organization or the group of those people who participate in the gathering and processing of news and who put together the news content of their medium. Cartoonists, photographers, librarians, technicians, camera operators, and anybody else who is not involved in the gathering and writing process was excluded from the study. It should be noted that the terms *journalists, news people, newsmen*, and *media practitioners* are used interchangeably.

Questionnaire Construction, Adaptation, and Pretesting

The questionnaire of this study builds on several others used in previous studies done on journalists as well as takes into consideration the main objectives of this study and the specific conditions in which the Algerian journalist lives. The questionnaires consulted are those of Johnstone, Slawski, and Bowman (1976); Burgoon, Burgoon, and Atkin (1982); Weaver and Wilhoit (1986); Tunstall (1977); and Tash (1983).

Administration of the Questionnaire and Data Collection

The questionnaire was distributed personally by the researcher to journalists and media managers. It was also sent to a score of news organizations and journalists. When the study was first designed it was intended to cover the whole Algerian journalistic population. However, after many problems, the researcher was able to gather only 75 questionnaires from 12 news organizations, including the national news agency, radio and television stations, the daily press (both in Arabic and French), weeklies, and magazines. The responses represent 10% of the Algerian journalistic workforce.

BASIC CHARACTERISTICS OF JOURNALISTS

The sample of this study consists of 75 journalists representing 12 news organizations. The daily press is represented by 30 journalists (40%); the radio network with its regional affiliates is represented by 10 journalists (13%); television is represented by 8 journalists (11%); the national news agency—APS—by 12 news people (16%); and the weekly publications by 15 (20%).

Geographic Distribution

The media in Algeria are heavily concentrated in the capital, and more than 80% of the journalists are based in Algiers; therefore, one would predict that a large proportion of journalists would come from the North-Central region where Algiers is located. However, in this study, the Eastern part of the country is the main provider of journalists (52%). The North-Central region comes in second with 31%. Only 4% of the Algerian journalistic workforce surveyed in this study comes from the Western part of the country. No one from the surveyed journalists was from the South, which is scarcely populated but represents 90% of the country's area.

It is clear that the geographic distribution of the journalists in this study generally reflects the geographic distribution of the population. The bulk of journalists in Algeria come from the North (East, North-Central, and West)—98%. However, the Eastern part, although less populated than the North-Central region and equally as populated as the Western area, provides slightly more than half of the Algerian journalists in this study.

Age, Sex, Marital Status

The Algerian journalist in this study has a median age of 30.5, and the majority of the surveyed journalists (73%) fall in the age bracket of 25 to 34 years old. This can be explained by the fact that older journalists are either retiring or receiving more remunerative positions outside the journalism and media business, and a new wave of media practitioners—mainly university graduates—are entering the profession. Almost one fourth of Algerian journalists are female (24%). This is a significant percentage given the fact that a high proportion of women in Algeria do not work. According to the 1977 census, the percentage of working women in the Algerian active population was only 6.75.

As for the distribution of women journalists by type of news organization, 62.5% of the television network journalists are women, in sharp contrast to radio and print media, in which men dominate at more than 75%. More than half of the journalists surveyed are single and never married (56%); 33%, however, were married.

EDUCATION AND TRAINING OF JOURNALISTS

Findings of the study suggest that more than three fourths of the Algerian journalists (79%) held a bachelor's degree, 17% had completed some graduate work, and 8% held advanced degrees (see Table 17.1). The majority of Algerian journalists (77%) went to college in Algiers. A large

Table 17.1. Journalists' Level of Education (N =75).

Level of Education	Percentage
Some high school or less	4
Completed high school	0
1-3 years of college	12
Graduated from college	54
Some graduate work	17
Advanced degree(s)	8
No response	4

number of those journalists holding a bachelor's degree majored in journalism (41%), political science (14%), and other majors such as law (8%), sociology (8%), psychology (5%), business (3%), and Arabic literature.

Concerning the variation among news organizations in the ratio of college graduates they employed, the data suggest that the more recently established news organizations (*Al-Massa, Horizons, Al-Mountakhab, Adhwa*) do not have a single journalist without a college education.

Slightly more than a quarter of the surveyed journalists had done some graduate work, most of them (84%) at Algiers University, majoring in journalism (36%) and social sciences and humanities such as Arabic literature, sociology, law, philosophy, and history. Only 36% of Algerian journalists had training before entering journalism. Almost a third of them had training abroad, 22% had training at the Ministry of Information, and 18% had an internship in print media.

Continuing Education

Fifty-six percent of the journalists expressed their interest in acquiring more training and working with veteran journalists. Nearly half of these journalists wanted training in writing techniques, and about one fourth wanted some training in media technology. Other journalists wanted to train in broadcast media (9.5%), and others wanted some training abroad (9.5%).

Nearly half of the surveyed journalists also wanted additional training or a refresher course. About 28% of them said they would like to take theoretical courses. The same percentage were interested in working on advanced media technology. About 14% were interested in seminars and workshops. This shows the strong desire of the Algerian journalists to learn more and to improve their talents and creativity. This may also indicate the lack of training and the weakness of the journalism school curriculum. New journalists with little media experience and of younger age were those most interested in continuing education. The older the journalist and the more experience, the less likely he or she was to want additional training or to participate in workshops and clinics.

Academic Versus Nonacademic Experience

Unlike law, medicine, engineering, and other professions that require a degree and an academic experience, journalism has no such requirements. Some of the best journalists in different countries of the world did not necessarily graduate from journalism schools, and journalism schools do not necessarily prepare skillful journalists.

To what extent did Algerian journalists agree or disagree with these theses? In general, Algerian journalists believe in the importance of academic studies. Fifty-one percent strongly agreed with the statement "academic study in journalism is important for journalists," and 35% said they agreed. Only 13% disagreed.

Algerian journalists also believe in the importance of nonacademic experience. Twenty-eight percent strongly agreed and 36% simply agreed. However, 29% disagreed. Almost half of the journalists (47%) disagreed—and 11% strongly disagreed—with the statement: "Academic study in journalism is more important than experience for journalists." Only 9% strongly agreed and 23% agreed with this statement.

Overall, Algerian journalists believe academic studies in journalism and nonacademic experience are important preconditions for a good journalist. However, when asked which one is more important than the other, the respondents tended to favor experience over academic studies. Only 32% of the respondents either strongly agreed or agreed that academic study in journalism is more important than experience, whereas 43% of the journalists either strongly agreed or agreed that nonacademic experience in journalism is more important than academic study for journalists.

The majority of Algerian journalists (84%) either strongly agreed or agreed that working journalists should be required to take some academic courses in journalism. Likewise, more than half of them (55%) strongly agreed and 43% agreed that new journalists should be required to have on-the-job training before starting their career.

Level of Education and Best Field of Study

One of the questions most frequently asked in the field of journalism is what level of education is needed for a person to practice journalism. Nowadays, the field is very competitive, and the impact of information technology is a daily challenge for journalists. Consequently it is believed that at least a college education is required. The majority of Algerian journalists suggested that a college education is needed (one third said at least some college and 53% said a college degree).

What are the fields of study that best prepare journalists to enter the field of journalism? More than a third (37%) of Algerian journalists chose journalism as the most suitable field for the profession. Almost a quarter selected political science, and 19% mentioned economics.

JOB SATISFACTION, COMMITMENT, AND WORKING CONDITIONS

With a median age of just over 30 years, the majority of Algerian journalists (79%) had not worked for another news organization besides their present one. News organizations in Algeria are sponsored by either the Ministry of Information or the unique political party, so the salary is the same from one medium to another. This reduces the job mobility of the journalists because the rewards are the same everywhere. Another factor explaining this pattern of lack of previous work in a different news organization among Algerian news people is their short job experience (an average of 4.15 years of work in journalism).

The respondents reported a wide range of job titles. The majority of them, however, were staff writers (37%), managing editors (16%), reporters (12%), and specialized editors (8%). A small proportion of the surveyed journalists did reporting regularly (11%), but a third of them reported occasionally. This can be explained by the low importance given to reporting by Algerian news organizations and their heavy dependence on the national and international news agencies for news.

The Algerian journalist worked an average of 35 hours a week. Asked about managerial responsibility, 61% of the respondents answered negatively, whereas only 16% said they had such a responsibility.

The data about reasons for becoming a journalist reveal that the majority of the respondents (79%) said they became journalists because they love journalism, 57% because they want to serve their country and their people, and 40% because it is a vocation.

Job Aspects

Asked about the importance of factors in judging a job, the respondents listed a wide range as very important and fairly important (see Table 17.2). Forty percent of the journalists said that the pay and fringe benefits were very important. The editorial policies of the news organizations were chosen as very important by 51% of the journalists; 52% chose job security, the chance to develop a specialty, and the degree of autonomy as very important. Overall, almost all factors listed were selected as very important or fairly important by more than two thirds of the respondents. Those most likely to be rated as "not too important" were the chance to get ahead and the fringe benefits. This implies that Algerian journalists were a bit more interested in the public service and journalistic aspects than in the financial rewards.

Table 17.2. Importance of Factors in Judging a Job (N = 75).

Factors	Very Important (%)	Fairly Important (%)	Not too Important (%)	No Response (%)
The pay	40	43	11	7
Fringe benefits	40	33	20	7
Freedom from supervision	47	27	16	11
The chance to help people	48	33	12	7
The editorial policies of the organization	51	28	13	8
Job security	52	24	15	9
The chance to develop a specialty	52	24	16	8
The amount of autonomy	52	21	16	11
The chance to get ahead in the organization	31	35	23	12

Journalists' Communication with Peers, Colleagues, and Audiences

Interaction of the journalist within and outside the news organization is very important and most likely has a strong impact on performance. Superiors were perceived to be the most likely to react to journalists' work occasionally (52% of journalists said so), then colleagues at the same level (49%), followed by readers, viewers, and listeners (35%). Audience members ranked first in reacting regularly to journalists' work (13%), whereas only 4% of the respondents said they got reactions from news sources.

Journalists with management responsibilities said that they do not interact very much with reporters. Only 10% of them said they met several times a day with reporters, 25% met daily, and the remaining managers met several times a week or close to weekly with journalists.

Asked about how much editing they get from others, almost half of the respondents (48%) said they get some editing from others, 12% said a great deal, and a third reported no editing from others at all. One third of the respondents said they do some editing and processing of other people's work, 19% said they edit a great deal, and the remaining respondents said not at all.

Journalists were asked about the kind of errors they find in the work they edit and process. The most frequently perceived faults, according to the respondents, were: poor editing (32%), lack of writing style (27%), and grammar, syntax, and sentence structure (2%). Other faults mentioned by journalists were lack of political orientation (12%), awkward and poor writing (11%), repetitious and redundant writing (8%), and tendency to editorialize (7%).

Journalists' Perceptions of Audiences

How do journalists think about their audiences? What kind of ideas do they hold about the people who are consuming their products? The majority of the respondents somewhat agreed (44%) or strongly agreed (27%) that audience members are more interested in the day's breaking news than in analysis of long-term trends. However, a large majority of the journalists believed (48% strongly agreed and 23% somewhat agreed) that audience members are also interested in news that criticizes the implementation of development plans and various government policies.

About one fourth of the Algerian journalists thought that audience members are gullible and easily fooled. More than 65% of the respondents agreed, either somewhat or strongly, that the majority of audience members have little interest in reading about day-to-day ordinary activities of various ministries and the government.

Do journalists think they know their audience and each other? Two thirds (68%) of the respondents agreed that journalists generally know what their audience wants, but one third agreed that journalists often have completely wrong ideas about what the public wants, suggesting considerable uncertainty among Algerian news people regarding knowledge of their audience desires. A large majority (89%) also agreed that it is very important for a journalist to be in touch with public opinion, and many of the Algerian news people in this study thought that journalists have very different political attitudes from one another (64% agreed with this statement). No significant differences were noted among journalists from different news organizations in their perceptions and opinions of their audiences.

Professional Autonomy and Freedom

Working in a developing country ruled by a single party, one can hypothesize that the Algerian journalist has to work under rather difficult bureaucratic and organizational constraints that limit freedom in terms of selecting news and interacting with sources. Sixteen percent of the journalists said they had almost complete freedom in selecting stories, 21% said they had a great deal, and 33% said they had some. Almost the same percentages were found regarding the level of freedom in emphasizing some aspects of a story. Twenty percent, 21%, and 33% said they had almost complete freedom, a great deal of freedom, and some freedom, respectively.

These patterns suggest that a minority of journalists have a relatively high level of freedom in selecting stories and choosing which aspects of any story should be emphasized. The routine, redundancy, and lack of investigative reporting and development journalism in the Algerian mass media may be due somewhat to a lack of autonomy and freedom of journalists, but it may also be explained by self-censorship and a lack of creativity of the journalists.

A delicate and sensitive issue in the practice of journalism is access to news sources. This is a problem that concerns journalists all over the world, including those in Algeria. Forty-four percent of the respondents said sometimes it is a problem, and 33% said it is a problem to get access to news sources. When journalists were asked about the process of investigating a critical issue, 48% said it is very difficult and a problem to investigate a critical issue, and 21% said sometimes it is a problem. Nearly half (48%) of the Algerian journalists said that almost always or more often than not they had the chance to follow up on stories, and 23% said they got such an opportunity only occasionally.

An important issue is the frequency of interference faced by the journalist when investigating a critical issue. Nearly three fourths (71%) of the journalists said they were subjected to interference from their bosses either regularly or occasionally, two thirds experienced interference from their news organizations, and nearly half were hindered by the Ministry of Information or the party either regularly or occasionally. Nearly two thirds said that it is not appropriate for others to interfere in journalists' investigations (63%), but 24% approved of such interference. Almost all journalists (92%) who approved interference justified their opinion by saying that interference is of importance to journalists because they need political orientation. The vast majority (93%) of those respondents who disapproved of interference said that interference either kills innovation and the personal initiative of the journalists or annihilates the freedom of the media practitioner.

Job Satisfaction

Half of the Algerian journalists (53%) said they were fairly satisfied with their job, but only 7% were very satisfied, and 38% said they are somewhat or very dissatisfied (Table 17.3). When asked about their working conditions, 57% of the respondents said they had some problems, and one fourth said their working conditions were very poor.

Table 17.3. Job Satisfaction of Journalists (N =75).

Level of Satisfaction	Percentage
Very satisfied	7
Fairly satisfied	53
Somewhat dissatisfied	31
Very dissatisfied	7
Don't know	1
No response	1

What accounts for such a low level of job satisfaction? Journalists were asked about their attitudes toward a variety of job-related aspects—stability, use of talents and creativity, freedom, salary and fringe benefits, and more. Twenty-three percent were strongly dissatisfied with the extent of their freedom and 28% with their living conditions. Forty percent were strongly dissatisfied with their sources of information and 49% with their housing. A fourth of the journalists were strongly dissatisfied with their peer relationships and a fifth with salary and job stability.

Opinions of journalists toward the performance of their news organizations were also somewhat negative. Almost two thirds (64%) rated their news media as doing a fair or poor job. Almost half of the journalists (49%) said that their news organization focuses too much on government activities, 45% said that there is too much emphasis on urban centers, and 40% said that there is a lack of interest and respect toward the profession.

When asked about what their news organizations ought to do, more than one third said they should provide facts and background information, put more emphasis on development journalism and economics, and reflect on problems, aspirations, and priorities of the masses. Respondents also mentioned more representation of both sides of the story, more critical and investigative journalism, and more respect shown to the profession and the journalist.

Journalists were also asked to comment on a list of criticisms of Algerian journalism. Almost two thirds either strongly agreed or agreed with the criticisms. Seventy-one percent of the respondents either strongly agreed or agreed that Algerian journalism is too ephemeral and lacks background information. Eighty percent of the respondents either strongly agreed or agreed that the press in Algeria is a government mouthpiece, and 83% said that Algerian journalism concentrates a lot on government routine activities. Nearly 80% agreed that there is not enough hard-biting investigative journalism.

In order to ascertain their job commitment, journalists were asked where they would prefer to work in five years. Almost two thirds of the respondents preferred to stay in the news media—37% in print media, 20% in broadcast media, and 9% in a news agency. Only 5% wanted to leave journalism to go into teaching, their own work, or work for the government. Given their job dissatisfaction and hard job conditions, one wonders why more journalists were not willing to leave journalism. It is likely that this attitude came from a belief on the part of the journalists that other jobs were not any better, and that the financial rewards were the same everywhere.

Media Performance, Press Law, and Improvement

What are Algerian journalists' opinions about the information policy and the press law in Algeria, and what are their suggestions for improving the performance of the mass media?

When journalists were asked about the weaknesses of the media, a large proportion listed a variety of problems and weaknesses such as unqualified personnel, poor management, unqualified managers, no clear communication policy, uncritical media, no investigative journalism, and lack of credibility. More than one third also mentioned a lack of legal protection for journalists, a lack of knowledge of the audience, poor distribution of the print media, and a shortage of modern equipment and facilities.

Respondents were also asked about their opinions toward information policy, and many journalists complained about the gap between theory (official documents and texts) and practice, lack of personnel and equipment, no clear definition of the role of the press, and no legal protection for journalists. More than two thirds said the press law in Algeria restricts the rights of the journalists, focuses on duties, and does not provide enough rights and protection to the journalist. Forty percent of the journalists in this study said that the press law is very flexible and can be interpreted in several ways, whereas 32% said the law is well thought out but not enforced in practice.

An important issue raised in the questionnaire is how to improve the media system in Algeria. Data show that more than half of the respondents suggested more protection, more freedom for journalists, more qualified news people, as well as a clear communication policy. Nearly half of the journalists also suggested the recruitment of good managers and the elimination of bureaucracy. A third said that the media should be at the service of the people first.

PROFESSIONALISM, NEWS VALUES, ROLES, AND ETHICS

Journalism as a profession in developing societies is still emerging and developing slowly. One indicator of professionalism is membership in a journalistic organization. Forty-eight percent of the Algerian journalists said they were members of the Union of Algerian Journalists and Writers—the only professional organization for journalists in the country. However, they argued that the organization is merely bureaucratic and is doing nothing to protect the noble cause of the profession of journalism and media practitioners.

Media Use

Another possible indicator of professionalism is readership of job-related publications. Algerian journalists were relatively heavy media consumers, reading an average of 6.7 domestic and foreign newspapers and magazines a week, watching newscasts 5.6 days a week, and listening to news on radio 4 days a week.

A striking finding concerning journalists' media use was the consumption of the foreign press. *Le Monde* was the most read publication, with 32% of the journalists mentioning it. *El-Moudjahid*, considered by many as the most prestigious Algerian newspaper, was second with 24%. Among the most preferred Algerian newspapers and publications were *El-Moudjahid, Algerie Actualite*, and *Ech-chaab*. Interestingly enough, these are the three publications that most Algerians would choose. All three publications are published in Algiers, have a relatively large circulation, have experienced journalists, and have relatively good quality journalism in comparison to other Algerian newspapers and periodicals.

How often do Algerian journalists read foreign publications? Many of them read the foreign press fairly regularly (45%), from time to time (22%), and regularly (19%). On a scale of 1 to 4, where 1 is never and 4 is regularly, the journalists averaged 2.04, fairly regularly. A large proportion said they bought them from newsstands (93%), and many got them from friends and colleagues (69%). Although one would think that the news organization library would provide such publications, only one fourth of the journalists mentioned this source. This sheds light on the kind of libraries, if there are any, that news organizations in Algeria have. Another problem is the scarcity of the foreign press in the newsstands in terms of quantity and choices. Algerian journalists also spent a good proportion of time watching and listening to electronic media.

News Values

Nearly one third of Algerian journalists viewed news as an event that is of interest to the nation and the people (29%). About one fourth defined news as events that have something to do with the government and as events that have effects on the nation and the people. One fifth defined news as stories that help raise the economic, cultural, and political education and awareness of the people. About one sixth said news is stories that help people acquire more education and knowledge. This indicates that some Algerian journalists conceived of the news within the realities of the country and viewed it as development journalism promoting social change and economic development. This is a healthy trend in Algerian journalism that suggests the possibility of conceiving of and using the mass media according to the needs and aspirations of the masses. This is true as far as the conception of news is concerned; the practice may be something else.

Media Roles

What are the most important roles of the media according to Algerian journalists? Nearly three fourths (71%) agreed that it is extremely important to get information to the public quickly, and more than half (55%) said it is extremely important to provide analysis and interpretation of complex problems (see Table 17.4). However, the percentage of those journalists who said it is extremely important to investigate claims and statements made by the government was notably lower (33%). This percentage in the Algerian context is very important, given the fact that the tradition of investigative journalism is not well developed in Algeria. Another significant finding was the relatively high percentage of journalists who said it is extremely important (45%) to criticize official agencies of the government when needed. This contradicts the realities of Algerian journalism in practice, in which very little criticism is found. This can be explained by the fact that journalists agreed with the Algerian communication policy that favors criticism and constructive journalism.

However, journalists argued that their access to the news sources was jeopardized, and that various pressures were exerted on them when they discussed sensitive and critical issues. Large proportions of the respondents strongly agreed with statements portraying the role of the media as perceived by the government: counterattacking foreign propaganda (73%), educating and forming a modern Algerian citizen (69%), enhancing the objectives of the socialist revolution (56%), and enhancing Islamic values among the population (48%).

Table 17.4. Perceived Importance of Media Roles (N = 75).

Tasks	Extremely Important (%)	Quite Important (%)	Somewhat Important (%)	Not Really Important (%)	Don't Know/ No Answer (%)
Get the information to the public quickly	71	21	4	0	4
Provide analysis and interpretation of complex problems	55	32	9	1	3
Provide entertainment and relaxation	40	27	13	4	16
Investigate claims & statements made by the government	33	25	13	7	21
Stay away from stories where factual content cannot be verified	60	24	9	4	3
Concentrate on news of interest to widest possible audience	43	35	11	4	8
Discuss national policy while it is still being developed	59	29	5	3	4
Develop intellectual & cultural interests of the public	20	23	5	15	37
Be an adversary of public officials by being constantly skeptical of their actions	51	29	12	0	8
Help in achieving the goals and objectives of development plans	65	25	4	3	3

Table 17.4. Perceived Importance of Media Roles (N = 75) (con't.).

Tasks	Extremely Important (%)	Quite Important (%)	Somewhat Important (%)	Not Really Important (%)	Don't Know/ No Answer (%)
Mobilize and politicize the masses to enhance economic development	29	19	12	16	24
Endorse government policies without any questions	44	20	13	13	9
Give the public what they want, not what the press decides what they need	36	32	11	7	15
Criticize official agencies of the government when needed	45	32	9	3	11
Should make a balance between government and the public interests and serve them both	56	32	4	4	4
Enhance the Islamic values among the population	48	32	7	5	8
Enhance the objectives of the socialist revolution	56	29	5	1	8
Educate and form a modern Algerian citizen	69	20	4	1	5
Counterattack foreign propaganda	73	16	3	0	8

Answers to the 19 questions in Table 17.4 about the level of importance of media roles were subjected to factor analysis to determine the patterns among the journalists' beliefs about their roles in society.

Two clusters of items emerged from the data. The first factor consisted of two items—Enhance the objectives of the socialist revolution" and "counterattack foreign propaganda—and can be called the supportive propaganda role. The second factor, consisting of the items "discussing national policy while it is being developed," "giving the public what they want not what the press decides they need," and "criticizing official agencies of the government when needed," can be labeled the investigative role. This factor, however, is not supported by the realities of Algerian journalism, in which little investigation and criticism are found. This factor may show the willingness and the desire of the journalists to perform investigative reporting. In practice, however, the Algerian media practitioner operates in an amalgam of organizational and institutional constraints that prevent her or him from performing the investigative role that the journalist dreams of.

As in the case of the definition of news, this is additional evidence that suggests that Algerian journalists agreed to a large extent with the overall communication policy of the government and viewed the tasks of the media within the specific condition of Algeria as a developing, Muslim, and socialist society. This suggests that news values do differ cross-culturally, and what may be news in the West is not necessarily so in Algeria, and vice versa. This, however, is not to say that the news values that journalists held were found in practice. Very often the reporter is reduced to a mere spokesman of government's activities and development projects without analyzing and criticizing what is going wrong.

As for how news values are linked to the practice of journalism, the findings of this study cannot answer this question. It can be speculated, however, that in terms of international news, the international news agencies and mainly Agence France Presse (AFP) set the agenda for the Algerian news organizations. With regard to domestic news, a lack of critical, investigative, and development journalism is notable.

News Conceptions

What is news and what is not is a controversial issue in the profession of journalism. Journalists were asked about what factors affected them the most in their conception of newsworthiness. Journalistic training (44%) and priorities of network news and prestige newspapers (32%) were most often mentioned as very influential by Algerian journalists. The day-to-day practice of journalism was the main factor shaping the ideas of journalists about what is news and what is not. In contrast, peers on the staff and supervisors were not perceived as very influential by very many journalists (12% and 17%).

To what extent have the journalists' conceptions of news changed since they entered the profession? On a scale of 1 to 4, where 1 is not at all (no change) and 4 very (a lot of change), journalists scored a mean of 2.43, meaning that they believed that the concept of news had changed somewhat. Twenty percent of the respondents said their conception of news had not changed at all, whereas 27%, 24%, and 17% said that it had slightly, somewhat, and very much changed, respectively.

Although audience research is almost nonexistent in Algeria, 29% of the respondents said that it had a strong influence on their conception of newsworthiness. This is a puzzling finding, but journalists might have taken audience research to mean their own contacts with the audience, its feedback, and its needs in terms of news.

Public Opinion

It is a common belief that the media are strong shapers of public opinion and that they influence the government heavily. Algerian media practitioners assigned the media a significant influence in shaping public opinion. On a scale of 0 to 10, where 0 is no influence and 10 is very great influence, respondents scored a mean of 7.24. The mean for how much media influence should be exerted on public opinion was 7.48 and 7.50 for media influence on government.

These results suggest that Algerian journalists believed that the media are strong and can play an important role in shaping public opinion and influencing the government. These findings are consistent with previous findings about the role of the media in society—to educate and form a modern Algerian citizen (69%) and to discuss national policy while it is being developed (59%).

Ethics

Journalism ethics is one of the most sensitive issues of the profession. Journalists interact with the society and with important sources of information. Many problems arise from the practice of the profession, and many issues are involved. Respondents were asked how influential different factors were on the journalist's sense of ethics. The most influential factor was the day-to-day newsroom learning. Forty percent said that this factor was extremely influential, and 24% said quite influential.

Religious training was the second highest factor mentioned by the journalists as extremely influential (20%) and quite influential (17%). Senior reporters, family upbringing, university teachers, and high school teachers were also mentioned as extremely or quite influential by a third or more of the Algerian journalists.

The findings suggest that the practice of journalism is more important than any other factor in shaping the journalist's ethics. Because religion plays an important role in the life of a Muslim, it was therefore mentioned as the second most important factor. Like the day-by-day newsroom learning, religion is also a daily practice and a daily learning.

CONCLUSIONS

This study was undertaken to draw a portrait of Algerian journalists and to understand the media system in Algeria from the angle of those who manufacture the news and shape the opinions. However, this portrait by itself is not enough to understand a given news system of a country. From the eight months spent by the researcher with the journalists, it was observed that in a developing country like Algeria, the political, economic, bureaucratic, and social institutions play an important role in the life and operations of both journalists and news organizations, and the communicator plays a very limited role in the delicate and sensitive world of journalism and communication.

It is unfortunate in a socialist developing nation like Algeria to find only six dailies, a poor regional press, the absence of community journalism, and a lack of logistics and equipment. In other words, it is clear that *la direction politique* of the Democratic and Popular Republic of Algeria (DPRA) has not paid a lot of attention to the sector of information. Paradoxically, the same *direction politique* has assigned a long list of tasks to the media. In this atmosphere, therefore, even with the most talented and skillful journalists in the world, the press in Algeria cannot do much because the socioeconomic and political institutions of the country are not ripe and efficient enough for the press to operate and function rationally and efficiently.

This profile of the Algerian journalist shows various aspects and facets of the Algerian media system. Some healthy trends as well as some major drawbacks and weaknesses were found. Among the most promising findings for a good and prosperous journalism in Algeria was the age composition of the journalists. The median age was 30.5 years old. Almost one fourth (24%) of the journalists were female. The Algerian journalist was a heavy media user reading an average of 6.7 local and foreign newspapers and magazines a week, watching newscasts 5.6 days a week, and listening to news on radio four days a week.

In terms of education, more than half of the Algerian journalists held a bachelor's degree, and almost half of them majored in journalism. Algerian news people agreed that both academic and nonacademic experience are important for journalists. They also agreed that working journalists should have on-the-job training and be required to take some academic refresher courses.

Algerian journalists conceived of press philosophy along the lines of the Algerian information policy. They viewed the role and the tasks of the news organizations within the context of Algeria as a developing, socialist, and Moslem society. They also believed that the media have a relatively high influence on the formation of public opinion and on the government.

More than two thirds of the journalists agreed that news people generally know what their audience wants. Algerian media practitioners had a relatively high level of freedom in selecting and emphasizing aspects of news stories. Almost half of them said that almost always or more often than not they had the chance to follow up on stories. Algerian journalists were committed to their jobs; two thirds of them wanted to remain in the media.

These positive trends suggest that Algeria has the raw material to have a good and effective press. The findings of this study refute the claims and theses that journalists in the Third World are either tied to the West or the East in conceiving of the philosophy and role of the press. Algerian journalists in this study were found to have their own, authentic philosophy and conception of the news and the role of the press. The young age of the journalists, their relatively high level of education, and the relatively high proportion of women practicing journalism are all good signs for a better and healthier journalism in Algeria.

Unfortunately, the other side of the coin reveals some negative aspects. The answers of the journalists concerning their working conditions, job satisfaction, and their rating of the news organizations' performance suggest that much is still needed to have a healthy and efficient media system in Algeria.

Among the negative aspects of Algerian journalism is the lack of training of journalists, whether before or after employment. Those journalists who graduated from journalism school in Algiers were not satisfied with the kind of education they got. More than half were not members of the Union of Algerian Journalists and Writers. The Algerian journalist lacked work experience, and interaction among journalists, managers, audience, people at the same level, and journalists from other news organizations was relatively low.

Another aspect of Algerian journalism's weakness was interference from others in the journalist's work. More than two thirds of the respondents said they were subjected to interference from their boss either regularly or occasionally. Almost three quarters of the journalists said they had some problems with their work, or their working conditions were very bad. More than half of the surveyed journalists were either dissatisfied or strongly dissatisfied with their job, their stability, the use of their talents and creativity, extent of freedom, living conditions, peer relationships, and relationships with sources of information.

In addition, almost two thirds of the respondents rated their media as doing either a fair or a poor job, almost half said their news organizations focus too much on government activities, and more than two thirds either strongly agreed or agreed that Algerian journalism is too ephemeral and lacks background information.

Algerian journalists were also disappointed with the communication policy and press law. Almost half of them said that the weaknesses of Algerian journalism lie in its bad management, the absence of a clear communication policy, lack of credibility, and lack of investigation and thorough analysis. Algerian journalists also cited a gap between the theory and practice of the information policy in the country. More than two thirds said that the press law restricts the rights of the journalist, does not protect him or her, and subjects him or her to a score of sanctions and penalties.

These negative trends and aspects cited by the respondents of this study by far outweigh the positive aspects. The findings, although suggesting some good and positive aspects in Algerian journalism, suggest that the news people in Algeria are working under rather critical and difficult conditions. Dissatisfied with their working conditions, peer relationships, and interactions with sources of information, one might wonder how the journalist could have the determination, devotion, and commitment to carry out his or her mission. With such dissatisfaction, the majority of journalists are not able to use their talents and creativity to fulfill their tasks and to serve the objectives of the socialist revolution and enhance socioeconomic change in developing Algeria.

Like previous studies done on mass communicators, this study was descriptive and presented some data about Algerian media practitioners. In order to put the data about the socioeconomic, demographic, and professional orientations of journalists in context, however, it is recommended that the organizational constraints in which the journalist operates, as well as the content of the news organizations, be studied. For instance, Dare (1983) studied the news content of the Nigerian news agency (NAN) as well as the role conceptions of its journalists. He concluded that the transnational wire services set the agenda of the news agency of Nigeria and that, although the journalists of NAN conceived of the role of the press within the Nigerian context, their practice of journalism shows their "uncritical acceptance of Western journalistic values."

Dare's and others studies refute the argument of Walter Gieber (1964) that "news is what newspapermen make it." News is more complex than that. Although it comes directly from the reporter, several factors and criteria play their role in its processing and dissemination. In fact in some settings, as in the case of Algeria, news is what the political and economic powers make it. For a quarter of a century, the political leadership—political factions, army, and financial groups—used and manipulated the media to serve their interests and to disseminate whatever messages suited their goals and objectives. In this case, the media were sacrificed to serve a handful of people at the expense of the large masses. Since the independence of the country, the media system in Algeria has failed to be an active, critical participant in the decision-making process. For a long time it has been the tool of those who rule and govern, but never the voice of the oppressed.

This implies that future mass communicator studies should not only look at the communicator but also at the media content and the institutional, legal, organizational, and political constraints within which the journalist carries out his or her mission. Looking at the organizational context of creativity in public television, Ettema and Whitney (1982: 103) argued that a range of factors affected the finished project in public television: "Professional perceptions and values, the demands of production routines and the compromises of organizational politics were all pieces of puzzles which the executive producer was called upon to solve."

This suggests that studies of mass communicators should be carried out on a macro level in order to understand the mechanisms of a given media system whether in the West, East, North, or South. Starck and Sudhakar (1979: 34) recommend:

> In studying journalists of a developing country, it may seem rhetorical to suggest the necessity of considering the very society in which they operate—the cultural, social, historical, political, and economic factors which influence performance, ideology, attitudes and ethics.

Several lessons were learned from this study. First, the poor performance of Algerian journalism is not due exclusively to journalists, but to the organizational and institutional constraints in which they work. Second, the findings of this study suggest that what ought to be investigated and looked at in the Algerian media system is its organization, management, politics, and bureaucracy.

This profile of the Algerian journalist suggests that much is needed to correct what is going wrong with the press system in the country. Journalists need more training and refresher courses; they should have more protection and the necessary means to fulfill their tasks adequately. The paradox in the Algerian press system lies in a score of contradictions and anomalies. The political leadership is using the media to disseminate its messages and defend its interests, unfortunately at the expense of the masses because the interests of the former are not necessarily compatible with those of the latter. In all of this the journalist is trapped also in a labyrinth and cannot serve both sides. Both the status of the news organization and that of the media practitioner in society reflect the willingness of the government to use both to maintain its politics, the status quo, and its interests.

The number of news organizations, the size of the journalistic workforce—very small compared to the size of the population—and the limited budget allocated to the media institutions demonstrate that there is a big gap between the roles and tasks assigned to the media in the official texts of the government and the means and infrastructure available to the media.

To conclude, the key solution to the critical situation of Algerian journalism is in institutional and organizational changes. The political leadership should make good use of the media system to promote development plans and the welfare of the masses and not to impose and dictate a vertical one-way communication system from the top to the bottom on the masses. The problem lies in the marginalization of the masses and their nonintegration into the media system in particular and the socioeconomic and political system in general. As a consequence, news organizations are functioning in a vacuum and serving the interests of a handful of Algerians, at the expense of an oppressed majority. The Algerian government should use its media system to integrate the masses into a democratic system, in which the people can participate in the decision-making process and in which the marketplace of ideas will prevail and open the doors to the best and the most competitive.

REFERENCES

Burgoon, Judee K., Michael Burgoon, and Charles K. Atkin. 1982. *The world of the working journalist*. East Lansing: Michigan State University.

Dare, Olatunji. 1983. *The news agency of Nigeria: A study of its impact on the flow of news and the role conceptions of its staffers*. Ph.D. dissertation, Indiana University.

Ettema, James S., and D. Charles Whitney, eds. 1982. *Individuals in mass media organizations: Creativity and constraint*. Beverly Hills, CA: Sage.

Gieber, Walter. 1964. News is what newspapermen make it. In *People, society and mass communication*, edited by Lewis Anthony Dexter and David M. White, pp. 173-82. London: The Free Press of Glencoe, Collier-Macmillan.

Johnstone, John W.C., Edward J. Slawski, and William W. Bowman. 1973. The professional values of American newsmen, *Public Opinion Quarterly* 36: 522-46.

Johnstone, John W.C., Edward J. Slawski, and William W. Bowman. 1976. *The news people: A sociological portrait of American journalists and their work*. Urbana: University of Illinois.

Kirat, Mohamed. 1993. *The communicators: A portrait of Algerian journalists and their work*. Alger: Office des Publications Universitaires.

Ottaway, David and Marina Ottaway. 1970. *Algeria: The politics of a socialist revolution*. Berkeley: University of California Press.

Starck, Kenneth and Anantha Sudhaker. 1979. Reconceptualizing the notion of journalistic professionalism across differing press systems. *The Journal of Communication Inquiry* 4, 2: 35-52.

Tash, Abdulkader T.M. 1983. *A profile of professional journalists working in the Saudi Arabian daily press*. Ph.D dissertation, Southern Illinois University at Carbondale.

Tunstall, Jeremy. 1970. *The Westminster Lobby correspondents*. London: Routledge and Kegan Paul.

Tunstall, Jeremy. 1977. *Journalists at work: Specialist correspondents, their news organizations, news sources and competitor colleagues*. London: Constable and Co. Ltd.

Weaver, David H. and G. Cleveland Wilhoit. 1986. *The American journalist: A portrait of U.S. news people and their work*. Bloomington: Indiana University Press.

Yu, Frederick T.C. 1977. Communication policy and planning for development: Some notes on research. In *Communication research: A half-century appraisal,* edited by Daniel Lerner and Lyle M. Nelson, pp. 167-190. Honolulu: University Press of Hawaii.

V

NORTH AMERICA

18

Canadian Women Journalists: The "Other Half" of the Equation

Gertrude J. Robinson
McGill University
Armande Saint-Jean
Université de Sherbrooke

Canada, which is frequently viewed as merely a northern extension of the United States, has in fact a number of sociopolitical and demographic differences that affect how its media are organized and function. Chief among these, according to Herschel Hardin (1974), are its large unevenly populated land mass. More than half of Canada's approximately 30 million people live in the area bounded by Quebec City, Montreal, and Toronto. Quebec and Ontario consequently have the largest concentration of print and broadcast outlets, 58 of 113 dailies (among them 13 of the country's 17 largest circulation papers) and 59 of Canada's 119 television stations. Historically, Canada is also a young nation, barely 125 years old. It was founded by two distinct cultural groups, the French and the English, whose political contract is reflected in the country's parliamentary institutions. Two parallel media networks in the two official languages signify this political fact. They serve two distinct viewer groups, the 25% French population in Quebec and in other provinces and the ethnically mixed audiences in English Canada.

---

*This research was funded by the Social Science Research Council of Canada Strategic Grants "Women and Change" theme, # 816-93-0026.

Another feature that differentiates Canada from the United States, according to Hardin, is its "corporate enterprise" culture. National political and informational infrastructures could not have been developed in Canada's five regions without state investment. This, together with private funds, built the national telephone, broadcast, and rail/air networks as well as the national health and social service infrastructures. Canada's dual public/private broadcasting system, which exists side by side with regionally focused private stations and newspapers, is a manifestation of this economic reality. The country's regionalism is also reflected in the fact that Canada lacks a national newspaper (the *Globe and Mail* is primarily read by urban elites in its five metropolitan centers), and that a majority of its newspaper outlets, 84 of 113, are small (less than 50,000 circulation) and regionally focused.

Communications historian Harold Innis (1951) points to the centrality of electronic communication technologies in Canada's national project resulting from these regional splits. Since the 1970s, the country has been linked by telecommunication satellites and cable; today a fiber-optic backbone and miniaturized telephones as well as computer ownership in one third of Canadian households make the country one of the most electronically sophisticated in the Western world.

Women's journey toward equality in the media professions was not chronicled until the early 1970s when Gertrude J. Robinson (1975) and others like Roger de la Garde (1971) began to survey their position in the daily press. This research demonstrated that women's status in the "prestige"—read "male"—profession of journalism was that of an "outsider," even though changes in North America's post-World War II economy and society had opened up the public world of "work" for women. In 1960, there were about 23 million working women who made up 30% of the U.S. workforce. By the 1990s, their labor force participation constituted 45% of all U.S. workers (Weaver and Wilhoit 1991). In Canada the figures are similar and indicate that more than 3 million women entered the labor force between 1970 and 1994, and that their workforce participation increased from 34% to 45% (Statistics Canada l995). Canadian media professionals benefited from this labor market shift (Robinson 1975). In the 20 years between 1974 and 1994, women increased their presence on daily newspaper staffs from 1 in 5 to almost 1 in 3 (21% to 28%), whereas in broadcasting women nearly doubled their participation from 20% to 37%. In spite of these advances, Canadian women professionals in the 1990s remained 11 percentage points behind their U.S. sisters in daily newspaper work, where participation had meanwhile grown from 22% to 39%. Canadian professionals, however, have a 3-point lead in television, where U.S. participation rates in the past 20 years increased to only 34% (Freedom Forum Media Studies Center 1993).

How to explain these participation rate differences in the Canadian and U.S. media professions, when both countries experienced a strong women's movement in the past 30 years and also provided better secondary education opportunities for its young women? Sociohistorical evidence suggests that Canadian women began their climb into the media professions from a lower starting point on the labor ladder. The 1970 Royal Commission on the Status of Women Report indicates that in 1960 women made up around 25% of the labor force in Canada, whereas it was 30% in the United States. College participation rates of 13% (Statistics Canada 1990) also lagged behind those of its southern neighbor. There are moreover fewer educational opportunities for women to acquire a journalism background in Canada than in the United States. Only eight universities offer programs, four in Quebec and four elsewhere.

A third reason for the smaller participation rates of Canadian than U.S. women in the media professions must be sought in French Quebec's unique media history. This shows that the province has always had proportionally fewer newspapers per population than English Canada: 10% of papers for 25% of the total population versus 41% of papers for 37% of the population in Ontario. The percentage of women working in these daily newspapers remained virtually stagnant in the past 20 years, growing a mere 3 percentage points from 18% to 21%. In television, however, women's participation rate of 37% is close to the national average, although still substantially below that in the Maritimes (44%) and Ontario (41%). These figures indicate that in both Canada and the United States broadcast organizations not only expanded their workforce more than print organizations, but that they were also under more pressure to hire women because of the affirmative action programs that had been put in place in the 1980s.

METHODS

To gain an up-to-date snapshot of women's professional progress in Canadian media, we restudied the role and position of Canadian female and male journalists in the daily press and television in 1994/1995. Survey I (the national sample) covered all of Canada's 114 dailies and 118 television outlets in a two-step process. The first involved a telephone interview to determine the number, distribution, and organizational position of female and male editorial staff in Canada's five regions: the Maritimes, Quebec, Ontario, Prairies, and British Columbia. The second sought more detailed staff information by means of a lengthy mail questionnaire on journalists' social backgrounds and education, work setting, average remuneration, professional beat (subject area), career patterns, and job satisfaction. One hundred ninety-six questionnaires were sent out and 186 responses received for a response rate of 95%.

Survey II (the attitude survey) was conducted in 1995. It constructed a regionally weighted proportionate representative sample of 134 female and male journalists, matched by age, position, and geographic location to probe gender differences in the workplace. To assess an organization's attitude toward women' diverse workplace experiences, management attitudes including affirmative action policies, journalistic self-perceptions, journalistic goals and values, as well as news production values were explored. The response rate to this in-depth quantitative and qualitative questionnaire was 92%. The inclusion of Quebec data and Weaver and Wilhoit (1991) questions guaranteed not only a Canada-wide picture, but also comparability with U.S. findings.

The national survey (survey I) demonstrates that the total number of Canadian daily print and television journalists increased significantly in the past 20 years, growing from 2,500 to 3,500, and that women comprised 28% of these totals. It also demonstrates that whereas women's participation doubled from 504 to 962, that of men increased by only 540 persons (Robinson and Saint-Jean 1995). These figures indicate that half of the new media recruits in the past two decades were women. Survey II confirms that the median age of women was lower than that of men in the profession in 1995, standing at 34 and 40, respectively. Comparative figures from the United States indicate that the median ages of both genders decreased between 1971 and 1982, dropping from 39.9 to 32.4 years (Weaver and Wilhoit 1991), a sign that the profession became younger during the 1980s. Although similar timeline comparisons are not available for Canada, our data indicate that a similar trend might have occurred here because broadcast hirings have been greater than those in the daily press. Younger median ages for professional women in both countries suggest that affirmative action programs were effective in recruiting more women and minorities into the media professions since the 1970s. This is a finding that is also corroborated in the Scandinavian countries, in which female professionals have made the greatest recruitment gains (Löfgren-Nilsson 1994).

WORKING CONDITIONS OF CANADIAN WOMEN JOURNALISTS: SUBSTANTIAL PROGRESS SINCE THE 1970S

Up to the beginning of the 1970s, the status of women in Canadian journalism and broadcasting was that of a minority. At that time, women constituted less than 20% of the workforce in print and about 12% in broadcasting (Robinson 1977). Minorities, as Ralph Turner demonstrated long ago, face systematic social barriers to entry into the professions, to promotion and pay, as well as to their effectiveness in leadership positions (Turner 1952). Our survey collected comparative evidence in all of these domains and is therefore able to document for the first time what kinds of progress Canadian media women have made in the past 20 years.

A great number of studies have shown that secondary education is one of the most important prerequisites for access to the media professions. In 1971, these prerequisites still disadvantaged women. At that time, William Bowman (1974) found that 60% of male journalists had a bachelor's degree, compared with only 50% of women. By 1982-83, however, the educational gap had been closed for U.S. journalists, and about 74% of both women and men held at least a bachelor's degree (Weaver and Wilhoit 1991). More recent U.S. surveys suggest that by the early 1990s, women began to be more educated than their male counterparts, a trend that also seems to hold for Canada, in which, in 1991, 10% of women aged 20 to 24 had a university degree versus 8% of men (Statistics Canada 1995). In Quebec, 77% of all media women have a university education, with 50% holding a bachelor's and another 21% an master's degree (Saint-Jean 1995). Our Canadian comparative sample puts these percentages at 58% for female and 53% for male media professionals holding a bachelor's degree, and 11% female versus 10% male journalists holding a master's degree.

Gender and Beats

The question of whether these advanced educational qualifications have raised the professional status of media women can be answered with a resounding "yes." In 1975, we wrote that "status in the media is defined in two ways, either through the kind of news one covers, or hierarchically, through the position one occupies in the organization" (Robinson 1975: 5). "Beat" assignments and positions are not linearly linked but become inflected by the multiple strands of gender, seniority, and trustworthiness. Our comparisons of the relationship between "beat" assignment and gender indicate that over the past two decades gender stereotyping of "beats" has decreased, and women have gained access to a larger number of subject areas. Using a cut-off point of 50%, in 1971, four subject areas were overwhelmingly covered by newspaper women (lifestyle, consumer affairs, religion, and social welfare). None of these ranked front page coverage and were therefore classified as less important "soft" news. Men in contrast had access to 12 subject areas, three times as many as their female counterparts. They included 10 front page or "hard news" areas such as sports, labor, business, urban affairs, outdoors, federal and provincial governments, real estate, agriculture, organizations plus the weather and travel domains. An additional six beats were covered by both genders—local, regional, and national news as well as human interest, entertainment, and minorities, a new subject made prominent by the women's movement and social activism in the late 1960s and early 1970s. This evidence indicates that in the early 1970s, newspaper "beats" were gender stereotyped both in terms of the smaller total number of subject areas women could report, 10 against men's 18, and in terms of their professional "usefulness" as stepping stones in building a journalistic career. Only 3 of the 10 subject areas offered "hard news" coverage experience—local, national, and regional news.

By the the early 1990s, not only the "beat" structure but also the gender stereotyping of subject areas had substantially decreased. In 1994, women journalists had become the major reporters of 10 subject areas. Among these 10, five were new (minorities, health, science, education, and environment), and two had been originally covered by a majority of males (organizations and labor). The number of male-dominated beats had meanwhile been reduced from 12 to 8. Six of these eight were holdovers from 1974—sport, outdoors, travel, weather, provincial government, and agriculture—whereas the other two were taken over from women (personalities and religion). Of the remaining five beats covered by both genders, four are the same as twenty years ago (local, regional, national news and entertainment) while one is new, the increased importance of business information.

The shifts in coverage areas between the genders indicate that in the 20 years between 1974 and 1994, five new subject areas were taken over by women (minorities, health, science, education, and environment), while one was taken over from them to be covered by men (religion). The subject-matter shifts have "mainstreamed" what used to be considered "women's news" (Marzolf 1993: 35). What is involved here is that issues that male editors had considered in the "private domain" of the home sphere in the 1970s such as education and the environment became prominent social issues in the 1990s and were shifted to the "public domain" of governmental concern.

Our Canadian comparison has also discovered that covering a beat has decreased in importance as a journalistic status indicator in the 20 years since the original study. This can be partially explained by the fact that there are far fewer reporters identified as "beat" reporters than was the case in the early 1970s. According to Weaver and Wilhoit (1991), in 1982-83, 48% of U.S. reporters who did reporting regularly were beat reporters. In Canada, the situation is different, only 33% of full-time reporters are defined as "beat" reporters. Although conclusive evidence is lacking, we speculate that the decrease in the number of "beat" reporters is partially explained by the predominance of small circulation dailies (under 50,000) in Canada and a general decrease in "beat" specialization in all types of media. "Beat" reporting has also been undermined by the use of personalized computers, which provide access to information (databases) that used to be available only through specialization and statistical analysis skills that are now supported by software.

Gender and Job Titles

Another indicator of women's progress in the media professions is provided by their advance up the occupational ladder. Table 18.1 indicates that in the two decades since 1974, newspaper women moved up into five of the six hierarchical levels and in 1994 were proportionally represented in all but the top editor-in-chief positions. Our comparison shows that in 1974, three quarters of women were reporters, whereas in 1994 this proportion was closer to that of men (57%). On the next three levels, women were close to the one-third level—star reporters (29%), desk heads (26%), and day/night editors (28%)—a significant increase from 1974. Assistant managing editors were also 22% female, indicating that women in 1994 were proportionally better represented across the position spectrum than they were 20 years earlier. Only the editor-in-chief positions still escaped their grasp, in which the male/female ratio was 89%/11%.

In television, women's progress was even more marked because a larger group of younger women were recruited into broad-

Table 18.1. Position of Journalists in Canadian Dailies by Gender (1974-1994).

	Total (1974)	Prop. of Men/Women (1974)	Total (1994)	Prop. of Men/Women (1994)
Reporters	1,291 (53%)	75%/25%	1,763 (51%)	70%/30%
Star Reporters	310 (13%)	76%/24%	246 (7%)	71%/29%
Desk Hds.	289 (12%)	81%/19%	130 (4%)	74%/26%
Day/Night Eds.	234 (9%)	92%/8%	975 (28%)	72%/28%
Asst. Man. Eds.	175 (7%)	89%/11%	160 (4%)	78%/22%
Eds.-in-Chief	151 (6%)	90%/10%	195 (6%)	89%/11%
Total	2,450 (100%)	79%/21%	3,451 (100%)	72%/28%

casting than print. Table 18.2 demonstrates that women achieved proportional representation in television journalism, but this time well over the one-third level where they will be able to affect organizational change. Women in 1994 held 41% of reporter, 33 percent of correspondent, 31 percent of desk head and 41 percent of producer/director positions. However, in television women were still excluded from the top executive producer positions, which were almost as overwhelmingly male occupied (82% vs. 18%) as they were in the newspaper sector. Comparable U.S. occupational breakdowns are not available. The Gannett Foundation's (1989) *Women, Men and Media* study gives only aggregated figures, noting that U.S. women constitute 25% of middle management and hold 10% of editor and 7% of general manager positions. Weaver and Wilhoit also fail to provide a breakdown of positions by gender, but they do compare the percentage of men and women in management positions in their 1982 and 1992 studies. The Gannett News Service figures suggest a less rosy picture south of the border and raise questions about whether U.S. affirmative action laws are less effective in promoting gender equity than their Canadian variants.

Table 18.2. Position of Television Journalists By Gender (1994) (N = 1,304).

	Men (1994)	Women (1994)	Prop. of Men/Women
News writers	43 (5%)	24 (5%)	64%/34%
Reporters	447 (55%)	305 (63%)	59%/41%
Correspondents	24 (3%)	12 (2%)	67%/33%
Desk Heads	110 (13%)	49 (10%)	69%/31%
Producers/Dir.	114 (14%)	79 (16%)	59%/41%
Exec. Producers	80 (10%)	17 (4%)	82%/18%
Total	818 (100%)	486 (100%)	63%/37%

Gender and Pay

Women's enhanced educational qualifications have also improved the income disparities between the genders, although parity is still far from being reached. In 1974, we found that the mean yearly salary of print journalists ranged between $9,200 at the rank-and-file reporter level and $16,600 at the top or chief editor level. Twenty years later these figures had increased to between $29,224 and above $45,500 in the top positions. A comparison of salary averages for the two periods indicates that salaries have more than tripled between 1974 and 1994, from $12,900 to $37,862. These figures are in line with George Pollard's 1985 survey of English language journalists for whom a mean salary of $33,009 was established.

The available salary information from our Canadian sample does not lend itself to a detailed comparison of female and male salary differentials, because all managing editors who filled out the questionnaire claimed that the 1986 Employment Equity Act required them to pay employees equally, while taking work experience, seniority, and education into account. Statistics Canada data, however, demonstrate that salary discrepancies between full-time employed females and males still exist in Canadian society, and that they vary by economic sector. Although the general earnings' rate of full-time, full-year female workers increased from 59.6% to 72.0% of male earnings in the past 20 years, women earn on average 63.7% of male salaries in managerial/administrative positions, 71.4% in social science and religion, and 77.7% in artistic/recreational occupations (Statistics Canada 1995). Wilhoit and Weaver (1991) found in 1983 that U.S. women journalists earned 71 cents to each male dollar which suggests that the 77.7 cents figure for Canada's artistic personnel may reflect the 1994 pay differential between women and men in the Canadian media professions.

Three other factors, according to Statistics Canada and our comparative data, affect the female/male earnings ratios. They are age, education, and employment in large rather than small media outlets. Women between the ages of 35 to 44, which is the largest group in our sample, had average earnings that were about $4,000 more than those of people 10 years younger or 10 years older. The same goes for women with university education or degrees, who were the majority in our sample. They earned an average of $5,000 more than women with diplomas (Statistics Canada, 1995).

Another factor that is positively associated with higher earnings is employment in large media outlets. Fifty-one percent of all daily newspaper women work in large circulation dailies versus 14% in medium and 35% in small ones. In television these proportions are even higher, with 62% of female professionals found in metropolitan markets and 19% in medium and 18% in small markets. The median weekly salary comparisons in Table 18.3 indicate that reporters in small circulation dailies receive only 64% ($562) of the weekly salary claimed by their colleagues in large circulation dailies ($883). In television a similar salary spread is found for personnel at the middle and top levels. Television outlets in large markets pay a median weekly salary of $812, which is 15% more than people earn in medium markets ($687) across the country.

Table 18.3. Comparative Median Weekly Salaries of Canadian Print Journalists by Outlet Size and Position (1974-1994).

Position	Small Circulation (Under 50,000) 1974	1994	Medium Circulation (50,000-100,000) 1974	1994	Large Circulation (Over 100,000) 1974	1994
Reporter	$162	562	$214	875	$228	$885
Star Reporter	178	625	227	926	252	1158
Desk Hd.	217	687	217	885	294	1135
Day/Night Ed.	214	687	270	979	337	1275
Asst. Man. Ed.	256	812	240	1,101	388	1513
Ed.-in-Chief	258	875	280	1,142	400	1560

Statistics Canada data indicate that although there has been a narrowing of the earnings gap between women and men, this gap continues to amount to between 18 and 22 percentage points for the highest paid professions in 1993 (Statistics Canada 1995). The narrowing gap, which has been fueled by equity legislation in the past 20 years, has also resulted from increases in the average earnings of women (8%) and decreases in earnings of men (2%) (Statistics Canada 1995). The upshot is that media industries continue to reap substantial benefits from employing the "other half" of their workforce at gender discounted prices.

ROLES, VALUES, AND ATTITUDES

Trends in professionalism have been described in *The American Journalist* (Weaver and Wilhoit 1991, 1994) and studied in different countries such as England and Germany, but in Canada such studies are rare. Our own second-stage survey replicated a number of questions related to aspects of professionalism as defined by Weaver and Wilhoit (1991, 1994). Among the indicators used are level of education, evaluation of news organization's performance, perception of the importance of different news media roles, views about ethically questionable reporting practices, indicators of perceived autonomy, importance ratings of different job aspects, membership in journalism or communication organizations, and readership of occupational or professional publications.

Our data therefore allow us to provide an overview of gender similarities and differences concerning journalists' views about their roles and their professional practice and the functions they assign to the media. Our study also allows us to draw a comparison between Canadian and U.S. journalists on some aspects related to professionalism. Because no similar study was ever conducted in Canada in the past, it is not possible to measure the evolution of trends that might have occurred in Canada over the past decades. Overall, our data confirm that some differences exist between men and women journalists, at least in the way in which the two groups perceive their roles, their profession, and the mission of the media they work for (Saint-Jean and Labarre 1995).

Roles and Performance of the Media

Defining the roles for journalists and the missions for the media have been matters of public debate for quite a number of years, actually ever since the proposals that led the media and the profession to endorse the Social Responsibility mandate in the late 1950s (Saint-Jean 1993). Today it is difficult to know exactly how journalists and media people define their social role in a democratic society. For these reasons previous studies (Johnstone, Slawski, and Bowman 1976; Weaver and Wilhoit 1991, 1994) have argued that it is important to explore these questions in greater detail. Respondents' answers from different countries would provide insights into national differences, as well as the role of gender in the construction of the profession's varying social role conceptions.

Our Canadian survey adopted Weaver and Wilhoit's methodology to respond to this challenge and furthermore added gender as an important variable to try to find out whether female and male professionals construct different role and attitude conceptions toward their profession. Using a list of "things that the media do or try to do today," respondents were asked to rate the importance of eight media roles on a 5-point scale, ranging from "very important" to "not important." Table 18.4, which records the percentage of female and male respondents considering a media role "most important," indicates that the two country's journalism corps assigned different importance ratings to the eight media roles.

Table 18.4 indicates that although women and men had similar response patterns in assessing these roles in the United States, this was not the case in Canada. In 1982-83, both U.S. female and male journalists assigned primary importance to investigating government claims (66%) and to getting information to the public quickly (60%). Their Canadian counterparts in 1995 made a different choice. For them, providing analysis of complex problems is in first place (63 %), whereas getting information to the public quickly is in second place (60%), followed by investigating government claims, which ranks third (52%).

These national differences, one might speculate, indicate that U.S. journalists are considerably more suspicious about their government

Table 18.4. Importance Journalists Assign to Various Mass Media Roles by Country and Gender (Percentage who rated each dimension very important).

Media roles	1982-83 U.S. Total (N=1,001) (%)	1982-83 U.S. Women (N=338) (%)	1982-83 U.S. Men (N=661) (%)	1994-95 Canada total (N=123) (%)	1994-95 Canada Women (N=62) (%)	1994-95 Canada Men (N=61) (%)
Investigate government claims	66	69	64	52	50	52
Get information to public quickly	60	63	58	60	64	57
Avoid stories with unverified content	50	58	46	29	29	28
Provide analysis of complex problems	49	49	49	63	61	63
Discuss national policy	38	40	39	32	39	27
Concentrate on widest audience	36	n.a	n.a.	20	14	23
Develop intellectual/cultural interests	24	26	23	14	14	14
Provide entertainment	20	23	18	7	2	10

agencies than Canadian professionals, and that the news agendas of the two countries differed markedly in the measurement periods of 1982-83 and 1995. In Canada the 1995 agendas were dominated by complex constitutional issues arising from Quebec's upcoming referendum on secession, which accentuated cultural differences, regional imbalances, and the like. No wonder that "providing analysis of complex problems" topped the list of media roles (63%) for Canadian professionals.

Additional differences in assessing the importance of media roles result from gender, a variable that does not seem to affect U.S. responses. Table 18.4 demonstrates that nearly two thirds of Canadian female journalists (64%) considered "getting information to the public quickly" very important as compared with 57% of their male counterparts. For the males, this order was inverted for analysis of complex problems, which they considered more important (63%). Moreover, a substantially larger proportion of women (39%) than men (27%) considered discussing national policy of great importance. Male professionals in contrast thought that reaching the largest audience (23%) and providing entertainment (10%) were other worthy media roles. A very broad interpretation of these gender differences suggest that Canadian male professionals focused more on the business aspects of media activity, favoring roles related to profit making, whereas female journalists favored content-oriented media roles that privilege the intellectual and social missions assigned to the media in democratic societies. Considerably more cross-cultural research is required to gain greater understanding of the effects of gender on media role expectations and journalistic attitudes.

Our evidence further suggests that subtle attitudinal differences appear between media practitioners in different types of media outlets. For instance, television journalists, we found, rated speed of transmission (getting information to the public quickly) slightly more favorably than newspaper journalists. The latter, in contrast, stressed the importance of the "analysis" and the "investigative" roles of the media vis-à-vis claims made by government. Another striking difference was the fact that television news people considered providing entertainment less important than newspaper journalists. This seems to indicate that print journalists are deeply aware of the competitive advantages of television as an "entertainment" medium with which they have to compete on a daily basis.

Weaver and Wilhoit's (1996) most recent U.S. survey has furthermore indicated that U.S. rank-and-file journalists have become more critical in their media performance ratings over time. In 1992, only 12.5% of their national sample felt that the media were performing their job in an outstanding manner, whereas 10 years earlier 17.9% had held this opinion. Our Canadian respondents seem to reflect a similarly critical attitude, with only 1 in 6 (15.6%) considering the media to have performed "outstandingly" in 1995. Significant differences exist, however, when editorial personnel and supervisory personnel responses are compared. In general, Canadian rank-and-file journalists seemed to be more critical of the media's performance than the supervisory staff. Our data on television respondents indicate that three quarters of all supervisory personnel (71%) believed the media were doing "outstandingly" well in getting information quickly to the public, while only half (50%) of the editorial journalists were of the same opinion. The two professional groups differed as well on television's "investigative" performance vis-à-vis government claims. Fully one third of supervisors (37.5%) gave them a "good" rating as opposed a mere 1 in 5 editorialists (19%) who believed it to be "outstanding."

Journalists' Roles and Professional Practices

Great importance is given in *The American Journalist* to journalistic role conceptions, using either Johnstone et al.'s 1971 binary scale of neutral and participant, or Weaver and Wilhoit's three-part model, based on a characterization of interpretive, disseminator, and adversarial roles. Neither of these models seems to be sophisticated enough to compare the complexities of professional role conceptions. In the researchers' opinion:

> The overwhelming conclusion from the intensive analysis of role conceptions among American journalists is that a large majority see their professional role as highly pluralistic. They cannot be described simply as interpreters or disseminators; they are *both*. Nor can it be said that they see no utility in the adversary role. (Weaver and Wilhoit 1991:144; emphasis in original)

Nowadays, journalists tend to blend all roles into their practice, and they generally consider theoretical categories as complementary aspects of the same outlook. To overcome the theoretical lacunae and develop new research criteria, we believe the ethical dimensions of reporting practices have to be investigated. It has already been pointed out (Weaver and Wilhoit 1991) that it is difficult to evaluate a reporting tactic when it is removed from the context of a specific news story. To guarantee comparability with previous U.S. research, we asked Canadian respondents to provide an approval rating (on a 5-point scale) of seven practices isolated by Weaver and Wilhoit in 1991.

Table 18.5 indicates that gender is relatively unimportant in evaluating general attitudes toward professional practices because both gen-

Table 18.5. Comparative Approval Ratings of Professional Practices by Country and Gender (Percentage who rated each practice "highly justified" or "justifiable" in Canada and "may be justified" in the U.S.).

Practices	U.S. 1992 (N = 1,156)	Canada 1994-95 (N=123)	Canada Women (N = 62)	Canada Men (N = 61)
	(%)	(%)	(%)	(%)
Getting employed in an organization to gain inside information	63	36	37	33
Using confidential business or government documents without authorization	82	60	59	63
Badgering unwilling informants to get a story	49	31	23	37
Making use of personal documents without permission (letters, photographs, etc.)	48	17	14	20
Paying people for confidential information	20	9	11	8
Claiming to be somebody else	22	7	7	7
Agreeing to protect confidentiality and not doing so	5	2	2	3

ders have received the same workplace socialization either in journalism schools or in their on-the-job training. Our data corroborate this thesis by indicating that both female and male professionals made the same ethical choices about which professional practices were more "justifiable" and which less so. To gain a better understanding of the "justifiability" scale used by Weaver and Wilhoit, which was tripartite (may be justified, would not approve, unsure), we expanded our scale to include five options. Two of these—"highly justified" and "justifiable"—were summed to approximate the "may be justified" option utilized in the Weaver and

Wilhoit survey (1991). We thus developed a means for distinguishing the strength of approval/disapproval manifested toward some of the methods used in the course of journalistic work. Although the question wording consequently was slightly different in the U.S. and Canadian surveys, we do believe that they probed the same ethical attitudes.

Feminist research on women's psychology and workplace behavior suggests that gender differences manifest themselves in a tendency for women to comply with authority more than their male counterparts (Löfgren-Nilsson 1994). Their socialization patterns that stress cooperation consequently lead them to reject actions that are legally or morally questionable, namely, using confidential documents, acting without permission, or badgering informants. Table 18.5 indicates that both Canadian women and men strongly disapprove of professional methods that involve lies or deception, like (6) claiming to be somebody else, which garnered only a 7% approval rating, or (7) failing to keep a promise of confidentiality for which the approval rating was a mere 2%. Beyond that, however, there were gendered differences in approval ratings, with between 6 and 14 percentage point spreads in (3) badgering unwilling informants to get a story, as well as (4) using personal documents without permission. Four-point differences in approval ratings existed with respect to (1) getting employed in an organization in order to gain inside information and (2) using confidential documents without authorization, although these differences may not be statistically significant.

One of the most interesting findings emerging from Table 18.5 concerning professional practices is the fact that Canadians seem to be more critical of certain types of professional practices than their U.S. counterparts. This is indicated by the fact that in Canada 6 out of 7 practices received approval ratings below 50%, whereas their U.S. colleagues were relatively approving of the same three practices (1, 3, and 4). They considered them "may be justified" and gave them ratings between 48% and 63%, respectively. Both groups disapprove strongly of paying people for confidential information, claiming to be someone else, and reneging on confidentiality. Beyond that Canadians and U.S. professionals agreed that "using confidential business or government documents without authorization" was somewhat justifiable. The discrepancies in approval ratings here (60% versus 82%) may be due to the Watergate experience and the difference in question wording. Overall, the national comparison indicates that Canadian journalists are more similar than different in ethical outlooks to what Weaver and Wilhoit (1991: 138) describe as the journalism corps of "three of the world's great democracies," the United States, Germany, and England.

Attitudes and Work Characteristics

The attitudes that encourage journalists to choose or remain in the profession can be subdivided into two categories. The first group of motivations can be labeled *material* considerations and includes salary, job security, chances of getting ahead in the organization, variety and stimulation in the workplace, as well as levels of stress. The second encompasses what might be called *professional* considerations and includes amount of autonomy, freedom from supervision, chances to excel and specialize, editorial policies, as well as chances to help others.

Table 18.6 indicates that gender plays a greater role in assessing the material conditions of journalistic work than in thinking about its professional characteristics. This is in line with the original finding that gender differences in the professional realm are eradicated through workplace socialization. Among the aspects that Canadian women value the most in their workplace, three belong to the material realm and show attitude spreads between 7 and 9 points. They are variety and stimulation,

Table 18.6 Comparison of Job Dimensions by Country and Gender (Percentage who rated each dimension very important).

	U.S. 1982-83 Women (N = 338) (%)	U.S. 1982-83 Men (N = 661) (%)	Canada 1995 Women (N = 62) (%)	Canada 1995 Men (N = 61) (%)
Material Dimensions				
Variety and stimulation	n.a.	n.a.	36	29
Salary	19	24	27	18
Fringe benefits	25	26	27	18
Job security	58	57	18	27
Chances for promotion	53	44	12	11
Level of stress	n.a.	n.a.	9	14
Professional Dimensions				
Amount of autonomy	51	50	36	32
Freedom from supervision	39	38	36	22
Chances to excel	n.a.	n.a.	30	27
Chances to help others	69	57	16	18
Editorial policies	62	54	16	11
Chances for specialization	50	42	12	11

salary, and fringe benefits. Only "freedom from supervision" in the professional realm registers an even greater 14-point, gender-related attitude spread. These comparative figures indicate that female journalists are considerably more concerned about the material aspects of their jobs than men. This makes sense when one considers that their median salaries are substantially lower than those of their male colleagues. Gender also affects the order of importance female and male professionals assign to the two dimensions of their work situation. For women journalists, variety and stimulation (M), amount of autonomy (P), and freedom from supervision (P) are at the top of the list, followed by chance to excel, salary, and fringe benefits, suggesting that women's workplace activities are more circumscribed by hierarchical rules than those of men.

Male Canadian journalists, however, have a different set of attitudes toward their working situation and thus consider different job dimensions important. In decreasing order of importance, they are amount of autonomy (P), variety and stimulation (M), chances to excel (P), and job security (M), which receive top billing, whereas freedom from supervision (P) and chances for specialization (P) are in fifth and sixth place. Interestingly, Canadian males are even less interested in the material conditions of their profession than their female colleagues, an assessment that reflects the workplace power of Canadian unions. Among their six choices, four professional considerations are paired with only two material ones: variety and stimulation as well as job security. The 9-point gender-related spread in the importance of job security, which males rate in third place (27 % vs. 18%) and females in seventh, may indicate that males are generally satisfied with their level of remuneration, but are becoming aware that female competition in the workplace may erode job security in the 1990s.

Table 18.6 also indicates that Canadian and U.S. journalists rate the job dimensions of their work setting very differently, and that gender affects these assessments. Our cross-cultural comparison indicates that U.S. female journalists choose four professional and two material dimensions as most important, which are different from those chosen by their Canadian counterparts. They include in order of importance: chances to help others, editorial policies, job security, chances for promotion, amount of autonomy, and opportunities for specialization. Although both U.S. males and females agree on the overall mix of these job aspects, gender affects the level of importance women and men assign to them. In general, women consider chances to help others and chances for promotion more important than men, registering a 12-point and an 9-point spread respectively along these two dimensions. Job security is valued by both genders equally, but editorial policies and chances for specialization were more salient for U.S. females than U.S. males as indicated by an 8-point spread in attitudes between the two groups. This seems to indicate that as in Canada, U.S. females face greater bureaucratic restrictions in the workplace than males, and that women place greater stress on the explanatory function of the media than men.

Overall, the cross-cultural comparison indicates that Canadian journalists evaluate their professional situation in terms of a different mix of characteristics than their U.S. counterparts. They seem to place less emphasis on autonomy, security, specialization, and chances for promotion than their U.S. counterparts. U.S. journalists seem to value more security in their workplace and define their job situation more altruistically. They view themselves as more consumer oriented and helpful, while at the same time rating as very important promotion, specialization, and job security in their profession. The striking difference in U.S. and Canadian assessments of the role of editorial policies in the professional setting, numbers 2 and 3 on the U.S. list and only number 8 on the Canadian requires further investigation. We hypothesize that journalists in the two countries have different ways of assessing the political orientation of the media outlet in which they work. In Canada the fact that more than half of all outlets are small circulation dailies or television markets makes it more difficult than in the United States to identify ownership with editorial policy.

Professional Organizations and Publications

Participation in professional organizations and readership of specialized trade publications are widely considered indicators, although minor ones, of the degree of professionalism. On these measures, our proportionate representative sample shows there are few gender differences. In Canada an overwhelming majority of journalists note that they read one or more professional publications; among men the percentage is only slightly higher (69%) than among women (63%). A much smaller proportion of Canadians belong to professional organizations: 48% of the female and 40% of the male respondents. A comparison with U.S. membership figures indicates that Canadian journalists join professional associations in greater numbers than their U.S. counterparts, whose rates have been declining constantly since 1971. In general, 44% of all Canadian respondents belonged to at least one journalism organization in 1995, whereas the percentage for U.S. journalists was 36 in 1992.

Because trade publications are scarcer in Canada than in the United States, our questionnaire asked only one question aimed at whether our respondents read any professional publications. It was followed by an open-ended question requesting respondents to list any publication they read. The evidence shows that Canadian journalists today read more trade or professional publications than their U.S. counterparts. In 1982-83, it was found that the oldest U.S. trade magazine, *Editor & Publisher*, was being read by about 60% of all U.S. journalists and 80% of daily newspaper journalists, at least "sometimes" (Weaver and Wilhoit 1991). However, recent data indicate substantial decreases in readership from 1982 to 1992, and the readership rate for *Editor & Publisher* is now down to about 40% (Weaver and Wilhoit 1994). In Canada gender differences seem to reflect two different cultures—in newspapers male journalists tend to read more professional publications than their female counterparts (74% vs. 64.5%), whereas both genders have the same reading rates in television newsrooms (60% for women and 59.1% for men).

CONCLUSIONS

Mapping a professional community for the first time in a country as large and diverse as Canada is a risky endeavor. Luckily some comparative landmarks do exist (Robinson 1975) to offer a framework for comparison of the professional progress women have made into the media professions. Past surveys of U.S. journalists (Johnstone et al. 1976; Bowman 1974; Weaver and Wilhoit 1991, 1994) provide further points of departure. The results of our two-stage research survey reveal that women have made substantial progress in moving into all aspects of this traditionally male-dominated profession. They are now proportionately integrated in all but the highest ranks of both print and electronic news organizations. Job assignments, "beat" coverage, and salaries have also become less discriminatory, although, as we have shown, women have still got a long way to go before they reach numerical and salary equality.

In addition, our findings have demonstrated that Canadian journalists, both women and men, are as highly professionalized as their counterparts elsewhere. They are highly educated and deeply conscious of their social responsibility, and they set high performance standards for the Canadian media as well as for themselves. This indicates that the social responsibility and the public service roles for media institutions are taken seriously in Canada, and that media performance is critically evaluated. Like their U.S. colleagues, Canadians overwhelmingly choose media work for professional reasons rather than for material gain.

Even though we as yet lack timeline data on changes in Canadian professional understandings and aspirations, this survey demonstrates that they share many characteristics with their colleagues in other Western democracies. Whether the noble ideals that Canadian journalists seem to value in 1995 will continue to prevail in the face of the media's growing race for efficiency, profits and ratings remains an open question that awaits further investigation in the 21st century. We are certain, however, that continued professional integration of women will depend on the commitment of employers to equal opportunity and of the federal government to antidiscrimination policies. Only well established, nationally mandated policies will counterbalance the unequal manner in which economic "downsizing" has traditionally affected female workers in the workplace.

REFERENCES

Bowman, William. 1974. *Distaff journalists: Women as a minority group in the news media.* Ph.D dissertation, University of Illinois at Chicago Circle.

de la Garde, Roger. 1971. *Pratique du journalisme au Québec* [The practice of journalism in Quebec]. Paper presented at Programme de journalisme, Université Laval.

Freedom Forum Media Studies Center. 1993. *The media and women without apology.* New York: Columbia University Press.

Gannett Foundation. 1989. *Women, men and media report.* Arlington: Gannett News Services.

Hardin, Hershel. 1974. *A nation unaware: The Canadian economic culture.* Vancouver: J. J. Douglas.

Innis, Harold. 1951. *The bias of communication.* Reprint. Toronto: University of Toronto Press.

Johnstone, John, Edward Slawski, and William Bowman. 1976. *The news people.* Urbana: University of Illinois Press.

Löfgren-Nilsson, Monica. 1994, July. Journalism, gender and newsroom working climate. *The working climate according to Swedish newsreporters—some preliminary results.* Paper presented at the International Association for Mass Communication Research Congress, Seoul, Korea.

Marzolf, Marion Tuttle. 1993, August. *Women making a difference in the newsroom.* Paper presented at the annual meeting of the Association for Education in Journalism and Mass Communication, Washington, DC.

Pollard, George. 1985. Canadian newsworkers: A cross-media analysis of professional and personal attributes. *Canadian Journal of Communication* 11, 3: 269-286.

Robinson, Gertrude J. 1975. *Women Journalists in Canadian Dailies: A social and professional minority profile.* Montreal: McGill Working Papers in Communications.

Robinson, Gertrude J. 1977. The future of women in the Canadian media. *McGill Journal of Education* 12, 1: 124-132.

Robinson, Gertrude J. and Armande Saint-Jean. 1995. *Women's participation in the Canadian news media : Progress since the 1970s. Phase I Report*. Montreal: McGill University, Montreal and Université de Sherbrooke.

Saint-Jean, Armande. 1993. *L'Évolution de l'éthique journalistique au Québec de 1960 à 1990* [The evolution of journalistic ethics in Quebec from 1960 to 1900]. Ph.D. thesis, Graduate Program in Communications, McGill University, Montreal.

Saint-Jean, Armande and Isabella Labarre. 1995. Le premier portrait des femmes journalistes au Québec [The first portrait of women journalists in Quebec]. *Le-30-19*, 10: 12-16.

Statistics Canada. 1990. *Women in Canada: A statistical report*, 2nd ed. Ottawa: Minister of Industry.

Statistics Canada. 1995. *Women in Canada: A statistical report*, 3rd ed. Ottawa: Minister of Industry.

Turner, Ralph. 1952. The foci of discrimination in the employment of non-whites. *American Journal of Sociology* 108, 4: 230-245.

Weaver, David H. and G. Cleveland Wilhoit. 1991. *The American journalist: A portrait of U.S. news people and their work*, 2nd ed. Bloomington: Indiana University Press.

Weaver, David H. and G. Cleveland Wilhoit. 1994, July. *Trends in professionalism of U.S. journalists, 1971 to 1992*. Paper presented to the Professional Education Section at the 19th Scientific Conference of the International Association for Mass Communication Research (IAMCR), Seoul, Korea.

Weaver, David H. and G. Cleveland Wilhoit. 1996. *The American journalist in the 1990s: U.S. news people at the end of an era*. Mahwah, NJ: Lawrence Erlbaum.

19

The Journalists and Journalisms of Canada

David Pritchard
University of Wisconsin-Milwaukee
Florian Sauvageau
Université Laval

Canadian journalism resists easy categorization. In many ways, it closely resembles the journalism practiced in the United States and other industrialized Western democracies. Canada has a highly developed media infrastructure, with 112 daily newspapers, 118 television stations, 550 radio stations, and more than 1,000 weekly newspapers (*Matthews Media Directory* 1996). Constitutional guarantees of press freedom are found in the Canadian Charter of Rights and Freedoms, and Canadian news operations such as the Toronto *Globe and Mail* and the Canadian Broadcasting Corporation often are considered to be among the world's finest.

In other ways, however, Canadian journalism is different. Like other sectors of economic and cultural life in Canada, the media have been shaped in important ways by government actions aimed at countering U.S. influence—a process summed up in one of the great slogans of Canadian history: "The State or the United States."

The multicultural nature of Canada also has shaped the country's journalism. About 60% of Canada's people are native speakers of English, while about 24% are native speakers of French. Most French

Canadians live in the province of Quebec. English Canadians, although a small minority in Quebec, are a powerful majority in the rest of Canada. Whether there is a single Canadian journalism, or whether there are two Canadian journalisms—one English, one French—is a much-debated question.

Canadian journalism, in short, is complex, multifaceted, and therefore quite interesting. Acting on the truism that one cannot understand journalism without first understanding journalists, we conducted a broad survey of Canada's journalists. In this chapter we present some highlights of our results, which are based on telephone interviews with a probability sample of 554 journalists from across Canada. The survey, conducted in May 1996, is the most extensive survey of Canadian journalists to date. (See Appendix A for details of method.)

BACKGROUND

A major theme in the development of Canada has been government action to counter U.S. influence. Indeed, long before Third World concerns about U.S. cultural imperialism became a high-profile issue on the international scene, the first government commission on media issues in Canada asserted that U.S. radio programming flowing into Canada had "a tendency to mold the minds of the young people in the home to ideals and opinions that are not Canadian" (Royal Commission on Radio Broadcasting 1929: 6). With the dual goals of replacing private commercial stations that were being established in Canada and providing a Canadian alternative to the powerful U.S. stations whose signals reached 90% of the Canadian population, the commission proposed the creation of a radio system based on the concept of public service. The government acted by establishing a national radio service, which in 1936 evolved into the Canadian Broadcasting Corporation (CBC), modeled on the British Broadcasting Corporation. However, the government did not abolish Canada's private stations.

The government's creation of the CBC was consistent with its creation of other institutions it considered essential to a modern nation. As Walter Stewart, a Canadian, noted: "History, custom and necessity have led us to recognize that, with so few people and so much geography, we had to use government agencies as major instruments of national development" (1986: 103)—a government-owned railway (Canadian National), a national airline (Air Canada), and a state-financed broadcasting service (CBC).

Although state-financed, the news and information broadcast on radio and later on television by the CBC and its French-language counterpart, la Société Radio-Canada, always has been independent of state control, despite occasional attempts by government officials to interfere. The independence of CBC/Radio-Canada is an important component of its reputation for quality journalism. Another reason for CBC/Radio-Canada's reputation for quality news is its public service orientation, often placed in stark relief to what many Canadians see as U.S. hucksterism. In a 1945 article prophetically titled "News—Entertainment or Information?", Dan McArthur, first chief news editor of the CBC, rejected what he called the "showmanship" of U.S. news broadcasts. News should not be a form of entertainment, wrote McArthur, who added that "a calm, factual presentation would enhance the CBC's reputation for accuracy and objectivity" (quoted in Albota 1991: 223).

It is difficult to overstate CBC/Radio-Canada's influence on Canadian journalists. It is by far the Canadian news organization Canadian journalists admire the most, our survey found. We also learned that a strong majority of Canadian journalists choose CBC/Radio-Canada over private Canadian networks or U.S. networks as their main source of television news.

CBC Radio has been a powerful influence in shaping the character of Canada. CBC Radio provides "a consistently nourishing menu of information and provocation for the mind," said *Globe and Mail* Editor William Thorsell. "As a country, we are much better educated and thoughtful as a result. It simply wouldn't happen without CBC Radio, as anyone who has spent any time in the United States can woefully attest" (1996: D-6). CBC Radio carries no advertising and is more distinctively Canadian than CBC Television, which does carry advertising and which has been much more influenced by U.S. formats and techniques.

CBC/Radio-Canada is the only major Canadian news organization actually owned by the state, but every sector of Canadian media has benefited from government action at some point in the 20th century. In 1917, for example, the Canadian government, unhappy with the war news supplied by foreign wire services, subsidized the creation and the first several years of operation of the national news service of the Canadian Press.

In the 1960s and 1970s, government action came to the rescue of Canadian magazines, which had always lost readers and advertising to U.S. magazines that targeted the Canadian market. To encourage Canadian businesses to advertise in Canadian-owned publications, changes in the tax code prevented businesses from claiming tax deductions for advertising in foreign-owned publications. The changes, which applied to newspapers as well as to magazines, had the effect of "encouraging advertisers to use Canadian rather than foreign publications to reach their Canadian audiences, and discouraging takeovers of Canadian publications by foreign interests" (Audley 1983: 42). An important effect of the changes in the 1970s was to steer advertising away from the Canadian edition of *Time*, an action which enabled Canadian-owned *Maclean's* to obtain enough advertising to become a weekly news magazine. In addition, federal regulations require ownership of broadcasting properties in Canada to be at least two thirds Canadian.

In general, the owners of Canadian media properties have welcomed government action to protect them from foreign-owned competition but have been much less receptive to limitations on ownership of their own properties. The restrictions on foreign ownership have contributed to high levels of concentration of media ownership in Canada, an issue that has concerned some journalists and policy makers for at least 30 years. The Special Senate Committee on Mass Media in 1970 and the Royal Commission on Newspapers in 1981 made proposals to limit concentration of media ownership, but many Canadian media owners lobbied hard against the proposals, and none was ever enacted into law. The result is that more and more Canadian news organizations are in the hands of fewer and fewer owners.

Although Canadian law protects Canadian media in many ways, law cannot guarantee cultural distinctiveness. Canadian journalists, like Canadian cultural workers generally, live and work in the cultural shadow of the United States. Apart from the CBC, there are relatively few differences between Canadian and U.S. media, at least in terms of format and presentation. British influence was important in Canadian newspapers well into the 20th century but had all but disappeared by the 1960s. In ownership structure, professional development, and even ethics, modern Canadian print journalism is "closer to Main Street, USA, than to Fleet Street," wrote Peter Desbarats (1990: 1), dean of the University of Western Ontario's journalism school.

Canadian journalism is not unidimensional, however. Many observers stress the differences between francophone and anglophone news organizations in Canada, and studies have documented that they cover events quite differently (Siegel 1977; Robinson 1984; Robinson and Charron 1989). The Royal Commission on Newspapers noted in 1981 that francophone journalists, "like the priest or politician," see themselves as "invested with a certain nationalist mission" (31).

Nowhere is the presumed nationalism of francophone journalists more controversial than in the context of the debate over whether Quebec should be independent, an issue that has been near the forefront of Canadian politics since the 1960s. The controversy was especially intense during the periods from 1976 to 1985 and again since 1994, when Quebec was governed by the Parti Québécois, a democratically elected political party committed to making Quebec an independent, French-speaking nation. Politicians who oppose independence sometimes claim that francophone journalists not only support independence, but slant their stories in favor of it. Systematic evidence to support such a claim is mixed, at best. Although one survey found that three quarters of the journalists at elite Quebec news organizations favored independence (Godin 1979), there is no evidence that they biased their stories. An investigation by the Canadian Radio-television and Telecommunications Commission in 1977 found no bias related to the independence issue in the news transmitted by CBC/Radio-Canada (Siegel 1977).

Although she does not assert that journalists are biased, Lysiane Gagnon, a veteran journalist at Montreal's *La Presse*, has argued that the French Canadian press inherited a style and direction from France's journals of opinion. According to Gagnon, legacies of the French tradition that persist in the modern French Canadian press include "the predominance of analysis, as opposed to simple reporting of events, (and) the tendency to treat matters conceptually rather than in terms of people and events" (Gagnon 1981: 28).

Gagnon's vision, widely shared in Canada, is not supported by research on francophone newspaper journalists in Quebec, which has documented their respect for hard facts (Langlois and Sauvageau 1982), nor by the results of our much broader survey, which found that Quebec journalists were significantly more likely than other Canadian journalists to think that it is important to accurately report sources' comments. Langlois and Sauvageau found considerable diversity among Quebec newspaper journalists, concluding that they could be grouped into four distinct categories: Educators, who try to persuade readers (21% of respondents); Investigators/analysts, who try to uncover hidden facts and/or provide a context for understanding known facts (31%); Reporters, who perceive their job as nothing more than the transmission of facts (32%); and Seducers, who place a high value on interesting and entertaining their readers (15%).

At times, especially during the 1960s and 1970s, many Quebec journalists saw news as a means of achieving social and political goals. However, the reasons for journalists' activism are easier to find in the social context of the times than in any historical tradition inherited from France. Although Quebec journalists are different in many ways from other Canadian journalists, there is little reason to believe that they are less "objective" than their U.S. or English-Canadian counterparts.

Newspapers in English Canada began as party organs, a tendency that persisted in some cases well into the 20th century. As late as the 1950s in Toronto, *The Telegram* and the *Globe and Mail* were clearly supportive of the Conservative party and the Toronto *Star* of the Liberal Party. Things were not much different in French Canada. In the 1950s, *Le Soleil* in Quebec City was still a Liberal daily, while as late as the 1960s a large-circulation tabloid, *Montréal-Matin*, was closely linked with l'Union Nationale, the conservative political party that governed Quebec for most of the 1940s, 1950s, and the latter half of the 1960s.

Even before the turn of the century, however, some newspapers—including Montreal's *La Presse*, founded in 1884, and Toronto's *Star*, founded in 1892—began orienting themselves more toward a mass public than toward partisan groups. These were newspapers for the people, and their focus slowly shifted away from advancing a particular point of view and toward building circulation and advertising. Although most newspapers maintained some links with political or religious factions, newspapers' increasing reliance on building circulation led to a new set of influences on journalistic practice (Desbarats 1990).

In the 1960s and early 1970s, as traditional newspapers were completing their transition away from partisanship and toward a more neutral stance, sensationalist tabloids emerged in Montreal, Toronto, and Quebec City. In 1964, a relatively unknown Montreal businessman named Pierre Péladeau took advantage of a strike at *La Presse* to launch *Le Journal de Montréal*. Three years later, Péladeau began publishing a similar tabloid, *Le Journal de Québec*, in Quebec City. By the end of the 1970s, *Le Journal de Montréal* was the largest circulation paper in Quebec, and Péladeau was no longer relatively unknown. His company, Quebecor, expanded rapidly to become a full-fledged international communications empire.

Tabloids also made their mark in English Canada. In 1971, the tabloid Toronto *Sun* rose from the ashes of the broadsheet *Telegram*, which had folded. Like the two Quebecor tabloids, the *Sun* stressed sex, crime, and sports. In the ensuing years tabloids emerged in Winnipeg, Edmonton, Calgary, and Ottawa, all owned either by Quebecor (Winnipeg) or the Toronto *Sun* (the others).

The tabloids competed vigorously with established broadsheets. At least in Quebec, they hired journalists more oriented toward entertaining and interesting readers than toward more traditional conceptions of public service (Langlois and Sauvageau 1982). The Toronto *Sun* and its clones also broadened the range of ideological debate in English Canada by featuring outspoken right-wing columnists.

PREVIOUS STUDIES

Given the social and political importance of journalism in Canada, it is somewhat surprising that Canadian journalists have been the object of little systematic study. Essays on the state of journalism in Canada and its regions have been frequent, but actual surveys have been rare and generally limited in scope. One of the first published surveys about Canadian journalists, for example, focused not on journalists but on *former* journalists in hopes of finding out why they had left their newspapers (Wilson 1966). The unsurprising answer? Low pay and lack of satisfaction with the routine nature of newspaper work.

Subsequent surveys focused on more interesting questions. Donald Wright attempted to find out whether Canada's journalists were really as unprofessional as the Special Senate Committee on Mass Media had claimed. Using scales of journalistic professionalism developed in the United States, Wright surveyed journalists at daily newspapers in the largest cities of Ontario, Manitoba, Saskatchewan, Alberta, and British Columbia (1974) and journalists at private radio stations in British Columbia (1976), finding relatively high levels of professionalism but fairly low levels of job satisfaction.

George Pollard followed Wright's interest in professionalism and job satisfaction with several national mail surveys (Pollard 1985, 1988/1989, 1994/1995a, 1995b). Although Pollard has been mostly interested in radio journalists, he conducted two surveys that included journalists at daily newspapers and television stations as well as radio journalists (1985, 1994/1995a). The 1985 survey, which focused only on English-language journalists, revealed higher levels of professionalism among broadcast journalists than among those who work at daily newspapers. Pollard also found that "Canadian newsworkers were quite satisfied and enthusiastic about their work, confident about their future in newswork and content with their current jobs" (1985: 29).

The results of the 1990 survey (which included francophone as well as anglophone journalists) mirrored those of the 1985 survey—newspaper journalists had lower levels of professionalism but higher levels of job satisfaction than broadcast journalists. Pollard speculated that this counterintuitive finding might not reflect traditional conceptions of job satisfaction, but rather that newspaper journalists were satisfied to have a steady job in difficult economic times. "Newspaper workers may have realigned work-related values and reward expectations to fit newsroom reality as a strategy to remain in the occupation or current job," Pollard wrote (1995a: 691; also 1994: 203).

The remaining published surveys of Canadian journalists have examined journalists in specific regions, most written in French and most focusing on Quebec. Some of the studies are little more than demographic profiles of various groups of Quebec journalists—those in the print media (de la Garde 1975), the broadcast media (de la Garde and Barrett 1976), and women (Dubois 1988; Saint-Jean and Labarre 1995; Saint-Jean, Labarre and Legault 1995). Other studies of journalists, however, deal with issues beyond demographics. Godin's study of the political attitudes of elite Quebec journalists, for example, was mentioned earlier in this chapter (Godin 1979), as was Langlois and Sauvageau's survey of journalists at Quebec's French-language daily newspapers.

Qualitative surveys based on open-ended questions have provided the data for several interesting articles. Pierre Fortin (1992) collected the thoughts of 58 Quebec journalists about matters of journalism ethics. Thierry Watine (1994) conducted lengthy interviews with 32 francophone journalists in Canada's Maritime provinces to learn how they balanced their roles as neutral reporters with their roles as advocates for greater recognition of the French presence in *l'Acadie*. Anne-Marie Gingras and Jean-Pierre Carrier (1995) were interested in whether the news media provide an adequate forum for unfettered discussion of public issues. After semi-structured interviews with 26 Quebec journalists who covered social and political news in Quebec City, Ottawa, and Montreal, the researchers concluded that the news media did not provide an adequate forum.

Scholars of journalism in Canada tend to speak only to members of their own linguistic community. Quite literally *none* of the studies mentioned previously, for example, cites a survey of Canadian journalists that was published in another language. The work published in English cites none of the work published in French, and vice versa—a stark example of how Canada's media scholars exist in two solitudes. This mutual ignorance not only impedes a full understanding of Canadian journalism but increases the likelihood that media scholars from one linguistic community will fail to grasp the richness and complexity of journalism in the other.

RESULTS

In this section we present preliminary results of our survey (details of the data collection are provided in Appendix A), broken down either by the media sector in which journalists work or by language. First, however, some hard facts are presented about Canadian journalists.

According to our study, Canada had about 12,000 full-time journalists in 1996. More than half of Canada's journalists worked for daily newspapers (30.2%) or radio stations (26.4%). Despite television's importance as a source of news for citizens, only two of nine Canadian journalists (22.2%) worked in television news, either for a local station or for a network. The rest of the full-time journalists in Canada worked for weekly newspapers (18%), wire services (2.6%), or news magazines (0.6%). The proportion of journalists working in any given province was very close to that province's proportion of the total Canadian population.

The typical Canadian journalist in our survey was a white (97%) male (72%) on the verge of middle age (about 40 years old), who made about $49,000 a year and who was slightly more likely than not to have a university degree. What was typical overall, however, was not necessarily typical of any single media sector.

Table 19.1 traces the portrait of Canadian journalists by the media sector in which they work—daily newspapers, radio, television, and "other" (a category dominated by weekly newspaper journalists). The highest proportions of women were in television (36%) and in the "other" category (34%). Journalists at daily newspapers and television stations were oldest (42 and 41 years old, respectively), whereas radio news people averaged 38 years old and "other" journalists 36.5. Not surprisingly, older journalists tended to have more years of experience in journalism.

Table 19.1 also shows that television and daily newspapers were more likely than other news organizations to employ journalists with university degrees and to pay them considerably more money. Well over half of the television and daily newspaper journalists had university degrees, and the salaries of television and daily newspaper people averaged about $20,000 higher than the salaries of journalists at other kinds of news organizations. Studying journalism or communication in universities was not directly related to salary. Television and daily newspaper journalists, who were the least likely to have taken university journalism or communication courses, earned the highest average salaries.

Table 19.1. Demographic Profile of Canadian Journalists, by Media Sector.

	Dailies	Radio	TV	Weeklies/others	Overall
Race (% white)	96.0	98.0	9.0	100.0	97.0
Sex (% male)	77.0	76.0	64.0	66.0	72.0
Age (years)	41.9	38.3	40.9	36.5	39.6
Experience (years)	17.5	14.2	16.8	11.8	15.3
% with degree from university	64.0	46.0	58.0	46.0	54.0
% who took journalism or comm. courses	58.0	75.0	60.0	63.0	64.0
1995 income from journalism	$58,185	$44,131	$58,708	$32,857	$49,176
N of respondents = (weighted)	152	133	112	107	504

Canadian journalists do consider further education to be important; a solid majority of respondents in all media sectors (61% overall) felt they needed additional training. Respondents who felt they would benefit from additional training were asked to name up to three subjects of special interest. One third mentioned journalism, with new technologies (25%), political science (24%), and economy (18 %) not far behind.

The desire for additional training may have been linked in part to changes in the workplace; responses to open-ended questions showed that at least 70% of Canadian journalists had learned to use computer-based or digital technologies in the previous two years. In general, journalists were enthusiastic about the new techniques, which 26% said had a very positive impact and 46% said had a somewhat positive impact on news content. Only 6% thought new technologies have had a negative impact.

Just as Wright in the 1970s and Pollard in the 1980s and 1990s were interested in journalists' job satisfaction, so were we. Like Pollard, we found high levels of job satisfaction. As Table 19 2 shows, the vast majority of Canadian journalists say they are either very satisfied (38%) or somewhat satisfied (47%) with their current jobs. Salary and job satisfaction do not appear to go hand in hand; journalists at daily newspapers have high salaries but the lowest level of job satisfaction. Journalists in television, the other media sector with high salaries, exhibit the highest levels of job satisfaction. Our findings differ from those of Pollard, who found that newspaper journalists had higher job satisfaction than radio or television journalists.

Table 19.2. Level of Job Satisfaction, by Media Sector.

	Dailies (%)	Radio (%)	TV (%)	Weeklies/ others (%)	Overall (%)
Very satisfied	36	40	43	34	38
Somewhat satisfied	45	48	47	51	47
Somewhat dissatisfied	16	9	9	12	12
Very dissatisfied	2	3	0	2	2
Average (1=min, 4=max)	3.16	3.24	3.34	3.18	3.22
N (weighted) =	152	133	111	107	503

In addition to having the lowest level of job satisfaction, daily newspaper journalists also have the least positive views about how well Canadian news organizations—their own as well as others—are informing the public, as Table 19.3 shows. Journalists in the other media sectors have much more positive views. Journalists from all sectors tend to think that their own news organization does a better job of informing the public than do the Canadian news media in general.

When asked their views about the editorial policies of their news organizations, daily newspaper journalists again differed sharply from journalists at other kinds of news organizations. Table 19.4 shows that journalists at daily newspapers consider their organizations to be considerably to the right of middle-of-the-road. Journalists in other media sectors typically perceived their news organizations to be just slightly left of center.

Journalists from all kinds of media organizations tended to be more "progressive" than they perceived their news organizations to be, but the gap was much larger for journalists at daily newspapers than for others. On a 100-point scale, daily newspaper journalists believed themselves to be 30 points more progressive than the editorial policies of their news organizations. Other journalists averaged about 10 points more progressive than their news organizations.

We oversampled Quebec journalists to be able to make precise comparisons between journalists from Canada's two major cultures. We estimated that 81% of Canadian journalists used English as their principal language, with 19% using French. Most francophone journalists (85%) said they speak fluent English, but only a few anglophone journalists (14%) could speak French. Fully 75% of anglophone journalists

Table 19.3. Evaluation of Media Performance, by Media Sector.

	Dailies	Radio	TV	Weeklies/others	Overall
Evaluation of own news organization (1 = min, 5 = max)	3.36	3.93	3.73	3.71	3.66
N (weighted) =	152	133	112	107	504
Evaluation of Canadian media (1 = min, 5 = max)	3.10	3.39	3.43	3.33	3.30
N (weighted) =	149	133	111	107	500

Table 19.4. Perceptions of Political Orientations, by Media Sector"(0 = very progressive, 50 = middle of the road, 100 = very conservative).

	Dailies	Radio	TV	Weeklies/others	Overall
Editorial policy of journalist's news organization	61	47	47	48	52
Journalist's own political views	31	41	35	38	36
Difference	30	8	12	10	16
N (weighted) =	143	121	107	99	470

could not speak any language other than English. The unilingualism rate among francophone journalists, by contrast, was only 14%. Clearly, most English Canadian journalists would have difficulty gaining firsthand information about the francophone culture in Quebec.

Canadian journalists had little language ability outside of English and French. Three percent could speak Spanish, 2% could speak German, but no other language was spoken by more than 1% of our respondents.

Francophone journalists' bilingualism enables them to sample English Canadian and U.S. media, and many take advantage of the opportunity. For example, more than a quarter (28%) of French-language journalists regularly read the *Globe and Mail*, published in Toronto. English Canadian journalists, in contrast, pay little attention to French-language newspapers, as Table 19.5 shows.

A question about which magazines journalists regularly read suggested that anglophone and francophone journalists in Canada are interested most by their own society (English Canadian or French Canadian), somewhat by U.S. society, and least by the Canadian culture to which they do not belong. The magazines most likely to be read by Canadian journalists are Canadian: A clear majority of francophone journalists (62%) read *L'actualité*, and a near majority (49%) of anglophone journalists read *Maclean's*. Next in popularity for both language groups are U.S. news weeklies. *Time* is read by 24% of francophones and 20% of anglophones; *Newsweek* is read by 10% of francophones and 14% of anglophones. Only 11% of francophone journalists read *Maclean's*, the most important news magazine in English Canada. Only 2% of anglophone journalists read *L'actualité*, the most important news magazine in French Canada.

Table 19.5. Daily Newspapers Read at Least Once a Week (percentages), by Language Group.

	Francophone	Anglophone
La Presse (Montreal)	74	3
Le Devoir (Montreal)	43	1
Journal de Montréal/Québec	37	1
Le Soleil (Quebec)	18	0
The Gazette (Montreal)	13	3
Globe and Mail (Toronto)	28	59
Toronto Star	3	32
Vancouver Sun	1	11
Toronto Sun	0	10
N of respondents	148	406

Note: Only the daily newspapers that were mentioned by at least 10% of either francophone or anglophone journalists are included in Table 19.5.

When asked which foreign news organization they most admire, anglophone and francophone journalists' top three choices were identical: CNN (the 24-hour cable news organization based in the United States), BBC, and the *New York Times*. Large numbers of anglophone journalists admired CNN and BBC most, with the *New York Times* ranking a distant third. Each of the three news organizations was most admired by 10% of the francophone journalists, whose admiration for English-language news organizations was strong. French-language news organizations were mentioned only by small percentages of francophone respondents: TV5 (7%), *Le Monde* (5%), and *Le Monde Diplomatique* (3%). Interestingly, a higher proportion of francophones than anglophones chose the *New York Times* (10% vs 8%) and the U.S. Public Broadcasting System (6% to 1%) as the news organizations they most admired, and a higher proportion of anglophones than francophones chose *Le Monde Diplomatique* (6% to 3%).

Although it is clear from the results just outlined that Canadian journalists' media habits are far from uniform, it also is clear that CBC and Radio-Canada play dominant roles in their lives. Canadian journalists overwhelmingly use CBC and Radio-Canada (or their 24-hour cable services, Newsworld and RDI) as their principal source of television news. Anglophone journalists are much more likely to rely on CBC or CBC Newsworld (61%) than are francophone (7%), and francophone are much more likely to rely on Radio-Canada (75%) than are anglophone (1%).

Canadian journalists' esteem for CBC and Radio-Canada is further revealed when they are asked which Canadian news organization they admire the most. Thirty-nine percent of francophone journalists and 45% of anglophone journalists admire the state-financed broadcaster more than any other Canadian news organization. No other news organization even came close.

As mentioned earlier in this chapter, concentration of media ownership has long been an issue in Canadian policy circles, even if the federal government has done little to limit concentration. Table 19.6 shows that Canadian journalists tend to agree that concentration of media ownership threatens the free flow of ideas, with daily newspaper journalists agreeing most strongly and radio journalists agreeing least strongly. Even radio journalists' agreement was fairly strong, however, averaging just over 7 points on a 10-point scale where 1 meant strong disagreement and 10 meant strong agreement.

Table 19.6 also shows that journalists tended to agree that government should act to limit media concentration, although their feelings were less intense on this issue (averaging 6.28) than on the issue of whether concentration threatens the free flow of ideas (7.35).

On the 10-point scale, anglophones (7.51) agreed more strongly than did francophones (6.68) that concentration threatens the free flow of ideas in Canada. Anglophones also favored government action more strongly (6.36 to 5.93).

Table 19.6. Journalists' Views about Concentration of Media Ownership, by Media Sector (1 = strongly disagree, 10 = strongly agree).

	Dailies	Radio	TV	Weeklies/ others	Overall
Concentration threatens free flow of ideas	7.68	7.04	7.43	7.19	7.35
Gov't should act to limit concentration	6.43	5.81	6.85	6.04	6.28
N (weighted) =	150	131	112	105	498

CONCLUSION

This chapter has provided an overview of preliminary results of the most extensive survey of Canadian journalists to date. In general, Canadian journalists are fairly satisfied with their jobs, think their news organizations are doing a fairly good job of informing the public, are somewhat more liberal/progressive than they perceive their news organization to be, and are quite concerned that media concentration may diminish the free flow of ideas.

Journalists at daily newspapers seemed to be systematically different from the journalists in other media sectors, according to our survey. Daily newspaper journalists tended to be older, better educated, higher paid, more liberal/progressive, less satisfied with their jobs, less likely to think their news organization is doing a good job of informing the public, and more concerned about media concentration than other journalists. The cumulative portrait suggests that daily newspaper journalists are both more privileged (at least in terms of education and salary) and more unhappy than other journalists.

Our results also documented differences in anglophone and francophone journalists' media habits. Neither group seems very interested in the media of the other, with the exception of francophone journalists' interest in the Toronto *Globe and Mail*. Rather, after paying attention to the media of their own cultures, journalists of both language groups tend to turn to U.S. media.

Our survey also helps put to rest the outdated idea that francophone journalists are somehow less factual than their English-speaking counterparts. If anything, the opposite may be true, given our study's finding that francophone journalists were more likely than anglophone journalists to agree that it is important to report sources' comments accurately.

A major finding of our study is the dominance of CBC/Radio-Canada, both as a source of news for journalists and as an ideal. By huge margins over other media, journalists from both of Canada's major cultures use and admire the public broadcaster most.

Events do not stand still, of course, and as we write in July 1996, Canadian journalism was in a state of turbulence. Shortly after our survey was conducted, Hollinger Inc., controlled by Canadian press tycoon Conrad Black, gained a decisive stake in Southam Inc., which owns 20 daily newspapers in Canada. The transaction left Black—whose press empire includes the *Daily Telegraph* in London, the Sydney *Morning Herald* and the Melbourne *Age* in Australia, the Jerusalem *Post* in Israel, the Chicago *Sun-Times*, and more than 100 small U.S. dailies—in charge of 58 of Canada's daily newspapers with almost 42% of Canada's daily-newspaper circulation. The transaction left Hollinger in control of every daily newspaper in Newfoundland, Prince Edward Island, and Saskatchewan, as well as the major dailies in Vancouver, Edmonton, Calgary, and Ottawa and the only English-language daily in Montreal.

Hollinger's actions renewed Canada's national debate about the possible political effects of press concentration. Black's conservative views are well known, and he often espouses them publicly in speeches and articles. That the person who owns a controlling interest in more than half of Canada's daily newspapers is such an ardent conservative worries many journalists at dailies, who our survey showed to be quite a bit more liberal/progressive than other journalists. Just as Black's views are well-known, so is his disdain for most journalists. The *Globe & Mail* described Black as "a man whose limited regard for reporters is as famous as his robust self-esteem" (Saunders & Mahood 1996: B-1). More generally, Hollinger has a reputation for reducing costs in news operations in order to maximize profit.

Concerns other than concentration of press ownership also were on the minds of Canadian journalists in mid-1996. The future of the Canadian Press (CP) was in jeopardy after Southam announced its intention to withdraw its 20 newspapers from the 88-newspaper cooperative, a move that would reduce CP's revenue by $7.2 million—more than 15% of its annual budget. If CP, seen by many as an essential element in Canadian unity, survives the crisis, it will be a much smaller organization in the future.

Meanwhile, crushing budget cuts at CBC/Radio-Canada throughout the 1990s have been accompanied by staff layoffs, program reductions, and even the closing of television stations. A government-appointed committee in the mid-1990s concluded that the very future of CBC/RadioCanada was at stake. The downsizing of CBC/Radio-Canada has taken place in the context of a crisis of government finances in Canada, as throughout the Western world, of regional free trade agreements in North America and of increasing economic globalization, all of which weaken both the will and the ability of governments to intervene in their countries' own economies.

Canada was successful in gaining the right to protect its cultural industries in free-trade negotiations with the United States in the late 1980s, but whether Canada will continue to intervene in its media system is a matter of serious doubt. Since the early 1980s, the private sector has been seen by successive Canadian governments as more efficient and better equipped than the state to serve the public interest. How the increasing reliance on the private sector will affect Canadian journalism remains uncertain. Will the state withdraw further from its historic role in supporting public service broadcasting aimed at helping Canadians understand and appreciate the social and cultural diversity of their complex nation? Will Canada maintain the regulations that effectively prohibit foreign ownership of Canadian news organizations, especially when foreign competition could reduce media concentration in Canada? More broadly, will Canada even remain a single country in the 21st century, or will the independence movement in Quebec be successful?

In addition to such questions are issues that affect journalists throughout the Western world generally. What is the future of mass-circulation newspapers? As new technologies make it easier and easier for fewer and fewer people to produce a publication or a newscast, will there be jobs for young journalists who might be able to speak to, and perhaps for, an increasingly alienated post-Baby Boom generation? Will the journalists of the 21st century be mostly freelancers working one day for a newspaper, the next for a television station, all the while doing some public relations work on the side? What is the role of public service journalism in an era when participation in mainstream political processes is declining?

Canadian journalists, like those in many other nations, live in an uncertain world.

REFERENCES

Albota, Robert. 1991. Dan McArthur's concept of objectivity for the CBC news service. In *Beyond the printed word: The evolution of Canada's broadcast news heritage,* edited by Richard Lochead, pp. 223-230. Kingston, Ontario: Quarry Press.
Audley, Paul. 1983. *Canada's cultural industries.* Toronto: Lorimer.
de la Garde, Roger. 1975. Profil sociodémographique des journalistes de la presse écrite québécoise [Sociodemographic profile of journalists in the Quebec print media]. *Communication et Information* 1: 31-52.
de la Garde, Roger, and Bernard Barrett. 1976. Profil sociodémographique des journalistes de la presse électronique québécoise [Sociodemographic profile of journalists in the Quebec broadcast media]. *Communication et Information* 1: 259-279.
Desbarats, Peter. 1990. *Guide to Canadian news media.* Toronto: Harcourt Brace Jovanovitch.
Dubois, Judith. 1988. Les femmes et l'information: Étude statistique de la place des femmes dans les médias québécois [Women and news: A statistical study of women's place in the Quebec media]. *Communication Information* 9: 111-122.
Fortin, Pierre. 1992. Quelques enjeux éthiques liés à la pratique du journalisme [Some ethical issues linked to the practice of journalism]. *Cahiers de Recherche éthique* 17: 59-83.

Gagnon, Lysiane. 1981. Journalism and ideologies in Quebec. *The journalists.* Vol. 2, Royal Commission on Newspapers. Ottawa: Supply and Services Canada.

Gingras, Anne-Marie, and Jean-Pierre Carrier. 1995. Les médias comme espace public: Enquête auprès de journalistes québécois [The media as public sphere: A study of Quebec journalists]. *Communication* 16: 15-36.

Godin, Pierre. 1979, May. Qui vous informe [They give you the news]. *L'actualité*, pp. 31-40.

Langlois, Simon, and Florian Sauvageau. 1982. Les journalistes des quotidiens québécois et leur métier [Daily newspaper journalists in Quebec and their craft]. *Politique* 1, 2: 5-39.

Matthews Media Directory. 1996. Toronto: CCN Communication.

Pollard, George. 1985. Professionalism among Canadian newsworkers: A cross-media analysis. *Gazette* 36: 21-38.

Pollard, George. 1988. The effects of profession and organization on decision acceptance among radio newsworkers. *Gazette* 41: 185-199. Results of this survey also published in Pollard, George. 1989. Profile of Canadian radio newsworkers. *Journalism Quarterly* 66: 80-86, 247.

Pollard, George. 1994. Social attributes and job satisfaction among newsworkers. Gazette 52: 193-208. Results of this survey also published in Pollard, George. 1995a. Job satisfaction among newsworkers: The influence of professionalism, perceptions of organizational structure and social attributes. *Journalism and Mass Communication Quarterly* 72: 682-697.

Pollard, George. 1995b. The impact of social attributes on professionalism among radio announcers. *Gazette* 56: 59-71.

Robinson, Gertrude J. 1984. Television news and the claim to facticity: Quebec's referendum coverage. In *Interpreting television: Current research perspectives*, edited by Willard D. Rowland, Jr. and Bruce Watkins, pp. 199-221. Beverly Hills, Calif.: Sage.

Robinson, Gertrude J. and Claude-Yves Charron. 1989. Television news and the public sphere: The case of the Quebec referendum. In *Communication for and against democracy*, edited by Marc Raboy and Peter A. Bruck, pp. 147-162. Montreal: Black Rose Books.

Royal Commission on Newspapers (Kent Commission). 1981. *Report.* Ottawa: Supply and Services Canada.

Royal Commission on Radio Broadcasting (Aird Commission). 1929. *Report.* Ottawa: Government of Canada.

Saint-Jean, Armande and Isabelle Labarre. 1995. Le premier portrait des femmes journalistes au Québec [The first portrait of women journalists in Quebec]. *Le 30*, November, pp. 12-16. Results of this survey also published in Saint-Jean, Armande, Isabelle Labarre, and

Alain Legault. 1995, November. La réalité des femmes journalistes au Québec [The reality of women journalists in Quebec]. *La Dépêche*, pp. 11-13.

Saunders, John and Casey Mahood. 1996, May. New layout, same story. *Globe and Mail*, 4, B1.

Siegel, Arthur. 1977. *Une analyse du contenu: Similitudes et différences entre les nouvelles des réseaux anglais et français de la Société Radio-Canada* [A content analysis: Similarities and differences in the news of the CBC's English and French language networks]. Ottawa: Canadian Radio-television and Telecommunications Commission.

Stewart, Walter. 1986. The seven myths of journalism. In *The forty-ninth and other parallels*, edited by David Staines, pp. 97-115. Amherst: University of Massachusetts Press.

Thorsell, William. 1996, March. CBC's commitment to the life of the mind helps make us Canadian. *Globe and Mail*, 16, D6.

Watine, Thierry. 1994. Médias acadiens: Fondements et limites d'une pratique journalistique militante [Acadian media: Foundations and limits of an activist journalism]. *Communication* 15: 199-222.

Wilson, C. Edward. 1966. Why Canadian newsmen leave their papers. *Journalism Quarterly* 43: 769-772.

Wright, Donald K. 1974. An analysis of the level of professionalism among Canadian journalists. *Gazette* 20: 133-144.

Wright, Donald K. 1976. Professionalism levels of British Columbia's broadcast journalists: A communicator analysis. *Gazette* 22: 38-48.

APPENDIX A: METHODS OF COLLECTING DATA

Our data came from 554 telephone interviews with a random sample of Canadian journalists. The interviews were conducted by CROP, a well-known polling firm in Montreal, and lasted an average of 28 minutes each.

We defined journalists as salaried full-time editorial personnel (reporters, writers, correspondents, anchors, columnists, news directors and editors) responsible for the information content of daily and weekly newspapers, more-than-monthly news magazines, news services, broadcast networks, and individual radio and television stations. We excluded photographers and camera operators because their function is more to illustrate news than to decide what will be news.

We generated the sample of journalists via a multistage process. The first stage involved compiling lists of all Canadian news organizations. We then used random sampling to generate a list of news organizations that included 37 daily newspapers (stratified by circulation so that we included roughly one third of the daily newspapers in each circulation category at random), 53 weekly newspapers (every 20th weekly newspaper chosen at random), 27 radio stations (every 20th one), 39 television stations (every third one), 4 news magazines, and a sample of wire service and private television network bureaus.

The second stage involved obtaining lists of the journalists who worked for the news organizations in the sample. We sent letters to the editors or news directors of the organizations, explaining the study and requesting the names and job titles of all journalists who worked for their organizations. Most news organizations were willing to supply lists of their journalists; overall, 85% did so. Weekly newspapers (98%) were most likely to comply with our request, followed by daily newspapers (86.5%), radio stations (76%), and television stations (73%). We also obtained lists of journalists from 6 of the 10 CBC/Radio-Canada network news and information services (chosen for maximum diversity). Small adjustments were made throughout the process to ensure proportional representation, including adding 18 radio stations and 12 weekly papers (chosen randomly) after initial returns indicated that we had underestimated the number of journalists working at such media.

Overall, 179 news organizations (including the six CBC/Radio-Canada network services) provided us with the names of 2,503 journalists. To obtain a probability sample of Canadian journalists—that is, one in which each journalist in Canada had an equal chance of being selected—we first had to estimate the number of journalists throughout Canada who worked for a given news organization. We calculated the proportion of each kind of media (e.g., daily newspapers, radio, television, etc.) that provided a list of journalists, and then divided the total number of journalists listed as working for each kind of media by the proportion of news organizations in that media sector that responded. We did a similar calculation to arrive at an estimate of the number of journalists who work in each Canadian region.

Our budget called for completed interviews with a probability sample of 500 Canadian journalists plus an additional 50 randomly chosen journalists from Quebec. We created a sampling frame of 832 journalists by choosing journalists randomly by media sector and region so that the sampling frame was representative of the distribution of Canadian journalists. Personalized letters were sent to each of the 832 journalists, informing them that the polling firm (CROP) would be phoning them to set an appointment for a telephone interview. The journalists' names and work telephone numbers were given to CROP, which attempted to contact each individual in the sampling frame. Forty-one people no longer worked at the news organization that had provided their names; they were excluded from the survey. So were 50 others who had either left journalism, did not work full time, were on long-term sick leave, or who could not be reached by phone.

Accordingly, a total of 741 journalists could be reached by phone. Interviews were completed with 554 journalists, while 33 refused to take part in the survey, and 3 others decided during the interview that they did not want to complete it. The resulting response rate could be considered to be 94% (554 completed interviews, 36 refusals or terminations). After they reached the contracted-for number of interviews, CROP stopped trying to set up interviews with the other 151 journalists in the sampling frame. Although none of those 151 journalists refused to take part in the survey, they could be considered as nonresponses, which would result in a response rate of 75% (554 completed interviews from a sampling frame of 741 journalists).

In the results section of this chapter, statements about journalists from all regions of Canada are based on analyses that correct for the disproportionately high number of Quebec journalists in the data set. Direct comparisons between English- and French-language journalists are based on the full data set.

20

Journalists in the United States*

David Weaver
G. Cleveland Wilhoit
Indiana University

In the United States, as never before, the news and the journalists who produce it are increasingly moving to centerstage. The "professional spirit" of journalists detected in Frank Luther Mott's classic history of U.S. journalism, and in the ideas of Pulitzer and the founders of the first schools of journalism, has not been forgotten but has never been fully developed, as documented in the 1971 national study of 1,328 U.S. journalists by Johnstone and colleagues (Johnstone, Slawski, and Bowman 1976) and by our 1982-83 follow-up study of 1,001 (Weaver and Wilhoit 1986).

---

*The authors appreciate the support and assistance of Charles Overby, President; Jerry Sass, Executive Vice President; Everette Dennis and Félix Gutiérrez, Senior Vice Presidents; and Brian Buchanan, Director of Journalism Programs, at The Freedom Forum. Trevor Brown, Dean of the Indiana University School of Journalism, encouraged us and gave us critical support. Graduate students Lars Willnat, Douglas Walker, Scott Lewis, Divya Punitha, and Wei Wu at Indiana University helped enormously in drawing the sample, corresponding with respondents, processing the data, and preparing charts. The support of the Roy W. Howard Chair is also much appreciated by David Weaver. We thank John Kennedy and his staff at the Center for Survey Research, Indiana University-Bloomington, for extremely thorough and professional telephone interviewing. And, finally, we thank most of all the 1,410 U.S. journalists who took the time to answer our many questions.

METHODS

Because this study was intended to be a follow-up to the 1971 and the 1982-83 national telephone surveys of U.S. journalists, we followed closely the definitions of a journalist and the sampling methods used by these earlier studies to be able to compare our 1992 results directly with those of 1971 and 1982. We also used many of the same questions asked in these previous studies, but we added some questions to reflect the changes in journalism and the larger society in the past decade (Weaver and Wilhoit 1996: Appendixes I and II).

Unlike the previous two studies, however, we deliberately oversampled journalists from the four main minority groups—Asian Americans, African Americans, Hispanic Americans, and Native Americans—to ensure adequate numbers for comparison with each other and with White journalists. We kept these oversamples of minority journalists separate from the main probability sample when making comparisons with the earlier studies.

The findings that we report here come from 45-minute telephone interviews with 1,410 U.S. journalists working for a wide variety of daily and weekly newspapers, radio and television stations, and news services and magazines throughout the United States. These interviews were conducted by telephone from June 12 to September 12, 1992, by trained interviewers at the Center for Survey Research at Indiana University's Bloomington campus.

Journalists in the main probability sample of 1,156 were chosen randomly from news organizations that were also selected at random from listings in various directories.[1] The response rate for this sample was 81%, and the maximum sampling error at the 95% level of confidence is plus or minus 3 percentage points. It is higher for the individual media groups.

The oversample of 254 minority journalists was chosen randomly from the membership lists of the four main minority journalism groups—the Asian American Journalists Association (AAJA), the National Association of Black Journalists (NABJ), the National Association of Hispanic Journalists (NAHJ), and the Native American Journalists Association (NAJA). The response rate for this sample was

---

[1]These directories include the 1991 *Editor & Publisher International Year Book*, *The Broadcasting Yearbook 1991*, the 1991 *Gale Directory of Publications and Broadcast Media*, and the Summer 1991 *News Media Yellow Book of Washington and New York*. We used systematic random sampling to compile lists of 181 daily newspapers (stratified by circulation), 128 weekly newspapers, 17 news magazines, 28 wire service bureaus, 121 radio stations, and 99 television stations, for a total of 574 separate news organizations.

61%, and the maximum possible sampling error is just above 6 percentage points but higher for the individual minority groups.

In drawing these samples, we had to make estimates of how many full-time journalists were working in general interest mainstream news media in the United States. We compared our final main sample percentages with the overall workforce percentages from these estimates, and found that we had slightly undersampled radio and television journalists by deliberately oversampling wire service and news magazine journalists to have enough from the wires (58) and news magazines (61) to analyze. However, no group was either under- or oversampled by more than 6 percentage points.

BASIC CHARACTERISTICS OF JOURNALISTS

There was very little growth in the number of full-time U.S. journalists in the 1980s, as compared with the 1970s. In fact, slightly less than 10,000 more full-time journalists were working for mainstream news media in the United States in 1992 (122,015) as compared with 1982 (112,072), a growth rate of just under 9%, as compared with a growth of 42,572 full-time journalists between 1971 and 1982, or a 61% increase. In terms of overall growth, then, the decade of the 1980s was one of very little change for U.S. journalists.

Profiles

Yet who were these journalists in 1992? As in 1982, it was difficult to talk in general terms about the "typical" U.S. journalist because there were more than 122,000 of them. Our 1992 national survey suggested that the "typical" U.S. journalist was a White Protestant male with a bachelor's degree from a public college, married, 36 years old, earning about $31,000 a year, working in journalism about 12 years, not belonging to a journalism association, and employed by a medium-sized (42 journalists), group-owned daily newspaper. Such a picture is inadequate, however, because our findings show that in 1992 there were substantial numbers of women, non-Whites, non-Protestants, single, young and old, and relatively rich and poor journalists working in the United States for a wide variety of small and large news media, both group and singly owned.

Many of these journalists differed from this profile of the typical journalist. For example, Black and Asian journalists were more likely to be women than men, not to be married, to have higher incomes ($37,000 to $42,000) than the typical journalist, to have worked in journalism 10 or 11 years, to be members of at least one journalism association, and to work for larger (100 to 150 journalists) daily newspapers.

Hispanic journalists were more likely to be Catholic than Protestant and to be more similar to Blacks and Asians than to the "typical" U.S. journalist on other characteristics. Native American journalists were more likely to be of some other religion besides Protestant or Catholic, to make much less than the other groups (median income of $22,000), and to work for very small newspapers or television stations (3 or 4 journalists).

Women journalists in general were likely to have worked in journalism three years less than men, to have somewhat lower incomes (about $27,000 a year), to be about a year younger than men, not to be married, and to be much more likely to identify with the Democratic Party than men.

How did the U.S. journalists of 1992 compare with those of 10 or 20 years ago?

Age

The median, or middle, age of U.S. journalists rose to 36 years old in 1992, about where it was in 1971, from a drop to almost 32 in 1982. In general, then, U.S. journalists returned in age to where they were 20 years earlier, before the massive hiring of young people during the 1970s. This was especially true for print journalists, with a median age of 37, compared to broadcast, where it was only 32.

This aging of U.S. journalists is more dramatically illustrated by looking at the proportions in each age group, as Table 20.1 illustrates. Those under 24 years old shrunk to only about 4% of all journalists, down dramatically from nearly 12% in both 1971 and 1982, mainly because of the small growth in number of new jobs during the 1980s.

Those 25 to 34 years old also declined from 45% to 37%, and those 35-54 grew the most (from 32% to 51%), becoming the largest age segment in U.S. journalism in 1992.

Those 55 to 64 years old have continued to decline since 1971, suggesting relatively fewer "elders" in U.S. journalism in 1992 as compared with the early 1970s. Whether that will change much in the next decade as many of those in the large 35 to 54 age group exceed 55 depends on how many stay in journalism and how many move on to other occupations. We do know from our survey that 21% of all journalists in 1992 said they would like to be working outside the news media in five years, compared to 11% in 1982-83 and only 7% in 1971.

Table 20.1. Age Distribution of U.S. Journalistic Workforce (Percentage in Each Age Group).

Age Groups	Journalists 1971[a]	Journalists 1982-1983[b]	Journalists 1992	U.S. Civilian Labor Force 1971[c]	U.S. Civilian Labor Force 1981[d]	U.S. Civilian Labor Force 1989[e]
Under 20	0.7	0.1	0.0	5.1	8.3	6.4
20-24	11.3	11.7	4.1	13.9	14.8	11.4
25-34	33.3	44.9	37.2	22.2	28.0	29.0
35-44	22.2	21.0	36.7	20.0	19.5	24.7
45-54	18.8	10.9	13.9	21.0	15.6	16.1
55-64	11.3	8.9	6.6	14.1	11.0	9.6
65 and older	2.3	1.6	1.5	3.9	2.8	2.8
Total	99.9f	99.1f	100.0	100.2f	100.0	100.0
Median age	36.5	32.4	36.0	39.2	33.6	36.1

[a]Data compiled from Johnstone et al. (1976: 197)
[b]Data compiled from Weaver and Wilhoit (1986: 19)
[c]Data compiled from U.S. Department of Labor (1971: Table A-3, p. 29).
[d]Data compiled from U.S. Bureau of the Census (1982-1983: 379).
[e]Data compiled from U.S. Bureau of the Census (1991: 392).
[f]Does not total to 100% because of rounding.

Gender

One thing that did not change much in U.S. journalism from 1982 to 1992, to our surprise, was the percentage of women working for all different news media combined. In spite of rapidly increasing enrollments of women in U.S. journalism schools during the 1980s, and the emphasis on hiring women since the late 1970s, the overall percentage of women in 1992 remained the same as in 1982—34.

When only those journalists with less than five years experience were considered, the proportion of women was much higher (about 45%). It was also higher for those with five to nine years experience, although not as much (about 42%). Because the growth rate in U.S. journalism was so small during the 1980s, and because there were far fewer women than men with 15 years or more experience, these increases in women hired during the 1980s did not change the overall percentage from 1982 to 1992.

It appears that women were successful in rising within the ranks of their organizations, as 42% of them said they had some supervisory responsibility for news editorial staff, a figure identical to that for males. These findings show that editors and news directors had some success in hiring and promoting more women during the 1980s, but this success was not reflected in the overall proportion of women journalists.

The percentage of women journalists in 1992 varied tremendously by medium, from about one fourth in the wire services and television to nearly one half in weekly newspapers and news magazines. Obviously, some news media did better than others in hiring and retaining women in the 1980s.

The proportion of women journalists also varied considerably by race, with all minority groups (especially Asians, Blacks, and Hispanics) represented by more women than the White majority group. This suggests that increased emphasis on hiring minority journalists is likely to increase the representation of women at the same time.

Race and Ethnicity

Although minority journalists can boast significantly higher percentages of women journalists than their White counterparts, it is clear that the proportion of minorities in U.S. journalism lags behind their proportions in the overall population. There has been some increase during the past decade, but the 8.2 percentage for 1992 still lags far behind the 24% estimated by the 1990 U.S. Census. In fairness, the proportion of qualified minorities (those with a bachelor's degree or more) was only about 9% in 1992, compared with more than twice that percentage among majority Whites (Hess 1992).

As with women, if only those journalists hired during the decade of the 1980s are considered, the overall percentage of minorities is considerably higher (about 12%), suggesting that there were increased efforts, and some success, in minority hiring during the 1980s. However, the percentage drops off sharply for those journalists with 10 or more years of experience, probably because of less emphasis on minority hiring during the 1960s and 1970s, and possibly because more minorities leave journalism after 10 years on the job.

As with women, some media did better than others in recruiting full-time minority journalists, most notably radio (14%) and television (12%), and some have done much worse. It is fairly certain that the very low percentage of minorities working on weekly newspapers (2%) reflects the fact that many minorities live in larger urban areas, but the same cannot be said for news magazines (5%) and wire services (5%).

In 1992, African Americans were the most numerous minority journalists, whereas Native Americans were the least common. When these percentages were projected to the total population of mainstream news media, we estimated about 4,500 Black journalists, 2,700 Hispanics, 1,200 Asians, and only 730 Native Americans. It should be remembered that these projections do not include special-interest or ethnic media, or any non-news magazines, so they are very conservative numbers.

Religion

In terms of religious backgrounds, U.S. journalists did not change much from the early 1980s to the early 1990s, and they reflected the overall population fairly closely. There was a drop of about 5 percentage points in Protestants, an increase of 3 points in Catholics, and an increase in "other" or "none" of about 3.5 points. The proportion of U.S. journalists rating religion or religious beliefs as "very important" in 1992, however, was significantly lower (38%) than in the overall U.S. population (61%).

Politics

Although there was not much change in religious backgrounds of U.S. journalists in the decade of the 1980s, there was a notable change in political party preference, with more journalists identifying themselves as Democrats (44%) and slightly fewer saying they were Republicans (16%). The proportion calling themselves Independents also dropped a bit to 34%.

When compared to the overall U.S. population in 1992, journalists were 5 to 10 percentage points more likely to say they were Democrats, and 10 to 15 points less likely to say they were Republicans, depending on which poll is used as a measure of the overall U.S. adult population's party preference. The percentage of journalists claiming to be Independents was very close to the overall population percentage of 31.

Part of the increase in journalists identifying with the Democratic Party came from the increase in minorities in U.S. journalism. In general, minorities were much more likely to call themselves Democrats than were White journalists, especially Blacks (70%), Asians (63%), and Hispanics (59%). There was also a wide gender gap for political party identification, with women journalists (58%) being much more likely than men (38%) to prefer the Democratic Party. Men were the most likely (40%) of all groups to say they were Independents. There was a pronounced shift of U.S. journalists from the center of the political spectrum in 1982-83 to the left in 1992, as Table 20.2 shows. Compared with the overall U.S. adult population, journalists were significantly more likely to lean to the left in 1992.

EDUCATION AND TRAINING

The proportion of U.S. journalists with at least a college bachelor's degree continued to increase during the 1980s to 82%, especially among those working for news magazines and wire services (95%). It is clear that a bachelor's degree has become the minimum qualification necessary for practicing journalism in all U.S. news media, even radio, which had about the same percentage (59) of college graduates in 1992 as existed in U.S. journalism overall in 1971.

However, a college degree with a major in journalism was still not held by a majority of U.S. full-time journalists in 1992, despite the large numbers of journalism school students graduating in the 1980s. In fact, there was no change overall in the percentage of college graduates who majored in journalism (40) during the previous decade, probably because of the very slow growth in number of mainstream journalism jobs and the aging of existing journalists. Yet when those who majored, minored, or took college classes in journalism were summed, the percentage rose from 40 to 62 in 1992.

Only in daily newspapers was a journalism degree almost the norm in 1992 (49%). Wire services and weekly newspapers were not too far behind at 38% and 34%. However, radio, television, and news magazine journalists were far less likely to hold journalism degrees (20% to 22%).

Table 20.2. Political Leanings of U.S. Journalists Compared with U.S. Adult Population (Percentage in Each Group).

Political Leanings	Journalists			U.S. Adult Population	
	1971[a]	1982-1983[b]	1992	1982[c]	1992[d]
Pretty far to left	7.5	3.8	11.6	—	—
A little to left	30.5	18.3	35.7	21	18
Middle of the road	38.5	57.5	30.0	37	41
A little to right	15.6	16.3	17.0	32	34
Pretty far to right	3.4	1.6	4.7	—	—
Don't know/refused	4.5	2.5	1.0	10	7
Total	100.0	100.0	100.0	100	100

[a]Data compiled from Johnstone et al. (1976: 93).
[b]Data compiled from Weaver and Wilhoit (1986: 26).
[c]Data compiled from George H. Gallup (1984: 82).
[d]Data compiled from Gallup Organization national telephone surveys of 1,307 U.S. adults, July 6-8, 1992, and 955 U.S. adults, July 17, 1992.

WORKING CONDITIONS

Income

One of the most important working conditions is, of course, salary. Our findings indicate that the median income of full-time journalists increased from $19,000 in 1981 (the year just before our 1982-83 study) to $31,297 in 1991. This was less than income estimates for other somewhat comparable occupational groups such as internal auditors and accountants.[2]

A decline in the rate of inflation over the decade of the 1980s enabled the increase in journalists' incomes to exceed the rise in the Consumer Price Index, but this progress in salary did not restore journalists' relative buying power to its level in the late 1960s.

One of the encouraging findings in our 1982-83 study was that the salary gap between men and women had decreased somewhat since 1970. From 1981 to 1991, that gap decreased even more than in the previous decade. Overall median salaries for women in 1991 were 81% of those for men, compared to 64% in 1970.

When years of experience in journalism was considered, the gender gap in income nearly disappeared. There was a notable gap among journalists of 10 to 14 years experience. Although we have no ready explanation for that difference, women with four years or less experience tended to work for slightly smaller news organizations than did men, helping to explain the small salary gap for the most recently hired journalists.

When a variety of predictors of income were controlled statistically (such as professional age, type of medium, size of news organization, managerial responsibilities, race, ownership of news organization, presence of a journalists union, region of country, and education level), gender predicted less than 1% of the variation in pay. There was no income gap by race of journalist, except for Native Americans, who made substantially less than others primarily because they worked for very small news operations.

Considerable differences in salary were found among the various news media. Journalists at news magazines and the wire services earned the most on average, and those at radio stations and weekly

---

[2]The mean salary for nonsupervisory management accountants in 1990 was $37,000. It was $36,800 for internal auditors (U.S. Department of Labor May 1992). The mean 1991 salary for all full-time U.S. journalists was $31,500, according to the data from our national probability sample of 1,156.

newspapers earned the least.[3] Not surprisingly, those at the largest organizations and those with the most experience tended to earn the highest salaries.

Job Satisfaction

Traditionally, U.S. journalists—despite considerable concern about pay scales—have ranked high on job satisfaction. That appears to have changed over the decades of the 1970s and especially the 1980s. Only 27% said they were very satisfied with their job in 1992, compared to almost half saying that 20 years ago, as Table 20.3 indicates. A majority in 1992 were at least fairly satisfied, but the overall decline in job happiness was considerable, with African-American and Asian journalists being the least likely to say they were very satisfied. The profile is somewhat less favorable than the picture of job attitudes for some other professions such as college professors (Russell, Fairweather, and Hendrickson 1991).

One of the most significant predictors of job satisfaction has been the extent to which journalists see their organization as informing

Table 20.3. Job Satisfaction.

Rating	1971[a] (%)	1982-83[b] (%)	1992 (%)
Very Satisfied	49	40	27
Fairly Satisfied	39	44	50
Somewhat Dissatisfied	12	15	20
Very Dissatisfied	1	2	3
	N = 1,328	N = 1,001	N = 1,156

[a]Data compiled from Johnstone et al. (1976: 238).
[b]Data compiled from Weaver and Wilhoit (1986: 89).

---

[3]The salary estimates for television journalists appear fairly close to those found by Vernon A. Stone (1992). Stone's estimates of median television salaries in 1991 were: reporters, $20,000; producers, $21,000; anchors, $34,500; and news directors, $45,000. Our estimates for radio appear to be higher than Stone's. He found these median salaries for radio: reporters, $13,620; anchors, $17,810; and news directors, $17,810.

their audience. There was a slight change in that estimate, with fewer journalists saying in 1992 that their newsroom was doing an outstanding job of informing the public, especially among Blacks and Asians. Reasons for this ranged from low quality of staff (being complacent or not aggressive enough) to limited resources.

The general picture, however, suggests most journalists did rate their organization as good or better on informing the public. Journalists for the wire services were most positive and cited high quality of editors and staff, and speed of news coverage. The least favorable ratings on informing the public were from television journalists, who mentioned small staffs and limited resources.

A majority of journalists said the editorial policies of their organization were very important in how they rated their job, an increase of 12 percentage points from 1982-83, as Table 20.4 shows. Journalists in the print media were more likely to say editorial policies were important than their colleagues in the broadcast media, and Native Americans were much more likely than other journalists to say so.

The chance to help people remained a very important aspect of work for a majority, but this altruism was somewhat more apt to be cited by journalists in broadcasting and on weekly newspapers than in other media, and especially by minority journalists. Table 20.4 shows that job

Table 20.4. Factors of Job Satisfaction (Percentage Saying Very Important).

Factors	1982-83[a]	1992
Helping people	61	61
Job Security	57	61
Editorial Policy	57	69
Autonomy	50	51
Chance to Advance	47	39
Developing a Specialty	45	40
Fringe Benefits	26	35
Pay	23	21
	N=1,001	N = 1,156

[a]Data compiled from Weaver and Wilhoit (1986: 93).

security and the extent of autonomy also were very important in how journalists rated their jobs. As in the past, though, fringe benefits and pay were much less likely than other factors to be cited as very important.

Commitment

Our 1982-83 study suggested that the number of journalists who planned to leave the field had increased from 6% to 11%, and that disgruntlement tended to be most visible among the more experienced and altruistic persons. The trend continued in the 1990s, as 21% of the sample—almost double that of 1982-83—said they planned to leave the field during the next five years mainly because of limited pay and the need for a change or a new challenge. Asian-American journalists were least likely (11%) to say they planned to leave journalism, and Native Americans were most likely to say this (29%).

PROFESSIONALISM

Roles

The journalists in our sample were asked a battery of 11 questions about the importance of various aspects of the possible roles of the news media. Specifically, each journalist responded to questions such as this: "How important is it for the news media to get information to the public quickly?"

For the most part, the perceptions of journalistic role were broadly similar to those in the early 1980s. Journalists tended to see their responsibilities as pluralistic, with wide majorities agreeing that there was at least some importance for roles as disparate as surveillance and entertainment. Which roles were seen as most important?

Table 20.5 indicates that two journalistic responsibilities were seen as extremely important by a majority: getting information to the public quickly and investigating government claims. There was no significant difference by race or gender on these journalistic roles, except that Native Americans were much less concerned about getting information to the public quickly.

Compared to a decade ago, journalists were somewhat more likely to rank their role in providing information quickly as extremely important, especially television and wire service journalists. Investigating the claims of government, which dropped in salience in the early 1980s,

Table 20.5 Importance Journalists Assign To Various Mass Media Roles (Percentage Saying Extremely Important).

Media Roles	1971[a]	1982-83[b]	1992
Investigate Government Claims	76	66	67
Get Information to Public Quickly	56	60	69
Avoid Stories with Unverified Content	51	50	49
Provide Analysis of Complex Problems	61	49	48
Discuss National Policy	55	38	39
Concentrate on Widest Audience	39	36	20
Develop Intellectual/Cultural Interests	30	24	18
Provide Entertainment	17	20	14
Serve as Adversary of Government[c]	—	20	21
Serve as Adversary of Business[c]	—	15	14
Set the Political Agenda[d]	—	—	5
Let People Express Views[d]	—	—	48
	N=1,313	N=1,001	N=1,156

[a]Data compiled from Johnstone et al. (1976: 230).
[b]Data compiled from Weaver and Wilhoit (1986: 114).
[c]Not asked in the 1971 survey.
[d]Not asked in the 1971 or 1982-83 survey.

was unchanged in relative importance and was ranked about the same by journalists on all media except radio. Journalists working for radio stations were much less likely to see this as extremely important.

The analytical function of news media—providing analysis of complex problems—also remained about the same, with 48% rating it extremely important. Journalists for the news magazines and daily newspapers were much more likely than those in other media to see this role as highly salient. Asian-American and African-American journalists were also more likely to rate it as extremely important.

In the post-Watergate climate of our earlier 1982-83 study, the question of journalists' perceptions of the importance of an aggressive stance toward government was of particular interest. We found the adversarial role was considered less salient in the minds of journalists in 1982-83 than many critics expected. Similar results were found in 1992.

Only a small minority of journalists in 1992 saw the adversary role—directed at either government or business—as extremely important. Print journalists, in general, were more likely to be adversarial than were broadcast. Asian Americans and African Americans were also more likely than other groups to rate the adversary role as extremely important.

In 1992, we asked a new question about the role of journalists in setting the political agenda, a topic that has received much attention during the 1980s. Few journalists saw their role in these terms, with only 5% ranking it extremely important and 41% rejecting it entirely. But three of the four minority groups (African Americans, Hispanics, and Native Americans) were more likely to say that this was an extremely important role. Even among these groups, however, only about 10% rated setting the political agenda as extremely important.

Another issue of currency is the extent to which journalists should attempt to give ordinary people a chance to express their views on public affairs. A little less than half of the sample said this was an extremely important role. Those working on daily and weekly newspapers were most likely to see this as extremely important.

As some prominent journalists join the critics in claiming that mainstream journalists are sometimes guilty of yielding too easily to the marketing values on the business side, our findings on the perceptions of the importance of entertainment are interesting. Fewer journalists in 1992 than a decade ago—especially among those in broadcasting—were willing to say that entertainment is extremely important to news organizations.

The effect of cable services and other new media in fragmenting the mass audience into specialized markets may explain one of the major shifts in journalists' perceptions of their work. When asked about the importance of trying to reach the widest possible audience, only a small percentage—significantly fewer than in 1982-83—agreed that this pursuit is extremely important.

Ethics

One of the most significant aspects of contemporary public debate about mainstream news media is questioning of the ethics of various reporting practices. This is an especially troublesome area for survey research because of the difficulty of asking a respondent to evaluate a reporting tactic that is removed from the context of a news story on which "it depends." Our study asked journalists to consider 10 practices individually and to say whether, given an important story, they may be justified on occasion or whether these practices would not be approved under any circumstances.

As Table 20.6 shows, the findings suggested a slight decline from the early 1980s in the number of journalists saying undercover

Table 20.6 Journalists' Acceptance of Various Reporting Practices (Percentage Saying May Be Justified).

Reporting Practices	(1982-83)[a]	(1992)
Getting employed in a firm or organization to gain inside information	67	63
Using confidential business or government documents without authorization	55	82
Badgering unwilling informants to get a story	47	49
Making use of personal documents such as letters and photographs without permission	28	48
Paying people for confidential information	27	20
Claiming to be somebody else	20	22
Agreeing to protect confidentiality and not doing so	5	5
Using hidden microphones or cameras[b]	—	60
Using recreations or dramatizations of news by actors[b]	—	28
Disclosing the names of rape victims[b]	—	43
	N=1,001	N=1,156

[a]Data compiled from Weaver and Wilhoit (1986: 128).
[b]Not asked in the 1982-83 survey.

reporting may be justified but a substantial increase in those tolerating the use of business, government, and personal documents without permission. Daily newspaper and wire service journalists were significantly more likely than others to justify the use of unauthorized documents, as were Asian journalists in general. Native Americans were the least likely to approve of this practice.

The change in the willingness of journalists to envision a circumstance for using confidential documents illustrated in Table 20.6 probably was based on a greater awareness of problems of government secrecy and the difficulty of access to computerized databases. However, there was a similar pattern in the opinions on use of personal documents and letters without permission that may have reflected increased competition among news media for exclusive stories regarding specific personalities.

There was a significant decline in the willingness to pay sources for information. African-American journalists were the most likely to say that this practice may be justified on occasion, but only 30% of them said this.

In the 1992 study, journalists were also queried about some recent reporting practices that have been widely debated. Not surprisingly, it was television journalists who were much more likely to justify using hidden microphones or cameras. The use of recreations or dramatizations was tolerated by a minority, again with broadcast journalists being more likely to say these techniques may be justified.

None of the practices assessed by the study is more complicated ethically than the question about disclosing the names of rape victims. Print journalists were more likely to be among the substantial minority saying that publishing the names of victims may be justified under some circumstances. Surprisingly, male and female journalists showed identical stances on this question, but Native Americans were much less likely to agree with this practice.

CONCLUSIONS

This data set of extensive interviews with more than 1,400 U.S. journalists has much more open-ended narrative from the respondents than our previous 1982-83 study. Much of that material can be found in the book, *The American Journalist in the 1990s* (Weaver and Wilhoit 1996). What we have provided here is only a brief sketch of some of the main findings, including the following points:

1. The substantial growth in the number of U.S. journalists working for the traditional news media that characterized the l970s has stalled in the 1980s. In spite of that, media organizations appear to have made some progress in attracting minorities. A minority workforce of 8%, up from 4% in our 1982-83 study, by no means indicates sufficient racial and ethnic diversity in U.S. newsrooms, but it is moving in the right direction.
2. Stalled growth in U.S. media employment appears to have affected the representation of women, as they are at the same proportion of the workforce (34%) as in the early 1980s. We

suspect the problem is one of retention, as well as limited growth in new jobs, because there is evidence of greater parity of representation of men and women at the entry levels of journalism.

3. The median age of journalists, 36, rose during the 1980s and is about the same as it was before the rapid influx of large numbers of young, entry-level employees in the 1970s. Professional identity appears to have declined, however, with a smaller minority of the workforce belonging to journalism organizations than in 1982-83.

4. Salaries have improved, with increases outpacing inflation over the decade. The median 1991 figure of $31,297 for the typical journalist, however, was still below pay levels of other somewhat comparable occupations. The salary gap between men and women narrowed, and none existed for the major minority groups (except Native Americans) in the field.

5. A serious problem of retention may be just over the horizon. More than 20% of those surveyed said they plan to leave the field within five years, nearly double the figure of 1982-83. This was tied to a significant decline in job satisfaction, with complaints about pay and the need for a different challenge being the major reasons for plans to leave.

6. Overall differences in ideas about journalistic roles and reporting practices, although not great, seemed to be related more strongly to working for a particular medium than a decade earlier. In addition, in the 1992 results, gender and racial differences appeared to account for fewer differences than did the types of news media for which U.S. journalists work.

Changes in media organizations and audiences appeared to be reflected in a perception among journalists that reaching the largest number of people was not as important in 1992 as it was a decade earlier. Speed in getting the news to the public—likely a reflection of new technology's capacity for immediacy—became more salient. Investigating government claims remained a high value. However, there was a tendency to downplay entertainment as an important aspect of the news.

Although recognizing the importance of the adversary role, U.S. journalists did not see it as their highest responsibility. In fact, there is evidence that they display considerable caution about playing an activist role in their news work. The idea of setting the policy agenda of the nation and their communities is also not one they saw as very salient to their job as journalists.

7. There seems to be recognition that some aggressive reporting practices may be more acceptable in an environment of gov-

ernment secrecy and the ease with which access to information is affected by computerized databases. Use of confidential government, business, and personal documents in 1992 was seen as justifiable on occasion by significantly more journalists than in the early 1980s.

There was about an even split on some complicated issues such as whether a rape victim's name may be published, but, as in many other aspects of journalism, gender (and race, for the most part) were not related to the position on the question. On one dimension, political party allegiance, both gender and race were pertinent.

8. Although more U.S. journalists in 1992 saw themselves as Democrats than in 1982-83, it was among women and minorities that the Democrats were strongest. Perhaps more important, however, was the perception by the U.S. journalists that the organizations for which they worked — regardless of their personal predilections—were middle of the road politically.

As in 1982, analysis of our 1992 data suggests that the newsroom, with all its constraints and daily hysteria of meeting deadlines, has more to do with the face of the news in the United States than does a statistical profile of U.S. journalists. This does not detract from the value of knowing who journalists are and how they compare with the public, however, because individual backgrounds, values, and perceptions undoubtedly have some influence on how the news is covered.

But these backgrounds, values, and perceptions influence news coverage within the constraints of individual news organizations, and our findings raise questions about whether these constraints are becoming more limiting in the 1990s than in the decades of the 1970s and 1980s.

For example, we find a significant decline in perceived autonomy of U.S. journalists since the early 1970s, as well as diminished job satisfaction. Other comparable occupations do not seem to have experienced this decline in those very satisfied with their work.

The perceived decline in the organizational incentives and resources to cover the news adequately—evident in the open-ended responses of the journalists in our study—has serious implications for the quality of news the public receives. Even if the constraints are more likely to be a result of a general anemia in the advertising industry than of a pervasive corporate culture that puts increased emphasis on profits, the result is the same. The sense of public service that has long been an attraction for U.S. journalists does seem threatened by many of the trends reported here.

U.S. journalists are likely to think their newsrooms are more successful at comprehensive and speedy coverage than at providing a real check on powerful officials and interests. The question that lurks, then, is whether the culture of the modern, corporate newsroom will sustain the democratic altruism and provide the resources for the searchlight of publicity to shine as brightly as before on powerful interests that often conflict with the public good. If not, there may be less real journalism—and fewer authentic journalists—in some of the major U.S. news media by the end of the 1990s.

REFERENCES

Gallup, George H. 1984. *The Gallup poll: Public opinion, 1983.* Wilmington, DE: Scholarly Resources.

Hess, Stephen. 1992. All the president's reporters: A new survey of the White House press corps. *Presidential Studies Quarterly* 22: 311-321.

Johnstone, John W. C., Edward J. Slawski, and William W. Bowman. 1976. *The news people: A sociological portrait of American journalists and their work.* Urbana: University of Illinois Press.

Russell, Susan H. James S. Fairweather, and Robert M. Hendrickson. 1991. *Profiles of faculty in higher education institutions, 1988.* Washington, DC: National Center for Education Statistics, U.S. Department of Education, 1991.

Stone, Vernon A. 1992, February. News salaries stand still. *Communicator*, pp. 14-15.

U.S. Bureau of the Census. 1982-1983. *Statistical abstract of the United States*, 103rd ed. Washington, DC: U.S. Government Printing Office.

U.S. Bureau of the Census. 1991. *Statistical abstract of the United States*, 111th ed. Washington, DC: U.S. Government Printing Office.

U.S. Department of Labor. 1971, December. *Employment and earnings*, 18(6). Washington, DC: U.S. Government Printing Office.

U.S. Department of Labor, Bureau of Labor Statistics. 1992, May. *Occupational outlook handbook*, Bulletin No. 2400. Washington, DC: Author.

Weaver, David H. and G. Cleveland Wilhoit. 1986. *The American journalist: A portrait of U.S. news people and their work.* Bloomington: Indiana University Press.

Weaver, David H. and G. Cleveland Wilhoit. 1996. *The American journalist in the 1990s: U.S. news people at the end of an era.* Mahwah, NJ: Erlbaum.

VI

SOUTH AND CENTRAL AMERICA

21

The Brazilian Journalist

Heloiza G. Herscovitz
University of Florida
Adalberto M. Cardoso
Universidade Federal do Rio de Janeiro

Brazilian journalists operate in a context that encompasses accelerated underdevelopment and compulsive modernization. It is common to say that there are many Brazils in the same territory because of great social inequalities. Although a wealthy elite enjoy the benefit of new technologies to access the Internet or to watch CNN through satellite dishes, about 40 million illiterate citizens are kept apart from the print media industry.

In addition, Brazilians' daily life is very much permeated by a nondemocratic legacy of a bureaucratic authoritarian regime that includes great political and economic dependency on the state, an inadequate welfare organization, and a political party structure prone to populism and clientelism (Mainwaring, O'Donnell, and Valenzuela 1992). These circumstances have deeply affected journalism in Brazil. At the same time, the country's emerging democracy, which is about a decade old, has redirected many journalistic concerns and opened up new avenues such as learning how to work under press freedom. Furthermore, new technologies in the newsrooms and the adoption of modern management practices by publishing companies have changed the business.

As expected in such a context, the media are highly concentrated. Ninety percent of all the media are controlled by nine family groups (Costa 1991). In spite of the fact that the media are primarily in private hands, the government has guaranteed its political influence through direct investment during the military rule and later through credit incentives, tax breaks, and government advertising.

The country has 295 daily newspapers, comprising 29% of all daily newspapers edited in Latin America and the Caribbean (Lopez 1991). They are read by the better educated people. The print media market has been closed to new publications since 1982. The same titles have fought for a stable portion of readers. Almost all larger newspapers increased circulation in the last decade, especially those published in the central areas of Sao Paulo and Rio de Janeiro, which extended their penetration to other regions. However, there has not been a similar increase in the educational level of the population in the same period. The explanation found for that increase in circulation is that typical readers are buying more than one newspaper, whereas most Brazilians still get their news from television. *Globo* TV network, the largest media group in the country, holds 60% of the total audience (Cardoso 1994).

A brief look at the history of Brazilian journalism helps one understand today's cultural setting. The first Brazilian paper appeared in 1808, almost two centuries later than in the United States, and it was controlled by the Portuguese monarchy. After Brazil's independence from Portugal in 1822, a partisan press expanded and was very much influenced by French journalism (Bahia 1990). Portuguese, British, and French influences were slowly replaced by U.S. influences after World War II. Since then Brazilian journalists trained in the United States have borrowed U.S. journalistic standards both in graphic and content forms as well as in management. Nonetheless, the workforce operates in a cultural context in which journalists are required to hold a bachelor's degree in journalism to get licensed before entering the occupation.

METHODS

This study is part of a major project about media and democracy in Brazil coordinated by sociologist Vilmar Faria of the Cebrap (Brazilian Center of Analyses and Planning) and financed by the Ford Foundation. The survey was designed, executed, and analyzed by sociologist Adalberto Cardoso of Cebrap. It attempted to replicate Weaver and Wilhoit's *The American Journalist* study (1986). The U.S. questionnaire was adapted to Brazilian reality. Some questions were eliminated and others were added. The sample was restricted to the print media. It included the seven daily newspapers and two weekly news magazines of Sao Paulo and Rio de Janeiro with the largest circulation as well as their branches in Brasilia, the country's capital.

The survey took place between March and April 1994. Mail questionnaires were sent to journalists who deal only with the production of news information and opinion. A total of 1,112 questionnaires out of 1,700 were distributed to journalists by their editors. The response rate was 31.9% (355 questionnaires). The response rate by media organizations was uneven, varying between 9% and 73% because of contrasting efforts by editors in distributing the questionnaires. Only one media organization insisted that all of its journalists participate in the study. As a pioneer study in Brazil, this survey's results can hardly be generalized to the journalist population because of its sample limitations. Nonetheless, it has opened an avenue for future research and has helped to roughly estimate some parameters in the field.

RESPONDENT CHARACTERISTICS

The sample consisted of 205 men (58%) and 150 women (42%) between the ages of 25 and 36. Younger people have filled the newsrooms since the last decade, possibly because of the journalism degree requirement in order to receive a professional license. Fewer than half of executive and managing editors were older than 36, and only among the columnists were there people older than 40.

Ninety-two percent of respondents were White, with only 1.7% identifying themselves as Black and 4.8% as mixed race. Respondents were mostly newspaper reporters—young, White, married without children, and with a bachelor's degree in journalism (84%). They had nine or more years of professional experience and had worked for more than six years for the same organization. Almost 80% of respondents said they had no religion.

The mean annual income for respondents in the first half of 1994 was US$21,415. However, income conversions from Brazilian currency to the dollar can be misleading because of monthly variations related to inflation, cost of living, and salary policies. Women had much lower salaries than men in all functions and in all categories of years of experience. For example, men with professional experience between 9 and 14 years had an annual average income of US$27,590, whereas women in the same category earned an average of US$18,353. Male journalists contributed 77% of the total family income, whereas women's contribution was estimated at 66%. These percentages vary according to journalists' marital situation. If married, journalists are responsible for

70% of family income; if single, 73%, and if divorced, they are responsible for 94% of the family income.

Table 21.1 shows percentages of men and women by function and suggests that women were nearly as likely as men to be executive editors and managers and more likely to be reporters.

Table 21.1. Gender.

Functions	Male (%)	Female (%)	Total (%)
Executive editors and managers	24.0	21.9	23.5
Editors and news processing functions	26.6	28.8	27.5
Reporters	40.9	48.6	44.1
Other functions	7.9	.7	4.9
N	203	146	349
Total	58	42	100

Respondents indicated a center left-leaning tendency regarding politics with a mean of 4.2 points on a scale of 1 to 10, where 1 was extreme left and 10 was extreme right. This trend to be more left than right on the political scale correlates with journalists' political party choice. Findings show that 30% supported the Workers' Party, a left-leaning political organization. Also, 32.5% indicated their intention to vote for the Workers' Party candidate in the 1994 presidential election, with only 11.6% supporting the Brazilian Social Democratic Party's candidate Fernando Henrique Cardoso, who won the election.

The tilt toward the left did not affect journalists' views that Brazil must be a capitalist country. When asked about socialism or capitalism as the best alternatives for Brazil, 37% chose capitalism, whereas 30% chose socialism; 8% mentioned "real capitalism with social justice," and 4% suggested social democracy.

WORKING CONDITIONS

The sample's large concentration of reporters derives from the predominant number of newspapers in the Southeast region. Most of the print media are concentrated in the Southeast.

Most journalists (85%) did not hold other jobs, although they did not earn much money at newspapers and newsmagazines. Those who did hold other jobs (15%) worked for other media outlets such as news wires or radio stations or as school teachers. There is a high rate of turnover in most newsrooms today, especially among the new generation of journalists. Respondents were split about turnover effects. Although 28% thought that disadvantages prevailed over benefits, 27% thought just the opposite. Another 25% said that turnover rates inhibited the consolidation of a staff of specialists familiar with beats and sources.

Asked about where they will be working in three years, 67% said they planned to remain in the field, with only 4% planning to pursue nonmedia jobs. Such results indicate a commitment to the profession. When asked why they chose journalism, 46% said they made a career decision to enter the profession. This attitude was consistent across all age brackets, suggesting that most journalists have felt a call to the field. The second most often mentioned reason for going into journalism was friends, families, and teachers, mentioned by about one fourth, followed by attraction of this type of work (18%), desire to effect change (15.5%), and famous journalists or writers (9%).

Brazilian journalists seem fairly satisfied with their jobs. Most of them made a conscious choice to enter the profession and plan to remain in the field. It is interesting to note that respondents who were 36 to 40 years old were the ones most likely to pick journalism because of a desire to effect change (19%). This attitude is partially explained by the fact that they went to school during the harshest period of Brazil's military dictatorship. Overall, 55.4% said they were fairly satisfied with their current job, and 11.6% said they were very satisfied, as shown in Table 21.2.

Table 21.3 indicates that the most important predictor of job satisfaction among 23 variables was work interaction. The more journalists shared news production with their coworkers, the more they seemed to be satisfied. Managerial responsibility and salary also appeared as pre-

Table 21.2. Job Satisfaction (in percentages).

Very satisfied	11.6
Fairly satisfied	55.4
Somewhat dissatisfied	20.7
Very dissatisfied	11.4
Don't know	.9
Total	99.1
N = 355	100.0

dictors of job satisfaction. These two variables are related—the more responsibility a journalist has, the higher is his or her salary.

Table 21.3. Predictors of Job Satisfaction.

Predictors	Standardized Regression Coefficient	Simple r
Co-workers' influence in news production	.27	.23
Comments from colleagues of other media organizations	.15	.11
Managerial responsibilities	.14	.18
Don't know where to be working in three years	-.13	-.16
Salary	.12	.21
Career Decision	-.11	-.15
Readers' comments on your work	-.10	-.05
Permissiveness in journalistic ethics	-.10	-.05

$R^2 = .19$

$N = 312$

Salary and perceived autonomy were most likely to be rated as very important to job satisfaction, as shown in Table 21.4. Salary appeared in first place, mentioned by 91% of the respondents. Perceived autonomy was mentioned by 74% of the respondents. When compared to U.S. journalists, salary and perceived autonomy were considered very important to more Brazilian journalists, but fewer Brazilians saw editorial policy and job security as very important to their jobs.

The majority of Brazilian journalists in this survey (60%) said they do reporting regularly no matter what job title they have. Doing special reporting or writing feature stories on a regular basis gives prestige to senior and managing editors. Some 55% said they "almost always" have freedom to cover the stories they want, and 31% claimed they have almost complete freedom to decide which aspects of a news story should be emphasized. About 42% said they have a lot of freedom to decide story emphasis.

Table 21.4. Factors of Job Satisfaction (Percentage Saying Very Important).

Factors	Brazilians	U.S.[a]
Pay	91.0	23
Autonomy	74.0	50
Helping people	69.5	61
Chance to advance	62.0	47
Developing a specialty	55.0	45
Job security	50.0	57
Fringe benefits	49.0	26
Editorial policy	43.0	57
	N = 352	N = 1,001

[a]Data compiled from Weaver and Wilhoit (1986: 93).
Note: Ns for both surveys vary slightly across factors.

Almost three fourths of the journalists (72%) said their stories were only "somewhat" edited by others. Such a high level of autonomy relates to the fact that print media organizations have cut costs in the last decade by eliminating staff—people who proofread all stories written by reporters. Today, all journalists are supposed to edit their own stories.

Journalists' perceived autonomy seems consistent with the relatively low level of comment they reported about their work. Only 34% said superiors commented frequently about their work. Frequent comment was even lower from peers (32.5%) and journalists outside their own organization (14%) as well as from news sources (29.5%) and readers (21.5%).

However, these results need to be carefully interpreted. In the first place, most journalists sampled did not have managerial responsibilities (69%). Those who did have (31%) said they met with reporters several times a day. It may be possible that journalists with managerial responsibilities receive more comment and feedback than do reporters. Historically, Brazilian media organizations have had great control over their contents and, therefore, over their staffs. Such a tradition—built over decades of nondemocratic regimes and the absence of a citizenship concept as it is known in more developed countries—began to change with the country's democratization in the mid-1980s.

Thus, on the one hand, it may not be true that journalists had the amount of internal autonomy inside the organization they claimed to have. On the other hand, the low perceived feedback from news sources and readers sounds like remnants of the old order. Respondents were perhaps somewhat isolated from each other and the society they reported on everyday as opposed to journalists in a stable democratic society, in which levels of accountability are higher.

The impact of new technologies among Brazilian journalists deserves a separate study based on the many views offered by respondents. Video Display Terminals (VDTs) were introduced to Brazilian newspapers by the mid-1980s. The media organizations that participated in this survey used VDTs and computer systems for writing and editing. Respondents answered in an open-ended question how VDTs and other new technologies had affected their work. The analysis separated positive from negative aspects. Under positive aspects, journalists said that new technologies improved work conditions (86%), speeded up writing and editing (69%), and gave journalists more independence (92%). Under negative aspects, respondents cited a decline in news quality (97%), reduction in staff size (97%), health problems (96%), and problems with adjustment to computers (94%).

PROFESSIONALISM

Most Brazilian journalists are unionized because they are compelled by law and state bureaucracy. In order to get a professional license, journalists must have a journalism degree. The license then is registered at the regional union where journalists have a job. A small percentage of their salaries are paid directly to their union, which played a political role during military rule. In this study, 96% of respondents said that people at their newsrooms were unionized. There are few other journalism associations and societies. More than half of the journalists in the sample (55%) did not belong to any associations, whereas only 28% were members of the most prestigious one, the Brazilian Press Association (*Associação Brasileira de Imprensa*).

There are few academic publications dedicated to journalism and only one media review in Brazil. *Imprensa*, the media review, was read regularly by 85% of the journalists in the sample. *Columbia Journalism Review* was read sometimes by 4.5% of the respondents.

MEDIA ROLES

Brazilian journalists began systematically discussing media roles and ethics in the 1990s, after the emerging democratization and the return of press freedom. The country's only media review, *Imprensa*, has contributed to this debate. More importantly, the role of the media in the impeachment of former president Collor de Mello for corruption in 1992 and the uncovering of so many cases of corruption involving regional and national politicians after that opened a new avenue closed to journalism during military rule. Similar to Weaver and Wilhoit's 1986 study, journalists in the sample were questioned about nine media roles as shown in Table 21.5.

Brazilian journalists seemed to embrace both the interpretive/investigative and the adversary roles much more than did U.S. journalists. Almost 80% considered it very important to investigate government claims, a percentage much higher than the one found among U.S. journalists (66%). This finding supports the role played by the Brazilian media in uncovering recent political scandals. Journalists in the sample considered it very important to provide analysis of complex problems

Table 21.5. Importance Journalists Assign to Media Roles (Percentage Saying Extremely Important).

Media Roles	Brazilians	U.S.[a]
Investigate government claims	79	66
Get information to public quickly	70	60
Provide analysis of complex problems	67	49
Serve as adversary of government	55	20
Develop intellectual/cultural interests	52	24
Serve as adversary of business	53	15
Provide entertainment	30	20
Concentrate on widest audience	30	36
Avoid stories with unverified content	26	50
N	352	1,001

[a]Data compiled from Weaver and Wilhoit (1986: 114).
Note: Ns for both surveys vary slightly across roles.

(66.5%) and to develop intellectual/cultural interests of readers (51.5%). These percentages were also higher than the ones found among U.S. journalists (49% and 24%, respectively).

Brazilian journalists endorsed the role of getting information quickly to the public (70%), but only 29% of the respondents considered it very important to concentrate on the widest audience. The most striking finding was the presence of an adversary mentality reflected in the ratings of the roles of adversary of government (54%) and business (51%). Statistical explorations of these variables were unable to determine clear patterns—separating interpretive/investigative-oriented journalists from adversary-oriented journalists. In fact, journalists held mixed-role orientations.

A second striking finding related to media roles reveals some ambiguity. Only 26% of Brazilian journalists considered it very important to avoid stories with unverified content, whereas 50% of U.S. journalists said the same. It appears that Brazilians are eager to investigate government claims and provide analyses of complex problems to be quickly delivered to the public, without caring very much about unverified content. Why? The reasons are complex. Brazil's journalism underwent a quick but profound change after regaining press freedom. It was like a volcano whose flames have erupted after some many years of forced silence. However, the end of censorship and the hunger for press freedom alone do not explain this disregard for verifying content of stories, especially those related to politics.

There are other factors playing a role here. The lack of penalties for publishing irresponsible news in Brazil prevents most lawsuits. The justice system is slow and lacks any tradition in favoring people or institutions hurt by biased news. As a result, people do not sue other people or organizations and, if they do, chances are that they will never get paid.

The current conflict between government and the press, with the latter alternating between interpretive/investigative and adversary roles, has its roots in history. Since the 18th century a tense relationship between the press and the government has existed, with the former denouncing political maneuvers that were unfavorable to newspapers and the latter trying to manipulate the press. The reasons behind this dispute may have changed, but there is an underlying tension between the press and the government in Brazil.

When asked about how much influence the media have on public opinion on a scale from 1 (no influence) to 10 (great influence), 36% chose 8, which suggests much perceived influence. Yet when asked how much of this influence there should be, 42% of respondents chose 5 on the scale. These findings suggest that journalists in the sample thought they had more influence on public opinion than they should have had. Subsequently, they were asked how much the influence public opinion should have on government, and 45% chose 10, great influence.

The survey also looked for the most influential factors affecting ethical orientations among respondents. Journalists said they had learned about journalistic ethics from newsroom routines (85%), more experienced editors (61%), more experienced reporters (60%), and other peers (42%). Journalism school teachers were also cited as very influential in ethics formation by 35% of the journalists, which makes sense because Brazilian journalists are required to hold a journalism degree to get in the profession. Also, it is from journalistic training (71%) that respondents have learned to develop their concept of newsworthiness as well as from readings and research (71%), supervisors (46.5%), and other newspapers (49%).

In sum, journalists perceived their organizational contexts, which include journalistic training, newsroom routines, more experienced professional and staff peers, as the most influential factor in their conceptions of ethics.

Brazilian journalists have a singular ethical perception about various reporting practices. As in Weaver and Wilhoit's (1986) study, journalists were asked to assume that they were dealing with an important story and were presented with eight reporting situations. Table 21.6 shows these results. The majority of journalists (87%) agreed on protecting confidential sources. Also, three fifths rejected the idea of paying for confidential information. However, Brazilian journalists were split regarding the use of personal documents without permission: 42% of respondents disapproved and another 42% said it may be justified.

Conversely, four fifths of the journalists considered justifiable the unauthorized use of confidential business or government documents. This finding is consistent with the sometimes investigative, sometimes adversary, work done by many Brazilian journalists since the early 1990s. During the coverage of former President Fernando Collor de Mello's link to a corruption ring, the press named the case "Collorgate." The investigative reporting developed by U.S. journalists in different cases involving the government have inspired much of the work developed by Brazilian journalists after the end of censorship.

Brazilian journalists did not have much problem with undercover employment: 68% said it may be justified as opposed to the 21% who disapproved of it. Using false identification also was supported by the majority of journalists.

Regression analysis of ethical perceptions according to factors influencing journalistic ethics did not reveal much. In other words, acceptance or disapproval of certain reporting practices did not vary according to college education or journalistic training. No significant variation in ethical perceptions occurred by age, years of experience, or job categories.

Table 21.6. Journalists Acceptance of Reporting Practices.

Reporting Practices	May be Justified (%)	Disapprove (%)	Not Sure (%)	N
Paying people for confidential information	24.0	62.0	14.0	351
Using confidential business or government documents without authorization	83.0	13.0	4.0	352
Claiming to be somebody else	63.0	31.0	6.0	352
Agreeing to protect confidentiality and not doing so	7.0	87.5	5.0	352
Making use of personal documents such as letters and photographs without permission	42.5	42.5	15.0	351
Getting employed in a firm or organization to gain inside information	69.0	21.0	10.0	350

Variation in ethical perceptions by years of experience was significant in one case only—the higher the number of years a journalist had worked, the less he or she was likely to approve of false identification. Seventy-five percent of those who were in the field for four years or less said it may be justified as opposed to 47% of those who worked as journalists for more than 15 years.

Men were more likely to subscribe to the eight practices presented in the survey than were women. Half of the men said it was justified to use personal documents without consent as compared with one third of the women. However, female journalists (67%) were slightly more likely to justify false identification than were men (60%). Comparing journalists who worked for newspapers and magazines, the latter were more likely to justify these reporting practices.

A comparison of Brazilian journalists in the sample with U.S., German, and British journalists (Weaver and Wilhoit 1986) reveals that Brazilians were more likely to justify various reporting methods than U.S. journalists, except for paying people for confidential information. This practice is unpopular among Brazilian newspapers and journalists. Brazilian cultural tradition asserts that people get what they want through a web of personal relations and influential backing known as *jeitinho*. Good personal relations and the dual ethic of the *jeitinho* have helped Brazilians to cope with a not so democratic, not so modern society. Journalists have used this strategy liberally.

A look at Table 21.7 suggests that Brazilian journalists are closer to the British, who were also more willing to accept the various questionable reporting practices investigated in cross-cultural studies. Although German and U.S. journalists enjoy special rights of access to government and business information, British journalists do not. As for the Brazilian journalists, although the new Constitution guarantees press freedom, they do not enjoy special rights to government information, much less to business information. Furthermore, Brazilian public institu-

Table 21.7. Acceptance of Reporting Methods (Percentage Saying May be Justified).

Reporting Methods	Brazil	U.S.[a]	German[b]	British[c]
Using confidential documents without authorization	83	55	57	86
Getting employed in a firm to gain inside information	69	67	36	73
Claiming to be somebody else	63	20	22	33
Using personal documents without permission	42	28	5	53
Paying people for confidential information	24	27	25	69
Agreeing to protect confidentiality and not doing so	7	5	1	4
N	350	1,001	450	405

[a] Data compiled from Weaver and Wilhoit (1986: 139).
[b] Data compiled from Institut fur Demoskopie Allensbach, Konstanz, Germany (see Donsbach 1983).
[c] Data compiled from Centre for Mass Communication Research, University of Leicester, England (see Donsbach 1983).

tions produce unreliable statistics about almost everything from public health to vote counting due to the lack of financial resources. For example, the last national census has been discredited for containing incomplete and contradictory information.

MEDIA ROLES, PUBLIC OPINION, AND DEMOCRACY

Journalists in the sample had mixed perceptions about their readers. Sixty-six percent agreed (somewhat or highly) that readers are more interested in breaking news than in the analysis of complex problems, and 34% disagreed. Also, 42% agreed that readers are easily deceived, and 58% disagreed. Nonetheless, 66.5% of respondents said that analysis of complex problems is an extremely important media role. It seems that journalists wanted to offer readers something that in their perception most readers did not really want. Adding the finding that only 26% of the journalists thought that it is extremely important to avoid stories with unverified content, one may infer that journalists might be willing to offer facts without proving them to readers they consider easily deceived.

Such contradictions in journalists' perceptions suggest that they lack a clear idea of the role of the media in Brazil's emerging democracy. Also, they tend to absolve the media for any responsibility in the country's social crisis and blame politicians (85%), business people (62%), and voters (53%) for that. These findings imply that journalists take an adversary role when dealing with politicians and business people. Politicians deceive voters, and both are highly blamed for the social crisis, according to the perspective of the respondents.

At the same time, journalists perceive the press as free from responsibility for the social crisis, with 40% saying it is not guilty at all and 52% saying it is somewhat guilty. They placed themselves on the "good side" of society, along with the Catholic church, unions, community associations, and organizations such as the Brazilian Bar, the Brazilian Press Association, and the Catholic Bishops' Association, which had an important role in opposing the military rule.

CONCLUSIONS

Brazilian journalists surveyed in 1994 were mostly young professionals who are required to have a bachelor's degree in journalism for licensing, according to the law passed in 1979 during the military rule. Licensing means being unionized for bureaucratic reasons, but it has little to do with creating a professional identity. There are few journalism associations and societies, and membership is low. Also, there are quite a few academic publications dedicated to journalism, but most journalists read the only media review published in the country.

They perceive themselves as a professional group that socializes mainly among themselves and are very independent from external influences. Brazilian journalists claim they are satisfied with their jobs and plan to remain in the field. Salary and perceived autonomy are important factors that keep these young people in technologically updated newsrooms. As in developed countries, the newsroom environment and journalistic training appear as the strongest influences in shaping their professional values and ethical perceptions.

Since the reestablishment of press freedom along with the country's emerging democratization, journalists have explored their own limits and searched for a role definition in a dynamic society. The role played by the media in the impeachment of former President Collor de Mello—the "Collorgate" scandal—and in subsequent political scandals have kept journalists' expectations very high. They feel too empowered and independent.

They seem to embrace both an interpretive/investigative role and an adversary role, with the latter mainly directed to politicians and business. Their ethical journalistic perceptions reflect the contradictions of their own society—one that is searching for its soul in a democratic, modern environment. At this point, their profile seems ambiguous in many aspects, but they certainly are moving toward the consolidation of attitudes and practices that will allow for more balance in their roles.

REFERENCES

Bahia, Juarez. 1990. *Jornal, história e técnica: História da imprensa brasileira* [Newspaper, history and technique: History of the Brazilian press]. Sao Paulo: Atica.

Cardoso, Adalberto M. 1994. *Journalistas: Ética e democracia no exercicio da profissão* [Journalists: Ethics and democracy in their profession]. Paper presented to the Anpocs annual conference in Caxambu, Brazil.

Costa, Caio Tulio. 1991. *O Relógio de Pascal /A Experiência do Primeiro Ombudsman da Imprensa Brasileira* [Pascal's watch/The experience of the first ombudsman in the Brazilian press]. Sao Paulo: Siciliano.

Donsbach, Wolfgang. 1983. Journalists' conceptions of their audience. *Gazette* 32: 19-36.

Lopez, Antonio. 1991. Panorama general de la prensa en America Latina [General view of the Latin American press]. *Chasqui* 3: 78-83.

Mainwaring, Scott, Guillermo O'Donnell, and J. Samuel Valenzuela. 1992. *Democratic consolidation/The new South American democracies in comparative perspective*. South Bend, IN: University of Notre Dame Press.

Weaver, David and G. Cleveland Wilhoit. 1986. *The American journalist: A portrait of U.S. news people and their work*. Bloomington: Indiana University Press.

22

Journalists in Chile, Ecuador and Mexico*

Jürgen Wilke
Johannes Gutenberg Universität

If the mass media are today attributed with a significant function for society and politics, then this also applies in Latin America. If one disregards the colonial origins, since the declarations of independence in the early 19th century, the press has gained increasingly in importance there. Since then, as in other countries, not only has the media sector expanded primarily because of the emergence of radio and television, but the role of journalists and their self-perception has also developed and changed. Profound difficulties had to be overcome because the history of this subcontinent is characterized by great political instability. The journalists especially suffered from authoritarian governmental structures, and in many cases they were subject to much repression.

In recent years, journalism and journalistic professional values have become the object of international research to a far greater extent (Weaver and Wilhoit 1986; Donsbach and Patterson 1992; Donsbach

---

*An earlier version of this chapter was presented to the Scientific Conference of the International Association for Mass Communication Research (IAMCR), July 3-8, 1994, Seoul, Korea.

and Klett 1993). To this end, journalists have been interviewed, especially in the Western industrialized countries. Up to the early 1990s, there have been few such studies of journalists in Third World countries. This can also be said of Latin America, even though a well-developed system exists for educating journalists at the university level, which could constitute the basis for such studies. However, Latin American quantitative, social-empirical communications research is still in the early stages. Thus, a lack of experience with this survey method of the social sciences hinders its implementation there.

Nevertheless, one should not leave it at that. For one thing the political circumstances in quite a number of countries have changed due to redemocratization and transitional processes that also affect the situation of journalism. Latin America deserves to be included in the flow of international comparative research efforts, and the examination of journalism and journalistic professional perception should not be delayed any longer, even if such studies do not comply in every respect with methodological standards often found in more developed research areas.

METHOD

This chapter reports on the results of interviews with journalists from three Latin American countries. These surveys were carried out in the early 1990s in Chilé (Rehbein González 1994), Mexico (Goehringer 1992), and Ecuador (Zwermann 1992). The surveys in the first two countries were largely synchronized so that a greater part of the results can be directly compared with each other. The survey in Ecuador used a somewhat different questionnaire so that direct comparisons are only possible in singular cases. Nevertheless, the results gained from this survey can shed new light on our subject.

Representative interviews of journalists in Latin American countries are complicated, as already indicated, for different reasons. First, there is usually no possibility of limiting the professional group in a reliable manner. Journalism for some of them is by no means their exclusive occupation. Also, the members of this population cannot be easily defined. Even if, as in Chilé, the journalists union controls access to the profession, not everyone who exercises this profession is a member of it. In view of these circumstances, it is difficult to build a full-scale representative (random) sample for a survey. There are also practical difficulties when carrying out the survey. A refusal to answer must be expected, based on political apprehensions.

A somewhat constructed design is unavoidable under the circumstances mentioned, as is a greater effort in the interviews themselves, which has consequences for the number of interviewees. In the studies reported on here, 116 journalists were interviewed in Chilé (in 1992), 100 in Mexico (in 1991), and 146 in Ecuador (in 1991). Of course, these samples are limited but are large enough to go beyond describing individual traits to saying something about their social distribution. When selecting the interviewees, particular attention was paid to the inclusion of representatives from all media and a dispersion of demographic features. Besides, the procedure was "coincidentally guided" insofar as those journalists who just happened to be working in the editorial offices were asked to participate in the interviews. Strictly speaking, the manner of the sample composition restricts the possibility of generalization or at least it prompts caution. Nevertheless, the findings add to our knowledge of journalists in these three countries. In Mexico the journalists were interviewed face to face; in Chilé and Ecuador, they filled in the written questionnaires.

BACKGROUND

The interviews with the journalists were carried out in three Latin American countries that have certain similarities. Nevertheless, there are of course some differences between them such as their historical traditions, ethnic compositions, economics, constitutions, and media systems.

For a long time, Chilé was one of the most stable democracies in Latin America, but the country was not saved from growing tensions that arose from the contradiction between a democratic social pluralism and both economic and social underdevelopment (Wilke 1994). The political changes that the leftist socialist, Salvador Allende, introduced after being elected to president in 1970 met with a military insurgence that resulted in a 17-year authoritarian dictatorship. Since 1990, the country has been able to free itself from this repression and to find its way back to a democratic order, with the help of an economic recovery.

Consequently, the media system revived itself. In Chilé, there were 42 daily newspapers with a total circulation of about one million copies in the early 1990s. *El Mercurio* in Santiago was dominant among them. New political magazines in particular appeared in the wake of redemocratization. The country had another 550 radio stations and 6 television channels. Although the latter were almost exclusively commercially organized in groups, in television along with private property (*Megavisión* above all) there was a relatively strong state and university presence. The journalist's union Colegio de Periodistas, to which in principle each member of this profession must belong, has more than 3,000 members. Yet, the core of active journalists whose main professional activity is journalism is probably lower than that. In view of the predominant entertainment in radio and television, journalistic reporting on radio and television takes up limited space.

For three quarters of a century, the political development in Mexico was defined by a one-party regime. A mixture of control and authoritarianism on the one hand and a limited democracy on the other preserved the system's stability. However, inner crises have not been lacking. Certain economic developments have transformed Mexico into a threshold country as evidenced by the common free-trade agreement with the United States (NAFTA). In Mexico, which is the second largest country in Latin America in population, 259 newspapers with a circulation of approximately 10 million copies were published in the early 1990s (Longin 1992). In 1991, there were 925 radio and 368 television stations. Nearly all of these belonged to certain chains or groups. The majority of the television stations broadcast the programs of the media giant *Televisa* and to a lesser extent those of the state organization *Imevisión*. According to a study in 1980, at that time there were approximately 21,000 journalists in Mexico, two thirds in newspapers, one tenth in radio, and only 3% in television (Hernández 1984). With regard to the active, main-profession journalists, there are similarities with Chilé.

Compared to other Latin American countries, Ecuador was often considered to be a "peaceful island," but the appearance is deceptive. Since its founding, Ecuador has also been marked by political instability and social conflicts that result mainly from the ethnic heterogeneity of the population. The political instability that caused the country to live through more than 30 governments from 1930 to 1970 influenced the development of the mass media, which for a long time had to operate under emergency laws and censorship. Since 1979, Ecuador again has a democratically elected government that has been led alternatively by a more social democratic and (since 1992) by a conservative president. Since then, its neoliberal economic policy has brought many inner conflicts out into the open.

In Ecuador, with scarcely 12 million inhabitants, 36 daily newspapers with a total edition of approximately 700,000 copies were published in the early 1990s (Zwermann 1992). *El Universo* (Guayaquil) had the biggest circulation. The country had 334 radio stations and 14 television stations. Some church and state stations operated alongside a large number of private radio stations. In 1992, there were 32 radio chains. The majority of the television stations were privately owned. Up until 1992, *Telecentro* was the only station whose technology enabled it to broadcast throughout Ecuador. All journalists in the country were obliged to be members of a regional professional association, but these organizations had not been established in all parts of the country. According to unofficial information by the Federación Nacional de

Periodistas, the number of persons working in news editorials in Ecuador was about 1,400 in the early 1990s.

DEMOGRAPHIC AND BASIC PROFESSIONAL FEATURES

In all three countries, the majority of journalists concerned were young people. On average, the youngest were in Mexico, in which two fifths of the interviewees were less than 29 years old and between 30 and 39 years old. By comparison, the "oldest" journalists were in Ecuador with barely one third of the two previously mentioned age groups and with one third over 40 years old. In Chilé, barely one third were up to 29 and between 30 and 39 years old. Whereas in Chilé, three fifths of the interviewees were men and two fifths were women; both in Mexico and Ecuador, three quarters were men and one quarter were women.

The length of the activity in journalism was correlated with age. In Chilé 38% of the interviewees said that they had been working as journalists for only one to three years. This indicates a new access to the profession since the democratic transition began in the country. In Mexico 56% of the interviewees had worked up to 10 years in the journalism profession. In both countries hardly one third of the interviewees worked between 11 to 20 years as journalists. The share of journalists who had been working in this field for more than 20 years fell between 20% (Ecuador) and 13% (Mexico).

Although three thirds of the interviewees in Mexico expressly stated their desire to become journalists, in Chilé only one third said so, but one half said that it had been a long process. Although in Chilé two thirds of the interviewees began their careers as journalists, this was true of only every second person in Mexico. This suggested a strong self-recruitment in favor of journalism in Chilé. Accordingly, half of the interviewees in Mexico referred to themselves as amateurs, whereas in Chilé only one third did so. Although the Mexican journalists stated most frequently that they were formerly laborers, the large part of the Chiléan amateurs were formerly teachers or assigned teachers or sales persons. Likewise, scarcely one tenth were civil servants in Mexico. In Mexico more journalists than in Chilé formerly worked in other media. Comparative data about journalists in Ecuador were not collected.

An indicator of professionalism is to what extent journalism is the main occupation for the interviewees. In Chilé only 17% cited other activities, but in Ecuador 42% did so. The majority of the interviewees worked for the press, mainly for newspapers. Newspaper journalists were most frequently represented in the sample of Mexican journalists, whereas radio journalists were most frequent in the sample of

Ecuadorian journalists. The share of television journalists ranged between barely 10% (Mexico) and 20% (Chilé and Ecuador).

Almost half of the Mexican journalists stated that they were responsible for domestic politics. In Ecuador barely two fifths were, and in Chilé only one sixth was responsible for domestic politics. In Mexico those journalists responsible for external politics, economics, culture, and sports followed those covering domestic politics. In Ecuador scarcely one quarter of the journalists worked in cultural or local areas. In Chilé a relatively high share stated that they worked for several editorial departments. In Chilé the most frequently mentioned task was editing, whereas writing was most frequently mentioned in Mexico.

EDUCATION AND TRAINING

Clear differences existed between the countries with regard to the educational levels of journalists. In Mexico, although 72% of the interviewees attended a university, 55% did not leave with a degree. This was different in Chilé and Ecuador, in which between 80% and 90% of the journalists said they had a university degree. In Chilé 70% completed academic journalism training. These differences are related to different access regulations concerning the journalism occupation. In Mexico access was open and not tied to any conditions, so in principle everyone had the chance to become a journalist. However, by the early 1990s, there were twice as many training facilities as there were 10 years previous. The majority of them operated on a private basis. In Chilé (until 1980) and in Ecuador, access to journalism was tied to prerequisites that included appropriate training. These differences were related to attitudes about the profession: Although in Chilé 72% of the interviewees thought journalism could be learned just like other professions, and only 15% thought a natural talent was necessary, in Mexico half adopted each position.

ATTRACTION TO JOURNALISM

What makes journalism attractive? In Chilé and Mexico the interviewees were presented with 17 options and agreed on more than one. Table 22.1 shows the results.

The findings indicate that journalists in Mexico were more likely to be attracted to journalism than those in Chilé by possible political influence, although the direct influence on political decisions plays a lesser role in both countries. However, the engagement for values and ideals, the

Table 22.1. Attraction to Journalism.

Question: "Which of these points do you find particularly attractive about your profession today?"

	Mexico (N = 100) (%)	Chilé (N = 116) (%)
The possibility to write, to phrase	76	60
The possibility to engage oneself for ideals and values	67	44
That there is little routine	57	76
The possibility of unfolding abuses and of criticizing	57	41
The varied, exciting element of this profession	54	49
The possibility of communicating knowledge to other people and broadening their horizons	52	64
The possibility of becoming acquainted with other people	45	43
The professional freedom of being able to decide one's own tasks and topics	44	45
To be one of the first to know what is really happening	38	30
Because it is fun to see one's name and work in print	32	11
The interesting people with whom one works, the colleagues	32	4
The possibility of influencing political decisions	26	19
Working under deadline pressure	12	12
The good future prospects	12	4
Good earning possibilities	7	2
The prestige of the profession	5	3

possibility of unfolding abuses and spreading one's own convictions are of stronger value in Mexico than in Chilé. The chance to write is uppermost in Mexico, whereas to Chilean journalists communicating knowledge was more important than to Mexican journalists, but even more important is the fact that there is little routine in this profession. In both countries a little less than half of the journalists found becoming acquainted with interesting people attractive or having professional freedom to determine one's own tasks and topics. All other reasons were mentioned considerably less frequently. Only very few were attracted by future prospects in journalism, profitable earning possibilities, or prestige. It was noticeable that working with colleagues (i.e., the professional socialization component) had far less attraction in Chilé than it had in Mexico.

The journalists were also asked directly about their role conceptions (i.e., how the tasks of this profession should be seen). Table 22.2 suggests that journalists in Mexico conceived of their profession as more active and more adversary than those in Chilé, although the journalists in Chilé were in favor of criticizing abuses. However, the other advocate-like motives were less dominant in Chilé. On the contrary, Chilean journalists were more likely to see themselves as neutral reporters and entertainers of the public. In Mexico the role of the journalist as an educator was chosen least frequently. In Chilé it was chosen with the same frequency but more often than some advocate-like orientations.

Table 22.2. Role Conceptions of Journalists.

Question: "In your opinion, how should a journalist conceive his task. As what should one see oneself as a journalist?"

	Mexico (N = 100) (%)	Chilé (N = 116) (%)
Critics of abuses	83	64
Communicator of new ideas	76	59
Watchdog of democracy	58	31
Population's mouthpiece	57	23
Someone who helps people	57	16
Neutral reporter	55	61
Lawyer of the underprivileged	35	13
Someone who should entertain	31	50
Politicians with other means	30	5
Educator	27	27

The opinions about the mass media as a "fourth estate" are in contrast to these trends. In Chilé 65% of the journalists questioned found this term justified, and 25% thought it unjustified; in Mexico 54% found it justified and 43% not so. The Mexican journalists may possibly have been responding to the actual rather than the normative role of the mass media in their country. More likely (and other survey results speak in favor of this), the journalists in Mexico were more dependent on other powers than in Chilé. The justification of the mass media as a "fourth estate" was much stronger, however, in Ecuador in which more than four fifths of the journalists agreed with this opinion. They saw the journalist more as a "watchdog" and less as a neutral reporter than in the other countries.

Journalists in Ecuador were also asked questions about other functions of mass media. More than 80% of the interviewees thought that one of the important tasks of the media in their country was educating and instructing the population. This and other answers speak in favor of a "developmental journalism" orientation. Yet political control functions—"discussing social problems" (79%) and "examining government contentions" (73%)—were mentioned second and third. However, two thirds thought it was their task to report about problems of people in the countryside (69%), to discuss disastrous development politics (64%), or to deal with other developing countries (64%). The option of supporting the government with development programs received the least consensus (25%), and fewer than half the journalists wanted to interfere with "national politics when they are emerging." Tasks of a more propagandistic nature such as "bringing national solidarity to the force" (59%) received a moderate rating as well as "portraying the future in a positive light in order to motivate people" (56%) and "mobilizing the population for development" (55%). The function of "supporting traditional values and customs" received little support (35%).

What influence do the media have on public opinion? This question was posed in a twofold manner. First, the respondents were asked to assess the actual influence of the mass media on public opinion in their countries and then the influence they thought it should have. An 11-point scale functioned as a measuring instrument, as Table 22 .3 indicates.

In general, there was a tendency to credit the mass media with a greater rather than lesser influence on public opinion regardless of the version of the question posed. Yet in the opinion of Mexican journalists, the mass media should exercise a greater influence on public opinion than they supposedly had. This was true also for Ecuador. In Chilé it was the opposite case—the mass media should have less influence on public opinion than they actually were thought to have. In both countries, the differences in average scores were not large.

Table 22.3. Perceived Influence of the Mass Media on Public Opinion.

Question: "How large do you rate the influence of journalists on the formation of public opinion?"
Question: "How large do you think the influence on the formation of public opinion should be?"

Rating between	Actual Influence Mexico (N = 100) (%)	Actual Influence Chilé (N = 116) (%)	Desired Influence Mexico (N = 100) (%)	Desired Influence Chilé (N = 116) (%)
0, no influence	-	1	-	2
1	-	1	-	-
2	2	-	-	1
3	4	1	-	4
4	10	4	2	2
5	15	7	22	30
6	14	11	7	12
7	17	22	12	13
8	20	32	21	15
9	10	13	18	9
10, very large influence	7	10	23	11
Average	6.54	7.48	7.44	6.46

OUTER AND INNER FREEDOM OF THE PRESS

In the early 1990s, freedom of the press existed in principle in all three countries concerned. At least, the constitutions had such directions, although press laws or other legal measures (e.g., for "national security") restricted freedom of the press in different ways. As far as redemocratization processes have taken place, initiatives have been taken to replace limits on press freedom with new, liberal rules. Nevertheless, the relationship between the state and the media in Latin America has been tense and subject to intervention, at least in times of crises. The scope for free journalistic affirmation has been constantly subject to change.

Journalists in Mexico and Chilé answered the question of whether freedom of the press is endangered very differently. Most Mexican journalists confirmed it (77%), and few denied it (18%), whereas in Chilé it was 40% and 48%, respectively. Although people had been released from the clutch of the Pinochet dictatorship for only a few years, half the Chiléan journalists did not consider freedom of the press to be endangered in their country. Obviously, there was a lot of trust in the political stability achieved by the early 1990s. In Mexico this was lacking to a far greater extent, although there were no comparable dictatorial circumstances there in the last few decades as there were in Chilé. However, this cannot be equated with a generally practiced democracy.

Those journalists who spoke of a threat to the freedom of the press in their country were asked from whom this threat came. In Mexico two thirds of the interviewees named the government or political institutions. In Chilé these were named by only 26%. However, in Chilé 45% named the military. In both countries, for two fifths of the journalists, dangers for freedom of the press lay in the economic interests of media enterprises and, for one third, from the economy in general. Other sources of danger (e.g., transnational enterprises, unions) were named only rarely. Journalists in Ecuador were asked about dangers for the freedom of the press in their country with slightly varying options. Here, the majority (72%) referred to economic interests of media enterprises, more than to bureaucracy and authorities (68%) or governments and political institutions (57%).

The journalists in Mexico and Chilé were also asked about the extent of their editorial freedom. In Mexico 11% said that they could "always" realize their own suggestions for topics, and in Chilé 15% said the same. In Mexico, 70% said that they could "nearly always" do so, and in Chilé 78% of the interviewees said the same. If the statements of the journalists are to be believed, then they obviously have quite a considerable scope of freedom, even more so in Chilé than in Mexico, in which 19% of them said that they could only "sometimes" realize their suggestions. Perhaps some of the dreaded threats to the freedom of the press were felt more strongly there. However, these fears may seem exaggerated to outsiders when four fifths of the interviewees can "always" or "nearly always" realize their suggestions for topics. Nonetheless, one could argue that journalistic suggestions were "clipped," or self-censored. Thus, only suggestions that could be implemented might be made.

For the possibility of choosing topics freely in journalism, it may be meaningful to determine whether journalists' political opinions correspond with those of the medium in which they work. To investigate this relationship, the journalists in Chilé and Mexico were asked to rate their own political attitude and then that of their editorial on an 11-point scale between "far left" and "far right." Table 22.4 shows the results of this rating.

Relatively speaking, although the greater number of journalists in Mexico and Chilé position themselves and their news medium in the center, it is noticeable that in both countries more journalists rated them-

Table 22.4. Own Political Opinion and Political Line of News Medium.

Question: "Media are sometimes categorized according to whether they are politically right, left, or center. Here is a scale from right to left. Where would you place: (a) the basic line of your editorial and (b) yourself on this scale?"

	Mexico (N = 100)		Chilé (N = 116)	
	Own Opinion	That of the Editorial	Own Opinion	That of the Editorial
0, far left	2	1	1	-
1	2	3	3	-
2	8	3	6	2
3	15	11	16	7
4	24	10	20	19
5, center	38	43	26	38
6	2	7	9	11
7	2	10	11	9
8	2	2	4	9
9	-	4	3	1
10, far right	4	4	1	4
Average	4.3	5.0	4.7	5.4

selves more left than right of the center (51 vs. 10 in Mexico and 46 vs. 28 in Chilé). More journalists in Chilé than in Mexico rated themselves right of the center (almost three times as many). The perceived editorial position of their news medium corresponds in both countries, although it is more centrist and more right than one's own opinion. In Chilé the position seemed to shift even more to the right than in Mexico. The differences between one's own editorial rating and between the countries are expressed in average values, although they hide some differences.

ACQUIRING INFORMATION AND REPORTING METHODS

Acquiring information in order to publish it is the prime task of journalists. The information cannot always be acquired to the extent desired, and often it is consciously withheld. The permissible means of acquiring information comprise a central question in the procedures and professional ethics of journalists. Therefore, this issue was included in the surveys in Mexico and Chilé. Table 22.5 shows how journalists in these countries rated different methods of gathering information.

The methods to gain information proposed in the survey were rejected for the most part by the journalists, but with varying unity. In Mexico, only one of the nine methods proposed was considered acceptable by a majority of journalists—the use of secret government documents. In Chilé, on the contrary, three methods were agreed to by a majority—using secret state papers, pretending to have a certain opinion to arouse confidence, and putting an informant under pressure. The greatest difference between the two countries was on this method, with Chilean journalists much more likely to consider pressuring informants acceptable, perhaps indicating a cultural difference between the countries. On the whole, the other methods were not approved. The journalists refused most decidedly to break their professional secrecy. The protection of informants appears to be the "toughest" professional norm, consistent with findings from surveys of journalists in other countries. The unexamined acceptance of information, as well as publishing private papers without permission, were also rejected by three quarters or more of the respondents. Obviously, the protection of private secrets is approved more than that of state secrets. Other reporting methods were rejected by scarcely one half to two thirds of the journalists (e.g., paying for documents and infiltrating an organization under cover in order to gain information). Although the Mexican journalists have diverging opinions on presuming a false identity to gain information, three quarters of Chiléan journalists do not consider this method to be acceptable.

Another question reinforces how seriously journalists in Mexico and Chilé (and probably elsewhere in Latin America) take the protection of informants. "A journalist," so the question goes, "has an appointment for an interview with a worldwide wanted member of a terrorist organization. What should the journalist do: Tip the police off or protect his informant?" Only 1 of 100 journalists in Mexico and 3 of 116 in Chilé said that the police should be informed. Conversely, 91 in Mexico and 86 in Chilé would not betray the interview partner to the police. The remainder were undecided or did not want to answer the question. The fact that journalists in these Latin America countries were less willing than German journalists (Köcher 1985) to name the terrorists probably had to do with their political experiences under a dictatorship and repression. Although almost all the Chiléan journalists assumed throughout that most other journalists in their country would behave likewise, in Mexico far fewer were convinced of this. Here, more than 10% believed that the identity of the interview partner would be disclosed, and one third were at least unsure of their colleagues' behavior.

Table 22.5. Assessment of Various Methods of Gaining Information.

Question: "Seeing as it is often difficult to gain important information, journalists use unwanted methods. Which of the following methods do you consider acceptable and which do you disapprove of totally?"

	Mexico (N = 100)			Chile (N = 116)		
	Yes (%)	No (%)	Don't know (%)	Yes (%)	No (%)	Don't know (%)
Using secret government documents	64	26	10	53	27	15
Giving false identity	45	44	11	22	73	2
Paying for documents	38	45	17	39	51	8
Pretending to have a certain opinion to arouse confidence	36	55	9	58	32	8
Forcibly entering an organization to get information	23	64	13	20	67	9
Pressuring informant	21	67	10	76	21	4
Publishing private papers without consent	13	78	9	14	73	11
Agreeing to (professional) secrecy, but then disclosing	5	91	4	2	97	-
Using unexamined information	4	90	6	10	79	7
Average	27.7	62.2	9.9	33.3	55.8	7.3

IMAGE OF THE AUDIENCE

What image do journalists in Mexico and Chilé have of their audience? This question, too, has a tradition in journalism research in which often a negatively shaded picture of the audience was observed (de Sola Pool and Shulman 1964; Donsbach 1981; Köcher 1985). However, this was not the case in these surveys.

Table 22.6 shows that most of Mexican and Chiléan journalists credited their audiences with positive characteristics, although the measures differed in places. The majority of journalists in both countries considered their audiences to be well informed and critical. However, the list of negative characteristics was rarely mentioned by the journalists themselves. That only one third (in both countries) considered the audience to be progressive may be evidence of the most criticism of the audience. Journalists in Chilé seemed to be more critical of their audience than those in Mexico. Fewer journalists in Chilé thought that their audiences participated in politics, and more thought audiences to be indifferent and greedier for sensations. However, Chilean journalists were more likely to think of their audiences as tolerant than were Mexican journalists.

Table 22.6. Journalists' Image of Their Audience.

Question: "If you think of the audience for whom you work, which characteristics apply?"

	Mexico (N = 100) (%)	Chilé (N = 116) (%)
Well informed	76	69
Partake politically	72	40
Critical	62	65
Open	48	41
Progressive	35	34
Tolerant	21	34
Easily influenced	10	17
Superficial, indifferent	6	22
Hungry for sensations	5	15
Reserved	3	13
Ignorant	2	8

CRITICISM OF PROFESSION, PRESTIGE, AND PROFESSIONAL SATISFACTION

The journalists in Mexico and Chilé were also asked what they criticized about their profession, that is, what bothered them and which aspects they found negative. On the one hand, standardized options were given. On the other hand, they were free to answer the question as they wished. This led to the results in Table 22.7.

All in all, the listed points of criticism were affirmed more in Chilé than in Mexico. The main criticism was not being really able to get the bottom of something. The danger of being misused scored second. Time pressure as well as the daily actuality were considered bothersome by fewer journalists, especially in Mexico. In addition to this list of professional aspects, three quarters of Chiléan journalists complained that they had the worst earnings and one half that they had the most irregular working hours. The journalists in Ecuador also complained of poor financial compensation. Only 13% of journalists in Mexico said likewise (on

Table 22.7. Negative Aspects of the Journalism Profession.

Question: "Here is a list of things that could bother you about journalism. Which of them especially bothers you personally?"

	Mexico (N = 100) (%)	Chilé (N = 116) (%)
That one cannot get to the bottom of any single thing	67	81
The danger of being used for the interests of an individual or a group	50	67
The mistrust that many people have of journalists	44	60
Being burdened with work that does not belong to the real work of a journalist	40	50
The time pressure under which one works	33	50
That one must often report about things without having any real background understanding of them	25	53
That daily actuality determines one's tasks	13	22
Criticism from the audience	4	33

their own initiative). However, Mexican journalists criticized other non-professional aspects, above all the danger of corruption. To the open-ended question, journalists in Chilé replied more self-critically (e.g., about professional ethics and ways of working than about the media themselves or other external powers).

How do journalists judge the respect and the reputation of journalists in general in their societies? Table 22.8 contains the responses of journalists in Mexico and Chilé to the question of perceived reputation.

Journalists in Chilé rated their reputation a bit better than those in Mexico. Two fifths perceived it as "satisfactory" and one fifth as "good." In contrast, half the journalists in Mexico thought that the reputation of journalism is "not particularly good" or even "bad" in their country. In Chilé two fifths said likewise. As in other countries, the journalism profession occupied a central position on the scale of professional prestige in these Latin American countries.

Does the criticism of journalism and its social reputation affect the professional satisfaction of journalists? Journalists from all three countries were asked about the degree of satisfaction with their profession. Table 22.9 shows their responses.

Mexican journalists rated the social reputation of their profession and themselves somewhat lower than their Chilean colleagues, but two thirds of the Mexican journalists said that they were completely satisfied with their profession. In Chilé fewer said so, but still more than half agreed. Of the three countries, the journalists in Ecuador were the least satisfied. Three quarters there said that they were not quite satisfied, and only one fifth were completely so. It should be kept in mind that the

Table 22.8. Perceived Reputation of Journalists.

Question: "In your opinion, how is the reputation of journalists in Mexico and Chilé?"

	Mexico (N = 100) (%)	Chilé (N = 116) (%)
Very good	1	3
Good	19	19
Satisfactory	29	39
Not particularly good	36	28
Bad	15	11
Total	100	100

Table 22.9. Journalists' Professional Satisfaction.

Question: "Are you completely satisfied with your profession as a journalist or not quite satisfied?"

	Ecuador (N = 146) (%)	Mexico (N = 100) (%)	Chilé (N = 116) (%)
Completely	22	67	54
Not quite	78	33	40
Undecided/Don't know/ No answer	-	-	6
Total	100	100	100

Ecuadorian journalists saw themselves most affected by the economic interests of media enterprises. In Chilé three quarters of the interviewees would opt for the journalism profession if they had to choose again. This, on its own, is also a good indicator of high professional satisfaction. Obviously, financial deficits are compensated by other gratifications.

SUMMARY AND CONCLUSIONS

The results of the surveys reported here are only a first approach to empirical, comparative interviews of journalists in Latin American countries. They can hardly do more than indicate certain tendencies that necessitate further examination, verification, or differentiation. As shown, the results do not form a coherent pattern; rather, they show certain discrepancies. However, the role of journalists and their role conceptions in other countries are not completely free of tension either. Although one is confronted with certain similarities between the countries examined, there are also some notable differences. The situation of journalists in Ecuador seems to be the most problematic; but the least data are available about this country to date. In Mexico and Chilé one is confronted with a mixture of positive and negative aspects. All in all, outsiders receive a better picture of journalism and its possibilities in these countries than expressed in some previous writings. Finally, some of the results can be put, in parts, in an even greater comparative context, whereby Mexico and Chilé would not come off badly. In certain ways the journalists there resemble those in more industrial countries, but they are distinguishable from them in other characteristics.

REFERENCES

Donsbach, Wolfgang. (1981). Journalisten zwischen Publikum und Kollegen [Journalists between their audience and colleagues]. *Rundfunk und Fernsehen* 29: 168-184.

Donsbach, Wolfgang and Thomas E. Patterson. 1992, May. *Journalist's roles and newsroom practices: A cross-national comparison.* Paper presented to the Conference of the International Communication Association, Miami, FL.

Donsbach, Wolfgang and Bettina Klett. 1993. Subjective objectivity: How journalists in four countries define a key term of their profession. *Gazette* 39: 53-83.

Goehringer, Sandra. 1992. *Journalismus und Journalistenberuf in Mexiko* [Journalism and the journalism profession in Mexico]. Master's thesis, Johannes Gutenberg-Universität Mainz.

Hernández, Rogelio. 1984. Desde la perspectiva de un reportero [Seen from a reporter's perspective]. In *Manuel Buendía: El oficio de informar*, p. 3. México: Fundación Manuel Buendía.

Köcher, Renate. 1985. *Spürhund und Missionar. Eine vergleichende Untersuchung über Berufsethik und Aufgabenverständnis britischer und deutscher Journalisten* [Bloodhound or missionaries: A comparative analysis of professionals' self-conceptions and ethics of journalists]. PhD Dissertation, Ludwig Maximilians Universität München.

McLeod, Jack M. and Ramona R. Rush. 1969a. Professionalization of Latin American journalists. Part I. *Journalism Quarterly* 46: 583-590.

McLeod, Jack M. and Ramona R. Rush. 1969b. Professionalization of Latin American journalists. Part II. *Journalism Quarterly* 46: 784-789.

Longin, Christine. 1992. Massenmedien in Mexiko [The mass media in Mexico]. In *Massenmedien in Lateinamerika*, Vol. 1, edited by Jürgen Wilke, pp. 267-312. Frankfurt am Main: Vervuert.

Rehbein González, Marcia. 1994. *Journalismus und Journalistenberuf in Chile* [Journalism and the journalism profession in Chilé]. Master's thesis Johannes Gutenberg-Universität, Mainz, Germany.

Sola Pool de, Ithiel and Irwin Shulman. 1964. Newsmen's fantasies, audiences and newswriting. In *People, society, and mass communication*, edited by Lewis A. Dexter and David M. White, pp. 141-159. London: Free Press of Glencoe/Collier-Macmillan.

Weaver, David and G. Cleveland Wilhoit. 1986. *The American journalist: A portrait of U. S. news people and their work.* Bloomington: Indiana University Press.

Wilke, Jürgen, ed. 1992. *Massenmedien in Lateinamerika. Vol. 1: Argentinien, Brasilien, Guatemala, Kolumbien* [Mass media in Latin American, Vol. 1: Argentina, Brazil, Guatemala, Columbia]. Frankfurt am Main: Vervuert.

Wilke, Jürgen, ed. 1994. *Massenmedien in Lateinamerika. Vol. 2: Chile, Costa Rica, Ecuador, Paraguay.* [Mass media in Latin American, Vol. 2: Chilé, Costa Rica, Ecuador, Paraguay]. Frankfurt am Main.: Vervuert.

Wilke, Jürgen, ed. 1996. *Massenmedien in Lateinamerika. Vol. 3: Bolivien, Nicaragua, Peru, Uruguay, Venezuela* [Mass media in Latin American, Vol. 3: Bolivia, Nicaragua, Peru, Uruguay, Venezuela]. Frankfurt am Main: Vervuert.

Zwermann, Beate. 1992. *Politische Rolle und berufliches Selbstverständnis des ecuadorianischen Journalismus* [The political role and professional self-conception of journalists in Ecuador]. Master's thesis, Johannes Gutenberg-Universität, Mainz, Germany.

CONCLUSION

23

Journalists Around the World: Commonalities and Differences

David Weaver
Indiana University

Comparing journalists across national boundaries and cultures is a game of guesswork at best. There are so many characteristics, attitudes, and behaviors that could be said to depend on the specific situation that some would argue against any attempt to look for more general patterns and trends. Yet there are also similarities that seem to cut across the boundaries of geography, culture, language, society, religion, race, and ethnicity. Not all journalistic (or human) experience is unique to a particular time and place.

Keeping in mind that many of the comparisons here are rough and post hoc, rather than carefully preplanned and controlled, this chapter attempts to look for similarities and differences in the basic characteristics, working conditions, and professional values of journalists from the 21 countries and territories represented in this book.

This task is made easier by the fact that many of the studies reported in these pages have borrowed questions from our original questionnaire (Weaver and Wilhoit 1986, 1996), which was modeled on a 1971 study of U.S. journalists conducted by sociologists at the University of Illinois at Chicago (Johnstone, Slawski, and Bowman 1976). However, some of the surveys employ their own questions and measures, or modify the original wordings somewhat. There is, in addition, always the slippage in meaning involved in translating from one language to another.

The point of trying to draw comparisons of journalists in these different areas of the world is the hope of identifying some similarities and differences that may give us a more accurate picture of where journalists come from, how they think about their work, and whether they are becoming more professional as we prepare to leave the 20th century behind and begin a new century and millennium. The major assumption is that journalists' backgrounds and ideas have some relationship to what is reported (and how it is covered) in the various news media around the world, in spite of various constraints, and that this news coverage matters in terms of world public opinion and policies.

BACKGROUNDS AND DEMOGRAPHIC PROFILES

In our latest study of U.S. journalists, conducted during the summer of 1992, we concluded that the statistical "profile" of the typical U.S. journalist in 1992 was much like that of 1982-83: a White Protestant male with a four-year bachelor's degree, married, and in his 30s (Weaver and Wilhoit 1996). However, there were some changes from the early 1980s—an increase of four years in median age to 36, more minorities, and more journalists earning college degrees, but no increase in those majoring in journalism in college (about 40%).

This demographic profile of U.S. journalists is similar in some ways to the profiles of journalists in other areas of the world, but there are some notable differences as well.

Gender

For example, men were more typical than women in newsrooms in all 19 countries or territories reporting gender proportions (see Table 23.1), although in some countries women were almost as numerous as men (New Zealand and Finland), whereas in others women lagged far behind (Korea, Algeria, Britain, and Spain). The average proportion of women journalists across these 19 countries and territories was one third (33%), almost exactly the proportion in the United States (34%).

Age

Another similarity between the United States and the rest of the world as represented here is that journalism is a young person's occupation, with

Table 23.1. Basic Characteristics of Journalists.

	Average Age	Female (%)	Total No. of Journalists	Married (%)	Minorities (%)	Holding College Degree (%)[a]	Majoring in Journalism (%)
I. Asia/Far East							
China	35	33	86,600	—[b]	11	47	32
Hong Kong	30	35	1,381+	41	—	78	48
Korea	37	14	40,900	—	0	94	14
Taiwan	36	38	5,500	—	1	60	32
II. Australia/Pacific							
Australia	32	33	4,500	—	—	35	33
New Zealand	—	45	1,738	—	5	44	—
Pacific Islands	—	36	—	—	Mixture	48	37
III. Europe							
Britain	38	25	15,175	71	2	49	4
Finland	40	49	8,000	—	—	40	25
France	—	—	—	—	—	—	—
Germany	35	41	36,000	46	—	65	—
Hungary	—	33	8,870	—	—	68	35
Poland	—	—	—	—	—	—	—
Spain	36	25	—	—	—	84	87[c]

Journalists Around the World 457

Table 23.1. Basic Characteristics of Journalists (con't.).

	Average Age	Female (%)	Total No. of Journalists	Married (%)	Minorities (%)	Holding College Degree[a] (%)	Majoring in Journalism (%)
IV. North Africa							
Algeria	30	24	800	33	—	79	41
V. North America							
Canada	40	28	12,000	—	3	54	—
United States	36	34	122,015	59	8	82	39
VI. South/Central America							
Brazil	—	42	—	—	8	—	84
Chile	—	40	3,000[c]	—	—	80-90	70
Ecuador	—	25	1,400	—	—	80-90	—
Mexico	—	25	21,000+	—	—	32	—

[a]Including four-year degree or higher.
[b]Not available from these studies.
[c]Including 1- to 3-year journalism programs.

most journalists between 25 and 44 years old. The average age of journalists ranges from 30 to 40 in the dozen places reporting it, with the youngest journalists coming from Hong Kong and Algeria, where the average age is 30, and the oldest living in Canada and Finland, where it is 40.

In most places, journalists are younger on average (35 years old) than is the workforce in general. In Chapter 3, Chan, Lee, and Lee argue that in Hong Kong many young people become journalists to earn some experience before deserting for more lucrative and stable jobs in other fields, especially public relations. This seems to be a fairly common pattern around the world.

Education

Although most journalists in the United States hold a four-year college degree, this is not the case in a number of countries, as Table 23.1 indicates. The countries with the lowest proportions of college graduate journalists are Australia, Finland, and Mexico—all well below one half. Those with the highest are Korea, Spain, and the United States, with Chile and Ecuador nearly as high. Eleven of 18 countries or territories report more than one half of their journalists holding a four-year college degree, so it is more common than not for journalists to be college graduates in this group, but the variation is substantial.

It is not typical, however, for journalists to be graduates of journalism programs in college. Only three countries reported more than half of their journalists had concentrated on journalism in college—Spain, Brazil, and Chile. In the other 11 countries or territories reporting this proportion, most did not exceed 40%, with the lowest figure from Britain (4%) and more typical figures hovering in the 30s.

Thus, whatever journalistic benefits or evils are attributed to journalism education must be tempered by the fact that most journalists are not graduates of college-level journalism programs in this sample of countries and territories. In fact, the average percentage among the 14 reporting was 41.5. Without including the extremes of Spain, Brazil, Chile, and Britain, it was one third, a bit under the U.S. percentage of 39.

Marital Status

Only five countries and territories reported the proportion of journalists who were married, and Table 23.1 indicates a fairly wide range—from one third in Algeria to nearly three fourths in Britain. Thus, it is not possible to draw any general conclusions about whether journalists tend to be married or not. Only two of the five reported figures are above one half, making it dubious to conclude, as in the United States, that the typical journalist tends to be married.

Race and Ethnicity

Less than half of the countries and territories represented in this study reported a figure for racial and ethnic minority journalists. Table 23.1 shows that the reported figures are small at best, ranging from 1% to 11% and reinforcing the conclusion of the 1971 U.S. study by Johnstone et al. (1976) that journalists come predominantly from the established and dominant cultural groups in society. This seems to hold true especially in Taiwan, Britain, and Canada and somewhat less so in Brazil, China, and the United States.

Size of Workforce

The estimated number of journalists working in the 16 different countries and territories reporting this figure varies tremendously, as one would expect given the great differences in the sizes and populations of these places (see Table 23.1). The two largest countries, China and the United States, have the most journalists, but it is striking that the United States has nearly one and a half times as many full-time journalists as does China, even though the U.S. population is only one fourth of that of China. It is also surprising that Korea has so many more journalists than Taiwan, Britain or Canada.

Some of these differences are undoubtedly due to different methods of estimating the total number of journalists, and some may reflect different definitions of who qualifies as a journalist. It does seem that those countries most advanced economically and most democratic politically tend to have larger numbers of journalists as compared to the population.

Thus, in terms of demographics, journalists from the various countries and territories were similar in average age and proportion of minorities, but varied considerably in gender, level of education, and whether they majored in journalism. They also varied substantially in marital status and in representation based on population.

WORKING CONDITIONS

Obviously the working conditions of journalists also differ widely in the 21 countries and territories represented in this book, not only in terms of material resources but also in professional autonomy, political pressures, and traditions of journalism that affect the subjects and approaches taken in reporting the news of the day. One of the most important indicators of the working conditions of journalists is their level of job satisfaction, which in many cases is linked to their perceived autonomy or freedom. In the United States, for example, declining levels of job satisfaction and perceived autonomy have gone hand in hand since the early 1970s (Weaver and Wilhoit 1996).

Job Satisfaction

The proportions of journalists considering themselves "very satisfied" with their jobs varies greatly among the 14 countries and territories that reported this attitude, as indicated in Table 23.2. Those countries or territories with the smallest percentages of very satisfied journalists were Hong Kong, Taiwan, and Algeria, with China and Brazil not far behind; those with the largest were Chile and Mexico. The average for the 14 reported figures was 25% very satisfied, just below the U.S. figure of 27%.

Perceived Autonomy

The leftmost column in Table 23.2 suggests that the proportions of journalists perceiving a great deal of freedom are related to the proportions claiming to be very satisfied. The lowest percentages for perceived autonomy are generally found for those countries or territories with the lowest job satisfaction percentages—Hong Kong, Taiwan, and China. This is not the case in Algeria, however, suggesting that other factors there contributed to lower levels of job satisfaction, such as housing shortages and scarce resources and, more recently, political terrorism.

In the case of the least satisfied journalists, Table 23.3 suggests other factors in addition to perceived autonomy. In China perceived freedom (or lack of it) was the leading predictor, but in Hong Kong dissatisfaction with pay was most prominent, followed by limited chances for creativity and learning. In Taiwan perceived freedom was the leading predictor of job satisfaction, followed by journalists' ratings of how well their news organization performed, salary and type of medium. In Brazil relationships with co-workers and comments from colleagues in other media were the most important predictors of job satisfaction. In Korea, which was below average in job satisfaction, supervisor's comments, pay, and job security were the main predictors of job satisfaction.

In the United States predictors of job satisfaction varied by age, with younger journalists more likely to emphasize freedom to choose stories to report and the performance of their news organizations in informing the public. Older U.S. journalists, however, stressed salary and the chance to advance—the tangible rewards of the job, as opposed to the more intangible ones favored by younger, more idealistic journalists.

Table 23.2. Working Conditions/Job Satisfaction.

	Perceived Autonomy (% saying a great deal/very satisfied)	Job Satisfaction (% saying very satisfied)	Commitment to Journalism (% saying they want to stay in journalism)
I. Asia/Far East			
China	8	10	57
Hong Kong	6	4	—[a]
Korea	22	17	—
Taiwan	6	6	71
II. Australia/Pacific			
Australia	—	29	—
New Zealand	—	—	82[b]
Pacific Islands	—	—	—
III. Europe			
Britain	10	33	40
Finland	81	19	47
France	—	—	—
Germany	—	—	—
Hungary	45	—	60
Poland	—	—	—
Spain	—	—	—
IV. North Africa			
Algeria	41	7	—
V. North America			
Canada	88	38	82
United States	85	27	78
VI. South/Central America			
Brazil	—	12	67
Chile	—	54[c]	—
Ecuador	—	22[c]	—
Mexico	—	67[c]	—

[a]Indicating data not available in these studies.
[b]This percentage was derived from the fact that 18% of journalists in the study indicated that they wanted to leave the field.
[c]Percentage saying they were "completely satisfied" with their profession as a journalist.

Table 23.3. Ranking of Predictors of Job Satisfaction.

China	1. Job autonomy
Hong Kong	1. Satisfaction with pay 2. Chance for creativity 3. Chance to learn 4. Gender (males more satisfied)
Korea	1. Supervisor's comments 2. Pay 3. Job security 4. Chance to serve social justice
Taiwan	1. Perceived autonomy 2. Rating of performance of the organization 3. Salary (pay) 4. Type of medium (daily newspaper, radio, TV)
Brazil	1. Co-worker's influence in news production 2. Comments from colleagues of other media 3. Don't know where will work in three years (-) 4. Pay
United States: Age 40 or Younger	1. Autonomy of story choice 2. Rating of performance of the organization 3. Supervisor's comments 4. Importance of pay (-)
Over 40	1. Actual Pay 2. Chance to advance (-) 3. Audience's comments 4. Supervisor's comments

Another indicator of job satisfaction among journalists is their commitment to the occupation. Table 23.2 shows that the greatest commitment was among journalists in Canada and New Zealand, where 82% said they planned to stay in journalism, followed closely by the United States, where 78% said so. The least commitment was found among journalists in Britain and Finland, where less than half said they wanted to continue working in journalism.

In contrast to the great differences in perceived autonomy and job satisfaction levels, the proportions saying they wanted to remain working as journalists did not vary as widely, and they did not seem to be systematically related to levels of perceived autonomy or job satisfaction, as Table 23.2 indicates. Apparently journalists have other reasons for wanting to stay in journalism besides perceived freedom and job satisfaction. One key consideration is likely to be the attractiveness of alternative jobs, in terms of pay, fringe benefits, privileges, and opportunities for advancement.

PROFESSIONAL VALUES

In *Journalists for the 21st Century*, based on surveys of about 1,800 first-year journalism students in 22 different countries in 1987-1988, Slavko Splichal and Colin Sparks (1994) argue that even though there is no strict definition of journalism as yet, the occupation seems to be moving from craft to profession (although not yet a true profession) because of changes in the education and specialist knowledge of journalists and an emphasis on autonomy and professional ethics.

The conclusion that journalists are not yet a true profession is similar to that by Cleveland Wilhoit and myself. We wrote at the end of our first U.S. journalist book (1986: 167) that "American journalists are unlikely ever to assume a formal professional status" because of their skepticism of institutional forms of professionalism such as certification or licensing, membership in organizations and readership of professional publications.

Looking across 22 countries, Splichal and Sparks (1994) noted in Chapter 5 that their initial hypothesis was that similarities across countries should prevail if journalism is really becoming a profession. They concluded in their last chapter that their major finding was a striking similarity in the desire of journalism students' for the independence and autonomy of journalism. In addition, they did not find evidence that journalism education and professional socialization were necessarily a function of politics or dominant ideology.

Based on these findings, they argued that some universal ethical and occupational standards were emerging in journalism, but this conclusion seems to contradict the differences in ethical reporting standards found in surveys of journalists in Britain, Germany, and the United States, and it may reflect the lack of specific questions about journalism roles, reporting practices, or ethical dilemmas in the Splichal-Sparks questionnaire more than the emergence of universal ethical and occupational standards in journalism.

There may be a fairly universal desire for more freedom among journalists in various parts of the world, although our findings on the importance of this job aspect are mixed, but that does not necessarily signal the emergence of any universal standards in journalism, nor is it necessarily anything new. A look at more specific professional roles or values, as well as reporting practices, may help to more precisely define the areas of agreement and disagreement among the 20,000 journalists of the world represented in this book.

Roles

In our latest study of U.S. journalists (conducted in the summer of 1992), we found, for the most part, that their perceptions of the roles of the news media were broadly similar to those a decade ago (Weaver and Wilhoit 1996). A majority of U.S. journalists tended to see two responsibilities as extremely important: getting information to the public quickly, and investigating government claims.

Among the 12 countries or territories reporting on the role of getting information to the public quickly, there was also considerable agreement. In most cases, as Table 23.4 indicates, two thirds or more agreed that it was very important, except in Taiwan (58%) and Canada (60%), but even in these places a clear majority agreed.

On investigating government claims (or being a watchdog on government) there was considerably less agreement, however, with journalists most likely to consider this very important coming from the more democratic countries of Australia, Britain, and Finland.

Those least likely to see this watchdog role as very important were from Taiwan, Algeria, and Chile, where there has not been a long history of democratic forms of government. However, there were exceptions to this pattern. In Germany, which has been a democracy since World War II, there was no more support for the watchdog role than among Algerian journalists. In China, which has never had a democratic system of government, there was more support among journalists for investigating government than in France and Canada.

The analytical function of news media—providing analysis of complex problems—remained about the same in the United States during the 1980s, with about half saying it was extremely important (Weaver and Wilhoit 1996). However, among the 14 countries or territories where this role was measured, there were considerable differences, with journalists in Taiwan and France least likely to consider it very important (40%), and those in Finland (96%) and Britain (83%) most likely to say so (see Table 23.4).

Another role over which there was some disagreement was the extent to which journalists should give ordinary people a chance to express their views on public affairs. A little less than half of the U.S. sample said this was an extremely important role, with journalists working on daily and weekly newspapers especially likely to say so.

Table 23.4. Professional Roles (in percentages).

	Report News quickly[a]	Provide analysis[a]	Be a watchdog on government[a]	Provide access for public[a]	Provide entertainment[a]	Report accurately or objectively[a]	Member of journalist organization
I. Asia/Far East							
China	79	72	61	24	19	—[b]	—
Hong Kong	65	55	58	41	16	71	18
Korea	—	—	—	—	—	—	—
Taiwan	58	40	27	—	16	76	65
II. Australia/Pacific							
Australia	74	71	81	—	28	45	86
New Zealand	—	—	—	—	—	—	—
Pacific Islands	86	67	67	—	22	37	—
III. Europe							
Britain	88	83	88	56	47	30	62
Finland[c]	—	96	87	53	—	77	—
France	69	40	40	—	8	—	—
W. Germany/E. Germany[d]	—	—	—	—	77/87	89/84	—
Germany[e]	73	74	33	40	47	74	—
Hungary	—	—	—	—	—	—	83
Poland	—	78	56	—	—	—	—
Spain	—	—	—	—	—	—	61

Table 23.4. Professional Roles (in percentages) (con't).

	Report News quickly[a]	Provide analysis[a]	Be a watchdog on government[a]	Provide access for public[a]	Provide entertainment[a]	Report accurately or objectively[a]	Member of journalist organization
IV. North Africa							
Algeria	71	55	33	—	40	—	—
V. North America							
Canada	60	63	52	—	7	—	—
United States	69	48	67	48	14	49	36
VI. South/Central America							
Brazil	70	67	79	—	30	—	—
Chile	—	—	31	—	50	61	—
Ecuador	—	—	—	—	—	—	—
Mexico	—	—	58	—	31	55	—

[a]Percentage saying very or extremely important.
[b]Indicating data not available for these studies.
[c]Percentage agreeing.
[d]Data from Schoenbach et al., this volume.
[e]Percentage agreeing or strongly agreeing; data compiled from Weischenberg et al., this volume, for all German journalists.

Although only six countries reported the importance of this role, there was some agreement among five—Hong Kong, Britain, Finland, Germany, and the United States—but Chinese journalists were notably less likely to see this role as very important, as Table 23.4 shows. Compared to other journalistic roles, this one was not seen as important by large proportions of journalists in any location. Only in Britain and Finland did slightly more than half of the journalists consider this a very important role.

There was great disagreement on the importance of providing entertainment among the 14 countries or territories reporting this role. Those journalists least likely to consider this very important were from Canada (7%) and France (8%), whereas those most likely were from Germany (77%—West; 87%—East) and Chile (50%). Clearly, this is one role where national differences in journalistic values are in sharp evidence. It seems that journalists from the Far East and North America were least likely to regard entertainment as an important function of journalism, but in Europe there were huge differences by country.

There was also disagreement on the importance of reporting accurately or objectively, with those journalists least likely to say so from Britain (30%) and the Pacific Islands (37%), and those most likely from Germany (89% and 84%), Finland (77%), and Taiwan (76%).

Thus, there was considerable agreement among journalists regarding the importance of reporting the news quickly and some agreement on the importance of providing access for the public to express opinions, but considerable disagreement on the importance of providing analysis and being a watchdog on government. There was most disagreement on the importance of providing entertainment and considerable variance in opinions on the importance of accurate or objective reporting.

Clearly, there was more disagreement than agreement over the relative importance of these journalistic roles considered together, hardly evidence to support the universal occupational standards mentioned by Splichal and Sparks (1994). The reasons for the disagreement are difficult to specify for so many possible comparisons, but a secondary analysis of the data from journalists in China, Taiwan, and the United States by Zhu, Weaver, Lo, Chen, and Wu (1996) suggests that political system similarities and differences are far more important than cultural similarities and differences, organizational constraints or individual characteristics in predicting the variance in perceptions of three roles (timely information, interpretation, and entertainment) by journalists in these societies.

Organizations

Another possible indicator of professionalism (or lack of it) is membership in organizations that encourage professional standards and values.

Only seven studies reported data on this, but Table 23.4 shows that among those there was a wide range—from 18% claiming to belong to a journalistic organization in Hong Kong to 86% in Australia and 83% in Hungary, followed fairly closely by Taiwan, Britain, and Spain, with the United States in between at 36%.

Most of these differences are likely explained by the requirement in some countries that journalists belong to a union to be able to work, but the large differences here also call into question whether journalists are becoming more professional around the world.

Ethics of Reporting

Still another measure of how professional journalists are is which reporting methods they consider acceptable.

Our surveys of U.S. journalists included questions about the acceptability of questionable reporting practices that were first asked in a 1980 study of British and West German journalists (Donsbach 1983; Koecher 1986) and also in public opinion surveys in the United States during the 1980s (Weaver and Daniels 1992; Weaver and Wilhoit 1986, 1996).

For example, a majority of U.S. journalists in 1992 said that getting employed to gain inside information may be justified on occasion. However, a national survey of 1,002 adults conducted for the American Society of Newspaper Editors (ASNE) in 1985 found that only 32% approved of journalists not identifying themselves as reporters (Gaziano and McGrath 1986), as did 32% in a 1981 Gallup national survey and 38% in a 1989 Indiana statewide survey (Weaver and Daniels 1992). The questions were somewhat different, but it is likely there was a considerable gap between the U.S. press and public on the acceptability of undercover reporting.

Another gap with the public appeared when U.S. journalists' opinions about the use of hidden microphones or cameras were compared with those of the public. Only 42% of the 1985 national sample of the public (and 46% of the 1989 Indiana sample) approved of using hidden cameras in 1985, compared with 63% of journalists in 1992 who said this practice might be justified. Again, the questions were not identical, but a gap seemed likely.

One practice that was approved by fewer U.S. journalists than the U.S. public was paying for information. Only 20% of the journalists in our 1992 study said this might be justified (Weaver and Wilhoit 1996), compared with 30% of the 1985 national sample and 33% of the 1989 Indiana sample who approved. On this score, then, U.S. journalists seemed less permissive (or more ethical) than the public at large.

If journalists are becoming more professional in a universal sense around the world, we should expect their views on the acceptability of various reporting practices to also become more similar.

In our earlier 1982 study of U.S. journalists, we found considerable differences between U.S., British, and German journalists on whether certain practices might be justified. The German journalists were much less likely to approve of badgering or harassing sources, using personal documents without permission and getting employed to gain inside information than were the U.S. and British journalists. The British journalists were especially likely to say that most of the questionable reporting practices could be justified, with the U.S. journalists in between the British and the Germans on most practices (Weaver and Wilhoit 1986: 139).

What about more recent times? Are journalists' views about which reporting methods are acceptable becoming more similar over time? In the United States we found some large increases from 1982 to 1992 in the percentage of journalists who thought that it might be justifiable to use confidential business or government documents without permission (up from 55% to 82%) and using personal documents such as letters and photographs without permission (up from 28% to 48% who thought this may be justified). However, the percentages approving the other methods stayed about the same (Weaver and Wilhoit 1996).

When journalists from different areas of the world are compared, Table 23.5 shows considerable differences, some very large, on the proportions saying that some reporting methods might be justified, as well as some agreement on other practices.

For example, on revealing confidential news sources, which has been the practice of most agreement (as unacceptable) among U.S. journalists from 1982 to 1992, journalists from 13 of the 14 countries or territories measuring this were very reluctant to say it might be justifiable (10% or less said so in Hong Kong, Korea, Taiwan, Australia, Pacific Islands, Britain, France, Germany, Canada, United States, Brazil, Chile and Mexico), but 39% of the journalists in Finland said it might be acceptable. On this practice, then, there was a high level of agreement among all journalists except those from Finland, suggesting a near-universal professional norm of protecting confidential sources.

On other reporting methods, however, Table 23.5 shows some very large differences of opinion. With regard to paying for secret information, the range is from 9% who think this is justifiable in Canada to 65% in Britain and 62% in Finland who think it may be justifiable. On undercover reporting (claiming to be someone else), the range is from 7% in Canada to 63% in Brazil and 58% in Chile who might find this practice justifiable. For badgering or harassing news sources the percentages vary from 12 in Germany to 84 in Hong Kong and 82 in France, and for using personal documents without permission the percentages range from 11 in Germany to 49 in Britain and 48 in the United States.

As for using business or government documents without permission, the range of those who might approve runs from 26% in Taiwan to

Table 23.5. Reporting Methods (Percentage Saying "May Be Justified").

	Reveal confiden- tial source	Pay for secret informa- tion	Claim to be someone else	Badger/ harass news sources	Use personal doc. w/o permission	Use personal or gov't doc. w/o permission	Get employed to gain inside information
I. Asia/Far East							
China	—[a]	—	—	—	—	—	—
Hong Kong	6	51	38	84	26	77	45
Korea	9	27	59	17	27	50	37
Taiwan	10	28	44	38	13	26	40
II. Australia/Pacific							
Australia	4	31	13	55	39	79	46
New Zealand	—	—	—	—	—	—	—
Pacific Islands[c]	3	20	14	14	12	43	29
III. Europe							
Britain	9	65	47	59	49	86	80
Finland	39	62	53	43	39	72	68
France	4	36	40	82	12	69	56
Germany[d]	10	41	45	12	11	54	54
Hungary	—	—	—	—	—	—	—
Poland	—	—	—	—	—	—	—
Spain	—	—	—	—	—	—	—

Table 23.5. Reporting Methods (Percentage Saying "May Be Justified") (con't.).

	Reveal confidential source	Pay for secret information	Claim to be someone else	Badger/ harass news sources	Use personal doc. w/o permission	Use personal or gov't doc. w/o permission	Get employed to gain inside information
IV. North Africa							
Algeria	—	—	—	—	—	—	—
V. North America							
Canada[b]	2	9	7	31	17	60	36
United States	5	20	22	49	48	82	63
VI. South/Central America							
Brazil	7	24	63	—	43	83	67
Chile	2	39	58	76	14	53	22
Ecuador	—	—	—	—	—	—	—
Mexico	5	38	36	21	13	64	45

[a] Indicating data not available in these studies.
[b] Percentages saying these practices are "highly justified" or "justifiable."
[c] Percentages are for those who "approve."
[d] Data compiled from Weischenberg et al., this volume, for all German journalists.

86% in Britain, 83% in Brazil and 82% in the United States. Finally, getting employed to gain inside information was seen as possibly justifiable by as few as 22% of journalists in Chile and as many as 80% in Britain.

Given these very large differences in the percentages of journalists who think that different reporting methods may be acceptable, it seems that there are strong national differences that override any universal professional norms or values of journalism around the world, except in the case of revealing confidential sources, where there is strong agreement, except in Finland, that this should never be done.

Aspects of Job

Another possible indicator of professionalism of journalists is which dimensions of their jobs they consider most important. Some would argue that salary, job security, and chance to advance are less professional aspects of an occupation than editorial policies, ability to develop a specialty, autonomy, and helping people (McLeod and Hawley 1964; Windahl and Rosengren 1978; Beam 1990).

Table 23.6 shows that there are wide disagreements among journalists from different countries on which aspects of the job are very important. Journalists in France and the former West Germany were more likely to emphasize freedom on the job than pay, job security and chance to advance, but this was not the case in Brazil, where journalists were more likely to say that pay was very important, followed by freedom and the chance to help people. Journalists in Algeria were likely to think that almost all job aspects were equally important.

Looking at Table 23.6 first by the "nonprofessional" job aspects, it is clear that Brazilian journalists were most likely to rate pay very important (91%), perhaps because of the very large rates of inflation in that country, followed by former East German journalists at 73%. Surprisingly, journalists in Chile (2%) and Mexico (7%) were least likely to say so. Whatever the reasons for these differences, there is not much agreement across countries on the importance of pay.

For job security, journalists in the United States were most likely to consider it very important (61%), no doubt because of the much more competitive job market and the lack of growth in journalism jobs during the 1980s, followed by those in East Germany (60%). Those least likely to say so were from Canada (18%) and France (21%), most likely reflecting the economic situations in their countries and illustrating a considerable range of disagreement across countries.

As for the chance to advance or to be promoted, those most likely to rate it very important were from Brazil (62%) and Australia (51%), again likely reflecting the economies of their countries. Those least concerned about advancement were from Finland (1%) and Mexico (4%).

Table 23.6. Job Aspects (Percentage Saying "Very Important").

	Pay	Editorial policy	Job security	Developing a specialty	Job autonomy	Helping people	Chance to advance
I. Asia/Far East							
China	—[a]	—	—	—	—	—	—
Hong Kong	—	—	—	—	—	—	—
Korea	—	—	—	—	—	—	—
Taiwan	—	—	—	—	—	—	—
II. Australia/Pacific							
Australia	23	55	58	40	51	44	51
New Zealand	—	—	—	—	—	—	—
Pacific Islands	39	61	57	51	54	62	48
III. Europe							
Britain	62	56	56	28	47	26	—
Finland	14	—	25	—	—	—	1
France	16	24	21	23	74	38	25
W.Germany/ E.Germany[b]	43/73	—	31/60	31/56	68/85	—	24/48
Hungary	—	—	—	—	—	—	—
Poland	—	—	—	—	—	—	—
Spain	—	—	—	—	—	—	—

Table 23.6. Job Aspects (Percentage Saying "Very Important") (con't.).

	Pay	Editorial policy	Job security	Developing a specialty	Job autonomy	Helping people	Chance to advance
IV. North Africa							
Algeria	40	51	52	52	52	48	31
V. North America							
Canada[c]	27	16	18	30	36	16	11
United States	21	69	61	40	51	61	39
VI. South/Central America							
Brazil	91	43	50	55	74	70	62
Chile	2	—	—	—	45	64	12
Ecuador	—	—	—	—	—	—	—
Mexico	7	—	—	—	44	52	4

[a] Indicating data not available in these studies.
[b] Data compiled from Schoenbach et al., this volume.
[c] Data for Canadian women journalists only.

On balance, then, it looks as if the Brazilian journalists were most likely to emphasize the "nonprofessional" material aspects of the job of journalist, and those from Mexico were among those least likely to rate these aspects very important. There are striking differences in the proportions of journalists from the different countries considering these aspects of their work as very important, suggesting little support for any universal motives of journalists.

Turning to the more "professional" job aspects, Table 23.6 shows that journalists from the United States (69%) and the Pacific Islands (61%) were most likely to rate editorial policy as very important, whereas those least likely to do so were from Canada (16%) and France (24%). As for developing a specialty, journalists in East Germany (56%) and Brazil (55%) were most likely to rate it very important, whereas those from France (23%) and Canada (30%) were least likely to do so.

Even on perceived freedom on the job, a journalistic norm that Splichal and Sparks (1994) identified as strikingly similar among the journalism students from 22 different countries, there were notable differences among the journalists interviewed in the studies reported here. Those from East Germany (85%), Brazil (74%) and France (74%) were most likely to say that freedom on the job is very important, whereas those in Canada (36%) were least likely (although this was the aspect of their jobs rated most highly as compared to others). There does seem to be more agreement on the importance of this aspect of the job than on others, as Splichal and Sparks (1994) argue, but there is still considerable variance between countries.

Finally, on the journalistic norm of helping people, those journalists most likely to consider this very important were from Brazil (70%) and Chile (64%). Those least likely were from Canada (16%), again suggesting a wide range of opinion on this indicator of professionalism.

On balance, then, it seems as if the Canadian and French journalists are least likely to emphasize the importance of these more professional aspects of the job, except for autonomy, and the journalists from Brazil, East Germany, and the United States are most likely to do so. As with most other indicators of professionalism, there appears to be no widespread agreement on the importance of these aspects of journalistic work.

Images of Audience

A final possible indicator of professionalism of journalists is their view of their audiences. Although only six countries included this measure in their studies, there were some striking similarities and differences, as Table 23.7 illustrates.

Table 23.7. Journalists' Images of Their Audiences (Percentage Saying "Strongly Agree").

	Audience Is Interested in Breaking News	Audience Is Interested in Politics & Social Problems	Audience Is Gullible
Algeria	27	—	9
Brazil	27	—	10
Chile[a]	—	40	17
Mexico[a]	—	72	10
W. Germany/ E. Germany	—	50/73	29/46
United States	26	33	3

[a]Percentages of journalists saying these characteristics apply to their audiences.

About one fourth of journalists from Algeria, Brazil, and the United States strongly agree that their audiences are interested in breaking news. But only one-third of the journalists in the U.S. strongly agree that their audiences are interested in politics and social problems, compared with nearly three fourths of the East German and Mexican journalists. Nearly one half of the East German journalists strongly agree that their audience is gullible, or easily fooled, and the U.S. journalists are the least likely to say so (only 3% strongly agree).

Again, on these measures of professionalism, there are some striking differences on two of the three, raising the question of whether journalists are becoming more professional around the world, as Splichal and Sparks (1994) argue.

CONCLUSIONS

Whether one thinks that journalists are becoming more professional around the world depends on the definition of professional and the indicators used. However, a variety of possible measures of professionalism reviewed here suggest that there are still many differences among journalists from the 21 countries and territories represented in this book.

Even though these are not a representative sample of all countries or territories in the world, they do include some of the largest and most influential, and they are located in most of the major continents and regions.

Further analysis is needed to uncover some of the reasons behind the differences reported here. Many of them seem to reflect societal influences, especially political system differences, more than the influences of media organizations, journalism education, and professional norms. The patterns of similarities and differences are not neatly classifiable along some of the more common political or cultural dimensions, however, lending some support to the conclusion of Splichal and Sparks (1994) that journalism education and professional socialization are not necessarily a function of politics or dominant ideology. Even so, cultural norms and political values do appear to have some influence on journalists' views of their roles and ethics.

In the end, it seems more important to discover who journalists are, where they come from (including their educational experiences) and what they think about their work, their roles, their methods and their publics than to try to classify them firmly as professionals or not.

The findings from the studies included in this book suggest that the typical journalist is still primarily a young college-educated man who studied something other than journalism in college and who came from the established and dominant cultural groups in his country. In some countries, such as Finland and New Zealand, women are almost as well represented as men in journalism, and it seems very likely that women will become as common as men in journalism in the early years of the next century, given their numbers in journalism schools. It seems less certain that ethnic and racial minorities will be represented in journalism according to their actual proportions in various societies in the near future. Those countries with the largest number of journalists, and the most opportunities, in relation to their populations tend to be those that are the most prosperous economically and the most democratic politically.

Job satisfaction of journalists in many countries is linked closely to perceived autonomy or freedom, but other conditions are also important, especially journalists' perceptions of how well their news organizations are doing in informing the public, how they view their pay, and their relationships with their supervisors and peers on the job. Intention to stay in journalism seems more dependent on the attractiveness of alternative jobs.

The single professional role that most journalists agree on is the importance of getting information to the public quickly. There is also some agreement on the importance of providing access for members of the public to express themselves. Beyond these roles, there is much disagreement over how important it is to provide entertainment, to report accurately and objectively, to provide analysis of complex issues and problems, and to be a watchdog on government. Although one might expect more journalists in democratically governed countries to consider the watchdog role very important, this is not a consistent pattern. In some less democratic countries, such as China, there are high proportions of journalists rating the watchdog role very important, perhaps because they know about cases of abuse of power that they think should be reported to the public. However, as the authors of Chapter 2 on Chinese journalists point out, what journalists in a survey say is sometimes inconsistent with what they do in daily practice, so it is important to distinguish between the two.

Journalists also sharply disagree on whether some ethically questionable reporting practices might be justified in the case of an important story. The only practice that seems almost universally agreed on is not revealing news sources who have been promised confidentiality. There are large differences of opinion on whether it might be justifiable to pay for information, to pose as someone else, to badger or harass news sources, to use documents without permission, and to get employed to gain inside information. These differences are not easily explained in terms of geography. They probably have more to do with the cultural norms of each country than with region of the world or differing political systems, in contrast to journalistic roles, which seem to be more closely linked to political system than to culture.

There is some agreement among journalists on the importance of autonomy and developing a specialty in their jobs, but considerable disagreement on the importance of pay, job security, the chance to advance, editorial policy, and helping people. Some of these differences seem to be due to different economic conditions in the various countries and territories, but the differences are not easily explained in terms of standard political and cultural categories based on language and heritage.

Because the similarities and differences among these journalists do not tend to follow geographic, political, and cultural patterns, and because there is not comparable data over time, it is difficult to say whether journalists around the world are becoming more professional or more ethical. The concerns of these journalists about the performance of their news organizations, freedom, getting information to the public quickly, and not revealing the identities of confidential sources are encouraging signs. However, the large proportions of journalists in some countries who consider providing entertainment very important, who might be willing to use deceptive and invasive reporting methods, and who consider their audiences gullible are not indicators of increased professional and ethical development.

In short, it seems that no country or territory has a monopoly on professionalism among journalists. There is a mixed picture in nearly all of the 21 societies represented in this book. Whether this picture will become clearer as we approach the end of the 20th century and the beginning of a new millennium remains to be seen. I hope this book will encourage more comparative studies of journalists to explore the reasons behind the similarities and differences documented here, as well as the patterns of development over time.

REFERENCES

Beam, Randal A. 1990. Journalism professionalism as an organizational-level concept. *Journalism Monographs* 121: 1-43.

Donsbach, Wolfgang. 1983. Journalists' conceptions of their audience. *Gazette* 32: 19-36.

Gaziano, Cecilie and Kristin McGrath. 1986. Measuring the concept of credibility. *Journalism Quarterly* 63: 451-462.

Johnstone, John W.C., Edward J. Slawski, and William W. Bowman. 1976. *The news people*. Urbana: University of Illinois Press.

Koecher, Renate. 1986. Bloodhounds or missionaires: Role definitions of German and British journalists. *European Journal of Communication* 1: 43-64.

McLeod, Jack and Searle Hawley Jr. 1964. Professionalization among newsmen. *Journalism Quarterly* 41: 529-538, 577.

Splichal, Slavko and Colin Sparks. 1994. *Journalists for the 21st century*. Norwood, NJ: Ablex.

Weaver, David H. and LeAnne Daniels. 1992. Public opinion on investigative reporting in the 1980s. *Journalism Quarterly* 69: 146-155.

Weaver, David H. and G. Cleveland Wilhoit. 1986. *The American journalist: A portrait of U.S. news people and their work*. Bloomington: Indiana University Press.

Weaver, David H. and G. Cleveland Wilhoit. 1996. *The American journalist in the 1990s: U.S. News people at the end of an era*. Mahwah, NJ: Erlbaum.

Windahl, Swen and Karl Erik Rosengren. 1978. Newsmen's professionalization: Some methodological problems. *Journalism Quarterly* 55: 466-473.

Zhu, Jian-Hua, David Weaver, Ven-hwei Lo, Chongshan Chen, and Wei Wu. 1996, July. *Individual, organizational and societal constraints on media professionalism: A comparative study of journalists in the U.S., China and Taiwan*. Paper presented to the Conference on Multiculturalism, Cultural Diversity and Global Communication, Rochester, NY. Published in *Journalism & Mass Communication Quarterly* 74: 84-96 (Spring 1997).

Author Index

A

Albert, P., 191, *208*
Albota, R., 375, *389*
American Society of Newspaper Editors, 102, *106*
Angiki, D., 132, *139*
Atkin, C.K., 127, *139,* 325, *347*
Atkinson, J., 118, *123*
Audley, P., 373, *389*

B

Bahia, J., 418, *431*
Bailly, C., 198, *208*
Balle, F., 193, 200, *208*
Banks, A.S., 129n, *139*
Barrett, B., 379, *389*
Beam, R.A., 473, *480*
Becker, B. von, 230, *252*
Becker, L.B., 213, *226*
Bellanger, C., 192, *208*
Bezunartea, C.C., 300n, *319*
Blume, M., 206, *208*
Blumler, J.G., 3, *6*, 299, *319*
Bowman, W.W., 1, 3, *6*, 41, *53*, 93, 100, *106*, 144, 145, 152, *160*, 194, *210*, 307, *319*, 327, *348*, 355, 361, 370, *371*, 395, 399n, 403t, 405t, *414*, 455, *480*
Bulletin, 99, *106*
Burgoon, J.K., 327, *347*
Burgoon, M., 327, *347*

C

Calder, P., 119, *123*
Cardoso, A.M., 418, *431*
Carrier, P., 380, *390*
Central Statistical Office, 147, 148, *160*

Author Index

Centre d'Etudes et de Recherches sur les Qualifications, 193, *208*
Chan, J.M., 32, 33, 34, 38, 44, 49, 50, 51, *52, 53*
Charon, J-M., 194, *208*
Chen, C-H., 469, *480*
Chen, L., 11n, *29*
Cheng, J-C., 72, 73, *88*
CNA, 72, *88*
Cocker, A., 118, *123*
Cohen, B.C., 307, *319*
Collins, R., 118, *123*
Commission de la Carte d'Identité des Journalistes Professionels, 193, 199, *209*
Costa, C.T., 417, *432*
Council for Industry and Higher Education, 149, *160*
Crocombe, R., 129n, *139*
Curry, J.L., 279, *297*
Czarnowski, S., 288, *297*

D

Daniels, L., 467, *478*
Dare, O., 345, *347*
de la Garde, R., 352, *371*, 379, *389*
Delano, A., 96, *106*, 145, *160*
Desbarats, P., 376, 378, *389*
Diezhandino, P., 300n, *319*
Donsbach, W., 152, 156, *160*, 194, *209*, 219, 229, 251, *252*, 429t, *431*, 435, 433, 447, *451*, 469, *480*
Douglas, N., 125, 129, *139*
Douglas, N., 125, 129, *139*
Drath, J., 230, *252*
Dubois, J., 379, *389*
Dygutsch-Lorenz, I. 230, *254*

E

Economist Intelligence Unit, 128, *139*
Erämetsä, H., 163, *188*
Ettema, J.S., 3, *6*, 346, *347*

F

Fairweather, J.S., 405, *414*
Fan, D., 13, *29*
Fishman, M., 305, *319*
Foerster, H. von, 231, *252*
Fortin, P., 380, *389*
Freedom Forum Media Studies Center, 352, *371*
Freiberg, J.W., 193, *209*
Freise, H., 230, *252*
Friedman, M., 204, *209*
Fung, A.Y.H., 51, *53*
Fusimalohi, T., 131, 133, *139*

G

Gagnon, L., 377, *390*
Gallup, G.H., 403n, *414*
Gannett Foundation, 356, *371*
Gans, H., 305, *319*
Gaziano, C., 469, *480*
Geserick, R., 230, *252*
Gingras, A-M., 380, *390*
Godechot, J., 192, *208*
Godin, P., 377, 379, *390-391*
Goehringer, S., 434, *451*
Gross, B., 229, *252*
Gruber, T., 229, *252*
Guiral, P., 192, *208*
Gurevich, M., 299, *319*

H

Hagan, I., 299, *319*
Hardin, H., 351, *371*
Harrell, S., 72, *88*
Harris, P., 32, *53*
Hart, B., 94, *106*
Hawley, S.E., Jr., 127, *140*, 473, *480*
Heinonen, A., 163, 164, 167, 168, 176f, 177, 178, 179, 180, 181, 182f, 183, 184, 185, 186f, *189*
Hemánus P., 169, *189*
Hendrikson, R.M., 405, *414*

Henningham, J., 52, 53, 92, 95, 96, 97, 105, *106*, 111, 115, *123*, 127, 128, 130, *139*, 144, 145, 151, 156, 157, *160*
Herman, F.,131, 132, *139*
Hernández, R., 436, *451*
Hess, S., 400, *414*
Hienzsch, U., 230, *252*
Huang, C-C., 72, *88*
Hudson, W.J., 96, *106*

I

Index of Hungarian Journalists, 258, *276*
Innis, H., 352, *371*
Institut Français de Press, 193, *210*
Institut National de la Statistique et des Etudes Economiques, 196, 197, *210*

J

Jacobi, U., 229, *253*
Jaffré, J., 198, *210*
Jeambar, D., 196, *210*
Johnson, O.V., 26, *30*
Johnstone, J.W.C., 1, 3, *6*, 93, 100, *106*, 144, 145, 152, *160*, 194, *210*, 307, *319*, 361, 370, *371*, 395, 399, 403t, 405t, *414*, 455, *480*
Journalisti, 175, *189*
Journalists Yearbook, 263, *275*
Jyrkiäinen, J., 162, *189*

K

Kanzleiter, G., 230, *254*
Karp, J., 10, *29*
Kehälinna, H., 163, 165, 16, 185, *189*
Kepplinger, H.M., 229, 251, *253*
King, M., 117, *123*
Kirat, M., 345, *348*
Kivikuru, U., 162, *189*
Klett, B., 434, *451*

Knight, R., 117, *123*
Köcher, R., 194, *210*, 229, 245, 248, *253*, 447, *451*
Koecher, R., 214, 215, 216, 219, 221, *226*, 469, *451*
Korea Press Center, 55, *69*
Korea Press Institute, 57, *69*
Korotynski, H., 296, *279*
Kovats, I., 258, 260, 263n, 276, *276*
Kuusava, S., 172, *189*
Kuusisto, O., 172, *189*

L

Laharre, A., 361, *372*, 379, *390*
Laitila, T., 179, *189*
La Depeche du Midi, 203, *209*
Langenbucher, W.R., 229, 230, *253*
Langlois, S., 377, 378, *390*
Lawrence, J., 131, *140*
Layton, S., 126, 127, 128, 132, *139*
Lazarsfeld, P.F., 26, *29*
Lealand, G., 110, *123*
Lee, C-C., 32, 33, 34, 35, 38, 44, 49, 50, 51, *52*, *53*, 72, 73, 74, 86, *88*
Lee, P.S.N., 32, 34, 35, 38, 49, *52*
Legault, A., 379, *391*
Lin, Y., 31, *53*
Lindon Commission, 193, *210*
Littlemore, S., 134, *140*
Liu, X., 16, *30*
Lloyd, C., 96, 100, *106*
Lo, V-H., 72, 73, 86, 87, *88*, 469, *480*
Löffelholz, M., 237t, 250, *256*
Löfgren, M., 181, *189*
Löfgren-Nilsson, M., 354, 366, *371*
Longin, C., 436, *451*
Lopez, A., 418, *432*
Lustarinen, H., 187, *189*

M

MacLennan, C., 120, *123*
Mahood, C., 388, *391*
Mainwaring, Sc., 417, *432*
Maka'a, J., 131, *140*
Mäkinen, A., 172, *189*
Marzolf, M.T., 358, *373*
Mast, C., 230, *253*
Masterton, M., 131, *140*
Matau, R., 132, *140*
Matthews Media Director, 373, *390*
McGrath, K., 469, *480*
McLeod, J.M., 3, *6*, 127, *140*, 473, *480*
McMane, A.A., 195, 204, *211*
Melin, H., 163, 164, 165f, 166, 167, 168, 169, 170f, 171, 172, 174, 174f, 185, *189*
Memo of the First National Seminar of Deans, 12, 13, *29*
Mermet, G., 199, *211*
Merrill, J., 92, *106*
Merton, R.K., 26, *29*
Min, A., 12n, *30*
Ministry of the Interior, 76, *88*
Missika, J-M., 198, *210*
Mühlberger, H., 229, *254*
Munro, M., 119, *123*
Murphy, K., 10, *30*

N

Nahr, G., 229, *253*
Nash, S., 138, *140*
Nayman, O.B., 127, *140*
NBR Consultus Poll, 122, *123*
Neilan, E., 87, *88*
Neverla, I., 230, *252*
News Media and Modernization in China Task Force, 13, *29*
Nicolás, J.D., 315n, *319*
Nikula, J., 163, 164, 165f, 167, 168, 169, 170f, 171f, 171, 172, 174f, 174, *190*

Noelle-Neumann, E., 229, *259*
Nordenstreng, K., 162, *189*
Nummijoki, S., 172, *189*

O

O'Donnell, G., 417, *432*
O'Keefe, G.J., 127, *140*
Oledzki, J., 290n, *297*
Opherden, R., 250, *255*
Ottaway, D., 324, *348*
Ottaway, M., 324, *348*

P

Padioleau, J-G., 193, *211*
Patterson, T.E., 433, *451*
Peng, B., 73, *88*
Petaia, U.L., 131, *140*
Phinney, R., 127, 128, *140*
Pollard, G., 371, *379*
Polumbaum, J., 12, 29, *30*
Prott, J., 229, 230, *254*

Q

Qiu, Z., 11, 12, *30*

R

Reese, S.D., 3, *6*
Rehbein González, M., 434, *451*
Rieffel, R., 193, 200, *212*
Ritova, S., 131, *140*
Robinson, G.J., 352, 354, 355, 370, *371*
Roegele, O.B., 229, 230, *253*
Rosengren, K.E., 3, *6*, 473, *481*
Royal Commission on Newspapers, 374, *390*
Royal Commission on Radio Broadcasting, 374, *390*
Royal Commission on the Press, 147, 149, *160*
Rühl, M., 230, *254*
Rush, R.R., 127, *140*
Russell, S.H., 405, *414*

S

Saint-Jean, A., 354, 355, 361, *372*, 379, *390*
Sassi, S., 162, *189*
Saunders, J., 388, *391*
Sauri, T., 163, *190*
Sauvageau, F., 377, 378, *390*
Savisaari, E., 162, *189*
Schneider, B., 52, *53*, 214, 215, 216, 218, 221, 222, *226*, 230, 248, *255*
Schoenbach, K., 52, *53*, 213, 214, 215, 216, 218, 221, 222, *226*, 230, 248, *255*
Scholl, A., 237t, 250, *256*
Schönhals-Abrahamson, M., 229, *253*
Schütt, B., 230, *255*
Schweda, C., 250, *255*
Semetko, H.A., 299, 315n, *319*
Shamir, J., 127, *140*
Shen, J., 32, *53*
Shoemaker, P.J., 3, *6*, 305, *319*
Shulman, I., 447, *451*
Sidel, M.K., 195, 204, *211*
Siegel, A., 376, 377, *391*
Sigal, L.V., 305, *319*
Siivonen, T., 172, *189*
Singletary, M.W., 278, *297*
Slattery, J., 150, *160*
Slawski, E.J., 1, 3, *6*, 41, *53*, 93, 100, *106*, 144, 145, 152, *160*, 194, *210*, 307, *319*, 327, *348*, 370, *371*, 399n, 403t, 405t, *414*, 455, *480*
Sola Pool, I. de., 447, *451*
Song, X., 11n, *29*
Sparks, C., 464, 468, 476, 478, *480*
Splichal, S., 464, 468, 476, 478, *480*
Starck, K., 32, *53*
Statistical Yearbook of China, 18, *30*
Statistics Canada, 353, 355, 359, 360, *372*
Stewart, W., 374, *391*
Stiehler, H-J., 230, *255*
Stone, V.A., 405n, *414*
Stuerzebecher, D., 214, 215, 216, 218, 221, 222, *226*, 230, 255, 248, *255*
Sudhaker, A., 346, *348*
Sun, C., 72, *88*
Sun, M-P., 87, *88*
Syndicat Nationale des Journalistes, 204, *212*

T

Tash, A.T.M., 327, *348*
Terrou, F., 191, 192, *208*
Tien, H-M., 73, *88*
Tolgyesi, J., 258, *276*
Tommila, P., 162, *190*
Tu, C-F., 87, *88*
Tuchman, G., 305, *319*
Tully, J., 119, 120, 121, *123*
Tunstall, J., 149, *160*, 327, *348*
Turner, R., 353, *371*

U

U.S. Bureau of the Census 129, *140*, 399n, *414*
U.S. Department of Labor 399, 404n, *414*
Untalan,-Munoz, F., 129, *140*

V

Valenzuela, J.S., 417, *432*
Vasarhelyi, M., 259, 265, 268, 271t, 272, 272t, *276*
Vohl, I., 229, 251, *253*
Voyenne, B., 193, *212*

W

Wackman, D.B., 3, *6*
Wasko, J., 299, *319*
Weaver, D.H., 1, 3, *6*, 13, 14, 23, 25, 29, *30*, 35, 37, 41, *53*, 74, 83, 84, 85, 86, *88*, 93, 95, 96,

100, 102, *106*, 127, 134, *140*, 144, 145, 152, 153t, 156, 156n, *160*, 200, *212*, 215, *227*, 237t, *255*, 299, 305, 306, *319*, 327, *348*, 352, 354, 355, 356, 359, 360, 361, 363, 364, 366, 370, *371, 372*, 395, 396, 403t, 406t, 410t, 411, *414*, 425t, 429, *432*, 433, *451*, 455, 456, 461, 465, 470, *480-481*
Weibull, L., 163n, *190*
Weischenberg, S., 229, 230, 237t, 250, *255*
Weiss, H-J., 230, *256*
White, R.A., 179, *190*
Whitney, D.C., 3, *6*, 346, *347*
Wilhoit, G.C., 1, 3, *6*, 13, 14, 23, 25, 29, *30*, 35, 41, *53*, 74, 83, 84, 86, *88*, 93, 95, 96, 100, 102, *106*, 127, 134, *140*, 144, 145, 152, 153t, 156n, 156, *160*, 200, *212*, 215, *227*, 237, *255*, 305, 306, *319*, 327, *348*, 352, 354, 355, 356, 359, 360, 363, 364, 366, 370, *372*, 395, 403t, 405t, 406t, 410t, 411, *414*, 418, 425t, 429t, *432*, 433, *451*, 455, 456, 461, 465, 469, 470, *480-481*
Wilke, J., 435, *452*
Wilson, C.E., 379, *391*
Wilson, G.D., 151, *160*
Windahl, S., 473, *481*
Winter, P., 113, *123*
Wright, D.K., 379, *391*
Wu, W., 469, *481*

Y

Yu, F., 16, 30, 325, *348*

Z

Zebrowska, A., 287, *297*
Zeiss, M., 229, *256*
Zhu, Q., 15, 26, *30*, 469, 477, *481*
Zwermann, B., 434, 436, *452*

Subject Index

A

Adhwa, 329
Adversarial role, 152-153, 159-160
Advertising, 11-12, 32, 119, 121, 192
Algerie Actualité, 337
Algerie Presse Service, 326-327
All Chinese Journalists Association (ACJA), 15
Al-Massa, 329
Al-Mountakhab, 329
Arbeitsgemeinschaft für Kommunikationsforschung (AfK), 230
Asian American Journalists, 385
Association of Hungarian Catholic Journalists, 273, 275
Association of Taiwan Journalists, 87

Audience (readers)
  journalists' image of, 61, 115-116, 219-220, 250-251
Australian Broadcasting Corporation (ABC), 93, 97
Australian Consolidated Press, 110
Australian Journalists Association (AJA), 91, 100
Autonomy, *see* Media autonomy

B

Beats, 151, 168
Beijing Review, 14
British Association of Journalists, 154
British Broadcasting Corporation (BBC), 144, 157, 385
Broadcasting Standards Authority (BSA), 120

487

C

Canadian Broadcasting Corporation (CBC), 373-374, 376, 385
Canadian Charter of Rights and Freedoms, 373
Canadian Press (CP), 388
CanWest Global Systems, 109
Catholic Bishops' Association, 430
Central People's Radio Station (CPRS), 10, 12
Chamber of Hungarian Journalists, 258
China Daily, 10
China News Service, 14
China Times, 73-74
Chinese Broadcasting Yearbook, 14
Chinese Central Television (CCTV), 10, 12
Chinese Communist Party (CCP), 10, 19-20, 32, 36, 44, 50
Chinese Journalism Yearbook, 14
Chinese Nationalist Party (KMT), 32, 36, 44, 50
Chonji, 62, 65
Clear Channel Communications, 110
CNN, 385, 417
Codes, *see* Professionalism - ethics
Colegio de Periodistas, 435
Collegi de Periodistes de Catalunya, 306
Commitment to profession, 28, 82-83, 100, 116, 145-146, 197, 273, 331, 336, 367, 407
Community of the Hungarian Journalists, 273
Continuing education, *see* Journalists—education

D

Daily Telegraph, 144
Democracy, 299-300
Democratic Progressive Party (DPP), 72, 77
Directory of the Korean Journalist, 57

E

Ech-chaab, 337
Editor & Publisher, 370
Education, *see* Journalists—education
El Mercurio, 435
El-Moudjahid, 337
El Mundo, 309
El Universo, 436
Employment, *see* also Journalists—working conditions, workforce
Ethics, *see* Professionalism - ethics

F

Fairfax Group, 92
Federación de Asociaciones de la Prensa de España (FAPE), 306
Federación Nacional de Periodistas, 436
Fiji Times, 133
Finnish Broadcasting Company (YLE), 162, 164, 172
Freedom, *see* Media autonomy
Front de Libération National (FNL), 324

G

Gannett News Service, 358
Gender, *see* Women journalists
Globe, 352, 373, 377, 384, 387
Globo TV, 418
Government Information Office (GIO), 74
Guardian, 144

H

Helsingin Sanomat, 162, 164, 185
Hollinger Inc., 387-388
Hong Kong Journalists Association, 41
Hong Kong News Executives Association, 41
Hong Kong Standard, 10
Horizons, 329
Hungarian Association of Journalists, 257-258, 268

I

Imevisión, 434
Impact of technology, 98, 118, 126, 158, 172, 424
Imprensa, 424
Income, 23, 150-151, 164, 238, 358-359, 382, 404
    gender gap in, 23, 80, 85, 164, 218, 238-239
Independent Evening Post, 87
Infomatin, 192
International Association for Media and Communication Research (IAMCR), 1
Internet, 172

J

Job
    aspects of, 101, 132, 154-155, 169-171, 198, 220-221, 239-240, 272, 294-295, 320-332
    commitment, *see* Commitment to profession
    titles of, 13, 16, 22-23, 37-38, 97, 126, 131, 167-168, 199, 239, 331
Job satisfaction, 25, 37-38, 61, 81, 97, 114, 145, 169, 197, 220, 240-241, 331, 334-335, 383, 405-406, 421-422, 450, 461
Journalism majors, 21, 37, 78-79, 93, 97, 149, 167, 197, 219, 238, 304-305, 329
Journalism Research Institute of the Chinese Academy of Social Sciences (CASS), 15
Journalisti, 175
Journalists,
    age differences, 19, 35, 58, 75-76, 94-95, 111, 147, 164, 195, 216, 259-260, 301, 328, 354, 380, 398, 419, 437, 459
    background, 17, 130, 145, 195
    basic/general characteristics, 16-21, 34-36, 57-59, 75-78, 944-96, 111-113, 128-130, 145, 147-149, 164-166, 195-196, 215-219, 236-237, 259-267, 301-304, 327-328
    economic status, *see* Income
    education, 13, 17, 21-22, 36-37, 59-60, 78, 96, 113, 130, 149-150, 166-167, 193, 196-197, 219, 237-238, 267-270, 304-305, 328-329, 381-382, 402, 437, 459
    ethnicity, 19, 23, 58, 77, 95, 98, 112, 117, 129, 148-149, 262-264, 398, 400-401, 460
    experience of, 35, 80, 94-95, 131, 145, 164, 237, 329-331
    political attitudes, *see* Politics—of journalists
    religious beliefs, 58, 95, 148-149, 262-264, 401
    self-censorship and, 49, 168
    training, 21-22, 36, 78, 114, 130-131, 166-167, 196, 219, 237-238, 267-270, 304-305, 328-330, 402, 437
    workforce, 16-17, 34, 57, 91-92, 111, 144, 164, 194, 215-216, 237, 258, 324, 460
    working conditions, 22-25, 37-41, 60-62, 78, 80-83, 97-99, 114-117, 131-133, 167-173, 197-199, 219-221, 238-242, 312-314, 331-336, 354-360, 420-421, 461

K

Kim Young Sam, 55-56
Korea Press Center, 57
Korea Press Institute (KPA), 57, 61
Kuomintang (KMT), 72-73, 77, 86

L

L'Actualité, 384
La Presse, 377
Laws, 10-11, 32, 71-73, 91, 120, 161, 191, 324-325, 336
Le Canard Enchaîné, 206
Le Monde, 192-193, 337, 385
Libération, 192
Liberation Daily, 11

M

Maclean's, 384
Mail, 352, 373, 377, 384, 387
Mandarin, 72
Media autonomy
   and the newsroom, 10-11, 24-25, 32, 47, 51, 60, 73, 80, 86-87, 133, 161, 167-169, 197-198, 271-272, 312-314, 334, 422-423, 442-443, 461
   limits on, 25, 49, 51, 60, 62, 64, 80, 86-87, 120, 126, 133, 198, 272, 333-334
   relation to professionalism, 138-139, 334
Media commercialization, 118
Media, Entertainment and Arts Alliance, 91, 100
Media influence on public opinion, *see* Public opinion
Media ownership/control
   concentration of, 386-388
   foreign ownership, 99
   privatization, 10, 33, 161-162
   propaganda, 10
   state-owned media, 10, 324-325

Media performance, 99, 110, 151-152, 185-187, 333, 335-336, 346-347
Media roles, *see* Professionalism—perception of media roles
Metro, 120
Minorities, *see* Journalists—ethnicity, Women journalists
MTV Oy, 162, 164
Murdoch, Rupert, 91-92, 110, 143, 158

N

NAFTA, 436
National Association of Black Journalists (NABJ), 396
National Association of Hispanic Journalists (NAHJ), 396
National Council for the Training of Journalists (NCTJ), 149
National Union of Journalists (NUJ), 149, 154
Nationalist Party, 72
Native American Journalists Association (NAJA), 396
New Party, 72
News Limited, 92, 99
News organization, *see* Media performance
News values/Newsworthiness, 47-48, 314-317, 338, 341-342
New York Times, 385
New Zealand Herald, 110
New Zealand Journalists Training Organization (NZJTO), 110, 114
New Zealand Qualifications Authority, 121
Nigerian News Agency (NAN), 345

O

Objectivity, 134, 296-297, 315-317
Ouest France, 192
Ownership of the media, *see* Media ownership/control

P

Pacific Islands Broadcasting Association (PIBA), 126
Pacific Islands News Association (PINA), 126, 133, 134
Pacific Journalists Association (PJA), 133
People's Daily, 10, 12
Political parties, 10, 32, 72-73, 96, 266, 268, 291
  journalists' identification with, 21, 96, 165, 218, 265-267, 302-303
Politics
  effects on media, 32-33, 36, 56, 126, 258, 374-378, 435
  of journalists, 21, 33, 35-36, 47, 49, 58, 77-78, 96, 113, 151, 164-165, 196, 218-219, 246, 264-267, 293, 302, 401-402
Polls, *see* Public opinion
Press and Information Agency, 214
Press Association, 144
Press laws, *see* Laws
Professionalism
  definition of, 278-279
  ethics, 12, 45-46, 62, 65, 85, 102-104, 120, 136, 155-158, 179-183, 204-206, 222-224, 246-248, 342-343, 409-411, 427-429, 445, 469-470
  membership, 306, 469
  partisanship and, 44-45, 47
  perception of media roles, 26-27, 29, 41-43, 61, 64, 83-84, 102, 116-117, 134, 136, 152-153, 175-177, 199-203, 222, 242-246, 290-291, 307-309, 314-315, 333, 337-341, 361-362, 407-409, 424-426, 440-441, 465

professional orientations, 100-101, 199, 220-221
Professional organizations, 100, 257-258, 273-274, 306
  memberships in, 41, 83, 100, 154, 199, 221, 258, 273, 276, 306-307
Professional roles, *see* Professionalism—perception of media roles
Public opinion, 2, 67, 69, 99, 122, 206, 342, 426, 441

Q

Quebecor, 378

R

Radio New Zealand, 110
Radio and Television Hong Kong (RTHK), 33
Reporting, 239-240
  accuracy of, 65-66
  area of, *see* Beats
  methods used in, 67-68, 85, 136, 138, 183-184, 204, 206, 222-224, 247
Reuter, 144
Robotnicza Spoldzielnia Wydawnicza (RSW), 289
Royal Commission on the Press, 147

S

Salaries, *see* Income
Sanoma Oy, 162
Satisfaction, *see* Job satisfaction
Sindicat de Periodistes de Catalunya, 306
Société Radio Canada, 375
State-Owned Enterprise (SOE), 109
Statistical Yearbook of China, 18
Syndicat National des Journalistes, 204

T

Telecentro, 436
Televisa, 436
TF1, 192
The Telegram, 377
Times, 144, 158
Toronto Star, 377
Toronto Sun, 378

U

Union of Journalists in Finland (UJF), 163-164, 173, 175, 179
Unions, trade, 154, 163, 173-175, 199, 306-307
United Daily News, 73-74
United Nations Educational, Scientific and Cultural Organization (UNESCO), 13, 131, 136
University of South Pacific (USP), 127
Uusi Suomi, 170

W

Women journalists, 18, 35, 58, 76-77, 93, 95, 98, 111-112, 122, 128-129, 147-148, 164, 172-173, 195, 199, 216-217, 237, 259, 261, 301-302, 328, 352-353, 355-357, 400, 456
 age, 95, 112, 128, 148, 164, 195, 261, 302, 328, 354, 380, 398, 419, 437, 459
 income disparities, *see* Income—gender gap in
 in management, 95, 112, 173, 199
Workforce, *see* Journalists—workforce
Working conditions, *see* Journalists—working conditions

X

Xinhua News Agency, 10, 14